Sir Gawain:

Eleven Romances and Tales

Middle English Texts

General Editor

Russell A. Peck
University of Rochester

Associate Editor

Alan Lupack
University of Rochester

Advisory Board

Rita Copeland
University of Minnesota

Thomas G. Hahn
University of Rochester

Lisa Kiser
Ohio State University

Thomas Seiler
Western Michigan University

R. A. Shoaf
University of Florida

Bonnie Wheeler
Southern Methodist University

The Middle English Texts Series is designed for classroom use. Its goal is to make available to teachers and students texts which occupy an important place in the literary and cultural canon but which have not been readily available in student editions. The series does not include those authors such as Chaucer, Langland, or Malory, whose English works are normally in print in good student editions. The focus is, instead, upon Middle English literature adjacent to those authors that teachers need in compiling the syllabuses they wish to teach. The editions maintain the linguistic integrity of the original work but within the parameters of modern reading conventions. The texts are printed in the modern alphabet and follow the practices of modern capitalization and punctuation. Manuscript abbreviations are expanded, and *u/v* and *j/i* spellings are regularized according to modern orthography. Hard words, difficult phrases, and unusual idioms are glossed on the page, either in the right margin or at the foot of the page. Textual notes appear at the end of the text, along with a glossary. The editions include short introductions on the history of the work, its merits and points of topical interest, and also include briefly annotated bibliographies.

Sir Gawain:

Eleven Romances and Tales

Edited by
Thomas Hahn

Published for TEAMS
(The Consortium for the Teaching of the Middle Ages)
in Association with the University of Rochester

by

Medieval Institute Publications

WESTERN MICHIGAN UNIVERSITY

Kalamazoo, Michigan — 1995

Library of Congress Cataloging-in-Publication Data

Sir Gawain : eleven romances and tales / edited by Thomas Hahn.
    p. cm. -- (Middle English texts)
    "Published for TEAMS, the Consortium for the Teaching of the
Middle Ages, in association with the University of Rochester."
    Includes bibliographical references and index.
    ISBN 1-879288-59-1 (pbk.)
    1. Gawain (Legendary character)--Romances. 2. English poetry-
-Middle English, 1100-1500. 3. Knights and knighthood--Poetry.
4. Arthurian romances. 5. Romances, English. I. Hahn, Thomas
(Thomas G.). II. Consortium for the Teaching of the Middle Ages.
III. University of Rochester. IV. Series: Middle English texts
(Kalamazoo, Mich.)
  PR2064.S57 1995
  821'. 108--dc20

                             95-31037
                                CIP

ISBN 1-879288-59-1
© 1995 by the Board of the Medieval Institute
Printed in the United States of America
P 5 4

Cover design by Elizabeth King

For

Jonathan Hahn

and

Geoffrey Hahn

Contents

Acknowledgments

Several years' work with these poems has left me with a sense of awe before the learning, meticulousness, and imaginative insight of their earlier editors, including Madden, Child, Amours, Hanna and others; although finding a small error or an unsolved crux in this earlier work provided small justifications for the present collection, it also made me falter at realizing how many errors must remain unnoticed or uncorrected in the volume. Despite all the help I record here, the final shape of the edition is my own responsibility.

Like many scholarly projects, this edition has expanded to take up much more time and space than I'd anticipated, with the result that I've had to rely on increasing numbers of people for help. The National Endowment for the Humanities, through a series of program grants to the Chaucer Bibliographies project, provided me with release time for my editorial work with that project, and helped thereby to allow continued attention to other matters, such as the present volume; I am deeply grateful for the Endowment's support. The Department of English at the University of Rochester furnished support for research assistance. Alan Lupack, Curator of the Rossell Hope Robbins Library at Rochester, put the Library's resources, and his own considerable intellectual energy, at my disposal. Russell A. Peck, the General Editor of the TEAMS Middle English Texts Series (and, as my colleague at Rochester, a contributor to every phase of my work), has taken an intense interest in the project from the outset, and has improved the volume enormously through his time, energy, enthusiasm, and, especially, his learning. In the early stages, I had help with typing from Nandini Bhattacharya, and with typing and other editorial decisions from Hsaio Ch'iu (Stella Kuo Wang). Betty Chasan read several of the texts with care and intelligence; Lynn Arner read final copy of almost all the poems, catching errors and inconsistencies, smoothing editorial snags, and drawing upon her scholarly expertise to improve the soundness and accuracy of texts, glosses, and notes. David Johnson of Florida State University kindly read the text of *Avowyng*, and offered me valuable and learned advice. Richard Barber of Boydell and Brewer read an early version of the Introduction, which has profited from his generous comments. Helen Cooper of University College, Oxford, carefully examined the edition of *Greene Knight* and provided many valuable suggestions. Several undergraduate and graduate classes at the University of Rochester tried out preliminary versions of these texts, and I am grateful for feedback that was both intelligent and practical. Alan Lupack read through a near-final copy, and offered many responses that improved the text. Karen

Acknowledgements

Saupe of Calvin College took over the last stages of production, and, amidst many other pressures and professional responsibilities, worked generously and efficiently on this project. John G. Roberts III has assisted in every step of the edition's long preparation, saving me from errors, showing me where improvements could be made, always pushing me to raise the scholarly, editorial, and critical standards for the project; as in other endeavors, I'm deeply grateful for his engagement. Geoffrey Hahn and Jonathan Hahn have done more than simply make space for the impositions this edition has made on their lives; they have also given me much positive encouragement, offering cheerful and often insightful advice on chivalry and on other rituals and narratives of violence, and helping me to keep a perspective on the place and meaning of literature as a feature of everyday life. Bette London has read and reread all of the introductory materials and much else besides, and her continuous support and responsiveness have helped me to think through broad issues and innumerable details, and finally to bring the edition to a conclusion.

The Consortium for the Teaching of the Middle Ages is grateful to the National Endowment for the Humanities for its generous support of the Middle English Texts Series.

Abbreviations

The following short titles are used to refer to the poems edited in this volume:

Avowyng	*The Avowyng of Arthur*
Awntyrs	*The Awntyrs off Arthur*
Carle	*The Carle of Carlisle*
Carlisle	*Sir Gawain and the Carle of Carlisle*
Cornwall	*King Arthur and King Cornwall*
Gologras	*The Knightly Tale of Gologras and Gawain*
Greene Knight	*The Greene Knight*
Jeaste	*The Jeaste of Sir Gawain*
Marriage	*The Marriage of Sir Gawain*
Ragnelle	*The Wedding of Sir Gawain and Dame Ragnelle*
Turke	*The Turke and Sir Gawain*

Other common abbreviations include:

OE	Old English
ME	Middle English
OED	*Oxford English Dictionary*
MED	*Middle English Dictionary*
EETS o.s.	Early English Text Society, original series
EETS e.s.	Early English Text Society, extra series
EETS s.s.	Early English Text Society, supplemental series

Introduction

Sir Gawain and Popular Chivalric Romance

Sir Gawain as Hero

All the glamour, mystery, and moral authority that chivalry might command were invested for late medieval audiences in the charismatic figure of Sir Gawain. Perhaps the most delightful and memorable testimonial to his celebrity is offered by Lady Bertilak the first morning she visits the knight in his bedroom, in *Sir Gawain and the Green Knight*. He alone, she says, possesses "The prys and the prowes that plesez al other" [line 1249: the worship and daring that gives everyone pleasure];

> For I wene wel, iwysse, Sir Wowen ye are,
> That alle the worlde worchipez quereso ye ride;
> Your honour, your hendelayk is hendely praysed
> With lordez, wyth ladyes, with alle that lyf bere

[lines 1226–29: for I know it well, you are Sir Gawain, whom all the world honors wherever you ride; your honor, your graciousness is courteously praised among lords and ladies, among all who are alive].[1] Though Lady Bertilak may intend to flatter (and perhaps compromise) Gawain by telling him that every living soul knows and admires his reputation for knightly virtue, it is hardly an exaggeration as far as late medieval readers and listeners were concerned; most English audiences, both courtly and popular, would think of Sir Gawain as the chief ornament of "Arthures hous . . . That al the rous rennes of thurgh ryalmes so mony" [*Sir Gawain and the Green Knight*, lines 309–10: Arthur's household, whose extravagant fame runs through so many kingdoms]. Chaucer, always attuned to popular taste despite

---

[1] All citations of medieval texts in the Introduction and in the introductions and notes to the individual poems refer to the editions listed in the Bibliography of Editions and Works Cited. I have usually provided line numbers in the text. Citations of editions or commentary specific to the poems edited in the present volume appear in the individual bibliographies preceding each poem.

his extraordinary bookishness, pays an equally telling tribute to the universality of Gawain's status as the paragon of knighthood. That most sentimentally chivalric of narrators, the Squire, praises the "reverence and obeisaunce / As wel in speche as in countenaunce" of a "strange knyght" by suggesting he is like "Gawayn, with his olde curteisye . . . comen ayeyn [again] out of Fairye" (lines 89 ff.). To equal Gawain was to be a knight indeed, though it's worth noting that even the Squire links such ideal chivalry to magic and fairy tale.

Gawain's stature and renown — if not in his own mythical lifetime, then among the flesh and blood listeners and readers of late medieval England — had as its source and substance the popular romances that make up the present volume. Almost all of these were composed or written down in the fifteenth century or later. Before these romances appeared, Gawain already enjoyed a reputation in England through two early fourteenth-century verse translations based upon twelfth-century French romances (Chrétien de Troyes' *Yvain* [c. 1175] and Renaut de Beaujeu's *Le bel inconnu* [c. 1190]). Moreover, the only surviving copy of a Latin pedigree produced for Gawain — *De ortu Waluuani* [The Origins of Gawain], an account (from the twelfth or thirteenth century) of his youth and early exploits modeled after the pseudo-history of Geoffrey of Monmouth (c. 1136) — was apparently copied in England in the fourteenth century.[2]

The *Alliterative Morte Arthure* (second half of the fourteenth century) extends the chronicle tradition of Geoffrey and Layamon's *Brut* (thirteenth century), exalting Gawain as a fierce and impetuous warrior, the greatest fighter in Arthur's troop. His slayer and half-brother Mordred eulogizes Gawain as "makles one molde," "the graciouseste gome . . . man hardyeste of hande . . . the hendeste in hawle . . . , the lordelieste of ledynge" [lines 3875–80: matchless on earth, the most courteous knight, hardiest in strength, most affable in hall, most gentle in conduct]. When King Arthur hears the news of Gawain's death, he cries, "thou was worthy to be kynge, thofe [though] I the corowne bare [bore] . . . I am uttirly undone" (lines 3962, 3966). *Sir Gawain and the Green Knight* elaborates upon this reputation, establishing its hero as the sterling exemplar of chivalry even as it probes the contradictory links between courtesy and violent death, private conscience and public honor, within the ethos of knighthood.

The glowing testimonials of the Gawain-poet and Chaucer do not, however, primarily pay tribute to a fame conferred upon Gawain by books and translations. The

---

[2] Again, the Bibliography of Editions and Works Cited provides full information for editions of poems mentioned here but not included in the present volume (except for Renaut's *Le bel inconnu*, which is not relevant to the traditions discussed here).

casual quality of their allusions depends for its resonance not upon reading know-
ledge, but upon pervasive recognition that the name of Gawain was the proverbial
equivalent of courtesy itself. The exploits, gallantries, and preternatural encounters
rehearsed in the eleven romances and ballads gathered here make plain the nature
and the extent of Gawain's appeal as all things knightly to all people of late medi-
eval England. Gawain's perfect courtesy does not, however, endow him with a coherent
identity; it simply serves as a touchstone, revealing the true or false chivalry of the
various antagonists who test him. To see this as deriving from some original core of
myth, or to argue that Gawain's charisma springs from his being before all else an
archetypal hero or solar deity, seriously distorts the miscellaneous character of
these adventures, ignores their deep and tangled roots in the social and cultural life
of late medieval England, and, perhaps worst of all, represses the episodic surges
and performative energy that animate these narratives and songs.[3]

Gawain's celebrity nonetheless stretches far back, beyond his appearances in high
medieval literary romances, or in later popular romances and ballads like those
collected here.[4] He appears initially to have been a legendary Celtic hero with
supernatural powers, though the precise origins of the figure who becomes the
knightly Sir Gawain are shrouded by typical Arthurian ambiguities. The waxing of
Gawain's strength before noon, and its waning thereafter (as in the *Stanzaic Morte
Arthur* and Malory) may reflect some prehistoric link with a sun god.[5] In his earliest

---

[3] Two notable monographs in English on Gawain as hero both relentlessly attempt to reach
back to an "original" meaning for the hero, and therefore regard the late medieval romances
as without significance except insofar as they provide pieces of evidence for the archetype. See
Jesse L. Weston, *The Legend of Sir Gawain: Studies upon Its Original Scope and Significance*,
Grimm Library, 7 (London: David Nutt, 1897), and John Matthews, *Gawain: Knight of the
Goddess — Restoring an Archetype* (Wellingborough, UK: The Aquarian Press, 1990). A brief
and reliable summary of surviving evidence is given in the entry for "Gawain," *New Arthurian
Encyclopedia*, ed. Norris J. Lacy (New York: Garland, 1991). The same volume contains
helpful entries for most of the poems in the present volume, and for the characters and places
they mention. The most thorough survey of Gawain's appearances in French and English
narratives remains B. J. Whiting, "Gawain, His Reputation, His Courtesy and His Appearance
in Chaucer's *Squire's Tale*," *Medieval Studies* 9 (1947), 189–234.

[4] Richard Barber offers a concise yet reliable account of Gawain's identity and his place
within larger Arthurian traditions in *King Arthur: Hero and Legend* (Woodbridge: Boydell,
1986).

[5] This special power is described in the *Stanzaic Morte Arthur*, lines 2802 ff., and Malory,
Works, pp. 1216–17.

3

adventures, Gawain seems to have had northern, often Scottish, affinities; he is the son of King Lot of Lothian and Orkney, connecting him through this ancestry with Edinburgh in the heart of Midlothian and with the Northern Isles. These associations may explain why the popular English Gawain romances consistently and distinctively set their action near the northern city of Carlisle, close to the border with Scotland.[6] Whether the earliest oral traditions (now lost) constituted a separate cycle of stories, or whether they associated him with Arthur, the legendary British warlord who fought against continental Germanic invaders in the fifth century, is not clear. Written versions of Welsh tales, including "Culhwch and Olwen," make Gwalchmai a companion of Arthur (the king's sister's son) and a figure equivalent to Gawain. Welsh translations of Geoffrey of Monmouth's Latin *History of the Kings of Britain* (c. 1136) endorse this identity of Gwalchmai with Geoffrey's Walwanus, nephew of Arthur. Gawain's heroism had, by the early twelfth century, become increasingly well known; a sculpture (dated before 1109) at the Cathedral in Modena,

---

[6] For both medieval and modern writers, considerable ambiguity, overlap, and confusion surround Arthurian place names. Carlisle is specified as a setting for *Wedding, Carlisle, Avowyng, Awntyrs, Greene Knight, Marriage,* and *Carle. Lancelot of the Laik,* the *Alliterative Morte Arthure,* the *Stanzaic Morte Arthur,* Malory, and perhaps *Libeaus Desconus* — all featuring Gawain's exploits, and linked with the popular romance tradition — are the only other Middle English romances to mention Carlisle. (*The Boy and the Mantle,* a Percy Folio MS ballad, also locates Arthur's court at Carlisle; see Child, I.257–274.) The remarkable geographical unity of the Middle English Gawain poems is discussed further below, pp. 29–33. In *Yvain* and *Perceval,* Chrétien places Arthur's court at "Carduel an Gales" indicating Carlisle, but in accord with ancient tradition locating this in Wales; *Ywain and Gawain,* the Middle English version of *Yvain,* casts Arthur as "Kyng of Yngland," conqueror of Wales and Scotland, and sets the romance "At Kerdyf [Cardiff] that es in Wales" (line 17). Other French romances also place Arthur's court at Carduel/Carlisle. The designation of Carlisle as the seat of Arthurian adventure in Middle English romances has sometimes been taken as a misnomer for, or corruption of, Caerleon-on-Usk, Monmouthshire (in the south of Wales, near the mouth of the Severn); Caerleon is prominently mentioned by Geoffrey of Monmouth (perhaps following Welsh oral traditions), and appears in both French romance and popular English tales, such as *Sir Launfal.* On the one hand, William of Malmesbury's remarks about the hero's tomb, which he places in Pembrokeshire, west of Caerleon on the coast of Wales, provide a further Welsh linkage for Gawain; yet in the same passage he identifies Gawain as the "miles" (knight) who ruled in that part of Britain hitherto called "Walweitha" (Galloway), confirming his northern, Scots affinity. (For this passage in William, see the following note.) Malory has Gawain buried "in a chapell within Dover castell . . . [where] yet all men may se the skulle of hym" (*Works,* 1232), and the sixteenth-century antiquary John Leland claimed to have seen Gawain's bones at Dover, and on this basis rejected the authenticity of the tomb in Pembrokeshire.

Italy, depicts Gawain undertaking a siege, together with Arthur and two other knights, and the historian William of Malmesbury (c. 1125) mentions Gawain in a way that assumes his learned readers' familiarity with this hero's adventures.[7] The transforming event in the literary history of Arthur and his knights, however, was the completion of *The History of the Kings of Britain* by the Welshman Geoffrey of Monmouth; in summarizing, synthesizing, and inventing a wide range of traditions, the *History* made available to learned and popular writers and their audiences the fundamental stories of the Round Table, in which Gawain figures prominently.[8] As the son of Arthur's sister (Morgause, or, in some accounts, Anna), he enjoys with the king the privileged relationship of mother's brother–sister's son (like Hygelac-Beowulf, or Charlemagne-Roland). Unlike Arthur, whose place at the center of things as the source of law and order sometimes makes him seem immobile — a *roi feneant* or do-nothing king — Gawain possesses the youthful freedom to take on strange adventures and exotic journeys, and can turn these exploits to his uncle's glory. In this crucial supporting role he stands in profound contrast to his dangerously restless brother Mordred (sister's son *and* biological son to the king through incest), who in many versions initiates an Oedipal, generational conflict that results in the downfall of the king, his father-uncle.

As knightly prowess, chivalric honor, and sexual love become central motifs in Arthurian narrative, Sir Gawain (Walwanus in Latin, Gauvain in French, with initial *G* and *W* sounds interchangeable in Middle English) becomes an increasingly favored hero. In the enormously influential and highly polished French romances of Chrétien de Troyes (late twelfth century), Gawain often serves as a companion and foil to the hero; his single-minded devotion to physical conquest, in combat and in love, makes him a less than ideal knight, in contrast to Perceval, Yvain, or even

---

[7] For the Modena archivolt, see *Arthurian Literature in the Middle Ages*, ed. R. S. Loomis (Oxford: Clarendon Press, 1959), pp. 60–62. In his remarks on Arthur and on Gawain's fourteen-foot long tomb by the seashore in Pembrokeshire in Wales, William of Malmesbury takes for granted his readers' interest in (and knowledge of) Gawain. William provocatively describes Gawain as occupying the undegenerate ("haud degener") relation to Arthur of mother's brother-sister's son, and as sharing properly in his uncle's fame, clearly indicating that by the early twelfth century the nephew was already a celebrity in his own right. See *De Rebus Gestis Regum Anglorum*, Book 3, section 287, ed. W. Stubbs, Rolls Series no. 90, vol. 2 (London, 1889), p. 342.

[8] For Geoffrey of Monmouth's portrayal of Gawain, see *The Historia Regum Britanniae of Geoffrey of Monmouth: I: A Single Manuscript Edition from Bern, Burgerbibliothek, MS 568*, ed. Neil Wright (Cambridge: Boydell and Brewer, 1984), pp. 144 ff., and *The History of the Kings of Britain*, trans. Lewis Thorpe (Harmondsworth, UK: Penguin, 1966), pp. 221 ff.

Lancelot. In later French medieval narratives, his character varies from comic inadequacy to moral imperfection (as in the *Queste del Saint Graal*) to complicity in the downfall of the Round Table, to outright villainy.[9] Sir Gawain's character in other medieval vernaculars was generally more favorable than in the French Arthurian romances that were their source. In German stories, for example, he plays a mixed role, and in romances from the Netherlands he enjoys an almost entirely positive portrayal.

Only in the popular romances in English, however, does a genuine cult of Sir Gawain emerge, making him the unsurpassed flower of chivalry. Like *Sir Gawain and the Green Knight*, these poems celebrate Arthurian chivalry in its glorious, even reckless youth, and the vigorous exploits of Sir Gawain offer only an occasional glimpse of the eventual downfall of the Round Table. Gawain's singular renown in these popular narratives — often drawn from traditional tales and oral stories, either with no known sources or with only a distant relation to a literary text — contrasts with the relatively minor role he plays in the two Gawain romances based directly upon French originals, both dating from the earlier fourteenth century. *Ywain and Gawain* condenses Gawain's role from Chrétien de Troyes' *Yvain*, leaving him less active both as a partisan of chivalry and as an obstacle to true love; *Libeaus Desconus* casts Gawain as the absent father and sometime instructor of Gingelein, "The Fair Unknown." The only other notable appearance of Sir Gawain in medieval English romance occurs in the three sustained chronicles of Arthur's death: the *Alliterative Morte Arthure*, the *Stanzaic Morte Arthur*, and Malory's prose *Morte Darthur* (which makes use of the two poems). Gawain's character parallels the later French tradition; though his courtesy and prowess remain prominent, he ap-

---

[9] Gawain's reputation in French romance as lover and sometime rake may account for his otherwise odd appearance as the hero of an academic satire in Latin verse, "On Not Taking a Wife" (before 1250). Here Gawain, planning marriage, has the spirits of three clerks attempt to dissuade him; they draw their arguments from biblical and classical exempla and from Latin misogynist writings, though their focus is not the virtues of celibacy but the disastrous results of secular marriage. The choice of Gawain as protagonist seems therefore something of a scholar's inside joke, though his role here suggests just how extensive his reputation was, reaching even to the precincts of learning. The poem survives in more than fifty manuscripts, and there are adaptations in French and Middle English. See A. G. Rigg, *Gawain on Marriage: The Textual Tradition of the "De Coniuge Non Ducenda" with Critical Edition and Translation*, Texts and Studies, 79 (Toronto: Pontifical Institute of Medieval Studies, 1986). The most comprehensive study of Gawain's role in Old French literature (with much attention to texts in other languages as well) is Keith Busby, *Gauvain in Old French Literature* (Amsterdam: Rodopi, 1980).

pears as frequently truculent, vindictive, and reckless, and takes a central part in the tragedy of the Round Table.

For the last one hundred and fifty years readers have come to know the medieval Sir Gawain through *Sir Gawain and the Green Knight*. This fourteenth-century alliterative poem (roughly contemporary with *Awntyrs*, the *Alliterative Morte Arthure*, and the *Stanzaic Morte Arthur*) presents the most elegant and subtle portrait of his chivalric courtesy and valor. Although the composer possessed extensive knowledge of Arthurian story, he only hints at the downfall of the fellowship. In this, he follows the almost unswervingly favorable view taken in the popular Gawain romances, which by far surpass in number those on any other Arthurian (or non-Arthurian) hero, and all of which are collected in this volume.[10]

Romance and Chivalry

The Middle English word *knight* derives from Old English *cniht*, a noun with a broad and variable range of meaning, including boy, servant, attendant, warrior. The abstract noun *knighthood* did not exist in Old English, for the social role and the code of values it describes did not come into being until the High Middle Ages (after the year 1000). *Knighthood* is the English equivalent for the French *chivalrie*, which in its primary sense meant a troop of mounted warriors; through the use of stirrups, swords, and lances, these fighters on horseback had awesomely increased the level of damage a warrior might inflict, and conferred upon knights as a group undisputed preeminence among the secular, land-holding aristocracy. But more and more, *chivalrie* came to mean the ideals — self-consciously proclaimed, but acknowledged by other classes in society as well — that gave a *chevalier* or knight his identity.[11] Knighthood did not just entail prowess or success as a fighter (mainly this was required, but sometimes not); it demanded as well the distinctive and deliberate

---

[10] I here follow the division already set out in the introduction, which separates the "popular" romances (gathered here) from those with a pronounced literary character or a notable textual source — namely, *Ywain and Gawain, Libeaus Desconus, Sir Gawain and the Green Knight* — as well as the chronicle narratives — Layamon, the *Alliterative Morte Arthure*, the *Stanzaic Morte Arthur*, and Malory. In all of these but *Gawain and the Green Knight*, Gawain plays roles of varying but subsidiary importance.

[11] On the historical development of knighthood, see the essays collected in Georges Duby, *The Chivalrous Society*, trans. Cynthia Postan (1977; Berkeley and Los Angeles: University of California Press, 1980), and Maurice Keen's *Chivalry* (New Haven and London: Yale University Press, 1984).

identification with a code that virtually all members of society endorsed as a source of privilege. So powerfully did the moral and social authority of this role enhance the identity of the secular aristocracy that by the later Middle Ages even kings and emperors considered themselves first of all knights.

Chivalry (or knighthood) therefore emerged as a code when those who already possessed power claimed this identity for themselves as proper, desirable, and exclusive. Though the first documents to mention knights ("milites," the Roman word for soldiers) occur in Latin, the official language of the Church, knighthood is clearly a secular or lay aristocratic form of life. The deeds of famous knights seem first to have been memorialized in vernacular oral poetry, like *The Song of Roland*, and great lords and noble fighters must have supported composers and singers who celebrated a warrior ethos in their own tongue before their own entourage. In this way, chivalry worked to define group consciousness, and so consisted not simply in great deeds but in their communal preservation. But chivalry as an identity possessed exclusively by members of a specific class is a social and historical impossibility, for any group's identity depends upon its place in a larger society where those outside validate its existence by acknowledging — adopting, or even rejecting — its distinctive values. The earliest literary versions of chivalry in themselves demonstrate that the leap had already taken place from oral, memorial poetry, celebrating a hero among his own group, to a culturally endorsed chivalry, presenting a hero whom an entire society, with its different estates and diverse interests, might celebrate as its ideal representative.[12]

---

[12] The question of precisely whose ideals or interests chivalric literature serves, whether asked openly or ignored, shadows every discussion of knightly romance, and admits no simple answer. Kings and powerful knights obviously perceived the value of romance and pageantry as a kind of "top-down" propaganda for their privileged political and economic position, as the proclamation of Edward III (see note 16, below) reveals, and one might therefore accurately claim that such tales were "popular" among this elite class because they maintained its hegemonic position. Yet the romances merit the label "popular" in the more common sense in that many (like *Ragnelle* and *Carlisle*) indisputably originate, become embellished and revised, and circulate among "the people," that is, broad and diverse audiences of various classes with overlapping and often conflicting interests. Moreover, as I suggest below (pp. 19–23), far from simply reproducing the values of the reigning culture, the romances open a space for satire or resistance in relation to elite values. Crucial questions concerning the nature of "popular" culture in the Middle Ages — about the social make-up of the audiences for medieval texts, the processes and effects of consuming romance, the overlaps of oral and literate, the determinants of taste for varying groups — have received relatively little extended historical analysis from critics and scholars. See Chandra Mukerji and Michael Schudson, "Introduction," in *Rethinking Popular Culture: Contemporary Perspectives in Cultural Studies*, ed. Mukerji and

Introduction

From its earliest historical origins, those concerned with chivalry as a code, including knights themselves, thought of it as stemming from some ideal, and therefore prehistoric and unhistorical, golden age. These ancient roots sanctioned its existence and strengthened its prerogatives, but also made every chivalric deed no more than a pale imitation of some lost perfection. Even the earliest Arthurian writings feature this element of nostalgia, and so present chivalry as a normative fantasy. This idealizing tendency continues to shape late medieval aristocratic institutionalization of chivalry as a class code, through the establishment of national and international Orders of Knights with written statutes. This legendary and literary influence is especially clear in Britain, the land of Arthur. In the late thirteenth century, when King Edward I wished to increase his prestige and power as a national figure and military leader in his struggles with the Welsh, he associated himself with Arthur, and held a number of tournaments and feasts that made the Round Table a central feature.[13] His grandson, Edward III, proposed to formalize this connection between knighthood and the Arthurian ethos: in 1344, influenced by the modern establishment of Orders of Knights in France and Spain, he proposed to initiate an English Order based upon the model of King Arthur, a "refounding" of the Round Table. Though Edward eventually abandoned these explicit Arthurian parallels in founding the Order of the Garter (1349), the interplay between social reality and literary mythification continued throughout the Middle Ages and into the early modern era, as the *Morte Darthur* and *Don Quixote*, for example, make clear.[14] The matter of Britain gave stirring articulation to the ideals of knighthood, and these idealizations in turn articulated for their audiences a sense of common

---

Schudson (Berkeley and Los Angeles: University of California Press, 1991) for a recent and helpful overview; and on the Gawain romances in particular, see comments below, pp. 10 ff. and 27 ff.

[13] It was during one of these Round Tables, while his courtiers were masquerading as Arthurian knights, that a loathly lady appeared to demand deeds of chivalry; see the Introduction to *Ragnelle*, and more particularly, R. S. Loomis, "Edward I, Arthurian Enthusiast," *Speculum* 28 (1953), 114–27.

[14] For an account of the Order of the Garter, and its place within the ideals and politics of late medieval chivalry, see D'Arcy Jonathan Dacre Boulton, *The Knights of the Crown: The Monarchical Orders of Knighthood in Later Medieval Europe, 1325–1520* (Woodbridge: Boydell, 1987), pp. 96–166. Boulton does not mention *Sir Gawain and the Green Knight*, with its appropriation of the Garter motto at its conclusion, though whoever added the phrase, "Hony soyt qui mal pence" (may he be shamed who evil thinks) certainly wished to associate chivalric romance with the codes and institutions of secular knighthood.

national interests and natural class divisions. In offering a vision of chivalry that is both timeless and nostalgic, the romances actively worked to mediate or veil the various conflicts embedded in such interests, at least for their most enthusiastic audiences. The motto at the end of *Sir Gawain and the Green Knight* in this way invokes the historical Order of the Garter as at once a prototype and a product of the poem's chivalry, and its derivative, *The Greene Knight*, similarly provides a "history" for the post-medieval Order of the Knights of the Bath.[15]

The historical Orders of knighthood, together with other less formal structures, were attempts to organize and regulate the behavior of a particular group, but they warmly invited the interest and affirmation of other classes. Knights, starting with the king, recognized the power of knightly spectacle to produce chivalric sentiment in all audiences. Edward III, "remembering the deeds of the ancients, and considering how much the use and love of arms has exalted the name and glory of knightly men, and how much the royal throne would be strengthened and dissentions reduced," offered his endorsement of a tournament as a festivity beneficial for all members of society.[16] Knightly conduct and ritual thus entailed the staged celebration of chivalry, and the appeal of knighthood as spectacle clearly extended beyond the class of knights themselves. Popular romances, in substituting idealizations of knightly conduct for the conduct itself, may have had greater impact in creating and reinforcing chivalric sentiment (in particular, among non-chivalric audiences) than anything knights did for themselves. In this way, stories like those of Sir Gawain perform social and political functions, making identification with chivalric values possible for a much wider spectrum of the king's subjects than an elite Order or an actual tournament might ever affect.

The Popular Appeal of Chivalric Romance

The dozen and more surviving Gawain romances form a unity not simply through their shared hero, but, perhaps even more, through their character as more popular than literary. As narratives, they manifest the features of *romance* in all its meanings: chivalry, Arthurian legend, prowess in combat, personal love, intrigue, encounters with the marvelous, and the decisive resolution of every real or potential conflict. These tales celebrate the idealized chivalry of some distant Arthurian past, but in so

---

[15] See Introduction to *Greene Knight*, together with the note at line 502 of that poem, for discussion of its connection to the Order of the Bath.

[16] Rolls of Parliament 18 Edward III, p. 1, m. 44; I quote here the translation published in Boulton, *Knights of the Crown* (note 14, above), p. 110.

doing they inevitably enhance the stature and prerogative of late medieval knighthood — an elite, aristocratic, warrior and land-owning class that largely controlled social, political, and military life. Yet the poems themselves do not originate in that class. These romances were composed for broad consumption, perhaps sometimes for audiences including knights, perhaps sometimes for readers, but mainly for listeners in large, diverse, and mixed groups. The manuscripts (and the single printed edition) in which they occur were not produced for the great households: they are in no way deluxe, but at best serviceable, and sometimes downright shabby.[17] The survival of individual romances must often have been chancy, depending upon the impulse of an unusually literate and literary listener — like the post-medieval compiler of the Percy Folio — who, for whatever reason, wished a record of such popular entertainment. The texts themselves are marked for oral recitation, with cues for the audience and reciter and conventional rhyme schemes associated with minstrelsy and oral performance. The narratives unfold through traditional plots and reiterated motifs, glorify a popular hero whom everyone knew, and eventuate in happy endings which bring the characters within the story to terms with one another, and which reconcile the audience outside the story to the structures and ideals epitomized by a "chivalric" (or hierarchically ordered) society.

The volume of surviving material, and the number of allusions in every kind of writing, make plain that the legends of Gawain's courtesy were widely known. Yet the precise nature and extent of this popularity within specific social contexts has remained vague. Two pieces of evidence (not much commented upon in the context of these Gawain stories) help to clarify the environment in which popular chivalric romances flourished — how, when, and by whom they were composed, performed, listened to, read, and copied. In the later 1470s Sir John Paston commissioned an "Inventory off Englysshe bokis" from his own library.[18] These included religious

---

[17] One other exception — besides *Sir Gawain and the Green Knight* — to the non-aristocratic context in which Gawain's legend prospers occurs in a heraldic roll with royal associations, which shows a figure labeled, "Sire Gawyn Mautrevers," connecting this hero with the Maltravers family, whose leading members were prominently connected to Edward II and Edward III. See Gerard J. Brault, *Early Blazon: Heraldic Terminology in the Twelfth and Thirteenth Centuries with Special Reference to Arthurian Literature* (Oxford: Clarendon Press, 1972), p. 43. See also the coats of arms attributed to Gawain in a fifteenth-century armorial album, referenced below in note 21.

[18] Sir John Paston of Norfolk (1442–79) is best known through the numerous letters he and other members of his family wrote. These have mainly to do with retaining and increasing the family holdings, and are usually considered as having little to do with, or as being diametrically opposed to, the world of chivalric romance. See, for example, the remarks of Larry D.

11

and devotional works, "a boke off nyw statutys from [King] Edward the iiii," Christine de Pisan's *Epistle of Othea*, some treatises by Cicero, an impressive collection of Chaucer's writings, and various romances; among the latter were *Guy of Warwick*, *Kyng Richard Cure de lyon* (i.e., "the Lionheart"), and *Guy and Colbronde* (perhaps in Lydgate's version). A series of volumes attests Paston's dedication to heraldry and chivalry: "myn olde boke off blasonyngys," "the newe boke portrayed and blasonyd," "a copy off blasonyngys off armys," "a boke wyth armys portrayed in paper" — altogether, an encyclopedia of coats of arms, which must have held urgent interest for the first member of a socially mobile family elevated to a knighthood.[19]

The list records as well "my boke off knyththod and therin . . . off making off knyghtys, off justys, off torn[aments, off] fyghtyng in lystys . . . and chalengys, statutys off weer [war]." For our purposes the crowning items in this collection are two other romances: the first title, "A boke . . . off the Dethe off Arthur," and, in the third group, "the Greene Knyght." The appearance of a narrative on the "Dethe off Arthur" in Paston's library is especially arresting since Malory composed his *Morte Darthur* less than a decade earlier (1469 or 1470), and Caxton published "thys noble and Ioyous book entytled le morte Darthur" only a few years after the compilation of this inventory, in 1485.[20] The pride of place awarded this volume within

----

Benson, *Malory's "Morte Darthur"* (Cambridge, Massachusetts: Harvard University Press, 1976), pp. 137–201. For the inventory of books discussed here, see *Paston Letters and Papers of the Fifteenth Century*, ed. Norman Davis, Part I (Oxford: Oxford University Press, 1971), pp. 516–18. Madden, with his usual encyclopedic knowledge, makes a passing reference to this inventory in his note to the *Greene Knight* (p. 352). G. A. Lester has discussed the inventory, and provided valuable commentary and background, in "The Books of a Fifteenth-Century English Gentleman, Sir John Paston," *Neuphilologische Mitteilungen* 88 (1987), 200–17.

[19] The most notable of these heraldic miscellanies has been described in great detail by G. A. Lester, *Sir John Paston's "Grete Boke": A Descriptive Catalogue, with an Introduction, of British Library MS Lansdowne 285* (Cambridge: D. S. Brewer, 1984). It contains, among many other items, a formulary (pp. 80–3) for creating Knights of the Bath (mentioned at the end of *Greene Knight*), descriptions of armor, accounts of particular battles (historical and fictional), passages from Geoffrey of Monmouth's *History*, proclamations for tournaments, and so on. For a more fanciful armorial album, recording two coats of arms associated with Sir Gawain, see note 21 below.

[20] This is the title Caxton gives in his colophon, *Works*, p. 1260. The notation that Paston's *Dethe off Arthur* has its "begynyng at Cassab . . ." suggests that he owned some English version of the Arthurian story ultimately derived from Geoffrey of Monmouth's *Historia Regum Britanniae*, which began with the conflicts between Julius Caesar and Cassivelaunus or Cassibellaunus, King of the Britons — Shakespeare's Cymbeline — (section fifty three of the Latin

the inventory perhaps implies the special value or interest that Arthurian romance held for Sir John (though it's unlikely that he actually possessed the Winchester Manuscript or any other copy of Malory's prose romance). The "Greene Knyght" which Paston had collected is almost certainly a retelling of the greatest of all English Arthurian poems. Nonetheless, the romance mentioned here as a single, anthologized item in "a blak boke" was probably neither *Sir Gawain and the Green Knight* nor the *Greene Knight*, but another, intermediary version of this Gawain story, probably more literary than the poem published in the present volume. Its place within Paston's library shows that the story circulated more widely than scholars have usually allowed, and that it was preserved through the interests of readers whose disparate tastes might range from folk narratives to proto-humanist translations of Cicero.

As a reader, an owner, and thereby even a sponsor of popular Arthurian romance, Sir John Paston represents a telling segment of the audience for such stories. Paston was a member of an influential and wealthy family, and may have studied at Cambridge University. Though perhaps less dedicated to the acquisition of property than his father, his possession of statute books and albums of armorial bearings reveals that his interest in knighthood was by no means anchored in fanciful romance.[21] His careful attention to the law and his jealous regard for his family

---

text). See *The Historia Regum Britanniae*, pp. 46–58, and *The History of the Kings of Britain*, pp. 106–19 (full citations in note 8, above). Among the English translations that Paston might have owned was that made at the end of the twelfth century by Layamon, though there is otherwise little evidence that Layamon influenced other Arthurian writers, or even found occasional readers, after his own time. For Layamon's account of the struggle see *Layamon: Brut*, ed. G. L. Brook and R. F. Leslie, EETS o.s. 250, 277 (London: 1963, 1978), vol. 1, pp. 214 ff. G. A. Lester has pointed out that the truncated spelling of Paston's inventory would also fit the *Chronicle* of Robert of Gloucester, that of Robert Mannyng, or the prose version of the *Brut*; see "The Books . . .," note 18, above, p. 203.

[21] The link between armorial bearings as the guarantor of identity, status, and entitlement to landed wealth and the celebration of arms in chivalric romance is apparent to some degree in Paston's own "Grete Boke" (see note 19, above). The mix of chivalric reality and fiction is much more striking and suggestive in the somewhat informal collection of "Aunciant Coates" that occurs in British Library MS Harley 2169; here alongside recognizably historical and ceremonial bearings appear the arms of the Nine Worthy, the Three Kings of Cologne, and other chivalric celebrities. Of greatest interest in the present context are the arms attributed to "Uter Pendragon," King Arthur, "Sir Lawncelot de Lake," and the two devices given to Gawain. The first of Gawain's arms consists of a green field with three golden griffins *passant* (number 29); the second, in an azure field with three golden lions' heads (number 39). The

arms (and for those of others in power or on the move) show his energetic engage-
ment with the harshly competitive life of the courts, both legal and royal. At the
same time, life as a courtier made him a devotee of chivalry: in 1473 he had himself
fitted for a complete suit of armor by the outfitter of the Bastard of Burgundy.
Earlier, in 1467, he took part in a tournament at Eltham on the King's side (slightly
injuring his hand), and later that year he made his own account of the jousting
between Lord Scales and the Bastard of Burgundy. Paston's enthusiasm for popular
chivalric romance seems then not to have been divorced from, but to have comple-
mented his personal, familial, and public ambitions. In glorifying a fabulous Arthur-
ian past, tales like Paston's "Greene Knyght" glorified the present as well, and their
stylized, even fantasized ideals of knighthood simply reinforced his own sense of
knightly identity and social order.[22]

A second private document, this one a description written some hundred years
after Paston's inventory, supplies still more striking clues about the social processes
that ensured the preservation and enjoyment of popular chivalric romances. Robert
Laneham published *A Letter* describing "the entertainment" presented before
Queen Elizabeth at Kenilworth Castle in 1575.[23] Among the festivities arranged by
the Earl of Leicester — the central theme of which was King Arthur and the Table
Round — was an "olld storiall sheaw . . . expressed in actions and rymes," an histor-
ical and carnivalesque pageant which ends with English women taking the invading
Danes captive. This was performed by players from neighboring Coventry, led by
Captain Cox, a mason by day who seems also to have been a performance artist of
sorts — "an od man I promis yoo . . . very cunning in sens, and hardy as Gawin,"
blustering about with his sword, acting, impersonating, singing, reciting, with "great

---

first device corresponds closely to descriptions in various of the Gawain romances; see for
example *Carle*, lines 55 ff. A description of the arms in Harley 2169, together with rough
facsimiles, is provided in *The Ancestor* 3 (1902), 185–213; see especially numbers 27–49.

[22] Benson (note 18, above) provides a stimulating and informative discussion of the con-
texts of late medieval chivalric romance in *Malory's "Morte Darthur,"* pp. 137–201.

[23] Robert Laneham, *A Letter: Whearin part of the entertainment untoo the Queens Maiesty . . .*
[1575], ed. R. C. Alston (Menston, UK: Scolar, 1968). The description of the festivities and
Captain Cox occurs on pp. 34–36 of this facsimile edition; I have imposed modern conventions
of orthography, capitalization, and word division in my quotations of the *Letter*. The Captain's
reputation as a performer was sufficiently extensive for Ben Jonson to mention him and "his
Hobbyhorse" in his *Masque of Owls* (1624); in his novel *Kenilworth* (1821), Sir Walter Scott
gives an account of the festivities. Madden also notes Laneham's mention of Gawain in his
Letter, and takes this as a reference to *Jeaste* (p. 349).

oversight . . . in matters of storie." Laneham's unthinking comparison of the Captain to Gawain attests that his popularity as the proverbial epitome of noble English manhood continued from Chaucer's time through Shakespeare's.[24]

So impressed was Laneham that he devoted several pages of his letter to the Captain's repertoire. These included an enormous "bunch of ballets [ballads] and songs all auncient," which Laneham records by their familiar first lines; "a hundred more [which] he hath fair wrapt up in Parchment and bound with a whipcord"; traditional tales like "Robin Hood," "Adam Bel," "Clim of the Clough," "The King and the Tanner," "The Seargeaunt that became a Fryar," "Skogan," and "The Nutbrooun Maid"; more current stories such as "Gargantua," "Collyn Cloout," "The Sheperds Kalender," and "The Ship of Fools"; and matters of "Philosophy both morall and naturall." The Captain could also draw upon a huge store of medieval chivalric romances — "Bevys of Hampton," "The Squyre of Lo Degree," "Syr Eglamoour," "Sir Tryamoour," "Syr Isenbras" — and he seems to have had particular knowledge of Arthurian narratives, namely "King Arthurs book" and "Syr Gawyn."[25] Although J. C. Holt has assumed that the last named romance was *Sir Gawain and the Green Knight*, it seems quite unlikely that a performance artist like Captain Cox would have access to, or any interest in, so highly literate a text.[26] On

---

[24] Laneham's descriptive phrase was surely proverbial. Though B. J. Whiting, *Proverbs and Proverbial Sentences* . . . (Cambridge, Massachusetts: Harvard University Press, 1968) gives no instances, passing references to Gawain's reputation for hardihood occur in "The Thrush and the Nightingale," *Sir Degrevant*, *The Squire of Low Degree*, and *Squire Meldrum*. See also the list of some one hundred thirty-five Arthurian allusions in non-Arthurian texts compiled by Christopher Dean, *Arthur of England* (full citation, below, note 26), pp. 130–56. The number and character of these allusions suggest that Gawain's proverbial stature may have been greater outside the literate tradition, within popular oral discourse.

[25] One striking title in the Captain's repertoire was "The Knight of Courtesy and the Lady Faguell" — not a version of *Gawain and Ragnelle*, but a sentimental romance that surivives in an Elizabethan print; see *The Knight of Curtesy and the Fair Lady of Faguell*, ed. Elizabeth McCansland, Smith College Studies in Modern Languages (Northampton, Massachusetts: Smith College, n.d. [?1922]).

[26] J. C. Holt, *Robin Hood* (London: Thames and Hudson, 1982), p. 140 and note 12. Madden (p. 349) also noted this reference, concluding "It is no doubt this romance [the *Jeaste of Syr Gawayne*, edited below, and not *Sir Gawain and the Green Knight*] which is alluded to. . . ." Christopher Dean, *Arthur of England: English Attitudes to King Arthur and the Knights of the Round Table in the Middle Ages and the Renaissance* (Toronto: University of Toronto Press, 1987), who mentions Cox, also assumes this is the *Jeaste*. For further bibliographical information on *Jeaste*, see the introduction to that romance.

the other hand, the skills and repertoire of the Captain and the mixed character of his audience — aristocratic, urban, and rural, consisting of women and men from the Queen to commoners — might well be taken as a heightened rendition of the diverse social environments in which Gawain romances like those in the present volume would thrive.

Laneham presents the Captain as capable of reciting not only romances like "Syr Gawyn," but "many moe [tales] then I rehears heere: I beleeve hee have them all at his fingers ends." Laneham refers to the bundle of written ballads that Cox carries, to the "omberty [abundance] of his books," and to his having "as fair a library for . . . sciences" as foreign competitors like "Nostradam of Frauns." On their face, these remarks seem to imply that Cox's performances were scripted and textual (though in the latter comments Laneham may have meant the abundance of titles in the "library" that Cox could reproduce memorially, "at his fingers ends"). Nonetheless, it is clear that what most impressed Laneham was the Captain's resources as an oral performer who could spontaneously produce "many goodly monuments both in prose and poetry and at afternoons can talk as much without book, as ony Inholder [inn keeper] betwixt Brainford and Bagshot, what degree soever he be."[27] The surviving copies of Gawain romances collected in this volume for the most part reflect

---

[27] William Matthews some time ago pointed out the features of orality — archaic diction, formulaic phrasing, alliterative linking, and so on — in the "sollem song" of an "auncient minstrell" of Islington, whose performance during the royal entertainment at Kenilworth in 1575, like that of Captain Cox, was described in Laneham's *Letter* (pp. 46–56; see above, note 23, for citation). His recital of "King Arthurz acts" was apparently based upon the published text of Malory's *Morte Darthur*, though whether he had read it for himself or heard it read is unspecified. His performance in any case unmistakably involved improvisation, and Matthews shrewdly adduced this as evidence that traditional techniques and materials (which may or may not have been written down) remained vital through the end of the sixteenth century. What is striking above all is the mixed character of the event — at once literate and oral, modern and traditional, reflecting French verse forms and native poetic practice, a popular improvisation yet part of a royal command performance. The avid interest — Laneham was a London merchant and courtier — attracted by Arthurian narrative in this mixed form perhaps offers a model for the kinds of responses medieval chivalric romances excited; in particular, it points to the diversity of audiences and occasions, and the range of feelings, from unselfconscious glee to patronizing smugness, that listeners might experience. See Matthews, "Alliterative Song of an Elizabethan Minstrel," *Research Studies* 32 (1964), 134–46.

just such a combined oral-literate context of performance.[28] The missing lines, gaps in the narratives, and the well-used (not to say dilapidated) quality of the manuscripts suggest that reciters must have carried them about — perhaps "bound with a whipcord" — and worked from them, beginning at the time of their composition and circulation in the fourteenth century, through the time of Captain Cox, and at least until the compiling of the Percy Folio Manuscript in the mid-seventeenth century.[29] And Laneham's elaborate tribute makes clear that for the occasional literate

---

[28] See Derek Pearsall, "Middle English Romance and its Audiences," *Historical and Editorial Studies in Medieval and Early Modern English for Johan Gerritsen*, ed. Mary-Jo Arn and Hanneke Wirtjes with Hans Jansen (Groningen: Wolters-Noordhoff, n.d. [?1985]), pp. 37–47, whose summary remarks on oral and literate preservation, on "re-composition" and improvisation in performance, and the "range of possible audiences" complement the presentation I offer here. In "The Myth of the Minstrel Manuscript," *Speculum* 66 (1991), 43–73, Andrew Taylor offers a careful review of surviving manuscript evidence for popular performance, emphasizing the interdependence of oral and written, official and unofficial cultural elements. Taylor does not consider the mixed nature of the Islington minstrel's performance of Arthurian romance (see Matthews' essay cited in the previous note), or the odd example of such mixed literate-oral material printed by Rossell Hope Robbins, "A Gawain Epigone," *Modern Language Notes* 58 (1943), 361–66; this comprises a fifty-three line fragment in garbled alliterative verse, apparently composed by Humphrey Newton. The formulaic phrasing seems repeatedly to imitate lines in *Sir Gawain and the Green Knight* (with parallels as well in *Awntyrs* and *Gologras* not noted by Robbins); it is not clear whether this is a purely literary excursion or a feeble record of some performance, but the deployment of alliterative linking is so mechanical and haphazard that the fragment seems completely incoherent.

[29] While I emphasize in this account the performance tradition that gave continuing life to the medieval chivalric romances, the sixteenth century also produced a significant number of printed romances that circulated among readers. Beginning with the materials produced by Caxton and his successors noted above, a string of knightly narratives issued from the presses, though relatively few were Arthurian. The two surviving fragments of the *Jeaste*, together with a license to issue another edition of the poem (dating from about 1529 to 1559), seem to be the only publication of verse romances; see the introduction to *Jeaste* in this volume for a full account. Malory's prose *Morte Darthur* was issued a number of times during the century, and a prose *History of . . . Arthur of lytell Brytayne*, translated by Lord Berners, appeared sometime before 1566. See Ronald S. Crane, *The Vogue of Medieval Chivalric Romance During the English Renaissance* (Menasha, Wisconsin: George Banta, 1919), who lists all editions chronologically; Dean, *Arthur of England* (note 24, above), offers a selective overview.

listener like himself, as well as for large audiences from all ranks and areas, their appeal remained undiminished into the lifetime of Shakespeare.[30]

Nonetheless, evidence that this appeal was *not* universal, that popular romance might be openly resisted, especially by those identified with high, literate, or official culture, survives in reactions from a variety of sources. Already in the mid-fourteenth century Robert Mannyng complained that "disours," "seggers," and "harpours" — reciters, story-tellers, minstrels, performance artists all — distorted some presumed authentic or original text ("But I here it no man so say / That of som copple some is away" [I never hear a performer speak, except that some part is missing]).[31] The *Speculum vitae*, versified instruction intended for oral presentation to (presumably non-literate) laity, starts out,

> I warne yow first at the begynnyng,
> I wil make no vayn spekyng
> Of dedis of armes ne of amours,
> As done mynstrels and gestours,
> That makyn spekyng in many place
> Of Octavyan and Isambrace,
> And of many other gestis,
> And namely when thei come to festis —
> Ne of the life of Bevis of Hamtoun
> That was a knyght of grete renoun
> Ne of Gy of Warwick . . . .[32]

Yet one manuscript of the *Speculum*, apparently intended for the urban bourgeoise, contains as well (together with other tales) complete copies of *Octavian*, *Beves*, and

---

[30] The preservation and lively performance of chivalric romances among urban working people — Captain Cox was "by profession a Mason, and that right skilfull" — recalls Shakespeare's cast of performers in *A Midsummer Night's Dream*. Coventry and Kenilworth are not far distant from Stratford-upon-Avon, and Cox was likely only one of the more notable of workers who could perform even classical stories, like "Virgils Life" or "Lucres and Eurialus."

[31] *The Story of England by Robert Mannyng*, ed. F. J. Furnivall, Rolls Series 34 (London: 1887), lines 101–02. Mannyng wrote his *Chronicle* in 1338.

[32] See *Cambridge University Library Manuscript Ff. 2.38*, ed. Frances McSparran and P. R. Robinson (London: Scolar Press, 1979). For discussion of the context of the shared and conflicted interests of popular religion and popular romance, see Eamon Duffy, *The Stripping of the Altars: Traditional Religion in England, c. 1400–c. 1580* (New Haven and London: Yale University Press, 1992), pp. 69–71.

Guy, the very chivalric romances denounced in this prologue. Clerical disdain found a counterpart in the literary scorn of popular narratives of knighthood that occurs in self-consciously artistic writers like Chaucer. "Sir Thopas," Chaucer's parodic narrative "Of bataille and of chivalry, And of ladyes love-drury [passion]," takes specific aim at the further layer of contradiction that "bourgeois" or "urban" brings to the already paradoxical genre of popular chivalric romance. Thopas, the improbable "flour [flower] / Of roial chivalry" shares his pedigree with other heroes of "romances of prys [great worth]," including "Horn Child," "Ypotys," "Beves," "Sir Gy," "Sir Lybeux," and "Pleyndamour." Satires like Chaucer's did not, however, discourage collectors like Sir John Paston from acquiring copies of *Guy of Warwyk,* *Guy and Colbronde,* and *Chylde Ypotis;* moreover, Caxton and his successors mass-produced such romances as *Beves, Eglamour, Guy, Ysumbras,* and *Tryamour* (as well as Malory's prose chronicle of Arthur), and a century after Caxton, Captain Cox still featured these chivalric tales in his repertoire of performances.[33] The scorn and satire that constitute a rejection of popular chivalric romance certainly did not end their vogue, and in themselves may be taken as a proof and tribute to their continuing power over audiences.

Evidence that Gawain romances were much enjoyed in the late Middle Ages is abundant in the extensive allusions to his knightly courtesy, in the multiple production of copies (for *Awntyrs* and *Gologras*), and in the multiple versions and retellings that survive (*Greene Knight, Marriage,* and *Carle* all reprise earlier medieval romances, and the other renditions of *Ragnelle* together with the ballad-style narratives of *Turke* and *Cornwall* prove the wide circulation of these stories). Moreover, the worn state of several of the manuscripts that contain single surviving copies of these poems suggests that they were literally read to death, perhaps often before live

---

[33] Among all the verse romances printed by Caxton and his immediate successors for English readers, none are Arthurian. (Malory's *Morte Darthur,* though it appropriates at least two English verse romances — the alliterative and stanzaic poems on the death of Arthur — is in prose.) Likewise, none of the poems satirized by Chaucer or dismissed in the *Speculum vitae* has Arthurian connections. The Gawain romances, and other popular Arthurian tales, seem therefore to have held sway mainly outside the world of print, and beyond the notice of literate and official culture (whether because more admired or beneath contempt seems unclear). Except for the print of *Gologras and Gawain,* and the two surviving fragments of *Jeaste,* all of the Gawain romances — including those in multiple copies and multiple versions — survive in manuscript copies only.

audiences.[34] But however broad their appreciation, can chivalric romances ever be taken as in any sense the literature of the people? Must we regard the celebration of knighthood as an imposition of the dominant culture, by which those largely outside political power are brought to celebrate secular society's most potent institution, and its symbol of the unequal division of estates or classes? When Captain Cox (or any one of his nameless predecessors) performed his "Sir Gawyn" before the Queen, a great lord, or even the Lord Mayor of Coventry, was he reinforcing the position of an elite class over him, or was he giving shape to an identity he as a stone mason shared with other workers, who must have constituted his chief audience?[35]

Such questions point to the elusive character of "popular" culture, and the difficulties that stand in the way of defining it in terms of the historical interests or lived experience of any distinct or exclusive social group or class. The censure of chivalric romance in high literary writing (Chaucer), popular burlesque (*The Tournament of Tottenham*), or ecclesiastical chastisement presents an emphatically negative view of popular culture; these imply that only the most simple and undemanding audience could sit through the exaggerations, absurdities, and contradictions of these tales, thereby making "popular" equivalent to ignorant or just plain bad. Yet the persistence of hostility towards chivalric romances from various quarters in itself proves that popular culture did not simply and irresistibly reproduce the values of a dominant order for mindless reception by a passive audience. Some medieval people — especially those in official positions, and those committed to refined or elite literacy — reacted to these tales as potentially subversive, and this

---

[34] For histories of medieval romance, and the place of chivalric romance in that larger context, see the individual books listed in the Bibliography of Editions and Works Cited by Barron, Mehl, Ramsey, Richmond, and Wittig.

[35] Questions surrounding romance as a literary genre, the nature of popular writing, and its relation to the reigning values of a society have been considered in a number of publications, none of which directly address medieval chivalric romance. These include Janice Radway, *Reading the Romance: Women, Patriarchy, and Popular Literature* (Chapel Hill, North Carolina: University of North Carolina Press, 1984); Colin MacCabe, "Defining Popular Culture," *High Theory / Low Culture: Analysing Popular Television and Film*, ed. MacCabe (New York: St. Martin's Press, 1986), pp. 1–10; and Bob Ashley, *The Study of Popular Fiction: A Source Book* (London and Philadelphia: University of Pennsylvania Press, 1989), which contains a number of classic analytical essays, with introductions and bibliographies.

rejection marks out one space for resistant or alternative readings and responses.[36] Modern readers have often followed this negative assessment of popular culture in their own reaction to the romances. A recent translator of the Gawain stories, for example, remarks that they are "primitive," "rustic," and "crude," though at times "charming" or "touching."[37] This critical perspective, in making the romances out to be failed attempts at psychological realism, too easily dismisses the potential in these narratives for laughter and disruption. The mixed character of the romances, their open disavowal of literary credibility in favor of the fantastic, their frequent comic tone and resort to extravagance and hyperbole, all have the effect of highlighting the absurdities, inequalities, and contradictions of a feudal order or chivalric ideals, even as they are idealized or celebrated. These seemingly naive and artless Arthurian stories, in giving pleasure and simple assurance to listeners at diverse social levels, exploit the paradoxical impulses that motivate the adventures of a bourgeois knight or a burger king, and in doing so they foreshadow the ultimate satire of this typically medieval hybrid, Cervantes' *Don Quixote*.

A fuller appreciation of the Gawain romances' popularity requires, then, a more vivid sense of the pleasure they gave to their sponsoring audiences. Though they may have appeared lacking in sophistication to committed readers of Chaucer's *Knight's Tale* or *Sir Gawain and the Green Knight*, the broad support for these stories among late medieval people reflects a deep enjoyment in listening or reading as

---

[36] Reactions to the romances as worthless or potentially damaging to one's character or soul come mainly from those associated with literacy — church officials, "serious" writers — rather than from the secular nobility. As Sir John Paston's literary interests imply, everyone within the gentry, from local knights to the royal household, enjoyed chivalric tales, and kings (and their image-makers) continued to see the useful connections between Arthurian legend and monarchical prestige throughout the late Middle Ages. In addition to the comments on the Arthurian interests of Edward I and Edward III above, which make clear the uses of chivalric pageantry in consolidating the interests of a dominant group and in naturalizing estate or class differences as a feature of cohesive national identity, see David Carlson, "King Arthur and Court Poems for the Birth of Arthur Tudor in 1486," *Humanistica Lovaniensia* 36 (1987), 147–83.

[37] See Valerie Krishna, *Five Middle English Arthurian Romances* (New York: Garland, 1991), pp. 24–26 (on *Carlisle*); though elsewhere in the introduction the point is made that these romances require appropriate standards for a proper appreciation, these remarks are on the whole representative. Similar assessments occur in the summary accounts of these tales in standard literary histories and in the *Manual of the Writings in Middle English* (see Bibliography of Editions and Works Cited).

a social (rather than solitary) event.[38] The circumstances of public performance make "audience" itself perhaps too confining a term, since listeners must have taken some active part in such readings (as implied by the frequent injunctions that the audience behave), or become storytellers in their own right on other occasions. Performance artists must have given boisterous and flamboyantly histrionic recitals, impersonating roles through change of voice and gesture, playing the melodramatic sentimentality and violence to the utmost, priming and inciting their listeners' responses to the wondrous (and perhaps even more, to the incredible) elements in their plots. Chivalric romances achieved popularity by combining the narrative obviousness of a television sit-com with the ambience of a professional wrestling match. Having to read these romances, rather than hear and watch them performed, makes their participatory spontaneity difficult for modern audiences to relish, all the more so because they are in Middle English. Yet it was clearly as popular performance art, with strong elements of mimicry and burlesque, that they initially brought pleasure to the majority of their earliest listeners.[39]

The performance-oriented character of these romances emerges also in their narrative technique and narrative content. Self-conscious writers considered the apparently simple meter of tail-rhyme and alliterative narratives to be chief among their literary offenses; Chaucer has his Host declare the romance of *Thopas* "rym dogerel" and "drasty rymyng . . . nat worth a toord," and his Parson refuses to

---

[38] The popular, or at least non-literary, character of the romances in the present volume appears strikingly in their complete lack of allusion to any other literary text. Though occasionally a poem refers to another Arthurian character or story, these narratives never demand, or even assume, that an imagined audience be prepared to make the textual associations that Chaucer, for example, assumed his readers would enjoy, and indeed would need to see any value in his writing. Even Malory's *Morte Darthur*, which for all its length makes no reference to a non-Arthurian text, is more *literary* than these romances simply because Malory created it in writing out of an encyclopedic array of French books (together with a handful of English poems).

[39] *Awntyrs* and *Gologras* in many respects constitute exceptions to the general remarks made here about the popular character of the Gawain romances. As their individual introductions make clear, both seem to have been produced by a self-conscious and literate composer, working from a written source, who made the fullest use of alliteration and formulas traditionally associated with native poetic traditions. Both poems enjoyed popularity in being reproduced in multiple copies — four manuscript versions of *Awntyrs* survive, and *Gologras* was one of the first Gawain romances in print — but the exceptional artfulness of their meter, verse forms, and descriptive detail separate them from the unchecked narrative movement of the other poems in this volume.

"geeste 'rum, ram, ruf' by lettre" — that is, to use the linking alliterative formulas of chivalric gests or tales. But partisans of popular romance did not seek the novelty of plot, individualized character, verbal ambiguities, subtle allusion, or variation in theme and image so dear to Chaucer. Like those who attend live musical concerts, they expected to hear lyrics they already knew, performed to a memorable beat that allowed them to vocalize along with the performer. Anyone who has attended a sporting event easily understands the power of rhythmic clapping, whether initiated by the crowd, the scoreboard, or the piped-in music of Queen ("We will, we will, rock you"). It was just this kind of participatory and moving experience that made the reading event so enjoyable for the audiences of chivalric romances, and made the romances so disreputable with the keepers of high culture.

The power of such simple meters remains obvious if one reads aloud the dense and richly echoic alliterative verse of *Awntyrs* or *Gologras*. There are elements of such alliteration in *Avowyng* as well as in some of the other romances, and a live performance (even by a solitary modern reader) softens the imputation of doggerel in the tail-rhyme romances as well. The strong beat that underlies the narrative and activates the audience is a striking residue of the orality that marks medieval (and later) popular culture. The performer's calls for order and participatory attention, the cues offered at narrative shifts or to control audience response, the relentless emphasis on surface description of clothing, accessories, armor, weapons, and other details demonstrate the public and social nature of these poems' reception. Just as the words of these tales try to present a vivid picture to listeners who can't review the text, so the words *in* the tales emphasize the importance of seeing and being seen; the array of synonyms for face, look, demeanor, appearance (which cannot be matched in the modern English glosses) helps convey the importance of direct contact and public self-presentation in the honor/shame culture of knighthood that the romances purport to describe. In the fiction as in its performance, identity abides in what one is seen to be or heard to say. What characters do or wear must be "ful clere" to all, and they must speak "on highe" so that all can hear, and so these frequently repeated phrases are hardly fillers; instead, they define the communal acknowledgment necessary for any action to have meaning or worth. The privileged role of spectacle within orality attaches as well to the rituals of combat, honor, and courtesy enacted by Gawain and the other knights. In a chivalric context, all speech and gesture (including, for example, laughter) require a proper form and an immediate response, or insult follows; knightly conduct therefore resembles the closed code of military speech, where each act demands a prescribed response, and only the unchivalric — Sir Kay, the Carle, Ragnelle — dare to overstep its limits, or speak out of turn.

The Gawain Romances

The Gawain Romances and Tales as a Group

In drawing together all but a few of the romances that feature Sir Gawain, the present volume to some degree assumes that the force of the hero's character is sufficient to overshadow the differences in texts produced over the course of several hundred years. This anthology omits the three earliest Gawain romances in Middle English, *Libeaus Desconus* (before 1350), *Ywain and Gawain* (before 1350), and *Sir Gawain and the Green Knight* (about 1375). All of these have impressive literary pedigrees and an ease of accessibility for the modern reader that separates them from most of the other Gawain tales. Yet even among the "popular" poems published here there are striking degrees of difference in literariness: in particular, *Awntyrs* and *Gologras* depend directly on literary sources, manifest intensely self-conscious artifice, and push traditional, oral poetic traits to the point of hyper-development. Nonetheless, these two poems shared in the popularity of their hero, for *Awntyrs* survives in four copies (an exceptional number for a romance) and *Gologras* was among the first printed books from the Scottish press.

Gawain does, then, represent the central presence in these romances. It is crucial to note, however, that he holds these narratives together not through some novelistic sense of "character," as a unique and consistent personality with individualized traits, complexly drawn motives, or psychologized feelings. Instead, Gawain plays a *role*; he routinely facilitates the extravagant adventures that happen around him, and does so to such an extent that one might even think of him almost as a narrative function. The romances emphatically mark out, in social as well as narrative terms, just what this role encompasses: Gawain is a generation removed from the father-figure of the king, to whom he stands in the crucial relation of mother's brother–sister's son. Gawain shares this slot in the social order with his brothers, Aggravayne and the illegitimate Mordred, but he is clearly the "good son"; despite his exuberance and superior physical prowess, he is unwilling to challenge the fatherly authority of the king. Gawain's courtesy, in both martial and domestic situations, in this way makes him the chief mediator of the father's law, the young man who offers the ultimate reassurance about the status quo in demonstrating the suppleness and strength of the rules governing the social order.

As the exemplary Young Man, Gawain remains unfettered by trammels of authority, the need to think hard about the future or make decisions of political consequence; he is on the loose, constantly ready for adventure. Over and over, Gawain proves the worth of familiar values by facing the marvelous or unknown, and rendering it manageable for the rest of his society. But his preeminence does not simply consist in unhesitating courage or unparalleled ability. Again it is Gawain's *courtesy* — perfect composure in moments of crisis — that endows him with heroic stature. Repeatedly, Gawain exhibits a willing restraint of available force or a refusal of the authority of position, which separates him from non-chivalrous opponents and also from the arbitrary bullying or domineering impertinence of Sir Kay. Each courteous conquest stages the general triumph of civility, ensuring that the rituals that organize social meaning prevail in spite of confusion or even threat to life. Gawain's exceptional performance of the precepts that bind everyday social existence thus conveys a stirring endorsement of the rightness of things as they are. Moreover, his courtesy makes his conquests all the more complete, for they entail not annihilation or brute suppression, but the ungrudging concession of Gawain's superiority by some previously hostile or unknown Other. Gawain's role in the romances works therefore to effect the reconciliation or reappropriation, rather than the destruction, of the strange or alien, and this happy resolution in turn secures the audience's identification with the hero, and with the naturalness of the social order he represents.

The two other characters who figure prominently in the Gawain romances are King Arthur and Sir Kay, Arthur's Steward. As the great king, Arthur establishes Gawain's heroic stature and authorizes what might otherwise seem capricious escapades as knightly quests. Yet in playing this background role to reckless adventure, Arthur seems sometimes less than dynamic and often ambiguous. If he remains apart from the action, he appears either inessential (as in *Carlisle* or *Jeaste*) or bordering on the ineffectual and ludicrous (as in *Ragnelle* and *Marriage*). If he joins in the action, he runs the risk of appearing silly or "childgered" (as in *Avowyng*) or tyrannical (as in *Gologras* and perhaps in *Awntyrs*).[40] His most kingly function is to appear in finales, confirming Gawain's successes and presiding over the reconciliation of conflict. Sir Kay cuts a still more ambiguous figure: he appears ambivalently aligned to both the older generation of King Arthur, and the reckless younger generation of Gawain, and is made to embody the worst tendencies of both. As Steward, he attempts to exploit the aristocratic privilege conferred through birth and position; he serves as Gawain's foil, trampling on courtesy and showing an arbitrary, impatient crabbedness to all he encounters. Kay lurches through each episode as an image of nobility out of control and in danger of self-destructing; as a character he is saved by unfailingly (and hilariously) receiving the comeuppance he so richly deserves, and by this same device the romances create a vision of chivalry as governed (and governing) through a rough but humane natural justice.

---

[40] Arthur is characterized as "childgered" in *Sir Gawain and the Green Knight* (line 86), as he anticipates adventure before the great feast. The word may imply a boyish merriness or a childish recklessness, or some combination of these traits.

The Gawain Romances

The Gawain romances achieve an obvious cohesion, then, through the name recognition of these central characters, through their repeated appearance and distinctive traits, and through the Arthurian associations most listeners would carry with them as part of their cultural baggage. Within the narratives predictable roles serve as powerful, stabilizing links that join rapid-fire episodes of marvels, violence, and mysterious confrontation, or extended and detailed description. The headlong sequencing of events, often apparently unmotivated or non-causal, and the lavish attention to surface realities equips the storytelling with a kinetic and spectacular quality that may leave a deeper impression on audiences than the characters themselves. This irruption of unforeseen wonders and threats is not, however, without pattern: these provide Gawain with the indispensable opportunity for heroic triumph, but they also illustrate recurrent settings, themes, and processes crucial to the social meaning of the romances. The unity that the poems attain is consequently often more the outcome of structural repetition and thematic variation than of character or event.

Among the scenes that the romances characteristically reproduce are encounters in the forest, on the battlefield, and in the bedroom. Unlike Dante's dark wood, Inglewood Forest is no thicket of inner spiritual crisis haunted by symbolic beasts; here hunters pursue English wild boar and deer, and occasionally meet up with weird or preternatural beings like Sir Gromer, the Carl, or the ghost of Guenevere's mother. Six of the poems in this collection begin with a forest episode; these clearly function as prologues, providing a familiar narrative space for the audience to quiet down and settle in. In each case, the woods at first are a place of aristocratic leisure and self-display, where members of the royal entourage can test their prowess against wild creatures and show their knowledge of hunting lore.[41] The holiday

---

[41] From the time of William the Conqueror, the forests were regarded as the special preserve of the king; by the time of Henry II, one third of England was subject to forest law. Hunting was at the king's prerogative only, and large game — specifically deer (the animals pursued in *Ragnelle, Carlisle, Awntyrs,* and *Marriage*), and wild boar (hunted in *Avowyng,* and together with deer and foxes, in *Sir Gawain and the Green Knight* and *Greene Knight*) — were reserved solely for the king. The *Dialogue of the Exchequer* (late twelfth century) describes the forests as "the sanctuary and special delight of kings, where . . . away from the turmoils inherent in a court, they breathe the pleasure of natural freedom"; justice in the forest comes not from the law, but from "the will and whim of the king." Any adventure occurring in a forest would therefore inevitably constitute a fundamental confrontation with the power invested in the person and the office of the king. See *Dialogus de Scaccario,* revised edition, edited and translated by Charles Johnson and others (Oxford: Clarendon Press, 1983); I have modified the translation slightly.

atmosphere furnishes, however, a pretext for adventure; the temporary respite from martial rigors and constant vigilance opens the court (and its great hero) to a test not simply of prowess but of mettle, and the unconstrained environs give the unexpected challenger a chance to probe the Arthurian ensemble in unguarded moments.

Battlefield encounters are an expected feature of chivalric romance, and so it is perhaps surprising that many of these poems contain no actual scenes of combat, or furnish only a bare, allusive description of fighting. Only *Awntyrs*, *Gologras*, and *Jeaste* offer sustained accounts of knightly struggle. Typically, all battles take the form of duels, enabling participants to prove their skill and expand their reputations, and giving the audience a concrete portrayal of armed violence. In all the romances, however, fighting constitutes primarily a symbolic, rather than a simply physical, activity: it insists upon the rule-bound character of mortal combat, stretches the limits of courtesy to the extremities of life, and demonstrates the overlaps between masculine rivalry and bonding, and between enmity and reconciliation within a politics of national cohesion. Bedroom scenes, on the other hand, may at first seem out of place in these martial romances, but events staged in this intimate, domestic space work similarly to strengthen the bonds of male solidarity. Pivotal or climactic episodes take place in women's beds in *Ragnelle*, *Carlisle*, and *Avowyng* (as well as in *Marriage*, *Carle*, and *Jeaste*), yet none of these have to do primarily with heterosexual passion; instead, these private spaces take on a theatrical ambience, making a trial of social ties — in the marriage contract between a woman and her husband, and even more in the ties between men within a fictionalized chivalric code. Courtesy's definition depends upon Gawain's response to the Carl's control of his wife's and daughter's sexual availability, or upon Baldwin's response to Arthur's bed trick, and the resolution of societal disruption comes about through the courteous and rule-bound exchange of women among men.

In *Ragnelle*, Gawain's bedroom scene enacts this reconciliation — between female and male, private and public, old and young, wretched and handsome, peasant and noble — through the outright physical transformation of the loathly lady into a beautiful young woman. Sympathetic audiences, medieval and modern, surely find pleasure in the singular improbability and the poetic justice of this spectacular turn of events. Just as surely, however, audiences recognize, if only subliminally, that such satisfying endings depend on the anticipation and endorsement of normative integration that these marvelous transformations symbolize; their reiteration in story after story is irrefutable evidence that they arise from the desire of listeners and readers, even as they assist in producing this desire. In *Ragnelle* and *Carlisle*, the threatening figures of hag and churl — rough, ugly, ignoble, menacing — are literally transformed by Gawain's *gentilesse* into refined, handsome figures who "naturally" take their place among the ruling elite. This plot recurs, with only slight structural variations, in *Marriage* and *Carle*, as well as in *Greene Knight* and *Turke*, which introduce elements of the exotic to the characterization of the outsider. In *Gologras* (and to a lesser extent in *Avowyng*, *Cornwall*, and *Jeaste*), the happy ending is achieved not through shape-shifting but through the transformative submission of enemies to the chivalric ethos.

These happy endings produce a "magical resolution" typical of romance: in this world of unmotivated marvels and fulfilled wishes, social interests quite opposed in the "real world" move into alignment. The stirring portrayals of triumphant courtesy and justice vindicated that mark the conclusions of romances potentially work to hold their diverse audiences together, to reproduce in them the feeling of integration that the narrated transformations dramatize, and to effect a *sense* of social cohesion (not at all dependent on social reality) that enables the established order to prevail.[42] In its crudest formulation, such a view of the romances would give them a crucial function in the conspiratorial imposition of dominant values upon a docile and homogeneous public; their reading would dull perceptions of social inequities and diminish the potential for political change. Yet spectacularly decisive resolutions, like those of the Gawain romances, do not inevitably or uniformly support the ruling order. As the magical realism of Latin American writers like Borges, Garcia Marquez, or Esquivel demonstrates, fantastic narratives can open a space for political critique; contradictions and absurdities, rather than being swallowed whole, constitute a basis upon which audiences — starting from a broad range of social positions — may formulate alternative or subversive understandings. Moreover, the romances themselves incorporate divergent, sometimes openly censuring, interpretations of knighthood: in *Awntyrs* Gawain self-consciously asks about the potential culpability of chivalric violence, and this romance and *Gologras* take a troublingly ambiguous outlook on the royal and aristocratic assumptions that underlie individual combat and the enterprise of warfare. Finally, the motifs of magical transformation that so strongly characterize the romances find social correlatives in the hybrid character of the poems. Their composition and consumption — as narratives about the nobility that circulate and are profoundly modified in popular milieux — imply a storytelling transmigration across elite, bourgeois, and laboring audiences, re-

---

[42] Raymond Williams employs the term "magical resolution" (as a kind of false consciousness that entraps those without power into agreement with social relations contrary to their interests) in his discussion of the social function of literature in the Industrial Revolution; see *The Long Revolution* (New York: Columbia University Press, 1961), pp. 65–71. For a general discussion of some of the main issues surrounding the analysis of popular culture from a social and historical perspective, together with excerpts from classic essays, see Ashley, *The Study of Popular Fiction* (note 35, above).

enacting the metamorphoses by which characters in the plots cross the boundaries of otherwise circumscribed groups.

A last characteristic that marks the Gawain romances as a unified group, and that again exemplifies the intersection of disparate elements within them, centers on their frequent resort to geography to locate their meaning. Almost all the poems explicitly set their adventures in or near Carlisle, a city with long-standing Arthurian associations, located in Cumbria (the north-westernmost territory of England, sharing the border with Scotland). Carlisle was in turn a Celtic and British stronghold, a Roman fortification, part of the area populated by Scandinavian invaders, and an outpost marking the edge of English (and Anglo-Norman) political claims. "Inglewood," the name of the forest in which so many encounters take place in the poems, seems originally to have signified "the woods or enclave of the Angles," a contested English foothold within mainly Celtic territories. A study of the personal names given in Cumberland indicates that the mixed character of the population carried through the central and late Middle Ages, with Celtic, Scandinavian, and English names all continuously in use.[43] In short, Carlisle with its environs is pre-eminently a border territory, a contested area of mixed populations and of shifting and changing alliances. The people of Cumbria — knights, clerks, peasants — were constantly exposed to feuding and factionalization, fueled by fiercely competitive local and national identities and by the struggle for land ownership as a means of social mobility.[44] Frontier society, prepared for war at all times and bred on tales of military prowess and conquest transformed into a nostalgic chivalry, made an ideal fictional setting for the marvels and adventures of romance.

These Arthurian romances themselves constitute a "border writing" of sorts, not so much because they are "about" Carlisle and the Anglo-Scottish marches as because they give literary expression to contending interests that intersect late medieval social, political, and intellectual life.[45] In specifically geographical terms,

---

[43] See John Insley, "Some Aspects of Regional Variation in Early Middle English Personal Nomenclature," *Leeds Studies in English* n.s. 18 (1987), 183–99, which provides evidence that surviving names exactly reflect "the heterogeneous nature of settlement patterns in this northern borderland" (p. 183).

[44] On the character of late medieval border territories, see Anthony Goodman, "Religion and Warfare in the Anglo-Scottish Marches," *Medieval Frontier Societies*, ed. Robert Bartlett and Angus MacKay (Oxford: Clarendon, 1989), pp. 245–66.

[45] I borrow the term "border writing" here from D. Emily Hicks, *Border Writing: The Multidimensional Text* (Minneapolis: University of Minnesota Press, 1991); for its usefulness in describing cultural situations of the medieval West, I am indebted to Kathleen Biddick. Border

poems oscillate between centripetal and centrifugal views of human activity. Almost every one of the Gawain romances shows a remarkably detailed and concentrated attention to Carlisle and adjoining areas.[46] Many choose Inglewood Forest or its famous lake, the Tarn Wathelene, as the setting of their principal action; from here, adventures move along the old Roman road, through local villages and to specific manors, whose names are sometimes still recognizable. *Turke* crosses to the Isle of Man, off the coast of Cumberland in the Solway Firth, and Galloway, the Scots territory north of the border, is frequently mentioned. This profusion of localizing detail furnishes the romances a setting that is at once compact and familiar-seeming, yet remote and wild.[47] Cumbria's reputation as romance territory may carry traces of earlier oral tales and of unrecorded border ballads; it continued in popular stories like that of the outlaw Adam Bell, and received belated tribute in Romantic attempts by Wordsworth and other Lake Poets to preserve popular traditions.[48]

The surviving Gawain romances, even those that appear only in a single manuscript, do not record the dialect of the composer, but are instead copies; nonetheless, linguistic evidence in the poems points to the northwest, and perhaps Cumber-

---

writing helps to suggest the ways in which popular chivalric romance joins discreet forms, miscellaneous subject matters, and potentially antagonistic audiences, and splits what might otherwise seem unified interests and groups. In this way, the romances define a border site of intersections and possible resistance to established regimes. Yet their crossover status consists chiefly in their openness to appropriation; in different ways and in differing situations they may well have offered a cheerful reinforcement of the status quo for many, perhaps most, audiences.

[46] The notable exceptions are *Gologras*, which sets its action on the continent, *Cornwall*, which takes place in Little Britain, and *Jeaste*.

[47] For a detailed description of the place of geography and geology in the economic, political, and social life of the area of the Gawain romances, see Angus J. L. Winchester, *Landscape and Society in Medieval Cumbria* (Edinburgh: John Donald, 1987).

[48] The earliest copy of the ballad of Adam Bell is a fragment of a print from 1536; it survives in five additional versions, including one in the Percy Folio manuscript (which contains *Greene Knight*, *Turke*, *Marriage*, *Cornwall*, and other narratives). At the outset of the ballad, Adam and his companions are, like Robin Hood, "outlawed for venyson" and "swore them brethen upon a day / To Englysshe-wood for to gone"; the odd spelling preserves the original sense of an English enclave in Celtic territories. See *The English and Scottish Popular Ballads*, ed. Francis James Child (1888; rpt. New York: Dover, 1965), vol. 3, pp. 22 ff. (stanza 4). In the context of such popular tales, it is worth noting that one of the Robin Hood ballads, *Queen Katherine*, has the knight whom Robin befriends, Sir Richard Lee, descend "from Gawiins blood"; see Child, vol. 3, p. 199 (stanza 22). This ballad also survives in the Percy Folio manuscript.

land itself, as the likely place of origin for several of them. Even if they reflect knowledge of a local landscape, however, their setting must be regarded as mainly fictional: it represents the centripetal tendency in these narratives to concentrate all meaningful action on the person of the king, and on the seat of royal power at Carlisle (however eccentric such a locale must have seemed in comparison to Westminster). At the same time, the romances provide a strong counterbalance to this tendency in the extraordinarily centrifugal thrust they project for Arthurian territorial ambitions. If Carlisle operates as the indispensable endplace in the plots, the centralized narrative site where everything is brought home and made secure, then all the other marginal, far-flung locations the romances name are the key symbols in the fantasy of world conquest. Gawain's role as the hero who faces the unknown and renders it manageable for the rest of his society is repeatedly figured in geographical terms; in a showdown at the court, or through a journey to a far-off realm, Gawain brings the socially or exotically monstrous under lawful rule, makes the strange recognizable, returns the outlying to the center. Yet, as fantasies of limitless monarchical control, these poems do not take an undifferentiated view of conquered kingdoms, but instead offer a precise, undeviating agenda for just which lands require subduing and colonization: all are Celtic territories that make up the periphery of England — Scotland, Wales, Cornwall, Ireland, the Isle of Man, Brittany. Their peripheral location defines a symbolic geography, and their conquest consequently enhances the myth of England's centrality and political dominion.[49] In locating fantasies of triumph in exoticized Celtic realms, the Gawain romances render these marginal spaces a proving ground for the superiority of centralized royal prerogative (in preference to any claims of local autonomy). Moreover, for English audiences at least, their combination of local and exotic (together with their other hybrid qualities) must have intensified the perception of a coherent and compelling national identity that crossed traditional boundaries of class and estate; in this way, nostalgic idealizations of chivalry and rousing tales of derring-do solicited enthusiastic engagement in an imagined community of the realm.

The efflorescence of Arthurian romance in England during the later Middle Ages, and in particular its regional association with the north, has provoked several attempts at explanation. William Matthews, confining his argument to alliterative

---

[49] Robert Bartlett has recently argued that armed expansion might be taken as a defining characteristic of European identity in the high Middle Ages; see *The Making of Europe: Conquest, Colonization, and Cultural Change, 950–1350* (Princeton: Princeton University Press, 1993). The extensive documentation Bartlett provides for this earlier period provides useful contexts for understanding the romances and their historical impact during the following two centuries and beyond.

poetry, claimed that the romances enunciated a coherent moral and political critique of contemporary conditions, most powerfully epitomized in the *Alliterative Morte Arthure*.[50] This poem, followed by *Awntyrs*, *Gologras*, and other non-chivalric romances, articulates a self-consciously anti-courtly, anti-national position, rejecting the centralization of power in a strong king and government bureaucracy, and rejecting the ambitions of a foreign policy based on warfare and increased taxation. *Awntyrs* and *Gologras*, according to Matthews, advance an ideal pattern of knighthood as a reproof against the appropriation of chivalric forms to justify territorial expansion, imperialistic foreign policy, and the abuse of feudal and governmental powers. Matthews' interpretation makes a strong case for the potential political dimension of chivalric romance, and for the possibility of reading these poems against the grain, thus turning them against the very institutions they purport to celebrate. Implicitly, his treatment makes clear the linkage of chivalric romance not merely to political interests, but to underlying ideological structures, and in emphasizing the regional character of the poems, Matthews reveals the splits that mark what might otherwise appear a unified noble estate. Matthews' arguments, however, leave a great deal out of account: they do not address non-alliterative poetry, and, by equating the value of poetry with high moral purpose, they effectively dismiss all "non-serious" poetry like *Ragnelle*, *Carlisle*, or even *Sir Gawain and the Green Knight*. Moreover, they imbue chivalric romance with a potent ethical vision without establishing any base in social history that would support such a critique, and they posit a geographical locus — the border country or simply the north — that is finally much less defined in terms of local realities than even the Cumbria of the Gawain romances.

Michael Bennett, in a detailed examination of the changing structure and mobility within county society in northwest England, describes circumstances that might well bear upon the hybrid character of chivalric romance.[51] According to Bennett, new modes affecting military service, the Church, and governmental administration multiplied the links between local society and the capital, and produced a new, relatively large class of educated careerists. The visible growth of cultural activities in the shires, and the increasing sophistication of architectural and literary productions, depend upon the cultural resources of Westminster and London, brought back to outlying districts by those with associations in the capital, and reshaped by

---

[50] William Matthews, *The Tragedy of Arthur: A Study of the Alliterative "Morte Arthure"* (Berkeley and Los Angeles: University of California Press, 1960). Matthews' passing commentary on the language and texture of the alliterative poetry is an invaluable feature of his study.

[51] Michael J. Bennett, *Community, Class and Careerism: Cheshire and Lancashire Society in the Age of "Sir Gawain and the Green Knight"* (Cambridge: Cambridge University Press, 1983).

local energies and interests. This interplay between national and local identities, cosmopolitan and provincial styles inevitably resulted in artifacts of mixed character, potentially including such border writing as the Gawain romances, which — given their mixed character and content, and their divergent audiences — might in themselves be taken as evidence of opposites in contact. Bennett, however, confines his scrutiny to the upper nobility, elite administrative personnel, and only the greatest of cultural monuments (such as *Sir Gawain and the Green Knight*), in part because surviving documents do not shed much light on the activities of those below this social rank. His study consequently leaves unexamined and unexplained what must certainly have been the most commonly enjoyed poetry of northwest England. Bennett's presentation of an emergent regional self-consciousness, of new classes of readers, writers, and patrons, and even of new modes of knighthood, give a vivid impression of the changes within an outlying society; yet it gives virtually no sense of how these significant changes correspond to a taste (differing with different audiences) for popular romance — perhaps the broadest medium for voicing local and national identities, for recycling traditional stories in new literary forms, and for trumpeting the ethos of chivalry.

Though the studies by Matthews and Bennett offer previously unexplored contexts for regional vernacular literature, they adhere, in their general outlook and in their specific critiques, to canonical assumptions about great writing as an integral feature of elite, literate culture. As a result, their approaches inevitably exclude even mention of popular chivalric romance, and make no attempt to assess, as a formative source of literary activity, the relations between the several official and popular cultures of the English Middle Ages. These gaps underscore the need to produce models of historical analysis that will address the miscellaneous traits that make chivalric romance border writing. But the relation of literature and history is elusive, especially when it attempts to specify the intersections of non-traditional narratives that must often have been presented as performances, or to articulate the experiences these narratives furnished people at different levels of society. A final case may help illustrate the impossibility of simple positions, either in reading romance as direct reflection of reality, or in insisting on its complete divorce from reality.

The life of Sir John Stanley (c. 1350–1414) helps clarify the familiarity and appeal of chivalric romance as both history and fantasy.[52] Stanley was a younger (and

---

[52] Bennett takes Sir John Stanley as one of the central figures in his discussion of "Power, Patronage and Provincial Culture," in *Community, Class and Careerism*, pp. 192–235, especially 215 ff. See also Bennett's discussion of the Stanleys in "'Good Lords' and 'King Makers': The Stanleys of Lathom in English Politics, 1385–1485," *History Today* 31 (1981), 12–17, and

therefore landless) son in a prominent northwest family, whose holdings included the forestship of Wirral (which Gawain traverses in *Sir Gawain and the Green Knight*). Through success in arms (whose highlights included an indictment for manslaughter), foreign adventure — at the court of the Grand Turk, for example — and tournament victories, Sir John won himself a knighthood and royal notice. Through his gallantry, he won the hand of the heiress Isabella, a crucial link in securing property rights and bonding him to other powerful men. From the 1380s, Stanley advanced the national ambitions of English kings, serving with distinction at the fringes of the kingdom — as an official on the Welsh and Scottish borders, as lieutenant of Ireland on three separate occasions, and finally through the hereditary title of King of Man (the office Gawain refuses in *Turke*). At various points in his career, Sir John was Constable of Windsor, a member of the Order of the Garter (whose motto occurs at the end of *Sir Gawain and the Green Knight*), Steward to the Prince of Wales, and (for almost the entire last decade of his life), Steward of the King's household, the role traditionally held by Sir Kay in Arthurian romance. Though Stanley hardly rose to his high eminence from the dust, his splendid and astonishing career illustrates a remarkable mobility and fame achieved through the characteristic forms of knighthood.[53] Sir John might stand as a paragon of chivalric ideals and achievement, and in fact a late sixteenth-century poem celebrates his deeds as founder of this branch of the family. At the same time, it's possible to imagine a figure with such powerful connections in the county and the court not simply as the subject but as a patron of literary activity; Sir John might have supported, like Richard II or John of Gaunt, the elite and prestigious writings of poets like Chaucer or the author of *Sir Gawain and the Green Knight*. But one wonders as well whether such a knight would not have enjoyed on many an unrecorded occasion performances of narratives like *Ragnelle* and *Carlisle*, or *Awntyrs* and *Gologras*,

---

the information on Sir John in *The Dictionary of National Biography*, entry for Thomas Stanley, Earl of Derby. The poem on the Stanleys appears in the *Palatine Anthology: A collection of Ancient Poems and Ballads relating to Lancashire and Cheshire*, ed. J. O. Halliwell (London, 1850), pp. 210–22.

[53] From the twelfth century, knights descended from non-noble families (especially those whose positions depended upon the favor of the king) frequently were attacked as "raised from the dust" (in the words of the twelfth-century historian Orderic Vitalis). Qualification for knighthood, or at least for membership in a formal Order of Knighthood, increasingly required proof of lineal nobility stretching back for two generations; as chivalric romances became more broadly popular, therefore, the highest aristocracy consciously intensified the exclusivity governing its ranks. See Keen, *Chivalry*, pp. 143 ff.

and whether he would not have patronized their makers for the pleasure of the court and countryside? Intensified reading and discussion of romances like those in this volume may begin the process of answering such questions.

All but one of the tales contained in this collection, along with *Sir Gawain and the Green Knight*, were brought together more than one hundred fifty years ago in one of the monumental works of Victorian scholarship, Sir Frederic Madden's *Syr Gawayne*. Though *Ragnelle* has been reprinted in paperback, and several of the others have received modern editions, it is a striking irony that these popular romances have remained generally inaccessible. Madden's volume has been difficult and expensive to come by, and the scholarly editions are neither inviting nor easily obtainable for general readers. To some degree, then, this gathering of Gawain romances is a redoing and updating of Madden's volume; its intention, however, is to make this group of popular stories newly accessible and enjoyable, and not just to antiquarian or scholarly audiences. The texts, introductions, and notes attempt to give reliable, accurate versions of the poems that survive from the Middle Ages, together with literary and historical information that will aid in their reading. I have tried to take account of all scholarly material relevant to these romances, from Madden's edition through the present. No doubt some of this will seem either too detailed or too general for different readers. Through the glosses, however, I have attempted to make the text of each poem completely accessible on its own.

Bibliography of Editions and Works Cited

Arthurian Encyclopedia. See *New Arthurian Encyclopedia.*

Aersten, Henk, and Alasdair A. MacDonald, eds. *Companion to Middle English Romance.* Amsterdam: VU University Press, 1990.

Alliterative Morte Arthure. See Benson, *King Arthur's Death.*

Amours, F[rancis] J[oseph], ed. *Scottish Alliterative Poems.* Scottish Text Society Publications, nos. 27, 38. Edinburgh and London: William Blackwood and Sons, 1897. [Contains *Awntyrs* (pp. 115–71) and *Gologras* (pp. 1–46).]

Barber, Richard W. *The Knight and Chivalry.* New York: Scribner, 1970.

———. *King Arthur: Hero and Legend.* Woodbridge: Boydell, 1986.

Barron, W. R. J. *English Medieval Romance.* London and New York: Longman, 1987.

Benson, Larry D. *King Arthur's Death:* The Middle English *Stanzaic Morte Arthur* and *Alliterative Morte Arthure.* Revised by Edward E. Foster. TEAMS Middle English Texts Series. Kalamazoo, Michigan: Medieval Institute Publications, 1994.

Chanson de Roland. See *The Song of Roland.*

Child, Francis James. *The English and Scottish Popular Ballads.* 5 vols. New York: Houghton, Mifflin, and Company, 1884–98; rpt. New York: Dover Publications, 1965. [Contains editions of *Cornwall* (I.274–88) and *Marriage* (I.288–96).]

Chrétien de Troyes. *Arthurian Romances.* Trans. D. D. R. Owen. Everyman's Library. London: J. M. Dent Ltd.; Rutland, Vermont: Charles E. Tuttle, 1987.

De ortu Waluuanii nepotis Arturi. See *The Rise of Gawain.*

Bibliography

Hales, John W., and Frederick J. Furnivall. *Bishop Percy's Folio Manuscript: Ballads and Romances*. 3 vols. London: N. Trübner and Company, 1868; rpt. Detroit, Michigan: Singing Tree Press, 1968. [Contains *Cornwall* (I.59–73); *Turke* (I.88–102); *Marriage* (I.103–118); *Greene Knight* (II.56–77); *Carle* (III.275–294).]

Hall, Louis B., trans. *The Knightly Tales of Sir Gawain*. Chicago: Nelson-Hall, 1976. [Contains prose modernizations of *Avowing, Awntyrs, Carlisle, Gologras, Ragnelle*.]

Keen, Maurice. *Chivalry*. New Haven: Yale University Press, 1984.

Krishna, Valerie, trans. *Five Middle English Arthurian Romances*. Garland Library of Medieval Literature, Series B, Vol. 29. New York: Garland, 1991. [Contains verse translations of the editions identified within brackets: *Awntyrs* [Hanna] (pp. 153–173); *Avowyng* [Dahood] (pp. 175–208); *Ragnelle* [Wilhelm] (pp. 209–234); *Carlisle* [Sands] (pp. 235–254). This edition contains no explanatory or textual notes, but does include a brief introduction (pp. 1–26) that summarizes the plots of each of the four poems, as well as a select bibliography.]

Lancelot of the Laik: A Scottish Metrical Romance. Ed. W. W. Skeat. EETS o.s. 6. London: Oxford University Press, 1865.

Layamon. *Brut*. Eds. G. L. Brook and R. F. Leslie. 2 vols. EETS o.s. 250 and 277. London: Oxford University Press, 1963 (Vol. I) and 1978 (Vol. II).

Libeaus Desconus. See *Lybeaus Desconus*.

Loomis, Roger Sherman, ed. *Arthurian Literature in the Middle Ages: A Collaborative History*. Oxford: Clarendon, 1959.

Lybeaus Desconus. Ed. M. Mills. EETS o.s. 261. London: Oxford University Press, 1969.

Madden, Frederic, ed. *Syr Gawayne: A Collection of Ancient Romance-Poems by Scottish and English Authors Relating to That Celebrated Knight of the Round Table*. London: Bannatyne Club, 1839. [Contains *Awntyrs* (pp. 95–128), *Carlisle* (pp. 187–206), *Gologras* (pp. 131–183), *Ragnelle* (pp. 298–298y), *Jeaste* (pp. 207–223), *Greene Knight* (pp. 224–242), *Turke* (pp. 243–255), *Carle* (pp. 256–274), *Cornwall* (pp. 275–287), and *Marriage* (pp. 288–297).]

Bibliography

Malory, Sir Thomas. *Works*. Ed. Eugène Vinaver. 2nd ed. 3 vols. Oxford: Clarendon, 1967.

A Manual of the Writings in Middle English: 1050–1500. See Newstead, "Arthurian Legends."

Matthews, William. *The Tragedy of Arthur: A Study of the Alliterative "Morte Arthure."* Berkeley: University of California Press, 1960.

Mehl, Dieter. *The Middle English Romances of the Thirteenth and Fourteenth Centuries*. [Trans. of *Mittelenglischen Romanzen des 13. und 14. Jahrhunderts*.] London: Routledge and Kegan Paul, 1969.

New Arthurian Encyclopedia. Ed. Norris J. Lacy. New York and London: Garland, 1991.

Newstead, Helaine. "Arthurian Legends." In *A Manual of the Writings in Middle English: 1050–1500: Fascicule I: Romances*. New Haven, Connecticut: Connecticut Academy of Arts and Sciences, 1967. Pp. 224–56.

The Quest of the Holy Grail. [*La Queste del Saint Graal*.] Trans. P. M. Matarasso. Baltimore: Penguin Books, 1969.

Queste del Saint Graal. See *The Quest of the Holy Grail*.

Ramsey, Lee C. *Chivalric Romances: Popular Literature in Medieval England*. Bloomington: Indiana University Press, 1983.

Richmond, Velma E. Bourgeois. *The Popularity of Middle English Romance*. Bowling Green, Ohio: Bowling Green University Popular Press, 1975.

The Rise of Gawain, Nephew of Arthur (De ortu Waluuanii nepotis Arturi), ed. and trans. Mildred Leake Day. Garland Library of Medieval Literature, vol. 15, series A. New York and London: Garland, 1984.

Robson, John, ed. *Three Early English Metrical Romances*. London, Printed for the Camden Society: J. B. Nichols and Son, 1842. [Contains *Avowing* (pp. 57–93) and *Awntyrs* (pp. 1–96).]

Bibliography

Sands, Donald B., ed. *Middle English Verse Romances*. New York: Holt, Rinehart and Winston, 1966. [Contains *Carlisle* (pp. 348–71) and *Ragnelle* (pp. 323–47).]

Sir Gawain and the Green Knight. Ed. J. R. R. Tolkien and E. V. Gordon. 2nd. ed. Rev. Norman Davis. Oxford: Clarendon Press, 1967.

The Song of Roland. [*Chanson de Roland*.] Trans. Frederick Goldin. New York: Norton, 1978.

Stanzaic Morte Arthur. See Benson, *King Arthur's Death*.

Weston, Jessie Laidlay. *The Legend of Sir Gawain: Studies upon Its Original Scope and Significance*. Grimm Library, 7. London: David Nutt, 1897.

Wittig, Susan. *Stylistic and Narrative Structures in the Middle English Romances*. Austin: University of Texas Press, 1978.

Ywain and Gawain. Ed. Albert B. Friedman and Norman T. Harrington. EETS o.s. 254. London: Oxford University Press, 1964.

The Wedding of Sir Gawain and Dame Ragnelle

Introduction

The episode that makes up the plot of *The Wedding of Sir Gawain and Dame Ragnelle* is one of the most popular stories of late medieval England. The transformation of the loathly lady — a story common in folktales, and here combined with motifs of fairy tales like the frog prince and sleeping beauty — occurs in a popular ballad (see *The Marriage of Sir Gawain*, below), and in more polished literary renditions from the late fourteenth century by Geoffrey Chaucer and John Gower. The story also served for the plot of an interlude performed at one of Edward I's Round Tables in 1299: a loathly lady, with foot-long nose, donkey ears, neck sores, a gaping mouth, and blackened teeth, rode into the hall and demanded of Sir Perceval and Sir Gawain (Edward's knights had assumed Arthurian identities for the occasion) that they recover lost territory and end the strife between commons and lords. The author of the interlude evidently assumed that Edward's court would recognize the story in its outlines.

Ragnelle may in fact have had its origins in some distant and lost Arthurian narrative, for both Chrétien de Troyes in the *Perceval* and Wolfram von Eschenbach in the *Parzival* describe a Grail messenger who is an ugly hag. A variety of early European vernacular stories retell the plot of a loathly lady who, in return for certain crucial information or power, demands some sign of sexual favor from a hero, and is then transformed by the hero's compliance. In the earliest Old Irish versions, the reward for the hero's offering his favor or making the right choice is kingship or political dominance; the late medieval English versions recast the tales' setting, from the realm of epic exploits to a domestic environment of personal love characteristic of romance. Sir Gawain's reputation as a chivalric hero rides to a large extent on his talent for "luf talkyng" (as in *Sir Gawain and the Green Knight*, line 927) and courtesy towards women, though according to *Ragnelle* these in turn are motivated by his fealty to the king.

At the heart of *Ragnelle* lies the question of how the unknown, the marvelous, or the threatening is brought into line with legitimate, normative, idealized chivalric society. Perhaps even more than the Green Knight in *Sir Gawain and the Green Knight*, Sir Gromer Somer Joure represents the forces of wildness and incivility: he

41

appears suddenly in the midst of the forest, he behaves in ways that violate knightly protocols, and, most of all, he has a name that connects him with the licensed anarchy of Midsummer's Day. But Ragnelle represents these threats no less than her brother. Her seemingly omnivorous appetite marks her as an outsider, both sexually and socially, to the aristocratic court. Despite the counsels of her betters, she *will* have Gawain, and the entire court, led by Arthur and perhaps including Gawain, fears she is a sexual predator (lines 722 ff.). Her appearance and behavior — her raggedness, poverty, and general unkemptness, and her antisocial and indiscriminate consumption of vast quantities of food at the wedding feast — make clear that her repulsiveness is a function of her low estate and not simply a wild monstrosity. What brands Ragnelle as a hag is, in the terms defined by the central question of the poem, a form of desire or lack — a lack of manners, beauty, deference; what certifies her as a lady at the end is her possession of these qualities and of Sir Gawain. Though for the bewitched Ragnelle a good man is hard to find, once found he satisfies all her heart's desire.

The plot of *Ragnelle*, then, turns on the transformation of its heroine both physically and symbolically, from an ugly hag to a beautiful lady, and from an enigmatic threat to a fulfilled woman. Her double role — both Beauty and the Beast — endows her with a deep ambiguity, enmeshing both attraction and revulsion, fatal danger and life-giving knowledge; such worrisome duplicity often attaches itself to women (and to femininity generally) in popular romance, and throughout Western culture. The poem proceeds to establish a stable and benign identity for Ragnelle by providing a satisfying answer to Gawain's rather frantic question, "What ar ye?" (line 644). This inquiry unmistakably rephrases *Ragnelle*'s pivotal question: "whate [do] wemen love best" (line 91), "whate [do] wemen desyren most" (line 406), what do "wemen desyren moste specialle" (line 465) — which itself uncannily anticipates the notorious formulation of Freud: *"Was will das Weib?"* — "What does Woman want?" It has sometimes been said that the fascination of this question and the wish to solve the enigma of Woman that it conveys express interests that are typically male (or, in more abstract, cultural terms, masculine). In the case of *Ragnelle*, the narrative unfolds in ways that have the heroine clearly serve the interests of the male chivalric society that the poem good-humoredly celebrates.

Through her relations with the various male characters — her kinship with Gromer, her compact with Arthur, her union with Gawain — Ragnelle literally holds the poem together, for *she* is their link with each other. She undoes the threat her brother poses for the court, and then reconciles him to the Round Table; she knows the answer to Arthur's problem and so saves his life and his kingship; she presents Gawain with opportunities to place his spectacular courtesy on display, first towards Arthur, and then towards women. Although Gawain performs his usual service as mediator, taming the strange (Ragnelle) and bringing it safely within the sphere of the court, even *his* success depends upon the more pervasive mediation of Ragnelle. By passing among these male characters, she becomes the nexus that ties them together and makes possible the fraternal and hierarchic bonds of chivalric solidarity.

Ragnelle explores the ties of chivalry through a structured repetition and variation of a fundamental pattern. This consists of a series of linked and interlocking oaths and commitments (a plotting device that distantly recalls the staggeringly complex interlacing of *Sir Gawain and the Green Knight*). In the first place, Arthur agrees (under duress) to a compact with Sir Gromer, though Gromer claims he imposes this trial because the king had already broken an obligation to him. Arthur then agrees with Ragnelle upon a second compact which will enable him to escape the first, though its fulfillment depends entirely upon Gawain's compliance. Gawain then agrees to the terms of the second compact, thereby obligating himself to Arthur and to Ragnelle. Ragnelle fulfills her promise, providing Arthur the knowledge that puts him out of Gromer's control (and puts Gromer in danger from Arthur and the court); Gawain fulfills his promise, marrying Ragnelle in a public ceremony and then agreeing to consummate the marriage. When Gawain, faced with what seems an impossible choice concerning Ragnelle's transformation, agrees to allow her to decide, he unwittingly fulfills the terms for setting her free from her enchantment. This outcome not only unites Ragnelle to Gawain, but to the King and Queen; she then uses this amity to bring Arthur and Gromer to reconciliation. *Ragnelle* ends therefore with everyone established in her or his proper place, and with courtesy restoring the Round Table's customary mutuality and hierarchy. Unmotivated marvels — meetings in the woods, monstrous apparitions, sudden transformations — work to bring about what everyone always wanted or expected, so that the link of fantasy and necessity seems (as it should in romance) inevitable.

Ragnelle deploys another common romance convention by setting the marvelous — especially the unanticipated but fatefully indispensable encounters and compacts that begin the poem — within a wood. The forest is a place for both recreation and mystery, where Arthur and his court go on holiday but where anything can happen. The hunt that starts the action constitutes a characteristic pastime for the English nobility of the late Middle Ages, an activity in which the necessities of survival are turned into a hierarchically nuanced display of strength and knowledge; the king is most a king when he sets off "wodmanly" (line 32) to stalk, kill, and then butcher the deer, conspicuously heedless of danger. *Carlisle*, *Avowyng*, and *Awntyrs* similarly begin with a hunt. The game or compact that Sir Gromer forces upon Arthur succeeds the chase. Though Sir Gromer's may seem an unchivalrous bargain, once Arthur has openly sworn his oath (line 99) he must abide by its rules on his honor, just as he must hold his word to Ragnelle (lines 294 ff.). In this way the romance orders events so that the force of civility and courtesy prevails, and the challenge of the wild is answered within the safe precincts of bedroom and court at the conclusion.

Although Sir Gromer alleges the justice of his complaint against King Arthur — like Sir Galeron in *Awntyrs*, he says that the king has unjustly stripped him of lands and given these to Sir Gawain (lines 58 ff.) — *Ragnelle* never stipulates the location of his estates. It does, however, identify the mysterious woods where he makes his appearance: he and his bewitched sister inhabit Inglewood Forest (lines 16, 152, 764, 835), the Cumberland setting for *Avowyng, Awntyrs*, and, by implication, for *Marriage*. In addition, the Round Table resides at Carlisle (lines 127, 132, 325), a center for Arthurian adventures in *Carlisle, Avowyng, Awntyrs, Greene Knight, Marriage*, and *Carle*. These allusions connect *Ragnelle* with other Gawain romances, and confer on the whole group a remarkable regional coherence.

Text

The Wedding of Sir Gawain and Dame Ragnelle survives in a sixteenth-century manuscript now in Oxford (Bodleian 11951, formerly Rawlinson C.86). Madden, in 1839, characterized the text of *Ragnelle* as recorded "in a negligent hand," "very carelessly written" (pp. lxiv, lxvii). The scribe leaves unclear whether he employs a word-ending stroke simply as a flourish, or as indication of final unstressed -e. Even more confusing is his formation of *i* and *y*, which are often indistinguishable; the interchangeability of *y* for *i* in Middle English writing often makes it impossible or pointless to choose between them in a modern transcription of this manuscript. Earlier editions have varied considerably on this score. I have transcribed as *y* those characters that seem clearly *y*; when the letter form appears ambiguous, I have rendered it as *i* in conformity with standard conventions of modern spelling. I have usually transcribed the scribe's frequent use of "Ff" and "ff" as "F," though occasionally in mid-line I have given lower case. Capitalization and punctuation are almost entirely editorial.

In the manuscript, *Ragnelle* appears without stanza breaks. Nonetheless, the poem clearly employs a tail-rhyme stanza common to many other Middle English romances. This consists of six lines rhyming *aabccb*, with the *a* and *c* couplets written in longer lines (often containing ten syllables, usually four stresses), and the *b*-lines shorter (usually three stresses). The surviving copy of the poem lacks a significant number of individual lines (many of which are tail-rhyme *c*-lines), and these absences make stanza divisions irregular and uneven. It would be possible to maintain a format of six-line stanzas, and to suggest where omissions fall (as Hartwell does in his edition). However, both the convenience of the reader and the sense of narrative movement seem better served by an editorial division into twelve-line stanzas. This is the format I have chosen, though missing lines do produce several stanzas of irregular length. The manuscript seems also to be lacking at least one leaf (after line 628), but the progress of the story remains clear nonetheless.

Select Bibliography

Manuscript

Oxford, Bodleian Library MS 11951.

Editions (arranged chronologically)

Madden, Frederic. 1839. See Bibliography of Editions and Works Cited.

Sumner, Laura, ed. *The Weddynge of Sir Gawen and Dame Ragnell*. Smith College Studies in Modern Language 5, no. 4. Northhampton, Massachusetts: Smith College Departments of Modern Languages, 1924.

Saul, G. B. *The Wedding of Sir Gawain and Dame Ragnell*. New York: Prentice-Hall, 1934. [Modernization with Introduction.]

Whiting, Bartlett J. *The Weddynge of Sir Gawen and Dame Ragnell*. In *Sources and Analogues in Chaucer's "Canterbury Tales."* Ed. W. F. Bryan and Germaine Dempster. New York: Humanities Press, 1958. Pp. 242–64. [Reprint of Summer's edition with "a few trifling misprints" corrected.]

Sands, Donald B. 1966. See Bibliography of Editions and Works Cited.

Hartwell, David Geddes. *The Wedding of Sir Gawain and Dame Ragnell: An Edition*. Columbia University Dissertation, 1973. *Dissertation Abstracts International*, 34:3343A.

Sir Gawain and the Loathly Lady. Retold by Selina Hastings. Illustrations by Juan Wijngaard. London: Methuen, 1981; Walker, 1988. New York: Lothrop, 1981; Lee and Shepard, 1985. [Children's version.]

Shibata, Yoshitaka. "The Weddynge of Sir Gawen and Dame Ragnell." *Tohoku Gakuin University Review: Essays and Studies in English Language and Literature (Tohoku Gakuin Daigaku Ronshu, Eigo-Eibungaku)* 72 (1982), 374–82. [Japanese translation.]

The Wedding of Sir Gawain and Dame Ragnelle

Garbáty, Thomas J., ed. *Medieval English Literature*. Boston: Heath, 1984. [Contains an edition of *Ragnelle* (pp. 418–39), based apparently on the published text of Whiting.]

Wilhelm, James J., ed. *Romance of Arthur III: Works from Russia to Spain, Norway to Italy*. New York: Garland, 1988. [Contains an edition of *Ragnelle* (pp. 99–116), apparently reprinted from Garbáty's text of Whiting.]

The Wedding of Sir Gawain and Dame Ragnell. Ed. J. Withrington. Lancaster Modern Spelling Text 2. Lancaster: Department of English, Lancaster University, 1991. [I have not been able to examine a copy of this edition.]

Shepherd, Stephen H. A., ed. *Middle English Romances*. New York: Norton, 1995. Pp. 243–67. [I have not been able to examine a copy of this edition.]

Criticism

Boffey, Julia, and Carol M. Meale. "Selecting the Text: Rawlinson C.86 and Some Other Books for London Readers." In *Regionalism in Late Medieval Manuscripts and Texts*. Ed. Felicity Riddey. Cambridge: D. S. Brewer, 1991. Pp. 143–69.

Coomaraswamy, A. K. "On the Loathly Bride." *Speculum* 20 (1945), 391–404.

Crane, Susan. "Alison's Incapacity and Poetic Instability in the Wife of Bath's Tale." *PMLA* 102 (1987), 20–28.

Dannenbaum, Susan [Crane]. "*The Wedding of Sir Gawain and Dame Ragnell*: Line 48." *Explicator* 40 (1982), 3–4.

Eisner, Sigmund. *A Tale of Wonder: A Source Study of "The Wife of Bath's Tale."* Wexford, Ireland: John English, 1957.

Field, P. J. C. "Malory and *The Wedding of Sir Gawain and Dame Ragnell*." *Archiv* 219 (1982), 374–81.

Fradenburg, Louise. "The Wife of Bath's Passing Fancy." *Studies in the Age of Chaucer* 8 (1986), 31–58.

Griffiths, J. J. "A Re-examination of Oxford, Bodleian Library, MS Rawlinson c.86." *Archiv* 219 (1982), 381–88.

The Wedding of Sir Gawain and Dame Ragnelle

	Lythe and listenythe the lif of a lord riche,	*Harken; listen to; noble*
	The while that he lyvid was none hym liche,	*like*
	Nether in bowre ne in halle.	*private room nor*
	In the tyme of Arthoure thys adventure betyd,	*occurred*
5	And of the greatt adventure that he hymself dyd,	*And [you will hear] of*
	That Kyng curteys and royalle.	
	Of alle kynges Arture berythe the flowyr,	*bears the prize*
	And of alle knyghtod he bare away the honour,	*knighthood*
	Wheresoevere he wentt.	
10	In his contrey was nothyng butt chyvalry	
	And knyghtes were belovid by that doughty,	*brave [warrior]*
	For cowardes were everemore shent.	*disgraced*
	Nowe wylle ye lyst a whyle to my talkyng,	*[if] you listen; performance*
	I shalle you telle of Arthowre the Kyng,	
15	Howe ones hym befelle.	*[adventure] once*
	On huntyng he was in Ingleswod,	*Inglewood*
	With alle his bold knyghtes good —	
	Nowe herken to my spelle!	*story (spiel)*
	The Kyng was sett att his trestylle-tree	*hunting station*
20	With hys bowe to sle the wylde veneré	*slay; game*
	And hys lordes were sett hym besyde.	
	As the Kyng stode, then was he ware	*waited; aware*
	Where a greatt hartt was and a fayre,	
	And forthe fast dyd he glyde.	*move*
25	The hartt was in a braken ferne,	*fern thicket*
	And hard the houndes, and stode fulle derne:	*heard; still*
	Alle that sawe the Kyng.	
	"Hold you stylle, every man,	*motionless*
	And I wolle goo myself, yf I can,	
30	With crafte of stalkyng."	
	The Kyng in hys hand toke a bowe	

	And wodmanly he stowpyd lowe	*as a woodsman*
	To stalk unto that dere.	*deer*
	When that he cam the dere fulle nere,	*quite*
35	The dere lept forthe into a brere,	*briar patch*
	And evere the Kyng went nere and nere.	*closer*

	So Kyng Arthure went a whyle	*for a time*
	After the dere, I trowe, half a myle,	*I guess*
	And no man with hym went.	
40	And att the last to the dere he lett flye	*at; took a shot*
	And smote hym sore and sewerly —	*sorely; surely*
	Suche grace God hym sent.	
	Doun the dere tumblyd so theron,	*on that spot*
	And felle into a greatt brake of feron;	*thicket; fern*
45	The Kyng folowyd fulle fast.	*very quickly*
	Anon the Kyng bothe ferce and felle	*fierce; eager*
	Was with the dere and dyd hym serve welle,	*butcher properly*
	And after the grasse he taste.	*afterwards; grease (fat); assayed*

	As the Kyng was with the dere alone,	*While*
50	Streyghte ther cam to hym a quaynt grome,	*strange man*
	Armyd welle and sure,	
	A knyght fulle strong and of greatt myghte.	
	And grymly wordes to the Kyng he sayd:	*fiercely*
	"Welle imet, Kyng Arthour!	*met*
55	Thou hast me done wrong many a yere	*year*
	And wofully I shall quytte the here;	*requite you*
	I hold thy lyfe days nyghe done.	*lifetime nearly*
	Thou hast gevyn my landes in certayn	*indeed*
	With greatt wrong unto Sir Gawen.	
60	Whate sayest thou, Kyng alone?"	

	"Syr Knyghte, whate is thy name with honour?"	
	"Syr Kyng," he sayd, "Gromer Somer Joure,	
	I telle the nowe with ryghte."	*by rights*
	"A, Sir Gromer Somer, bethynk the welle;	*consider*
65	To sle me here honour getyst thou no delle.	*slay; not a bit*
	Bethynk the thou artt a knyghte:	
	Yf thou sle me nowe in thys case,	

	Alle knyghtes wolle refuse the in every place;	
	That shame shalle nevere the froo.	*leave you*
70	Lett be thy wylle and folowe wytt	*recklessness; reason*
	And that is amys I shalle amend itt,	*whatever*
	And thou wolt, or that I goo."	*If you wish before*

	"Nay," sayd Sir Gromer Somer, "by Hevyn Kyng!	
	So shalt thou nott skape, withoute lesyng;	*escape, no lie*
75	I have the nowe att avaylle.	*at [my] advantage*
	Yf I shold lett the thus goo with mokery,	*after mocking [you]*
	Anoder tyme thou wolt me defye;	*Another; challenge in combat*
	Of that I shalle nott faylle."	*In [preventing] that*
	"Now," sayd the Kyng, "so God me save,	
80	Save my lyfe, and whate thou most crave,	*whatever*
	I shalle now graunt itt the;	
	Shame thou shalt have to sle me in veneré,	*in hunting*
	Thou armyd and I clothyd butt in grene, perdé."	*green, by God*

	"Alle thys shalle nott help the, sekyrly.	*surely*
85	For I wolle nother lond ne gold, truly,	*want*
	Butt yf thou graunt me att a certeyn day	*Unless; agree [to meet] me*
	Suche as I shalle sett, and in thys same araye."	*specify; gear*
	"Yes," sayd the Kyng; "Lo, here my hand."	
	"Ye, butt abyde, Kyng, and here me a stound.	*hear; moment*
90	Fyrst thow shalt swere upon my sword broun	*bright*
	To shewe me att thy comyng whate wemen love best in feld and town	*women*
	And thou shalt mete me here withouten send	*summons*
	Evyn att this day twelfe monethes end;	*twelve*
	And thou shalt swere upon my swerd good	
95	That of thy knyghtes shalle none com with the, by the Rood,	*Cross*
	Nowther fremde ne freynd.	*stranger nor*

	"And yf thou bryng nott answere withoute faylle,	
	Thyne hed thou shalt lose for thy travaylle —	*head; effort*
	Thys shalle nowe be thyne othe.	*oath*
100	Whate sayst thou, Kyng? Lett se, have done!"	*Come on, do it*
	"Syr, I graunt to thys! Now lett me gone.	*agree; [be] gone*
	Thoughe itt be to me fulle lothe,	*distasteful*
	I ensure the, as I am true kyng,	*assure*

To com agayn att thys twelfe monethes endyng
105 And bryng the thyne answere."
"Now go thy way, Kyng Arthure.
Thy lyfe is in my hand, I am fulle sure;
Of thy sorowe thow artt nott ware.   *plight; aware*

"Abyde, Kyng Arthure, a lytell whyle:
110 Loke nott today thou me begyle,   *trick*
And kepe alle thyng in close —   *to yourself*
For and I wyst, by Mary mylde,   *if I knew*
Thou woldyst betray me in the feld,
Thy lyf fyrst sholdyst thou lose."
115 "Nay," sayd Kyng Arthure, "that may nott be.
Untrewe knyght shalt thou nevere fynde me —
To dye yett were me lever.   *would even be preferable to me*
Farwelle, Sir Knyght, and evyll mett.   *met through bad luck*
I wolle com, and I be on lyve att the day sett,   *if I'm alive; appointed*
120 Thoughe I shold scape nevere."   *escape [alive]*

The Kyng his bugle gan blowe.   *did*
That hard every knyght and itt gan knowe;   *heard; did know*
Unto hym can they rake.   *did; hasten*
Ther they fond the Kyng and the dere,
125 With sembland sad and hevy chere,   *countenance; distressed look*
That had no lust to layk.   *Who; desire to play*
"Go we home nowe to Carlylle;   *Carlisle*
Thys huntyng lykys me nott welle,"   *pleases*
So sayd Kyng Arthure.
130 Alle the lordes knewe by his countenaunce
That the Kyng had mett with sume dysturbaunce.

Unto Carlylle then the Kyng cam,
Butt of his hevynesse knewe no man;   *[the cause] of his sadness*
Hys hartt was wonder hevy.   *heart; exceedingly*
135 In this hevynesse he dyd abyde
That many of his knyghtes mervelyd that tyde,   *So that; at that time*
Tylle att the last Sir Gawen
To the Kyng he sayd than: *then*
"Syr, me marvaylythe ryghte sore   *[it] puzzles me greatly*

50

140   Whate thyng that thou sorowyst fore."

     Then answeryd the Kyng as tyghte: *immediately*
     "I shall the telle, gentylle Gawen knyght.
     In the Forest as I was this daye,   *while*
     Ther I mett with a knyght in his araye,   *in full armor*
145   And serteyn wordes to me he gan sayn   *certain; did say*
     And chargyd me I shold hym nott bewrayne;   *not give him away*
     Hys councelle must I kepe therfore,   *confidence*
     Or els I am forswore."   *forsworn*

     "Nay, drede you nott, Lord! By Mary flower,   *fear*
150   I am nott that man that wold you dishonour
     Nother by evyn ne by moron."   *evening; morning*
     "Forsothe I was on huntyng in Ingleswod;   *In fact*
     Thowe knowest welle I slewe an hartt, by the Rode, *Cross*
     Alle mysylf alon.
155   Ther mett I with a knyght armyd sure;   *heavily*
     His name he told me was Sir Gromer Somer Joure:
     Therfor I make my mone.   *lament*

     "Ther that knyght fast dyd me threte   *pressingly; threaten*
     And wold have slayn me with greatt heatt,   *passion*
160   But I spak fayre agayn.   *Except that; in turn*
     Wepyns with me ther had I none;   *Weapons*
     Alas! My worshypp therfor is nowe gone."   *honor*
     "What therof?" sayd Gawen.   *What came of it*
     "Whatt nedys more? I shalle nott lye: *can I say*
165   He wold have slayn me ther withoute mercy —
     And that me was fulle lothe.   *to me was most hateful*
     He made me to swere that att the twelfe monethes end *twelve*
     That I shold mete hym ther in the same kynde;   *manner*
     To that I plyghte my trowithe.   *pledged my troth (good faith)*

170   "And also I shold telle hym att the same day
     Whate wemen desyren moste, in good faye;   *faith*
     My lyf els shold I lese.   *otherwise; lose*
     This othe I made unto that knyghte,
     And that I shold nevere telle itt to no wight;   *man*

175	Of thys I myghte nott chese.	*In this [matter]; choose*
	And also I shold com in none oder araye,	*other gear*
	Butt evyn as I was the same daye.	*first day*
	And yf I faylyd of myne answere,	
	I wott I shal be slayn ryghte there.	*know*
180	Blame me nott thoughe I be a wofulle man;	*Chide; if*
	Alle thys is my drede and fere."	*[the cause of] my doubt*
	"Ye, Sir, make good chere.	
	Lett make your hors redy	*Have; prepared*
	To ryde into straunge contrey;	
185	And evere wheras ye mete owther man or woman, in faye,	*either; faith*
	Ask of theym whate thay therto saye,	*to that [question]*
	And I shalle also ryde anoder waye	
	And enquere of every man and woman and gett whatt I may	*inquire; learn*
	Of every man and womans answere;	
190	And in a boke I shalle theym wryte."	*book*
	"I graunt," sayd the Kyng as tyte;	*immediately*
	"Ytt is welle advysed, Gawen the good,	*considered*
	Evyn by the Holy Rood."	*Cross*
	Sone were they bothe redy,	
195	Gawen and the Kyng, wytterly.	*truly*
	The Kyng rode on way and Gawen anoder	*one*
	And evere enquyred of man, woman, and other,	*others*
	Whate wemen desyred moste dere.	*dearly*
	Somme sayd they lovyd to be welle arayd,	*accoutered*
200	Somme sayd they lovyd to be fayre prayed,	*beseeched*
	Somme sayd they lovyd a lusty man	
	That in theyr armys can clypp them and kysse them than.	*hug*
	Somme sayd one, somme sayd other;	*one [thing]*
	And so had Gawen getyn many an answere.	
205	By that Gawen had geten whate he maye	*Finally*
	And come agayn by a certeyn daye.	*returned*
	Syr Gawen had goten answerys so many	
	That had made a boke greatt, wytterly.	*for sure*
	To the courte he cam agayn.	
210	By that was the Kyng comyn with hys boke,	*At the same time; had come*

And eyther on others pamplett dyd loke. *pamphlet*
"Thys may nott faylle," sayd Gawen.
"By God," sayd the Kyng, "I drede me sore; *fear greatly*
I cast me to seke a lytelle more *resolve; seek*
215 In Yngleswod Forest.
I have butt a monethe to my day sett;
I may hapen on somme good tydynges to hitt — *hit [upon]*
Thys thynkythe me nowe best." *seems to*

"Do as ye lyst," then Gawen sayd, *please*
220 "Whatesoevere ye do I hold me payd; *satisfied*
Hytt is good to be spyrryng. *enquiring*
Doute you nott, Lord, ye shalle welle spede; *Fear; fare*
Sume of your sawes shalle help att nede, *sayings*
Els itt were ylle lykyng." *Otherwise; unlikely*
225 Kyng Arthoure rode forthe on the other day *next*
Into Yngleswod as hys gate laye, *path led*
And ther he mett with a Lady.
She was as ungoodly a creature *uncouth*
As evere man sawe, withoute mesure. *beyond measure*
230 Kyng Arthure mervaylyd securly. *marveled transfixed*

Her face was red, her nose snotyd withalle, *snotted as well*
Her mowithe wyde, her tethe yalowe overe alle, *mouth; teeth yellow*
With bleryd eyen gretter then a balle. *bleary; than*
Her mowithe was nott to lak: *oversmall*
235 Her tethe hyng overe her lyppes, *hung*
Her chekys syde as wemens hippes. *broad; hips*
A lute she bare upon her bak; *hump; back*
Her nek long and therto greatt; *equally broad*
Her here cloteryd on an hepe; *hair clotted; heap*
240 In the sholders she was a yard brode.
Hangyng pappys to be an hors lode, *breasts [large enough]*
And lyke a barelle she was made.
And to reherse the fowlnesse of that Lady, *recount*
Ther is no tung may telle, securly; *surely*
245 Of lothynesse inowghe she had. *ugliness enough*

She satt on a palfray was gay begon, *palfrey [that] was richly draped*

53

With gold besett and many a precious stone.   *adorned*
Ther was an unsemely syghte: *incongruous*
So fowlle a creature withoute mesure
250   To ryde so gayly, I you ensure,   *handsomely; assure*
Ytt was no reason ne ryghte.   *neither proper nor*
She rode to Arthoure and thus she sayd:
"God spede, Sir Kyng! I am welle payd   *satisfied*
That I have with the mett;
255   Speke with me, I rede, or thou goo,   *advise before*
For thy lyfe is in my hand, I warn the soo;   *promise you*
That shalt thou fynde, and I itt nott lett."   *if; prevent*

"Why, whatt wold ye, Lady, nowe with me?"   *what do you desire*
"Syr, I wold fayn nowe speke with the   *eagerly*
260   And telle the tydynges good.
For alle the answerys that thou canst yelpe,   *Despite; sing out*
None of theym alle shalle the helpe.
That shalt thou knowe, by the Rood.   *Cross*
Thou wenyst I knowe nott thy councelle,   *think; secret*
265   Butt I warn the, I knowe itt every dealle.   *promise; bit*
Yf I help the nott, thou art butt dead.   *all but*
Graunt me, Sir Kyng, butt one thyng,
And for thy lyfe I make warrauntyng,   *stand as guarantor*
Or elles thou shalt lose thy hed."

270   "Whate mean you, Lady? Telle me tyghte,   *quickly*
For of thy wordes I have great dispyte;   *indignation*
To you I have no nede.   *Of*
Whate is your desyre, fayre Lady?
Lett me wete shortly —   *know right away*
275   Whate is your meanyng?
And why my lyfe is in your hand?
Telle me, and I shalle you warraunt   *guarantee*
Alle your oun askyng."   *own*

"Forsothe," sayd the Lady, "I am no qued.   *wicked person*
280   Thou must graunt me a knyght to wed:
His name is Sir Gawen.
And suche covenaunt I wolle make the,

54

Butt thorowe myne answere thy lyf savyd be,   *Except that through*
Elles lett my desyre be in vayne.   *Otherwise*
285 And yf myne answere save thy lyf,
Graunt me to be Gawens wyf.
Advyse the nowe, Sir Kyng.   *Consider*
For itt must be so, or thou artt butt dead;   *are as good as*
Chose nowe, for thou mayste sone lose thyne hed.   *may*
290 Telle me nowe in hying."   *haste*

"Mary!" sayd the Kyng, "I maye nott graunt the   *"Good heavens!"*
To make warraunt Sir Gawen to wed the;   *guarantee*
Alle lyethe in hym alon.   *rests with him*
Butt and itt be so, I wolle do my labour   *if it may be*
295 In savyng of my lyfe to make itt secour;   *[that outcome] secure*
To Gawen wolle I make my mone."   *lament*
"Welle," sayd she, "nowe go home agayn
And fayre wordes speke to Sir Gawen,
For thy lyf I may save.
300 Thoughe I be foulle, yett am I gaye;   *gracious*
Thourghe me thy lyfe save he maye
Or sewer thy dethe to have."   *ensure*

"Alas!" he sayd; "Nowe woo is me
That I shold cause Gawen to wed the,
305 For he wol be lothe to saye naye.
So foulle a Lady as ye ar nowe one   *you are*
Sawe I nevere in my lyfe on ground gone;   *to go*
I nott whate I do may."   *do not know*
"No force, Sir Kyng, thoughe I be foulle;   *No matter*
310 Choyse for a make hathe an owlle.   *mate [is allowed even to]*
Thou getest of me no more.
When thou comyst agayn to thyne answere   *for your*
Ryghte in this place I shalle mete the here,
Or elles I wott thou artt lore."   *know; lost*

315 "Now farewelle," sayd the Kyng, "Lady."
"Ye, Sir," she sayd, "ther is a byrd men calle an owlle...
And yett a Lady I am."
"Whate is your name, I pray you, telle me?"

	"Syr Kyng, I highte Dame Ragnelle, truly,	*am named Lady*
320	That nevere yett begylyd man."	*deceived a man*
	"Dame Ragnelle, now have good daye."	
	"Syr Kyng, God spede the on thy way!	
	Ryghte here I shalle the mete."	*you meet*
	Thus they departyd fayre and welle.	
325	The Kyng fulle sone com to Carlylle,	*soon came*
	And his hartt hevy and greatt.	*painful*

The fyrst man he mett was Sir Gawen,
That unto the Kyng thus gan sayn,   *did say*
"Syr, howe have ye sped?"   *you fared*

330   "Forsothe," sayd the Kyng, "nevere so ylle!
Alas, I am in poynt myself to spylle,   *ready; destroy*
For nedely I most be ded."   *of necessity*
"Nay," sayd Gawen, "that may nott be!
I had lever myself be dead, so mott I the.   *rather; may I prosper*
335   Thys is ille tydand."   *bad news*

"Gawen, I mett today with the fowlyst Lady
That evere I sawe, sertenly.   *certainly*
She sayd to me my lyfe she wold save —
Butt fyrst she wold the to husbond have.   *desires you as*
340   Wherfor I am wo begon —
Thus in my hartt I make my mone."   *lament*
"Ys this alle?" then sayd Gawen;
"I shalle wed her and wed her agayn,
Thowghe she were a fend;   *fiend*
345   Thowghe she were as foulle as Belsabub,   *the devil*
Her shalle I wed, by the Rood,   *Cross*
Or elles were nott I your frende.

"For ye ar my Kyng with honour
And have worshypt me in many a stowre;   *honored; battle*
350   Therfor shalle I nott lett.   *hesitate*
To save your lyfe, Lorde, itt were my parte,   *role*
Or were I false and a greatt coward;
And my worshypp is the bett."   *honor; more*
"Iwys, Gawen, I mett her in Inglyswod.   *Indeed*

355	She told me her name, by the Rode:	*Cross*
	That itt was Dame Ragnelle.	
	She told me butt I had of her answere,	*unless; from*
	Elles alle my laboure is nevere the nere —	*Otherwise; nearer [success]*
	Thus she gan me telle.	*did*
360	"And butt yf her answere help me welle	*unless*
	Elles let her have her desyre no dele —	*Otherwise; not at all*
	This was her covenaunt.	
	And yf her answere help me, and none other,	*no other [answer]*
	Then wold she have you: here is alle togeder	
365	That made she warraunt."	*guarantee of*
	"As for this," sayd Gawen, "itt shalle nott lett:	*get in the way*
	I wolle wed her att whate tyme ye wolle sett.	*whatever; will*
	I pray you, make no care.	*have no concern*
	For and she were the moste fowlyst wyghte	*if; person*
370	That evere men myghte se with syghte,	
	For your love I wolle nott spare."	*stint*
	"Garamercy, Gawen," then sayd Kyng Arthor;	*Many thanks*
	"Of alle knyghtes thou berest the flowre	*take the prize*
	That evere yett I fond.	*knew*
375	My worshypp and my lyf thou savyst forevere;	*honor*
	Therfore my love shalle nott frome the dyssevyr,	*from you be severed*
	As I am Kyng in lond."	*While*
	Then within five or six days	
	The Kyng must nedys goo his ways	
380	To bere his answere.	*offer*
	The Kyng and Sir Gawen rode oute of toun —	
	No man with them, butt they alone,	
	Neder ferre ne nere.	*Neither far; near*
	When the Kyng was within the Forest:	*[he said]*
385	"Syr Gawen, farewelle, I must go west;	
	Thou shalt no furder goo."	*further*
	"My Lord, God spede you on your jorney.	*quest*
	I wold I shold nowe ryde your way,	*wish*
	For to departe I am ryghte wo."	*very distressed*
390	The Kyng had rydden butt a while,	

Lytelle more then the space of a myle,

Or he mett Dame Ragnelle.   *Before*

"A, Sir Kyng! Ye arre nowe welcum here.

I wott ye ryde to bere your answere;   *perceive*

395   That wolle avaylle you no dele."   *will; not at all*

"Nowe," sayd the Kyng, "sithe itt wolle none other be,   *not otherwise*

Telle me your answere nowe, and my lyfe save me;   *save for me*

Gawen shalle you wed.

So he hathe promysed me my lyf to save,   *in order to save*

400   And your desyre nowe shalle ye have,

Bothe in bowre and in bed.   *chamber*

Therfor telle me nowe alle in hast —   *haste*

Whate wolle help now att last?

Have done, I may nott tary."   *Be quick*

405   "Syr," quod Dame Ragnelle, "nowe shalt thou knowe

Whate wemen desyren moste of highe and lowe;   *high and low rank*

From this I wolle nott varaye: *deviate*

"Summe men sayn we desyre to be fayre;

Also we desyre to have repayre   *traffic*

410   Of diverse straunge men;   *With*

Also we love to have lust in bed;   *pleasure*

And often we desyre to wed.

Thus ye men nott ken   *do not understand*

Yett we desyre anoder maner thyng: *Also; another*

415   To be holden nott old, butt fresshe and yong,   *regarded as*

With flatryng and glosyng and quaynt gyn —   *cajolery and special art*

So ye men may us wemen evere wyn

Of whate ye wolle crave.   *whatever; will*

"Ye goo fulle nyse, I wolle nott lye;   *act very foolishly*

420   Butt there is one thyng is alle oure fantasye,   *fancy*

And that nowe shalle ye knowe.

We desyren of men above alle maner thyng

To have the sovereynté, withoute lesyng,   *mastery, no lie*

Of alle, bothe hyghe and lowe.

425   For where we have sovereynté, alle is ourys,

Thoughe a knyght be nevere so ferys,   *fierce*

And evere the mastry wynne. *mastery*
Of the moste manlyest is oure desyre:
To have the sovereynté of suche a syre, *a lord*
430 Suche is oure crafte and gynne. *skill; art*

"Therfore wend, Sir Kyng, on thy way, *go*
And telle that knyght, as I the saye, *you tell*
That itt is as we desyren moste. *What*
He wol be wrothe and unsoughte *angry; bitter*
435 And curse her fast that itt the taughte, *stoutly; you*
For his laboure is lost.
Go forthe, Sir Kyng, and hold promyse, *keep [your]*
For thy lyfe is sure nowe in alle wyse, *secure; ways*
That dare I welle undertake." *well declare*
440 The Kyng rode forthe a greatt shake, *at headlong speed*
As fast as he myghte gate *go*
Thorowe myre, more, and fenne, *moor; bog*
Whereas the place was sygnyd and sett then. *assigned*

Evyn there with Sir Gromer he mett, *Right*
445 And stern wordes to the Kyng he spak with that: *right away*
"Com of, Sir Kyng, nowe lett se *Come on*
Of thyne answere, whate itt shal be,
For I am redy grathyd." *all prepared*
The Kyng pullyd oute bokes twayne: *two books*
450 "Syr, ther is myne answer, I dare sayn; *say*
For somme wolle help att nede." *one [of these] will have to help*
Syr Gromer lokyd on theym everychon: *every one*
"Nay, nay, Sir Kyng, thou artt butt a dead man; *as good as*
Therfor nowe shalt thou blede." *bleed*

455 "Abyde, Sir Gromer," sayd Kyng Arthoure,
"I have one answere shalle make alle sure." *settle everything*
"Lett se," then sayd Sir Gromer, *see*
"Or els, so God me help, as I the say, *tell*
Thy dethe thou shalt have with large paye, *to my great pleasure*
460 I telle the nowe ensure." *surely*
"Now," sayd the Kyng, "I se, as I gesse, *think*
In the is butt a lytelle gentilnesse,

59

By God that ay is helpand.   *ever; helping*
Here is oure answere, and that is alle
465   That wemen desyren moste specialle,   *especially*
Bothe of fre and bond: *unfree*

"I saye no more, butt above al thyng
Wemen desyre sovereynté, for that is theyr lykyng.   *their pleasure*
And that is ther moste desyre,
470   To have the rewlle of the manlyest men,   *control*
And then ar they welle. Thus they me dyd ken   *Thus they did teach me*
To rule the, Gromer Syre."
"And she that told the nowe, Sir Arthoure,
I pray to God, I maye se her bren on a fyre;   *burn*
475   For that was my suster, Dame Ragnelle,
That old scott, God geve her shame.   *nag*
Elles had I made the fulle tame;   *Otherwise*
Nowe have I lost moche travaylle.   *effort*

"Go where thou wolt, Kyng Arthoure,   *you wish*
480   For of me thou maiste be evere sure.   *may rest assured*
Alas, that I evere se this day!
Nowe, welle I wott, myne enimé thou wolt be.   *know*
And att suche a pryk shall I nevere gett the;   *plight*
My song may be 'Welle-awaye!'"   *alas*
485   "No," sayd the Kyng, "that make I warraunt: *[of] that; guarantee*
Some harnys I wolle have to make me defendaunt,   *armor; ready for combat*
That make I God avowe!   *an oath*
In suche a plyghte shalt thou nevere me fynde;
And yf thou do, lett me bete and bynde,   *have me beaten*
490   As is for thy best prouf."   *As living proof*

"Nowe have good day," sayd Sir Gromer.
"Farewele," sayd Sir Arthoure; "so mott I the,   *as I prosper*
I am glad I have so sped."   *fared*
Kyng Arthoure turnyd hys hors into the playn,
495   And sone he mett with Dame Ragnelle agayn,
In the same place and stede.   *spot*
"Syr Kyng, I am glad ye have sped welle.
I told howe itt wold be, every delle;   *part*

60

	Nowe hold that ye have hyghte:	*hold [to] what; promised*
500	Syn I have savyd your lyf, and none other,	*Since*
	Gawen must me wed, Sir Arthoure,	
	That is a fulle gentille knyght."	*Who*

	"No, Lady; that I you hyghte I shalle nott faylle.	*what; promised*
	So ye wol be rulyd by my councelle,	*As long as*
505	Your wille then shalle ye have."	
	"Nay, Sir Kyng, nowe wolle I nott soo;	*will I not [have it] so*
	Openly I wol be weddyd, or I parte the froo	*Publicly; from*
	Elles shame wolle ye have.	*Otherwise; will*
	Ryde before, and I wolle com after,	
510	Unto thy courte, Syr Kyng Arthoure.	
	Of no man I wolle shame;	*Upon; [do] I wish*
	Bethynk you howe I have savyd your lyf.	
	Therfor with me nowe shalle ye nott stryfe,	*strive*
	For and ye do, ye be to blame."	*if*

515	The Kyng of her had greatt shame,	*was ashamed*
	Butt forth she rood, thoughe he were grevyd;	*grieved*
	Tylle they cam to Karlyle forth they mevyd.	*onward; rode*
	Into the courte she rode hym by;	*alongside*
	For no man wold she spare, securly —	*hold back surely*
520	Itt likyd the Kyng fulle ylle.	*pleased*
	Alle the contraye had wonder greatt	*Everyone*
	Fro whens she com, that foule unswete;	*whence; unlovely*
	They sawe nevere of so fowlle a thyng.	
	Into the halle she went, in certen.	*indeed*
525	"Arthoure, Kyng, lett fetche me Sir Gaweyn,	*have summoned [for] me*
	Before the knyghtes, alle in hying,	*haste*

	"That I may nowe be made sekyr.	*have surety*
	In welle and wo trowithe plyghte us togeder	*let us pledge [our] troth*
	Before alle thy chyvalry.	*knights*
530	This is your graunt; lett se, have done.	*pledge; come on, do it*
	Sett forthe Sir Gawen, my love, anon,	*Bring*
	For lenger tarying kepe nott I."	*longer; suffer*
	Then cam forthe Sir Gawen the knyght:	
	"Syr, I am redy of that I you hyghte,	*for what; promised*

61

535	Alle forwardes to fulfylle."	*agreements*
	"God have mercy!" sayd Dame Ragnelle then;	
	"For thy sake I wold I were a fayre woman,	
	For thou art of so good wylle."	
	Ther Sir Gawen to her his trowthe plyghte	*troth*
540	In welle and in woo, as he was a true knyght;	
	Then was Dame Ragnelle fayn.	*glad*
	"Alas!" then sayd Dame Gaynour;	*Guenevere*
	So sayd alle the ladyes in her bower,	*chamber*
	And wept for Sir Gawen.	
545	"Alas!" then sayd bothe Kyng and knyght,	
	That evere he shold wed suche a wyghte,	*person*
	She was so fowlle and horyble.	
	She had two tethe on every syde	*each*
	As borys tuskes, I wolle nott hyde,	*boar's; dissemble*
550	Of lengthe a large handfulle.	*In; hand's breadth*
	The one tusk went up and the other doun.	
	A mowthe fulle wyde and fowlle igrown,	*foully grown*
	With grey herys many on.	*hairs; one*
	Her lyppes laye lumpryd on her chyn;	*lumpish*
555	Nek forsothe on her was none iseen —	
	She was a lothly on!	*one*
	She wold nott be weddyd in no maner	
	Butt there were made a krye in all the shyre,	*Except; proclamation*
	Bothe in town and in borowe.	*borough*
560	Alle the ladyes nowe of the lond,	
	She lett kry to com to hand	*did summon; to visit*
	To kepe that brydalle thorowe.	*wedding feast*
	So itt befylle after on a daye	
	That maryed shold be that fowlle maye	
565	Unto Sir Gawen.	
	The daye was comyn the daye shold be;	*date had arrived [when]*
	Therof the ladyes had greatt pitey.	
	"Alas!" then gan they sayn.	
	The Queen prayd Dame Ragnelle sekerly —	*steadfastly*
570	"To be maryed in the mornyng erly,	

As pryvaly as ye may."   *privately*
"Nay!" she sayd; "By Hevyn Kyng,
That wolle I nevere, for no thyng,
For oughte that ye can saye.   *anything*

575   "I wol be weddyd alle openly,
For with the Kyng suche covenaunt made I.
I putt you oute of dowte,   *assure you*
I wolle nott to churche tylle Highe Masse tyme
And in the open halle I wolle dyne,
580   In myddys of alle the rowte."   *midst; company*
"I am greed," sayd Dame Gaynour;   *agreed*
"Butt me wold thynk more honour   *Only I am thinking about*
And your worshypp moste."   *worship*
"Ye, as for that, Lady, God you save.
585   This daye my worshypp wolle I have,   *honor*
I telle you withoute boste."   *boast*

She made her redy to churche to fare
And alle the states that there ware,   *As did all those of noble rank*
Syrs, withoute lesing.   *no lie*
590   She was arayd in the richest maner,
More fressher than Dame Gaynour;
Her arayment was worthe thre thowsand mark
Of good red nobles, styff and stark,   *coin; hard*
So rychely she was begon.   *done up*
595   For alle her rayment, she bare the belle   *Despite; took the prize*
Of fowlnesse, that evere I hard telle —   *For; heard*
So fowlle a sowe sawe nevere man.   *sow*

For to make a shortt conclusion,
When she was weddyd, they hyed theym home;   *As soon as; hastened*
600   To mete alle they went.   *dinner*
This fowlle Lady bygan the highe dese;   *occupied first place on the dais*
She was fulle foulle and nott curteys,   *courteous*
So sayd they alle verament.   *truly*
When the servyce cam her before,   *platters*
605   She ete as moche as six that ther wore;   *were there*
That mervaylyd many a man.   *[At] that*

	Her nayles were long ynchys thre,	*inches three*
	Therwith she breke her mete ungoodly;	*broke her bread unmannerly*
	Therfore she ete alone.	*she didn't wait for anyone*
610	She ette thre capons, and also curlues thre,	*curlews*
	And greatt bake metes she ete up, perdé.	*roasts; by God*
	Al men therof had mervaylle.	
	Ther was no mete cam her before	
	Butt she ete itt up, lesse and more,	*But she did not*
615	That praty, fowlle dameselle.	*crafty*
	Alle men then that evere her sawe	
	Bad the deville her bonys gnawe,	*Bade; bones*
	Bothe knyght and squyre.	
	So she ete tylle mete was done,	
620	Tylle they drewe clothes and had wasshen,	*cleared tables*
	As is the gyse and maner.	*custom*
	Meny men wold speke of diverse service;	*various courses*
	I trowe ye may wete inowghe ther was,	*trust; know enough*
	Bothe of tame and wylde.	*[meats]*
625	In Kyng Arthours courte ther was no wontt	*lack*
	That myghte be gotten with mannys hond,	*[Of] what*
	Noder in Forest ne in feld.	*Neither*
	Ther were mynstralles of diverse contrey.	

[The manuscript is here missing one leaf, containing about seventy lines; the narrative continues at the moment of Ragnelle's and Gawain's wedding night.]

	"A, Sir Gawen, syn I have you wed,	*since*
630	Shewe me your cortesy in bed;	
	With ryghte itt may nott be denyed.	*By*
	"Iwyse, Sir Gawen," that Lady sayd,	*Surely*
	"And I were fayre ye wold do anoder brayd,	*If; take another tack*
	Butt of wedlok ye take no hed.	*Unless; regard*
635	Yett for Arthours sake kysse me att the leste;	*least*
	I pray you do this att my request.	
	Lett se howe ye can spede."	*fare*
	Sir Gawen sayd, "I wolle do more	*will [undertake to] do*

Then for to kysse, and God before!"
640 He turnyd hym her untille.   *towards*
He sawe her the fayrest creature
That evere he sawe, withoute mesure.   *compare*
She sayd, "Whatt is your wylle?"

"A, Jhesu!" he sayd; "Whate ar ye?"
645 "Sir, I am your wyf, securly.   *without doubt*
Why ar ye so unkynde?"   *aloof (unnatural)*
"A, Lady, I am to blame.
I cry you mercy, my fayre madame —
Itt was nott in my mynde.   *(I was not thinking)*
650 A Lady ye ar fayre in my syghte,
And today ye were the foulyst wyghte   *person*
That evere I sawe with mine ie.   *eye*
Wele is me, my Lady, I have you thus" —
And brasyd her in his armys and gan her kysse   *embraced; did*
655 And made greatt joye, sycurly.   *surely*

"Syr," she sayd, "thus shalle ye me have:
Chese of the one, so God me save,   *Choose*
My beawty wolle nott hold —
Wheder ye wolle have me fayre on nyghtes   *Whether*
660 And as foulle on days to alle men sightes,
Or els to have me fayre on days
And on nyghtes on the fowlyst wyfe —   *wife [of all]*
The one ye must nedes have.   *of necessity*
Chese the one or the oder.
665 Chese on, Sir Knyght, whiche you is levere,   *one; preferable*
Your worshypp for to save."   *honor*

"Alas!" sayd Gawen; "The choyse is hard.
To chese the best, itt is froward,   *confounding*
Wheder choyse that I chese: *Either*
670 To have you fayre on nyghtes and no more,
That wold greve my hartt ryghte sore,
And my worshypp shold I lese.   *lose*
And yf I desyre on days to have you fayre,
Then on nyghtes I shold have a symple repayre.   *dismal relations*

65

675	Now fayn wold I chose the best:	*happily*
	I ne wott in this world whatt I shalle saye,	*don't know*
	Butt do as ye lyst nowe, my Lady gaye.	*[it] pleases you*
	The choyse I putt in your fyst:	*hand*
	"Evyn as ye wolle, I putt itt in your hand.	*Just*
680	Lose me when ye lyst, for I am bond;	*Release; bound*
	I putt the choyse in you.	
	Bothe body and goodes, hartt, and every dele,	*part*
	Ys alle your oun, for to by and selle —	*buy*
	That make I God avowe!"	
685	"Garamercy, corteys Knyght," sayd the Lady;	*Many thanks courteous*
	"Of alle erthly knyghtes blyssyd mott thou be,	*may*
	For now am I worshyppyd.	*honored properly*
	Thou shalle have me fayre bothe day and nyghte	
	And evere whyle I lyve as fayre and bryghte;	
690	Therfore be nott grevyd.	*grieved*
	"For I was shapen by nygramancy,	*transformed; necromancy*
	With my stepdame, God have on her mercy,	*By*
	And by enchauntement;	
	And shold have bene oderwyse understond,	*otherwise [as a hag] perceived*
695	Evyn tylle the best of Englond	*Until; best [knight]*
	Had wedyd me verament,	*truly*
	And also he shold geve me the sovereynté	*mastery*
	Of alle his body and goodes, sycurly.	*surely*
	Thus was I disformyd;	*On such conditions*
700	And thou, Sir Knyght, curteys Gawen,	
	Has gevyn me the sovereynté serteyn,	
	That woll nott wrothe the erly ne late.	*Who; hurt*
	"Kysse me, Sir Knyght, evyn now here;	
	I pray the, be glad and make good chere,	
705	For well is me begon."	*I am well-off*
	Ther they made joye oute of mynde,	*beyond imagining*
	So was itt reason and cours of kynde,	*So far as it accorded with nature*
	They two theymself alone.	
	She thankyd God and Mary mylde	
710	She was recovered of that that she was defoylyd;	*which had defiled her*

So dyd Sir Gawen.
He made myrthe alle in her boure   *chamber*
And thankyd of alle Oure Savyoure,   *for everything*
I telle you, in certeyn.

715   With joye and myrthe they wakyd tylle daye   *stayed awake; dawn*
        And than wold ryse that fayre maye.   *arise; woman*
        "Ye shalle nott," Sir Gawen sayd;
        "We wolle lye and slepe tylle pryme   *mid-morning*
        And then lett the Kyng calle us to dyne."

720   "I am greed," then sayd the mayd.   *agreed*
        Thus itt passyd forth tylle middaye.
        "Syrs," quod the Kyng, "lett us go and asaye   *find out*
        Yf Sir Gawen be on lyve.   *alive*
        I am fulle ferd of Sir Gawen,   *fearful for*
725   Nowe lest the fende have hym slayn;   *fiend*
        Nowe wold I fayn preve.   *gladly make sure*

        "Go we nowe," sayd Arthoure the Kyng.
        "We wolle go se theyr uprysyng,
        Howe welle that he hathe sped."
730   They cam to the chambre, alle incerteyn.   *unsure*
        "Aryse," sayd the Kyng to Sir Gawen;
        "Why slepyst thou so long in bed?"
        "Mary," quod Gawen, "Sir Kyng, sicurly,   *surely*
        I wold be glad, and ye wold lett me be,   *if you would*
735   For I am fulle welle att eas.   *ease*
        Abyde, ye shalle se the dore undone!
        I trowe that ye wolle say I am welle goon;   *trust; well-off*
        I am fulle lothe to ryse."   *completely averse*

        Syr Gawen rose, and in his hand he toke
740   His fayr Lady, and to the dore he shoke,   *hastened*
        And opynyd the dore fulle fayre.   *widely*
        She stod in her smok alle by that fyre;   *night dress right by*
        Her here was to her knees as red as gold wyre.   *hair*
        "Lo, this is my repayre!   *source of comfort*
745   Lo!" sayd Gawen Arthoure untille —   *unto*
        "Syr, this is my wyfe, Dame Ragnelle,
        That savyd onys your lyfe."   *once*

67

	He told the Kyng and the Queen hem beforn	*in their presence*
	Howe sodenly from her shap she dyd torne —	*monstrousness; revert*
750	"My Lord, nowe be your leve" —	*by*
	And whate was the cause she forshapen was	*transformed*
	Syr Gawen told the Kyng both more and lesse.	*in all details*
	"I thank God," sayd the Queen;	
	"I wenyd, Sir Gawen, she wold the have myscaryed;	*thought; harmed*
755	Therfore in my hartt I was sore agrevyd.	
	Butt the contrary is here seen!"	
	Ther was game, revelle, and playe,	
	And every man to other gan saye,	*did*
	"She is a fayre wyghte."	*person*
760	Than the Kyng them alle gan telle	
	How did help hym att nede Dame Ragnelle,	
	"Or my dethe had bene dyghte."	*assured*
	Ther the Kyng told the Queen, by the Rood,	*Cross*
	Howe he was bestad in Ingleswod	*beset*
765	With Sir Gromer Somer Joure,	
	And whate othe the knyght made hym swere,	*oath*
	"Or elles he had slayn me ryghte there	
	Withoute mercy or mesure.	
	This same Lady, Dame Ragnelle,	
770	From my dethe she dyd help me ryght welle,	
	Alle for the love of Gawen."	
	Then Gawen told the Kyng alle togeder	*fully*
	Howe forshapen she was with her stepmoder	*transformed; by*
	Tylle a knyght had holpen her agayn.	*helped*
775	Ther she told the Kyng fayre and welle	
	Howe Gawen gave her the sovereynté every delle,	*part*
	And whate choyse she gave to hym.	
	"God thank hym of his curtesye;	
	He savid me from chaunce and vilony	*mischance; evil*
780	That was fulle foulle and grym.	
	Therfore, curteys Knyght and hend Gawen,	*gracious*
	Shalle I nevere wrathe the serteyn,	*hurt you surely*
	That promyse nowe here I make.	

	Whilles that I lyve I shal be obaysaunt;	*obedient*
785	To God above I shalle itt warraunt,	
	And nevere with you to debate."	

	"Garamercy, Lady," then sayd Gawen;	*Great thanks*
	"With you I hold me fulle welle content	
	And that I trust to fynde."	*will ever be the case*
790	He sayd, "My love shalle she have.	
	Therafter nede she nevere more crave,	*Beyond that*
	For she hathe bene to me so kynde."	
	The Queen sayd, and the ladyes alle,	
	"She is the fayrest nowe in this halle,	
795	I swere by Seynt John!	
	My love, Lady, ye shalle have evere	
	For that ye savid my Lord Arthoure,	
	As I am a gentilwoman."	

	Syr Gawen gatt on her Gyngolyn	*begot; Guinglain*
800	That was a good knyght of strengthe and kynn	*ancestry*
	And of the Table Round.	
	Att every greatt fest that Lady shold be.	
	Of fayrnesse she bare away the bewtye,	*the [prize for] beauty*
	Wher she yed on the ground.	*went*
805	Gawen lovyd that Lady, Dame Ragnelle;	
	In alle his lyfe he lovyd none so welle,	
	I telle you withoute lesyng.	*no lie*
	As a coward he lay by her bothe day and nyghte.	*Submissively; stayed*
	Nevere wold he haunt justyng aryghte;	*pursue jousting as usual*
810	Theratt mervaylyd Arthoure the Kyng.	

	She prayd the Kyng for his gentilnes,	
	"To be good lord to Sir Gromer, iwysse,	*indeed*
	Of that to you he hathe offendyd."	*Insofar as*
	"Yes, Lady, that shalle I nowe for your sake,	
815	For I wott welle he may nott amendes make;	*know; offer restitution*
	He dyd to me fulle unhend."	*acted towards; uncourteously*
	Nowe for to make you a short conclusyon,	
	I cast me for to make an end fulle sone	*undertake*
	Of this gentylle Lady.	

820	She lyvyd with Sir Gawen butt yerys five;	*five years*
	That grevid Gawen alle his lyfe,	
	I telle you securly.	
	In her lyfe she grevyd hym nevere;	*offended*
	Therfor was nevere woman to hym lever.	*dearer*
825	Thus leves my talkyng.	*ends; performance*
	She was the fayrest Lady of alle Englond,	
	When she was on lyve, I understand;	*dare say*
	So sayd Arthoure the Kyng.	
	Thus endythe the adventure of Kyng Arthoure,	
830	That oft in his days was grevyd sore,	*sorely harassed*
	And of the weddyng of Gawen.	
	Gawen was weddyd oft in his days;	
	Butt so welle he nevere lovyd woman always,	*constantly*
	As I have hard men sayn.	*heard*
835	This adventure befelle in Ingleswod,	
	As good Kyng Arthoure on huntyng yod;	*went*
	Thus have I hard men telle.	
	Nowe God, as thou were in Bethleme born,	
	Suffer nevere her soules be forlorne	*their; lost*
840	In the brynnyng fyre of helle!	*burning*
	And, Jhesu, as thou were borne of a virgyn,	
	Help hym oute of sorowe that this tale dyd devyne,	*make up*
	And that nowe in alle hast,	*[do] that*
	For he is besett with gaylours many	*jailors*
845	That kepen hym fulle sewerly,	*guard; securely*
	With wyles wrong and wraste.	*tricks; powerful*
	Nowe God, as thou art veray Kyng Royalle,	*true*
	Help hym oute of daunger that made this tale	
	For therin he hathe bene long.	
850	And of greatt pety help thy servaunt,	*out of; pity*
	For body and soull I yeld into thyne hand,	
	For paynes he hathe strong.	

Here endythe the weddyng of
Syr Gawen and Dame Ragnelle
For helpyng of Kyng Arthoure.

Notes

As I have mentioned in the introduction to the text, the scribe's letter forms are often interchangeable, and strokes ambiguous. Often transcription will therefore be somewhat arbitrary. Where the scribe's forms are clear, I have reproduced them in my readings; where they are unclear, I have opted for forms closer to modern conventions of spelling. This has resulted in some inconsistencies, such as a mix of spellings like *his* and *hys*. In general, I have regarded final flourishes as meaningless, and so given, for example, *knyght* and *with* (in agreement with Madden and Hartwell) in preference to *knyghte* and *withe* (the usual readings in Sumner, Whiting, and Sands). In cases of double *l* with a stroke, I have retained a final *e* (i.e., *welle, fulle, Ragnelle*). These ambiguities of writing practice are not uncommon in medieval and Renaissance vernacular manuscripts, and the scribe certainly did not regard them as affecting the meaning of the text in any essential way. Consequently I have not recorded in these notes all the instances where spelling differs from edition to edition because the scribe's forms can legitimately be read in a variety of ways. *Ragnelle* has been edited more times than most other Middle English romances; I have benefitted greatly by consulting these earlier editions, and at the same time I have had to make choices among confusing, confused, and sometimes contradictory readings. These differences among editions have the effect of making the text of *Ragnelle* seem even more unpredictable in its orthography than it actually is. This has been complicated by attempts at editorial "normalization"; this is especially the case with Sands (likely the best known print of the poem), where standardization is itself inconsistent, and new spellings and word forms are added to the manuscript's readings. The present edition tries to offer a readable text that leaves the manuscript readings unaltered wherever possible. I have modernized spellings, giving "j" for "i," "u" for "v" and "w," "v" for "u" and "w," and "w" for "u" and "v" in accord with current usage.

Abbreviations: R = Rawlinson MS, M = Madden, S = Sumner, W = Whiting, Sands = Sands, H = Hartwell. See Select Bibliography for these editions.

11   *belovid by that.* R: *belovid that*; M adds *by* for sense, which I follow.

16   *Ingleswod.* The story is set in Inglewood Forest, near Carlisle (see lines 127, 132, 325) in Cumberland, in northwest England, on the border of Scotland. Inglewood Forest (whose Anglo-Saxon name, meaning "the wood of the

Angles," suggests an English settlement in contested British territory) ceased to exist in the nineteenth century. Its mention connects *Ragnelle* with the settings for *Avowyng* (line 65) and *Awntyrs* (line 709). The Tarn Wathelene (mentioned in *Avowyng*, *Awntyrs*, and *Marriage*) was located within Inglewood Forest; see *Awntyrs*, line 2 and note. For these tales of Sir Gawain, the woods and lakes of Inglewood and the environs of Carlisle were locales with strong Arthurian and marvelous associations.

26   *houndes.* R: *goundes*; M reads as *houndes*, H reads as *hounds*; S, W emend to *g[r]oundes*.

43   *theron.* R: *deron*. The manuscript reading has presented a puzzle to editors. Most have taken *deron* (see line 26) to mean "covertly," though such a spelling is not, so far as I know, attested elsewhere. Again, *deron* might seem a past participle of *derien*, "to wound," though, likewise, no spellings resembling *deron* occur. I have taken it therefore as a case in which the scribe substitutes *d* for *th*; other instances occur at lines 176 (*oder*), 196 (*anoder*), 383 (*Neder*), 386 (*furder*), and so on, though in all of these cases the scribe substitutes *d* for a voiced, intervocalic *th*, not for an initial unvoiced sound. I take the line to mean that the wounded deer fell down on the spot. To read this as a form of *derne* would suggest either that the deer fell blindly into a thicket, or fell into a blind thicket (which concealed Sir Gromer).

47   *serve welle.* R: *s̆vell*. The scribe writes *s* with *-er* abbreviation stroke over the letter, followed by *well* with a stroke through the ascenders. M reads *serve well*, which makes good sense in this context; I follow scribal spelling of this reading as in S, W. H reads *sirvell*, and emends to *quell*.

48   *grasse.* S derives the meaning of this word from the Old English word for "grass," and is followed by W. Sands calls it "a puzzling line," and, following S, suggests the deer touched the grass (i.e., died). It seems certain, however, that this scene is an "assay," in which the hunter measures the deer's fat (*grasse*, meaning grease or fat) as a preliminary to the ritualized "breaking" or butchering of the animal. Such scenes occur in Gottfried von Strassburg's *Tristan*, in which the hero proves his royal identity by demonstrating his knowledge of the ritual, and in the Middle English *Parlement of the Thre Ages* and *Sir Gawain and the Green Knight*. Instructions for the assay are given in several hunting manuals; see notes to lines 1325 ff. of *Sir Gawain and the Green Knight* in the Tolkien-Gordon-Davis edition, where the "gres" of the "fowlest" deer is

two fingers in breadth. H also notes this connection, as does Susan Dannen-baum [Crane] in her note on the line (*Explicator* 40 [1982], 3–4).

62   *Gromer Somer Joure.* H reads *Jourer* (with expanded abbreviation) and emends to *Jour.* The name seems less connected with chivalry than with folklore. Malory in the *Morte Darthur* names Sir Gromore Somyr Joure (or Sir Gromoreson in the Winchester manuscript) among the faction of twelve knights who align themselves with Gawain's brothers Mordred and Aggravayne in the ambush of Lancelot (see *Works*, p. 1164, and also pp. 343, 346, 1148). Among the others in the faction are Sir Gyngolyne, the son of Sir Gawain and (according to the present romance) Ragnelle (see line 799). In *Turke* (see text and notes at lines 320 ff. in this volume), Sir Gawain transforms the pagan "Turk" by beheading him, and he becomes Sir Gromer. But here his dangerous-ness, his sudden appearance deep in the woods, and his name would seem to connect Sir Gromer Somer Joure to the festivities of midsummer's day and night, and to the spirits and the "great and ugly gyants marching as if they were alive" associated with this occasion in England through the sixteenth century (George Puttenham, *The Arte of English Poesie*, ed. Gladys Doidge Willcock and Alice Walker [Cambridge: Cambridge University Press, 1936], p. 153). In this respect, he shares some traits with the Green Knight, in *Greene Knight* (text and notes in this volume) and still more with the eerie intruder of *Sir Gawain and the Green Knight*, who exhibits striking similarities to the partici-pants at celebrations of the agricultural year. The name *Gromer* may simply be a version of "groom," i.e., "man," as in "bridegroom" (compare line 50, where this term is applied to Sir Gromer), or a derivative from "gram," "angry." In *Marriage*, the lady tells Gawain that her wicked stepmother not only cast a spell on her, but "witched my brother to a carlish" shape (line 179). In *Ragnelle*, there's no evidence that Sir Gromer is bewitched, and he is without doubt a knight, as Arthur's greetings and descriptions make clear. See also note on Gyngolyn, line 799 below.

75   *I have the nowe att avaylle.* For the use of this phrase to express triumph, see OED, "avail," sb., 1b.

77   *defye.* The word *defy* carries a quasi-technical meaning in the context of chival-ric honor; it implies a public challenge, which is simultaneously a denunciation and a demand for open, physical vindication of one's honor, and is therefore quite the opposite of what Sir Gromer Somer Jour does here. See MED, "defien" v. 1, 2.

80   *whate thou most crave.* Arthur's offer to Sir Gromer anticipates the riddle the latter poses to the King — to name "whate wemen love best" (line 91). In the same way, Sir Gromer's remark — "Thy lyfe is in my hand" (line 107) is directly echoed in Ragnelle's identical claim (line 256).

86   *certeyn.* M, S, W, Sands: *certayn.*

91   *best in feld and town* is written into margin; this hypermetrical tag may be part of a lost line.

96   *fremde.* R: *frende*; M reads *fremde*, which I follow.

104   *endyng.* R: *end*; I emend for the sake of rhyme.

128   *huntyng.* W misprints *hyntyng.*

149   *By Mary flower.* This is an elliptical phrase, meaning, "Mary, flower among women," or "flower of womanhood."

172   *lese.* R: *leve*; M reads *lese.* H reads R as *lose*, but follows M's emendation, as I do.

194   *they.* R: *the*; M reads *they*, which I follow.

212   *faylle.* R: *ffayd*; M reads *faylle*, which I follow.

235   *her.* R: *he*; M reads *her*, which I follow.

256 ff.   Ragnelle's warning here precisely repeats the boast her brother, Sir Gromer, had made to Arthur at line 107 and so emphasizes the parallel between the compacts into which the king is forced. See also line 80 and note.

266   *Yf I help the nott, thou art butt dead.* R: *Butt I warn the yf I help the nott, thou art butt dead*; I follow M in omitting the phrase repeated from previous line, as a probable copyist's error.

273   *Whate is your desyre, fayre Lady.* Arthur's question ironically solicits from Ragnelle a concrete reply to the enigma Sir Gromer has set for him. In fulfil-

ling her desire for Gawain, Arthur presumably obtains the answer to what all women desire, and answers Sir Gromer's challenge as well (see lines 467–72).

280   *a knyght to wed.* The line involves a pun: a knight to marry, and a knight as pledge of good faith ("to wed"). See OED, *wed* sb., 2a.

293   *Alle lyethe in hym alon.* In making individual consent — rather than family or state interests, or priestly authority — the ultimate basis for a valid marriage, the poem reflects central doctrinal positions taught from the twelfth century; see R. H. Helmholz, *Marriage Litigation in Medieval England* (Cambridge: Cambridge University Press, 1974). Ragnelle makes the same point, concerning her own right to choose, at line 310.

302   *sewer.* S (followed by Sands) glosses this word adverbially, as "surely," but it seems more likely a form of the verb *sure*, "to assure": through me Gawain may save your life, or assure that your death comes about.

314   *lore.* R: *lore fowll*; I follow M in omitting the final word, which seems a confused rhyme.

316   *ther is a byrd men calle an owlle.* The precise import of this line is unclear; it may be that a part of the text is missing here. In echoing herself from line 310, Ragnelle seems to mean *owlle* to refer both to her own monstrousness (the owl was chiefly a negative symbol in late medieval writings) and to her natural rights as a human being, or to her repellent appearance and her assertion that she is in reality *a Lady* (line 315).

319   *Dame Ragnelle.* The name is otherwise unknown in Arthurian romance. In *Patience*, a poetic version of the Jonah story usually attributed to the author of *Sir Gawain and the Green Knight*, the gentile sailors on whose ship the Hebrew prophet tries to escape from the Lord curse him by "Ragnel" (line 188), apparently intended to be taken as the name of a pagan god or devil. See the note in J. J. Anderson's edition (Manchester, 1969), p. 59. In the Digby play of *Mary Magdalen* a heathen priest and his servant perform a comic exorcism in broken Latin, and then call on the gods "Ragnell and Roffyn" (line 1200; *Late Medieval Religious Plays of . . . Digby 133*, ed. Donald C. Baker and others, EETS o.s. 283 [Oxford, 1982], p. 64). The Chester play of "Balaam" has that gentile prophet invoke his gods "Ruffyn and Reynell" (line 213); the latter is

given as "Ragnell" in one manuscript. Likewise, the Chester play of "Antichrist" has Antichrist call for aid:

> Helpe, Sathanas and Lucyfere!
> Belzebubb, bould batchellere!
> Ragnell, Ragnell, thou art my deare! (lines 645–47)

(*The Chester Mystery Cycle*, ed. R. M. Lumiansky and David Mills, EETS s.s. 3 [Oxford, 1974], pp. 87 and 434; see also commentary by the same editors, EETS s.s. 9 [Oxford, 1986], pp. 69 and 347.) This widespread equivalence between the name *Ragnelle* and an exotic pagan god or devil may be echoed in Gawain's intentionally exaggerated comparison of Ragnelle to "a fend" and "Belsabub" (lines 344–45), or Arthur's reference to "the fende" (line 725), by which he may mean that he takes Ragnelle to be an evil spirit. In *Marriage*, the lady does not have a name, but she says her stepmother "witched me" so that "I must walke in womans liknesse, / Most like a feeind of hell" (lines 181–82). These associations may have made Ragnelle seem more spectral and frightening for a late medieval audience (like the ghost of Guenevere's mother in *Awntyrs*), and may have increased the ambiguity that surrounds her in the poem.

342 ff. Gawain's vow to "wed her and wed her agayn" out of friendship and fealty to Arthur gives the motive of male chivalric loyalty precedence over romantic personal love, and makes clear how women operate in romance as the intermediate term in the bonds between men.

366 *itt*. M supplies *it* before *shalle* as necessary for grammar and sense; the present emendation follows M's suggestion, though the spelling has been brought into accord with the scribe's convention.

419 *Ye goo fulle nyse, I wolle nott lye*. H emends the line to echo more fully Chaucer, Wife of Bath's Tale (line 931): "He gooth ful ny the sothe, I wol nat lye." This resemblance is one of the most striking evidences of direct connection between the two versions of the story.

439 *welle*. M, S, W, Sands emend to *well*.

440 *shake*. S takes the word to mean distance, and is followed by Sands. H rearranges lines 440–42, so that *shake* becomes a verb, "to go" (compare *shoke*, line 740).

But the phrase seems clearly adverbial, a variation on the still-current idiom, "no great shakes," and means "quickly"; see OED, "shake," sb. 1, 1.

456   *alle.* R: *ale*; M reads *all*; I follow S, W in preserving the usual spelling.

476   *her.* R: *he*; M reads *her*, which I follow.

499   *that ye have.* Sands misprints *that he have.*

508   *wolle ye have.* W misprints *wolle y have*; Sands misreads *welle ye have.*

525 ff.   Ragnelle here addresses Arthur.

528   *us togeder.* Sands misreads *un togeder.*

536   *God have mercy.* R: *Godhavemercy*, written as one word.

548 ff.   The description of Ragnelle here complements the initial portrait (lines 231 ff.) in its extravagant hideousness, though the specific details are sometimes at odds ("Her nek long," line 238, as against no neck at all, line 555, for example).

562   *thorowe.* S glosses this word as "thoroughly," and Sands and H reproduce this. It is certainly a form of *throw*, meaning a specific time, an interval, or an occasion; see OED, *throw* sb. 1.

564   *fowlle maye.* R: *fowlle*; M inserts *lady* for rhyme and sense, followed by S, W, Sands. I follow H's insertion of *maye*, which duplicates the rhyme at lines 715–16 and better maintains the meter.

571   *ye.* R: *we*; I emend for the sake of sense.

592   *thre thowsand mark.* R: *thre mlle mark.* I have expanded the abbreviation (a form of Latin *mille*). The figure (about two thousand pounds) signifies not a specific amount, but simply the extravagance of Ragnelle's clothing.

612   *Al.* W: *All.*

635   *for Arthours.* Sands misreads *of Arthours.*

644   *he.* R: *she*; M reads *he*, which I follow.

650   *ar.* W: *are*.

652   *ie.* R: *ien* (plural); M reads *ie*, which I follow.

656 ff.   The choice offered by Ragnelle — "fayre on nyghtes" (line 659) or "fayre on days" (line 661) — is the same in *Marriage* and in Gower's "Tale of Florent" (See G. C. Macaulay, *Confessio Amantis* in *The English Works of John Gower*, EETS e.s. 81, Vol. I [Oxford, 1900], I.1411 ff.) The choice in the *Wife of Bath's Tale* is "foul and old" and "true, humble wyf" or "yong and fair" and "take youre adventure" on sexual faithfulness (lines 1220 ff.). Chaucer's version makes more explicit the conflict embedded in the other three versions, namely public vs. private male enjoyment of the lady's sexual attractions. The happy ending allows the hero (putting it crudely) to have his cake and eat it too.

659   *nyghtes.* R: *nyght*; M reads *nyghtes*, which I follow.

672   *lese.* R: *lose*; M reads *lese*, followed by S, W, H.

677   *do as ye lyst.* Gawain's disposing himself to Ragnelle's desire brings to convergence a crucial array of themes and verbal echoes in the poem. By this accord, Ragnelle has *sovereynté* (line 697), which breaks the spell; Ragnelle had said to Arthur that women most desire *sovereynté*, and Arthur in turn had promised her fulfillment of her "desyre" (line 400). This knowledge of women's "rewlle" had given Arthur "rule" over Gromer (lines 470, 472), whose own desire of Arthur was to know "what wemen love best" (line 91). When Gawain has given "her sovereynté every delle" (line 776), Ragnelle puts her desire at his will (line 784), just as Arthur (at Ragnelle's wish) makes peace with Gromer (lines 811 ff.).

691   *nygramancy.* This use of a learned word to give credibility to the magical transformation is repeated in *Carle*, line 405, suggesting that even specialized Latin terms might be appropriated for specific functions within the popular romances.

716   *maye.* R: *mayd*; M reads *maye*, followed by S, W, H.

722   *Syrs.* R: *syr*; M reads *syrs*, followed by S, W, H.

730   *incerteyn*. Previous editors have taken *in certeyn* as two words (meaning "without doubt"), partly because of the slight gap between them in the manuscript. Such a space often occurs between components that modern print conventions present as unbroken words (i.e., *be fell*, line 15, *be think*, line 66, *I wys*, line 354), just as separate forms are joined (*Almen*, line 612). The form *incertain* is unusual but not rare, and makes good sense as specifying the state of mind of the royal entourage at this point. See OED, *incertain*, and MED, *incertain(e)*.

737   *goon*. Sands reads *gon*, perhaps emended for sake of rhyme.

743   *here*. R: *hed*; M (followed by S, W, Sands, H): *her*; I adjust spelling for scribal convention.

759   *is a fayre*. Sands misprints *is faire*.

761   *help*. R: *held*; so M, S, W, Sands. I emend to the common idiom on the basis of sense, as does H.

773   The responsibility of Ragnelle's stepmother for her enchantment links the romance to traditions of domestic intrigue and intergenerational, interfamilial hostility characteristic of fairy tales. *Marriage* and Gower's "Tale of Florent" also assign the responsibility to the "Stepmoder for an hate" (Macaulay [see note on line 656 above], *Confessio Amantis* I.1844), while the Wife of Bath's Tale seems to imply that the lady acts on her own.

799   *Gyngolyn*. Sir Gawain's son (French *Guinglain*) is the hero of the Middle English romance *Libeaus Desconus* (the Englishing of "Le bel inconnu," The Fair Unknown), which survives in six different versions (ed. M. Mills, EETS 261 [Oxford, 1969]). In the romance, the hero is begotten by Gawain "be [by] a forest syde" (line 9); his mother, who is unnamed, rears him in secret, not revealing his identity, "For douute of wykkede loos" (line 17) — for fear of shame attaching itself to her or to her son. The Lambeth version contains a title: "A tretys of one Gyngelayne . . . that was Bastard son to sir Gaweyne" (ed. Mills, p. 75). In Malory, "sir Gyngalyn, Gawaynes sonne" is defeated by Tristram in his madness (*Works*, pp. 494–95); in the climactic action of the story, syr Gyngalyne makes one of the twelve accompanying his uncles Mordred and Aggravayne in the ambush of Lancelot (*Works*, p. 1164). Among the other knights in this group are Gawain's other sons, Florence and Lovell (who, according to Malory, "were begotyn uppon Sir Braundeles syster"; *Works*, p.

1147, and see *Jeaste* line 320 and note), Sir Galleron of Galway (see *Carlisle*, line 43 and *Awntyrs*, line 417 and note), and Sir Gromore Somyr Joure, the antagonist of the present romance whom Malory's Gawain brings to the Round Table. As Malory notes, all of Lancelot's antagonists "were of Scotlonde, other ellis of sir Gawaynes kynne, other wel willers to his bretheren."

805   Gawain's unflagging devotion here contrasts with his behavior in French stories, where he tirelessly pursues knightly adventure, as in Chrétien de Troyes' *Yvain*; in the latter poem, Gawain's taste for exploits disrupts the hero's love of his lady. *As a coward* (line 808) ironically recalls line 12 above, "For cowardes were everemore shent"; Ragnelle's transformation has also changed the nature of chivalric virtue, or at least the court's view of it.

810   *mervaylyd.* S, W read *movaylyd* and emend to present reading; I follow M, H in transcribing as *m* with superior abbreviation stroke.

           Arthoure the Kyng. R: *kyng Arthoure*; M reads *Arthoure the kyng*, which I follow.

832   This reference to Gawain's many liaisons obliquely recalls his reputation as roué in French romance, which appears in *Jeaste* as well.

838   *born.* Sands misprints *boren.*

844   *besett with gaylours.* The claim that the composer of *Ragnelle* is imprisoned recalls Malory's description of himself as "a knyght presoner," and his request that readers "praye for me . . . that God sende me good delyveraunce" (*Works*, pp. 180, 1260). Field (see Select Bibliography, above) suggests that Malory may have been the author of this poem.

847   *Royalle.* R: *Ryoall.*

Sir Gawain and the Carle of Carlisle

Introduction

The romance of *Sir Gawain and the Carle of Carlisle* demonstrates Gawain's surpassing chivalry in what seems a most unlikely setting, a carl's castle. *Carl* (from Old Norse) means simply "man" in Middle English, but is almost always used in a contemptuous or condescending way, identifying someone who is not only low on the social scale, but often also crude and physically violent; Chaucer's drunken Miller, who knocks doors off their hinges with his head, is a "stout carl." *Carl* is a cognate of the Old English *churl*, a word meaning the opposite of "noble" or "gentle," and referring to someone of low estate, without rank or consequence — a boor, or a "boy" (see, for example, lines 193, 209, 216, and so on in *Turke*). A "carl's castle" is therefore as much a contradiction in terms as "popular chivalric romance," and such a locale could only exist inside this hybrid literary form. As an imaginative space, however, it turns out to be a wonderful place for defining popular notions of chivalric conduct, for it shows that Gawain retains his knightly courtesy even when he is not exclusively among gentles — or at least when he *seems* not to be among his noble peers, for the Carle of Carlisle turns out to be a gentle knight after all.

The adventure of *Carlisle* begins with a royal hunt (as in *Ragnelle, Marriage, Avowyng,* and *Awntyrs*). The pursuit of a deer leads Gawain, Kay, and Baldwin (the trio linked by oaths in *Avowyng*) to become lost in a wood, and then to seek an unlikely refuge with the Carle. Even the knights' initial conversations, among themselves and with the porter, set up contrasts between Baldwin's apprehensive uncertainty, Kay's haughty sense of the rights of lordship, and Gawain's unwavering courtesy. The Carle presents several tests, implicit and explicit, of the Arthurian knights' chivalry; these include the knights' reactions to the porter and to the Carle's wild menagerie, Gawain's courteous genuflection before the Carle, the treatment of the horse at the barn, the hurling of the deadly spear, the drinking and feasting, and the love scenes (first with the wife, then the daughter). The last and most important of these episodes is missing in *Carlisle*, though it appears in the later *Carle of Carlisle* (in this volume); in this crucial scene, Gawain courteously accedes to the Carle's request for beheading, which breaks the spell that had bound him to "carllus corttessy" (line 278) and transforms him to a gentle knight. Gawain's success in

81

these tests consists in the conspicuous restraint he exercises over his own powers and prerogatives, his perfect willingness to concede the Carle's rights of property and control within his own domain, even when his fellow knights see no need to do so. As in *Ragnelle*, the hero gains control over his situation by giving up the power that he apparently possesses. *Carlisle* makes a glowing testimonial to the ineluctable rightness of chivalric values as practiced by a true knight (as opposed to the reckless Kay and Baldwin).

Sir Gawain's mediation of the tension between the knightly prerogatives of the Round Table and the local power of an individual subject makes up the central story of *Gologras*, and arises as well in *Ragnelle* and *Awntyrs*. But *Carlisle* shapes its plot so that such issues are not defined in terms of lordship, territorial control, or individual knightly prowess, but rather within a peculiar framework of personal or even domestic chivalry. The bedroom scene, where (under the Carle's watchful instruction) Gawain restrains himself from making sexual advances to the naked wife (lines 445 ff.), epitomizes this emphasis in *Carlisle*. It resembles the episode with Baldwin's wife in *Avowyng*, the wedding night in *Ragnelle*, or the bedroom encounters — more masked and more suggestive — in *Sir Gawain and the Green Knight*. Here in *Carlisle*, the bed temptation enacts a crude but unmistakable demonstration of Sir Gawain's courteous respect for the Carle and for his proprietary rights over his wife and household. The ensuing union between Gawain and the Carle's daughter confirms the relationship of equality between the two men: it establishes the Carle's right to give her in marriage to a noble husband, and Gawain's acceptance of her as a legal and proper wife (lines 565 ff.) makes clear that the match entails no "disparagement" or social disparity between husband and wife.

The woman given in marriage reconciles father and husband; the wedding formally draws Gawain from Arthur's family into the Carle's household, marks the restoration of the Carle to his proper identity, and looks forward to the more elaborate feast that rounds off the poem (lines 591 ff.), where the former Carle courteously kneels to King Arthur and becomes a knight of the Round Table. Because *Carlisle* does not contain a beheading-disenchantment scene (like that in *Carle*, *Turke*, *Greene Knight*, and *Sir Gawain and the Green Knight*), the knight's initial transformation or restoration appears less striking and less motivated. Yet through the Carle's vow to establish a chantry for the souls of his slain victims (lines 517 ff.), the romance makes his changeover a part of its overall drive towards reunion and communal solidarity; his desire to effect a reconciliation with the dead gives shape to his rejection of his former behavior, or, in fact, his entire former identity as the "churlish" Carle. As in the two episodes of *Awntyrs*, the memorialization of the dead, as both a religious and chivalric act, demonstrates and even increases the honorable renown of the living.

Introduction

The monstrous bearing of the Carle, his wild animal companions, and the challenges he poses to the Arthurian knights may all have been associated in earlier narratives with a preternatural or mythic figure. In *Carlisle*, however, these details function to make him appear an antagonist of chivalry, as does his social status as *carl* in the views of Kay and Baldwin. The poem begins with Arthur's court at Cardiff in Wales (lines 19 ff.); again, an English popular romance places the King in residence in a peripheral Celtic territory. The Carle's castle seems remote and mysterious, surrounded by "myst" and "mor" (line 121), though it turns out he is lord of Carlisle in Cumberland, a center for Arthurian adventure (and Arthur's own court) in so many of the Gawain romances. As usual, Gawain's role is to bring the strange, the threatening, and the resistant within the ambit of the Round Table; he does this by acting out his "olde curteisye" (as Chaucer's Squire calls it), imposing home values on the unfamiliar, making the antagonists of chivalry its allies. In the course of its narrative, however, *Carlisle* makes clear that the Carle was never the enemy of proper lordship or genuine courtesy; the deference performed within his household and family reproduces an ideal version of the values that prevail at Arthur's court. Gawain's courtesy therefore does not so much convert the strange into the familiar, as show how the uncourteous mistake the universality of the familiar: the Carle turns out to be a proper knight and lord awaiting the transformation that will make his true nature and status visible to all.

The codes of conduct practiced in the court of the greatest king of Britain and the "castle" of a carl could fundamentally agree only in a chivalric romance. The unity of *Sir Gawain and the Carle of Carlisle* consists in its coherently popular rendition of ostensibly aristocratic, chivalric values, embodied equally in Sir Gawain and a metamorphosed churl. Moreover, the poem is stylistically all of a piece, so that Arthur's call to the hunt, the somewhat spurious roster of knights of the Round Table, Kay's crankiness, Baldwin's mincingness, Gawain's steadfastness, the Carle's bluffness, or the daughter's frank concern about her noble sexual partner — all are given in the same lively register. The boisterous and blunt manner of the Carle and his household is itself a central feature of the poem's narrative effect, and this is in turn a main source of enjoyment for readers of *Carlisle*.

Text

Sir Gawain and the Carle of Carlisle was probably composed in the northwest of England around 1400, and copied by a scribe from the northwest midlands. It survives in a single manuscript, Porkington MS 10 (also known as Harlech MS 10, and Brogyntyn MS), in the National Library of Wales at Aberystwyth; this copy, made perhaps in Shropshire, dates from about 1460 or a little later. *Carlisle* occurs near the beginning, at folios 12–26v. The manuscript is truly a miscellany, containing lyrics, Christmas carols, prophesies, prognostications, a chronicle, meteorological, astrological, botanical, and agricultural tracts, moral, devotional, and instructional writings, a saint's life, popular bawdy tales, and a prose romance. The scribe of *Carlisle* has drawn lines and brackets to mark the standard three-line unit (couplet plus tail-rhyme); these markings are themselves sometimes irregular, however, and do not give clear guidance for larger units or stanza breaks. Nonetheless, the rhyme scheme and the movement of the narrative clearly indicate that *Carlisle* is written in twelve-line tail-rhyme stanzas, ordered *aabccbddbeeb*, though rhymes are sometimes defective and stanzas irregular. I have followed the practice of earlier editors in inserting stanza breaks, though because of the text's uncertainties the present edition sometimes differs in where stanzas begin or end.

Select Bibliography

Manuscript

National Library of Wales, Porkington MS 10 (also known as Harlech MS 10 or Brogyntyn MS).

Editions (arranged chronologically)

Madden, Frederic. 1839. See Bibliography of Editions and Works Cited.

Ackerman, Robert W., ed. *Syr Gawane and the Carle of Carelyle*. University of Michigan Contributions in Modern Philology, 8. Ann Arbor: University of Michigan Press, 1947.

Kurvinen, Auvo, ed. *Sir Gawain and the Carl of Carlisle: In Two Versions*. Suomalaisen Tiedakatemian Toimituksia (Annales Academiae Scientiarum Fennicae). Series B.71.2. Helsinki, 1951.

Sands, Donald B. 1966. See Bibliography of Editions and Works Cited.

Shibata, Yoshitaka. *"Sir Gawain and the Carl of Carlisle*: A Japanese Translation." *Tohoku Gakuin University Review: Essays and Studies in English Langauge and Literature (Tohoku Gakuin Daigaku Ronshu, Eigo-Eibungaku)* 75 (1984), 1–37.

Sir Gawain and the Carle of Carlisle

	Lystonnyth, lordyngus, a lyttyll stonde	*Listen; while*
	Of on that was sekor and sounde	*one; sure and true*
	And doughgty in his dede.	*strong*
	He was as meke as mayde in bour	*humble; chamber*
5	And therto styfe in every stour;	*in addition unyielding; battle*
	Was non so doughtty in dede.	
	Dedus of armus wyttout lese	*Deeds; lie*
	Seche he wolde in war and pees	*Seek; peace*
	In mony a stronge lede.	*strange country*
10	Sertaynly, wyttoutyn fabull	*Certainly; falsehood*
	He was wytt Artter at the Rounde Tabull,	*with*
	In romans as we reede.	*romance; read*
	His name was Syr Gawene:	
	Moche worschepe in Bretten he wan,	*honor; Britain; earned*
15	And hardy he was and wyghte.	*strong*
	The Yle of Brettayn icleppyde ys	*Isle; [the area] is called*
	Betwyn Skotlond and Ynglonde iwys,	*(That takes in); indeed*
	In storry iwryte aryghte.	*history written*
	Wallys ys an angull of that yle;	*Wales; corner*
20	At Cardyfe sojornde the Kynge a whylle	*Cardiff sojourned*
	Wytt mony a gentyll knyghte	*With*
	That wolde to Ynglonde to honte,	*wished to go; hunt*
	As grete lordys dothe and be wonte,	*are accustomed*
	Wytt hardy lordys and wygghte.	*With; strong*
25	Kinge Arttor to his lordis gan saye	*did*
	As a lorde ryall that well maye,	*royal*
	"Do us to have a Masse.	*Let there be*
	Byschope Bawdewyn schall hit don;	*Baldwin; perform*
	Then to the forrest woll we gon,	*will; go*
30	All that evyr her ys,	*here*
	For nowe is grece-tyme of the yeer,	*[animals'] sleek time*

	That baruns bolde schulde hont the der,	*barons; deer*
	And reyse hem of her reste."	*start them from their cover*
	Wondor glad was Syr Mewreke;	*Exceedingly; Marrok*
35	So was the knyght Sir Key Caratocke,	*Kay Caradoc*
	And other mor and lase.	*greater (in rank); less*
	Glade was Launccelet de Lacke,	*Lancelot of the Lake*
	So was Syr Percivall, I undortake	*Percevall; dare say*
	And Lanfalle, I wene.	*Lanval; think*
40	So was Syr Eweyn the Uyttryan	*Ywain son of Urien*
	And Syr Lot of Laudyan,	*Lothian*
	That hardy was and kene;	
	Syr Gaytefer and Syr Galerowne,	*Gadiffer; Galleron*
	Syr Costantyn and Syr Raynbrown,	*Constantine; Reinbrun*
45	The Knyght of Armus Grene.	*Green*
	Syr Gawen was Stwarde of the halle;	*Steward*
	He was master of hem all	*them*
	And buskyde hem bedenne.	*readied them right away*
	The Kyngus uncull, Syr Mordrete,	*King's uncle; Mordred*
50	Nobull knyghttus wytt hym gan lede,	*with; did lead*
	In romans as men rede.	
	Syr Yngeles, that genttyle knyghte,	*Engely*
	Wytt hym he lede houndys wygght	*strong*
	That well coude do her dede.	*perform their work*
55	Syr Lebyus Dyskonus was thare	*Le Bel Inconnu*
	Wytt proude men les and mare	
	To make the donne der blede;	*dun deer bleed*
	Syr Pettypas of Wynchylse,	*Petipace; Winchelsea*
	A nobull knyght of chevalré,	*chivalry*
60	And stout was on a stede.	*steed*
	Syr Grandon and Syr Ferr Unkowthe,	*Fair Unknown*
	Meryly they sewyde wytt mouthe,	*pursued with shouts*
	Wytt houndys that wer wyght;	
	Syr Blancheles and Ironsyde,	*Brandelys; Ironside*
65	Monny a doughty that day con ryde	*Many; warrior; did*
	On hors fayr and lyghte.	*swift*
	Irounsyde, as I wene,	*understand*

	Gat the Knyght of Armus Grene	*Begot; Green*
	On a lady brygght —	
70	Sertenly, as I undurstonde,	*Certainly; dare say*
	That fayr may of Blanche Lonnde,	*maid; Blanchland*
	In bour that lovely wyghte.	*chamber; person*
	Ironsyde, as I wene,	*understand*
	Iarmyd he wolde ryde full clene,	*Armed; completely*
75	Wer the sonn nevyr so hoot.	*Were; sun; hot*
	In wyntter he wolde armus bere;	*bear*
	Gyanttus and he wer ever at were	*Giants; were; war*
	And allway at the debate.	*always; strife*
	Favele Honde hyght ys stede.	*"Tawnyfoot" is named his steed*
80	His armys and his odir wede	*other gear*
	Full fayr and goode hit was:	
	Of asur for sothe he bare	*[A shield] of azure truly*
	A gryffyn of golde full feyr	*[Displaying] a griffin; fair*
	Iset full of golde flourrus.	*Embellished; fleurs-de-lis*
85	He coude mor of venery and of wer	*knew; hunting; war*
	Then all the kyngus that wer ther;	*Than*
	Full oft asay hem he wolde.	*put them to trial*
	Brennynge dragons hade he slayn,	*Fiery*
	And wylde bullus mony won	*many overcome*
90	That gresely wer iholde.	*grisly; regarded*
	Byge barrons he hade ibonde.	*Strong; captured*
	A hardyer knygght mygght not be fonde;	*found*
	Full herdy he was and bolde.	*courageous*
	Therfor ha was callyd, as I hard say,	*he; heard*
95	The Kyngus fellowe by his day,	*in his time*
	Wytt worthy knyghttus itolde.	*Among; reputed*
	A lyon of golde was his creste;	
	He spake reyson out of reste;	*reason beyond the*
	Lystynn and ye may her.	*hear*
100	Wherever he went, be est or weste,	*by east*
	He nold forsake man nor best	*would not forego [the chance]; beast*
	To fyght fer or ner.	*far*

	Knyghttus kene fast they rane;	*ran [on the hunt]*
	The Kynge followyd wytt mony a man,	
105	Fife hunderd and moo, I wene.	*more*
	Folke followyd wytt fedyrt flonus,	*People; feathered arrows*
	Nobull archarrus for the nons,	*archers for that occasion*
	To fell the fallow der so cleyn.	*kill; cleanly*

	Barrons gan her hornnus blowe;	*did their horns*
110	The der cam reykynge on a rowe,	*running in a crowd*
	Bothe hert and eke heynde.	*hart; also hind*
	Be that tyme was pryme of the day	*By; [it] was mid-morning*
	Fife hunderd der dede on a lond lay	*dead; clearing*
	Alonge undur a lynde.	*In a row; linden tree*

115	Then Syr Gawen and Syr Key	
	And Beschope Baudewyn, as I yow say,	*tell*
	After a raynder they rode.	*reindeer*
	Frowe that tym was prym of the day	
	Tyl myde-undur-non, as I yow saye,	*late afternoon*
120	Never styll hit abode.	*stayed*
	A myst gan ryse in a mor;	*moor*
	Barrons blowe her hornis store.	*blew their; loudly*
	Meche mon Syr Key made:	*Great lament*

	The reyneder wolde not dwelle.	*stop*
125	Herkon what aventer hem befelle;	*Listen; adventure them*
	Herbrow they wolde fayn have hade.	*Lodging; gladly*

	Then sayde the gentyll knyght Syr Gawen,	
	"All this labur ys in vayne,	*labor*
	For certen, trowe hit me.	*For sure; believe*
130	The dere is passyde out of our syght;	
	We mete no mor wytt hym tonyght,	*meet*
	Hende, herkon to me.	*Gentle sirs; hearken*
	I reede that we of our hors alyght	*advise; off*
	And byde in this woode all nyght,	*stay*
135	And loge undur this tree."	*lodge*
	"Ryde we hens," quod Keye anon;	*away said; then*

"We schall have harbrowe or we gon.   *before we go [far]*
Dar no man wern hit me."   *Dare; refuse it to me*

Then sayd the Beschope: "I knowe hit well —
140 A Carle her in a castell   *(i.e., non-noble warrior) [lives] here*
    A lyttyll her ner honde.   *here nearby*
    The Karl of Carllyll ys his nam: *name*
    He may us herborow, be Sent Jame,   *give us lodging by Saint James*
    As I undurstonde.   *dare say*
145 Was ther nevyr barnn so bolde   *fellow*
    That ever myght gaystyn in his holde   *be a guest; household*
    But evyll harbrowe he fonde.   *experienced*
    He schall be bette, as I harde say,   *[The guest] will be overcome*
    And yefe he go wytt lyfe away   *if; alive*
150 Hit wer but Goddus sonde.   *only through; will*

"Nowe ryde we thedyr all thre."   *thither*
Therto sayd Key, "I grant hit the,   *go along with you*
    Also mot I well far;   *And may I prosper*
    And as thou seyst, hit schall be holde.   *it; done*
155 Be the Carle never so bolde,
    I count hym not worthe an har.   *consider; hair*
    And yeyf he be never so stoute,   *if*
    We woll hym bette all abowt   *beat thoroughly*
    And make his beggynge bar.   *stronghold bare*
160 Suche as he brewythe, seche schall he drenke;   *brews such*
    He schall be bette that he schall stynke,   *beaten [so fiercely]; stink*
    And agenst his wyll be thar."   *(i.e., won't wish to stay)*

Syr Gawen sayd, "So hav I blyse,   *bliss (i.e., by heaven)*
I woll not geystyn ther magre ys,   *stay; against his wish*
165 Thow I myght never so well,   *Though; easily*
    Yefe anny fayr wordus may us gayn   *If; avail*
    To make the larde of us full fayn   *lord with us pleased*
    In his oun castell.
    Key, let be thy bostfull fare;   *behavior*
170 Thow gost about to warke care,   *make trouble*
    I say, so have I helle.   *health (i.e., may I prosper)*
    I woll pray the good lorde, as I yow saye,

	Of herborow tyll tomorrow daye	*morning*
	And of met and melle."	*food for a meal*
175	On her way fast they rode.	*their*
	At the castell yat they abode —	*gate; stopped*
	The portter call they schulde.	*needed to*
	Ther hynge a hommyr by a cheyn.	*hung; hammer*
	To knocke therat Syr Key toke dayn;	*with that; felt disdain*
180	The hommyr away he wold have pold.	*pulled*
	The portter come wytt a prevey fare	*secret step*
	And hem fonde he ther;	*them examined*
	He axid what they wolde.	*asked*
	Then sayd Gawen curttesly,	
185	"We beseche the lorde of herbory,	*for lodging*
	The good lord of this holde."	*household*
	The portter answerd hem agayn,	*back*
	"Your message wold I do full fayn;	*undertake with pleasure*
	And ye have harme, thanke hyt not me.	*If; don't blame me*
190	Ye be so fayr, lyme and lythe,	*limb and body*
	And therto comly, glad therwytt,	*moreover*
	That cemmely hyt ys to see.	*agreeable*
	My lorde can no corttessye;	*knows*
	Ye schappyth notte wyttout a vellony,	*escape; villainy*
195	Truly trow ye mee.	*believe*
	Me rewyth sor ye came this waye,	*I sorely regret*
	And ar ye go, so woll ye say,	*before*
	But yefe mor grace be."	*Unless; special dispensation*
	"Portter," sayde Key, "let be thy care;	*put aside*
200	Thow sest we mey no forther fare —	*say; go*
	Thow jappyst, as I wene.	*joke; guess*
	But thou wolt on our message gon,	*Unless; with*
	The kyngus keyis woll we tane	*king's; take*
	And draw hem doun cleyn."	*them (the gates)*
205	The portter sayde, "So mot I thryfe,	*As I may prosper*
	Ther be not thre knyghttus alyve	
	That dorst do hit, I wene.	*dare; it; guess*
	Wyst my lorde your wordys grete,	*[If] knew; lofty*

90

	Some your lyvys ye schold forlete	*Several [of] your; give up*
210	Or ellus full fast to flen."	*else; flee*
	The portter went into the hall;	
	Wytt his Lord he mett wyttall,	*right away*
	That hardy was and bolde.	
	"Carl of Carllhyll, God loke the!	*watch over you*
215	At the yatt be barnnus thre,	*gate; men*
	Semley armus to welde:	*Capable; wield*
	To knyghttus of Arterys in,	*Two; Arthur's house*
	A beschope, and no mor men,	
	Sertayn, as they me tolde."	
220	Then sayd the Carle, "Be Sent Myghell,	*By Saint Michael*
	That tythingus lykyth me ryght well.	*tidings pleases*
	Seyth thei this way wolde."	*should come*
	When they came befor that syr,	
	They fond four whelpus lay about his fyer,	*young animals; fire*
225	That gresly was for to see:	*grisly*
	A wyld bole and a fellon boor,	*bull; lethal boar*
	A lyon that wold bytte sor —	*bite*
	Therof they had grete ferly.	*wonder*
	A bege ber lay louse unbounde.	*big bear; loose*
230	Seche four whelpus ther they founde	
	About the Carllus kne.	*knee*
	They rose and came the knyghttus agayn,	*towards*
	And soun thei wold hem have slayn;	*immediately; them*
	The Carle bade hem let bee.	*commanded; hold off*
235	"Ly doun," he sayd, "my whelpys four."	
	Then the lyon began to lour	
	And glowyd as a glede,	*glowed; coal*
	The ber to ramy, the boole to groun,	*growl; snort*
	The bor he whett his toskos soun	*tusks; at once*
240	Fast and that good spede.	*immediately*
	Then sayd the Carle, "Ly style! Hard yn!"	*Lie still! Stay back!*
	They fell adoun for fer of hyme,	*fear*
	So sor they gan hyme drede.	*did fear him*
	For a word the Carle gan say	*For a single word*

91

245 Under the tabull they crepyd away;
    Therof Syr Key toke hede.   *heed*

    The Carle the knyghttus can beholde,   *did*
    Wytt a stout vesage and a bolde.   *look*
    He semyd a dredfull man: *terrifying*
250 Wytt chekus longe and vesage brade;   *visage broad*
    Cambur nose and all ful made;   *Turned up; foully*
    Betwyne his browus a large spane;   *span*
    Hys moghth moche, his berd graye;   *mouth large*
    Over his brest his lockus lay   *hair*
255 As brod as anny fane;   *winnowing basket*
    Betwen his schuldors, whos ryght can rede,   *whoever; understand*
    He was two tayllors yardus a brede.   *in breadth*
    Syr Key merveld gretly than.   *then*

    Nine taylloris yerdus he was hyghtht   *in height*
260 And therto leggus longe and wyghtht,   *With; powerful*
    Or ellus wondor hit wer.   *Amazing as it sounds*
    Ther was no post in that hall,   *tree-post*
    Grettyst growand of hem all,   *grown; them*
    But his theys wer thycker.   *thighs*
265 His armus wer gret, wyttoutyn lese,   *lie*
    His fyngeris also, iwys,   *surely*
    As anny lege that we ber.   *leg; have*
    Whos stoud a stroke of his honde,   *Whoever withstood*
    He was not wecke, I undurstond,   *weak I dare say*
270 That dar I safly swer.   *safely swear*

    Then Syr Gawen began to cnele;   *kneel*
    The Carle sayd he myght be knyght wylle,   *indeed*
    And bad hyme stond upe anon.
    "Lett be thy knellynge, gentyll knyght;   *Cease*
275 Thow logost wytt a carll tonyght,   *lodge; churl*
    I swer, by Sennt Johnn.
    For her no corttessy thou schalt have,
    But carllus corttessy, so God me save —   *Except*
    For serttus I can non."   *Surely; know*
280 He bad brynge wyn in gold so der;   *wine; precious vessels*

Anon hit cam in coppus cler —   *cups bright*
  As anny sonn hit schon.   *sun*

Four gallons held a cop and more;   *one cup*
He bad brynge forthe a grettor —   *larger*
285 "What schall this lyttyll cope doun?   *What [good]; do*
This to lyttyll a cope for me,   *too*
When I sytt by the fyr onn hy   *fire; high*
  By myself aloun.
Brynge us a gretter bolle of wynn;   *bowl*
290 Let us drenke and play syne   *then*
  Tyll we to sopper goun."   *go*
The butteler brought a cope of golde —
Nine gallons hit gane holde —   *did*
  And toke hit the Carle anon.

295 Nine gallons he hyld and mare;   *it held; more*
He was not weke that hit bare   *weak*
  In his won honde.   *one*
The knyghttus dronkon fast about,   *all around*
And sethe arose and went hem out   *then; made their exit*
300   To se her hors stond.   *see how their horses were stabled*
Corne and hey thei had reydy.   *hay; nearby*
A lyttyll folle stod hem bye   *small horse (foal); by them*
  Wytt her hors fast ettand.   *their; eating*
The Besschope put the fole away: *moved*
305 "Thow schalt not be fello wytt my palfray   *equal; saddle-horse*
  Whyll I am beschope in londe."

The Carll then cam wytt a gret spede
And askyde, "Who hathe doun this dede?"
The Beschope seyd, "That was I."
310 "Therfor a bofett thou schalt have,   *buffet*
I swer, so God me save,
  And hit schall be sett, wytterly."   *made even, truly*
"I ame a clarke of ordors hyghe."   *cleric of high orders*
"Yett cannyst thou noght of corttessyghe,   *know; courtesy*
315   I swer, so mott I trye!"   *so far as I can tell*

	He gafe the Besschope a boffett tho	*gave; then*
	That to the ground he gan goo;	*did go*
	I sonynge he gann lyghe.	*In a faint (swoon) he did lie*
	Syr Key came in the sam cas	*way*
320	To se his stede ther he was;	*steed where*
	The foll fond he hym by.	*war horse*
	Out att the dor he drof hym out	
	And on the backe yafe hym a clout.	*gave*
	The Carle se that wytt hys yghe.	*saw; eye*
325	The Carll gaffe hym seche a boffett	*gave*
	That smertly onn the grond hym sett;	*swiftly; dropped*
	In sonynge gan he lyghe.	*faint; lie*
	"Evyll-taught knyghttus," the Carl gan sey;	
	"I schall teche the or thou wend away	*before you go off*
330	Sum of my corttessye."	
	Then they arose and went to hall,	
	The Beschope and Syr Key wytall,	*in company*
	That worthy was iwroght.	*impressively; built*
	Syr Gawen axyd wer they had byne;	*asked; been*
335	They seyd, "Our horssys we have sene,	*seen to*
	And us sor forthoght."	*we are sorely grieved*
	Then ansswerd Gawen full curttesly,	
	"Syr, wytt your leyf then wyll I."	*leave; [take stock]*
	The Carll knewe his thought.	*intention*
340	Hett reynnyd and blewe stormus felle	*It rained; fierce*
	That well was hym, be bocke and belle,	*by book*
	That herborow hade caught.	*lodging had obtained*
	Wyttout the stabull dor the foll gan stond.	*Outside*
	Gawen put hyme in agayn wytt his honde;	
345	He was all wett, I wene,	*guess*
	As the foll had stond in rayne.	*stood*
	Then keveryd he hym, Sir Gawene,	*covered*
	Wytt his manttell of grene:	*green*
	"Stond upe, fooll, and eette thy mette;	*eat your fodder*
350	We spend her that thy master dothe gett,	*use here what; provide*
	Whyll that we her byne."	*are here*

The Carle stode hym fast by
And thankyd hym full curtteslye
Manny sythis, I wene.   *times I guess*

355   Be that tyme her soper was redy dyght: *By; their; prepared*
       The tabullus wer havfe upe an hyght;   *raised up on high (on trestles)*
       Icovert they were full tyte.   *Covered; quickly*
       Forthwytt, thei wolde not blynne: *And then; pause*
       The Besschope gan the tabull begynne   *(sit in first place)*
360   Wytt a gret delytte.   *delight*
       Syr Key was sett on the tother syde   *other*
       Agenst the Carllus wyfe so full of pryde,   *Opposite; grandeur*
       That was so feyr and whytte: *Who*
       Her armus small, her mydyll gent,   *waist delicate*
365   Her yghen grey, her browus bente;   *eyes; arched*
       Of curttessy sche was perfette.   *complete*

       Her roode was reede, her chekus rounde,   *complexion; rosy*
       A feyrror myght not goo on grounde,   *fairer; go (exist)*
       Ne lovelyur of syghte.   *to see*
370   Sche was so gloryis and soo gay: *handsome*
       I can not rekon her araye,   *describe; clothing*
       Sche was so gayly dyghte.   *decked out*
       "Alas," thought Key, "thou Lady fre,   *noble*
       That thou schuldyst this ipereschde be   *thus lost*
375   Wytt seche a foulle weghtht!"   *person*
       "Sytt styll," quod the Carl, "and eete thy mette;
       Thow thinkost mor then thou darst speke,   *dare*
       Sertten, I the hyght."   *promise*

       I do yow all well to wette   *give; understand*
380   Ther was noo man bade Gawen sitte,
       But in the halle flor gann he stonde.   *on; did*
       The Carle sayde, "Fellowe, anoun!   *quick*
       Loke my byddynge be well idoun!   *done*
       Go take a sper in thy honde   *spear*
385   And at the bottredor goo take thy passe   *to the pantry door pass over*
       And hitt me evyn in the face;   *right*
       Do as I the commande.   *you*

And yeyfe thou ber me agenst the wall *if; drive*
Thow schalt not hort me wyttalle, *hurt me at all*
390   Whyll I am gyaunt in londe." *hereabout*

Syr Gawenn was a glade mann wytt that; *good-humored at that*
At the bottredor a sper he gatte *got*
  And in his honde hit hente. *grasped*
Syr Gawen came wytt a gret ire. *moved; fervor*
395   Doun he helde his hede, that syre,
  Tyll he hade geve his dentte. *given; blow*
He yafe the ston wall seche a rappe *gave*
That the goode sper all tobrake; *shattered*
  The fyer flewe out of the flente. *fire; flint*
400   The Carl sayde to hym ful soune, *at once*
"Gentyll knyght, thou hast well doune,"
  And be the honde hyme hente. *by; him grasped*

A cher was fette for Syr Gawene, *chair; fetched*
That worthy knyght of Bryttayne;
405   Befor the Carllus wyfe was he sett.
So moche his love was on her lyght, *fixed*
Of all the soper he ne myght
  Nodyr drynke nor ette. *Neither; eat*
The Carle sayde, "Gawen, comfort the, *console yourself*
410   For synn ys swete, and that I se. *sin is*
  Serten, I the hete, *assure you*
Sche ys myn thou woldyst wer thynn. *[whom] you wish; yours*
Leve seche thoghttus and drenke the wynne, *Leave such*
  For her thou schalt nott geytt." *have*

415   Syr Gawen was aschemmyde in his thowght. *ashamed*
The Carllus doughtter forthe was brought,
  That was so feyr and bryght.
As gold wyre schynde her here. *wire shone her hair*
Hit cost a thousand pound and mar, *more*
420   Her aparrell pertly pyghte. *beautifully adorned*
Wytt ryche stonnus her clothus wer sett, *jewels*
Wytt ryche perllus about her frete, *all over adorned*
  So semly was that syghte.

	Ovyr all the hall gann sche leme	*radiate*
425	As hit were a sonbeme —	*sunbeam*
	That stonnus schone so bryght.	
	Then seyde the Carle to that bryght of ble,	*[woman]; face*
	"Wher ys thi harpe thou schuldist have broght wytt the?	
	Why hast thou hit forgette?"	
430	Anon hit was fett into the hall,	*Soon; fetched*
	And a feyr cher wyttall	*chair as well*
	Befor her fador was sett.	*father*
	The harpe was of maser fyne;	*maple wood*
	The pynnys wer of golde, I wene;	*tuning pins*
435	Serten, wyttout lett	*pause*
	Furst sche harpyd, and sethe songe	*then*
	Of love and of Artorrus armus amonge,	*all the while*
	How they togeydor mett.	*fit*
	When they hade soupyde and mad hem glade	*themselves*
440	The Beschope into his chambur was lade,	*led*
	Wytt hym Syr Key the kene.	*[And]; bold*
	They toke Syr Gawen, wyttout lessynge;	*lie*
	To the Carlus chamber thei gan hym brynge,	
	That was so bryght and schene.	*splendid*
445	They bade Syr Gawen go to bede,	
	Wytt clothe of golde so feyr sprede,	
	That was so feyr and bryght.	*fair*
	When the bede was made wytt wynn,	*joy*
	The Carle bade his oun Lady go in,	*own; get*
450	That lovfesom was of syghte.	*lovely; to see*
	A squyer came wytt a prevey far	*secret step*
	And he unarmyde Gawen ther;	*disarmed*
	Schaply he was undyght.	*Duly; disrobed*
	The Carle seyde, "Syr Gawene,	
455	Go take my wyfe in thi armus tweyne	*two*
	And kys her in my syghte."	*kiss*
	Syr Gawen ansswerde hyme anon,	
	"Syr, thi byddynge schall be doune,	

	Sertaynly in dede,	*indeed*
460	Kyll or sley, or laye adoune."	*strike [me]; knock [me]*
	To the bede he went full sone,	
	Fast and that good spede,	
	For softnis of that Ladys syde	
	Made Gawen do his wyll that tyde;	*[the Carl's] will; time*
465	Therof Gawen toke the Carle goode hede.	*Then; heed*
	When Gawen wolde have doun the prevey far,	*private act (intercourse)*
	Then seyd the Carle, "Whoo ther!	*Whoa there*
	That game I the forbede.	*engagement; forbid*
	"But, Gawen, sethe thou hast do my byddynge,	*since*
470	Som kyndnis I most schewe the in anny thinge,	*kindness; in some way*
	As ferforthe as I maye.	*Insofar*
	Thow schalt have wonn to so bryght	*one [woman] just as*
	Schall play wytt the all this nyghte	*[Who]*
	Tyll tomorrowe daye."	*at daylight*
475	To his doughtter chambur he went full ryght,	*immediately*
	And bade her aryse and go to the knyght,	
	And wern hyme nott to playe.	*not hinder him from [sexual]*
	Sche dorst not agenst his byddynge doun,	*command act*
	But to Gawen sche cam full sone	*right away*
480	And style doun be hyme laye.	*softly; by*
	"Now, Gawen," quod the Carle, "holst the well payde?"[1]	
	"Ye, for Gode, lorde," he sayde,	*before*
	"Ryght well as I myghte!"	*as completely*
	"Nowe," quod the Carle, "I woll to chambur go;	
485	My blessynge I geyfe yow bouthe to,	*give; both two*
	And play togeydor all this nyght."	
	A glad man was Syr Gawen	
	Sertenly, as I yowe sayne,	
	Of this Lady bryght.	*Because of*
490	Serten, sothely for to say,	
	So, I hope, was that feyr maye	*dare say; woman*
	Of that genttyll knyght.	

---

[1] *"Now, Gawain," said the Carle, "do you hold yourself well paid (pleased)?"*

"Mary, mercy," thought that Lady bryghte,
"Her come never suche a knyght   *Here came*
495   Of all that her hathe benne."
Syr Key arose uppon the morrown
And toke his hors and wolde a goune   *have gone*
    Homwarde, as I wenne.   *guess*
"Nay, Syr Key," the Beschope gann seye,
500   "We woll not so wende our waye
    Tyll we Syr Gawen have sene."
The Carll arose on morrow anon
And fond his byddynge reddy doune: *command already done*
    His dyner idyght full cleyne.   *prepared completely*

505   To a Mas they lett knelle;   *For a Mass; commanded the knell*
    Syr Gawen arose and went thertyll
    And kyst that Lady bryght and cler.
    "Maré, marcé," seyde that Lady bryght,   *Mary*
    "Wher I schall se enny mor this knyght   *Wherever; any*
510   That hathe ley my body so ner?"
When the Mese was doune to ende,   *Mass*
Syr Gawen toke his leve to wende   *go*
    And thonkyde hym of his cher.   *hospitality*
"Furst," sayde the Carle, "ye schall dynn   *dine*
515   And on my blessynge wende home syne,   *upon receiving; afterwards*
    Homward al yn fere.   *together*

"Hit is twenti wynter gon," sayde the Karle, "nowe   *years ago*
That God I maked a vowe,   *[to]*
    Therfore I was fulle sad: *For which*
520   Ther schulde never man logge in my wonys   *lodge; dwelling*
But he scholde be slayne, iwys,   *Except that; surely*
    But he did as I hym bad.   *Unless; bade*
But he wolde do my byddynge bowne,   *Unless; quickly*
He schulde be slayne and layde adowne,   *low*
525   Whedir he were lorde or lad.   *servant*
Fonde I never, Gawen, none but the.   *Found [true]; but you*
Nowe Gode of hevyn yelde hit the;   *reward you for it*
    Therfore I am fulle glade.

    "He yelde the," sayde the Carle, "that the dere boughte,[1]

530   For al my bale to blysse is broughte   *misery*

    Throughe helpe of Mary quene."   *the queen*

    He lade Gawen ynto a wilsome wonys,   *led; desolate dwelling*

    There as lay ten fodir of dede menn bonys.   *cartloads; bones*

    Al yn blode, as I wene,   *bloody*

535   Ther hynge many a blody serke,   *hung; shirt*

    And eche of heme a dyvers marke.   *them [bore] a heraldic design*

    Grete doole hit was to sene.   *sorrow*

    "This slowe I, Gawen, and my helpis,   *These slew; helpers*

    I, and also my foure whelpis.

540   For sothe, as I the say,

    Nowe wulle I forsake my wyckyd lawys;   *customs*

    Ther schall no mo men her be slawe, iwys,   *more; slain*

    As ferthforthe as I may.   *Insofar*

    Gawen, for the love of the

545   Al schal be welcome to me   *everyone*

    That comythe here by this way.   *along*

    And for alle these sowlys, I undirtake,   *souls; make promise*

    A chauntery here wul I lete make,   *church; have made*

    Ten prestis syngynge til domysday."   *[With]*

550   Be that tyme her dyner was redy dyghte: *By; their; all prepared*

    Tables wer hovyn up an hyghte;   *raised up*

    Ikeverid thei were fulle clene.   *Covered*

    Syr Gawen and this Lady clere,   *[the Carle's daughter]*

    They were iservyd bothe ifere.   *served; together*

555   Myche myrthe was theme bytwene;   *Much*

    Therfore the Carle was full glade.

    The Byschop and Syr Kay he bad   *bade*

    Mery that thei scholde bene.

    He yafe the Bischop to his blessynge   *gave; for*

560   A cros, a myter, and a rynge,   *mitre*

    A clothe of golde, I wene.   *guess*

    He yaf Syr Kay, the angery knyght,   *gave; irascible*

---

[1] *"May He reward you," said the Carle, "who you dearly redeemed."*

A blode rede stede and a whight;   *blood red; powerful*
Suche on had he never sene.   *a one*

565   He gaf Syr Gawen, sothe to say,
        His doughter, and a whighte palfray,   *white riding horse*
         A somer ichargid wyth golde.   *[And] a pack horse laden*
        Sche was so gloryous and so gay
        I kowde not rekyn here aray,   *describe her clothing*
570   So bryghte was non on molde.   *earth*
        "Nowe ryde forthe, Gawen, on my blessynge,
        And grete wel Artyr, that is your Kynge,   *greet*
        And pray hym that he wolde,
        For His love that yn Bedlem was borne,   *love of Him; Bethlehem*
575   That he wulle dyne wyth me tomorne."   *will*
        Gawen seyde he scholde.

        Then thei rode syngynge away
        Wyth this yonge Lady on her palfray,
        That was so fayre and bryghte.
580   They tolde Kynge Artir wher thei had bene,
        And what wondirs thei had sene
        Serteynly, in here syght.   *their*
        "Nowe thonkyd be God, cosyn Gawyn,   *kinsman*
        That thou scapist alyve unslayne,   *escaped*
585   Serteyne wyth alle my myght."
        "And I, Syr Kynge," sayd Syr Kay agayne,   *in response*
        "That ever I scapid away unslayne
        My hert was never so lyght.

        "The Carle prayde you, for His love that yn Bedlem was borne,   *Bethlehem*
590   That ye wolde dyne wyth hym tomorne."
        Kynge Artur sone hym hyght.   *immediately; promised*
        In the dawnynge forthe they rade;   *rode*
        A ryalle metynge ther was imade   *royal; took place*
        Of many a jentylle knyght.   *gentle*
595   Trompettis mette hem at the gate,   *greeted them*
        Clarions of silver redy therate,   *right there*
        Serteyne wythoutyn lette —   *ceasing*
        Harpe, fedylle, and sawtry,   *fiddle; psaltery*

	Lute, geteron, and menstrelcy.	gittern; minstrelsy
600	Into the halle knyghtis hem fett.	fetched them
	The Carle knelyd downe on his kne	
	And welcomyd the Kynge wurthyly	
	Wyth wordis ware and wyse.	prudent
	When the Kynge to the halle was brought,	
605	Nothynge ther ne wantyd nought	was lacking
	That any man kowde devyse.	mention
	The wallys glemyd as any glasse;	
	Wyth dyapir colour wroughte hit was —	varied [rich]
	Of golde, asure, and byse;	azure; gray
610	Wyth tabernacles was the halle aboughte,	canopies; [trimmed all] about
	Wyth pynnacles of golde sterne and stoute;	spires; sturdy
	Ther cowde no man hem preyse.	praise [sufficiently]
	Trompettys trompid up in grete hete;	with vehemence
	The Kynge lete sey grace and wente to mete,	had grace said; the meal
615	And was iservyde wythoute lette.	a snag
	Swannys, fesauntys, and cranys,	pheasants; cranes
	Partrigis, plovers, and curlewys	Partridges
	Before the Kynge was sette.	
	The Carle seyde to the Kynge, "Dothe gladly!	Enjoy
620	Here get ye no nothir curtesy,	other
	As I undirstonde."	dare say
	Wyth that come yn bollys of golde, so grete	bowls
	Ther was no knyght sat at the mete	meal
	Myght lyfte hem wyth his on honde.	one
625	The Kynge swore, "By Seynte Myghelle,	Michael
	This dyner lykythe me as welle	pleases
	As any that evyr Y fonde."	experienced
	A dubbyd hym knyght on the morne;	He
	The contré of Carelyle he gafe hym sone	gave; at once
630	To be lorde of that londe.	
	"Here I make the yn this stownde	you; moment
	A knyght of the Table Rownde:	
	Karlyle thi name schalle be."	

102

On the morne when hit was daylyght
635 Syr Gawen weddyid that Lady bryght,
    That semely was to se.

Than the Carle was glade and blythe
And thonkyd the Kynge fele sythe,   *many a time*
    For sothe, as I you say.
640 A ryche fest had he idyght   *feast; prepared*
That lastyd holy a fortenyght   *an entire (i.e., wholly)*
    Wyth game, myrthe, and playe.
The mynstrellis had geftys fre   *gifts liberal*
That they myght the better be   *[disposed]*
645 To spende many a day.
And when the feste was broughte to ende,
Lordis toke here leve to wende   *their leave to go*
    Homwarde on here way.

A ryche abbey the Carle gan make   *did build*
650 To synge and rede for Goddis sake
    In wurschip of Oure Lady.
In the towne of mery Carelyle
He lete hit bylde stronge and wele;   *caused; to be built*
    Hit is a byschoppis see.   *(i.e., a cathedral)*
655 And theryn monkys gray   *[he enjoined] Cistercian monks*
To rede and synge tille domysday,
    As men tolde hit me,
For the men that he had slayne, iwis.   *On behalf of; indeed*
Jesu Cryste, brynge us to Thy blis
660 Above in hevyn, yn Thy see.   *on Your throne*

    Amen.

Notes

I have normalized orthography (giving "th" for thorn; "gy," "g," or "y" for yogh as appropriate; "j" for "i", "u" for "v" and "w," "v" for "u" and "w," and "w" for "u" and "v") to accord with modern usage. I have expanded numerals and abbreviations ("wtt" as "wytt," "&" as "and," and so on). Punctuation (including capitalization) is editorial, and word division reflects current standard use ("undur stonde" is given as "undurstonde," for example). Some of the scribal abbreviations are ambiguous; I follow Kurvinen in rendering terminating flourishes as "us" (rather than "ys," as Ackerman represents them). I have also interpreted the ambiguous series of four minims (usually following "o") as "un" (following Kurvinen) rather than as "nn" (as Ackerman renders them). I have interpreted the ambiguous superior stroke at word endings as "e" in cases where rhyme or usage make it seem appropriate, though for the most part I have disregarded this sign.

Abbreviations: P = Porkington MS; M = Madden's edition; A = Ackerman's edition; K = Kurvinen's edition; S = Sands' edition. See Select Bibliography for these editions.

1   *Lystonnyth*. A reads *lystenneth*.

3   *doughgty*. P gives *douȝgty*, with ȝ added above line.

20   *At Cardyfe*. Cardiff, just southwest of Caerleon at the mouth of the River Severn, has some Arthurian associations; its great distance from Carlisle, however, makes the geography of the poem impossible to imagine. In order to restore geographical coherence, K suggests changing *Cardyfe* to *Carllyll*, and *Ynglonde* to *Ynleswode*.

21   *gentyll*. M reads *gentylle*.

28   *Byschope Bawdewyn*. This Baldwin differs from the Bowdewynne of Bretan whose exploits are celebrated in *Avowyng* (line 74) in being an ordained clerk and a high church official; yet it seems likely that the popular romances meant "Bawdewyn" and "Bowdewynne" to name the same prominent companion of Arthur. In Malory, Arthur names as his "chieftains" before undertaking the

campaign against Lucius "Sir Bauden of Bretayne" and "Sir Cadore," father of "Sir Constantyne that aftir was kynge, aftir Arthurs dayes" (*Works*, p. 195; see also *Avowyng*, line 914 and note); see below, line 44 and note. Malory also has Lancelot cured of a deadly wound by "the ermyte [hermit], sir Bawdewyn of Bretayne" (*Works*, p. 1086), who says of himself, "sometyme I was one of the felyship" of the Round Table (*Works*, p. 1075). That Malory takes these two Baldwins, knight and holy man, as identical seems clear in his further remark that "there were none ermytis in tho dayes but that they had bene men of worship and of prouesse, and tho ermytes hylde grete householdis and refreysshed people that were in distresse" (*Works*, p. 1076). In *Avowyng* Baldwin is distinguished for the great household he keeps and for his willingness to refresh all who come to him. In *Turke* (lines 152 ff.; see note at line 154), the King of Man scorns equally Gawain's "unckle King Arthur" and "that Bishopp Sir Bodwine," who by this title seems both church official and knight.

31   *grece-tyme of the yeer.* The hunting season for the buck or hart (or stag) — the male deer — ran from about midsummer (or perhaps a bit earlier) to the middle of September; its height seems to have come in August, when deer have fattened and can be hunted without danger to the herd. (The hind and doe — the female deer — were hunted from September through February, according to medieval hunting manuals.) In *Ragnelle*, after Arthur has taken his deer, he "dyd hym serve welle, / And after the grasse he taste" (lines 47–48; see note). Arthur's butchering of the deer (see *Carle*, line 20) and his assay of its fat is appropriate to the "grece tyme." *Sir Gawain and the Green Knight* contains similar references to the hunt and the woodsman's knowledge of the ritual of "breaking" the deer.

34   *Syr Mewreke.* Here begins a catalogue of Arthurian knights whose names are drawn from a variety of sources. Some of the most prominent companions of the Round Table — Gawain above, Kay, Lancelot, Percivale, Ywain, Lot, Mordred — are named. Many of these became the central figures in popular Middle English verse romances, as did Launfal, Libeaus Desconus (line 55), and Galerowne (line 43 and note). Some of the names mentioned here are not identifiable as Arthurian characters, and may be completely improvised for a performance of *Carlisle*, or legendary names garbled beyond recognition. *Awntyrs* mentions *Marrake* as one of the knights who rushes to the aid of Galeron and Gawain; see line 655, and note at lines 654 ff.

35   *Caratocke.* A reads *cantocke*.

43   *Syr Gaytefer and Syr Galerowne. Gologras* several times mentions *Gaudifeir* as a companion of Arthur; see line 545 and note. Sir Galeron of Galloway plays a major role as Gawain's opponent in the second episode of *Awntyrs* (see line 417 and note). In Malory, Galeron is numbered among the knights of Scotland affiliated with Gawain's kin and the other "wel willers" of his brothers Aggravayne and Mordred, who oppose Lancelot. These knights include Sir Petipace (line 58 and note), Sir Gromer Somyr Joure (see *Ragnelle*, line 62 and note, and *Turke*, line 320 and note), and Gawain's sons Gyngalyne, Florence and Lovell (the latter two also being nephews of Brandles, line 64 and note below). See *Works*, p. 1164.

44   *Syr Costantyn.* Perhaps the son of Sir Cador and king after Arthur's days; see above, line 28 and note, and *Avowyng*, line 914 and note.

48   *bedenne.* A reads *bedene.*

49   *The Kyngus uncull, Syr Mordrete.* A mistake for *cosyn* (K) or "nephew" (A), which potentially inverts the crucial relation of mothers' brother – sister's son between Arthur and Mordred. In some narratives, Mordred is not merely Arthur's nephew by his sister Morgawse, wife of King Lot of Orkney, but Arthur's own son through incest. Mordred causes the dissension that turns his brother Gawain against Lancelot, and begins the disintegration of the Round Table; he attempts to overthrow the rule of his uncle (in some versions taking Guenevere as his own wife), and fatally wounds Arthur in the combat that brings about his own death. *Carlisle*, in celebrating Gawain's chivalry, seems little concerned with the ultimate fall of the Round Table, and making Mordred Arthur's uncle (whether a mistake or a conscious change) further distances those dire events to which *Awntyrs*, for example, deliberately alludes (lines 286 ff.). *Carle* (line 31) groups Arthur with "his cozen Mordred," and *Marriage* (line 24) refers to Arthur's "cozen Sir Gawaine"; in both cases, *cozen* simply means kinsman, and might easily include the relation of a nephew.

55   *Dyskonus.* K reads *dyskoniis.* Libeaus Desconus (Old French "Li Biaus Descouneus," French "Le Bel Inconnu," English "The Fair Unknown") is Gawain's son Gyngalyne. *Ragnelle* makes the heroine of that poem his mother; see line 799 and note. His mysterious identity seems to have led to his being presented in *Carlisle* as two different knights, for he appears again at line 61 as "Syr Ferr Unkowthe." See line 43 above and note for his associates in Malory.

58   *Syr Pettypas*. Another of the knights identified by Malory (*Works*, p. 1164) as "of Scotlonde" or aligned with Gawain's brothers Aggravayne and Mordred. See lines 43 and 55 and notes.

64   *Syr Blancheles*. Though *Carlisle* provides no details, this is almost surely *Sir Brandles*, Gawain's chief opponent in *Jeaste* (see introduction to that poem, and line 320 and note). Malory names Sir Braundeles the uncle of Gawain's sons Florence and Lovell (*Works*, p. 1147), clearly drawing upon a version of the story that lies behind *Jeaste*. See also *Ragnelle*, line 799 and note. Madden (p. 347) noted this possible connection.

    Ironsyde. In Malory, Sir Ironsyde is the last of the knights Gawain's brother Sir Gareth of Orkney encounters on his quest. He presents himself as the Rede Knyght of the Rede Laundis, but reveals his true identity at Arthur's court (*Works*, pp. 319, 336–37); he is the father (or brother) of the other knights in colored liveries, including the Grene Knyght, whom Gareth defeats. *Carlisle*, in making him the father of "the Knyght of Armus Grene" (lines 45, 68), perhaps relies upon a popular story, now lost, that Malory (whose source for the adventures of Gareth remains unknown) had read as well — a story that, among other things, connected Gawain's family with Green Knights. See also introduction to *Greene Knight* in the present volume.

79   *Favele Honde*. P gives *Fabele Honde*; the emendation is suggested by A.

80 ff.   Sir Ironside's arms consist of a golden griffin on a field of blue, surrounded by fleurs-de-lis. Ironside bears arms that strongly resemble those traditionally associated with Gawain and his kin. In one album of arms, Gawain's device is said to have been three golden lions' heads on an azure field, or, alternatively, three golden griffins on a green field; Ironside's arms combine these elements. (See the details provided in the Introduction, note 21). It may be that Ironside's armorial bearings have been confused in the transmission of *Carlisle* with those of "Syr Ferr Unkowthe" (line 61), Gawain's son Libeaus Desconus or the Fair Unknown; see especially *Carle* lines 55 ff. and note, as well as *Awntyrs*, line 509 and note.

86   *kyngus*. M emends to *knights*.

99   *Lystynn*. M reads *lystyne*.

145   *barnn.* A reads *barun* ("baron").

154   *thou.* A reads *thu*, here and in lines 202, 277, 310, 329, 373, 374, 388, and 401.

160   Kay here uses a proverb meaning he'll get what he asks for, or, he'll take the consequences of his own actions. See B. J. Whiting and H. W. Whiting, *Proverbs, Sentences, and Proverbial Phrases* (Cambridge, Massachusetts: Harvard University Press, 1968), B259.

162   *thar.* A reads *thor*; M reads *there*.

167   *larde.* M reads *lorde*

177   *call.* P gives *callyd*.

202   *wolt.* M reads *wolle*.

203   *kyngus keyis.* The meaning of this phrase remains a puzzle; the most convincing suggestion is that this is a popular, sarcastic idiom for the crowbars and other tools used by the king's agents in making a forcible entry while serving a warrant.

204   *cleyn.* M reads *certeyn*.

215   *barnnus.* M: *barnuns*; A: *barunys*.

218   *beschope.* A reads *beschape*.

222   *thei.* A reads *thi*, here and in lines 233, 301, 358, and 443.

233   *slayn.* A reads *sleyn*.

241   *Hard yn!* P gives *hardyn* as one word; a space is inserted by K. "Stay back!" or some similar command seems appropriate here, though this meaning is not attested. Another possibility would be *Herd, in!*

251   *ful.* P gives *full*. I follow the emendation K suggests in her note.

257   *yardus a brede.* P gives *ʒardus brede*; I follow K's emendation.

tayllors yardus. A tailor's yard is the common measure of three feet, making the Carle six feet across the shoulders and twenty-seven feet tall — a true giant, but a dwarf next to the hero of *Carle*, who is nine feet broad and seventy-five feet tall.

259   *hyghtht*. P gives *hyʒthent*; emended by M.

261   The point of this line — literally, "Or else it would be a wonder" — seems to be that, given his bulk, if the Carle's limbs were any smaller, that would be still more astonishing.

263   I have glossed *growand* as past (rather than the present) participle of *growen*.

267   *anny*. M reads *any*.

271   *Gawen*. P gives only *G*; I have expanded to *Gawen* here and in lines 337, 344, 380, 394, 415, 442, 445, 457, 464, 465, 469, 479, 481, 501, 512, 526, 532, 538, 544, 553, 565.

290   *syne*. P: *sethyn*; I adopt *syne* (suggested in K's note) for the sake of rhyme.

314   The Carle's judgment on Bishop Baldwin here contrasts ironically with his own regulations (lines 193 ff.) and outright claim (lines 277 ff.) that he "can no corttessye."

315   *trye*. P: *tryne*. For this meaning of *try*, see OED, "try," v. 13.

337   *answerd*. A reads *answered*.

341   *be bocke and belle*. This proverbial phrase derives ultimately from the rite for excommunication; see *Awntyrs*, line 30 and note.

342   *That*. P gives *The*; emended by K.

349   *Stond*. P gives *Sstond*; A reads *G[awain]: stond*.

356   *havfe*. A reads *hovfe*.

374   *That*. M suggests emending to *Thus*.

377   This line is proverbial, as K points out, though Whiting, in his *Proverbs*, offers no medieval instances.

379 ff.   The narrator makes a pointed contrast between Gawain's courteous refusal to sit at table before he is invited, and Baldwin's and Kay's impulsive indulgence of their hunger (lines 358 ff.).

385   *passe.* A form of *pace*, so that the phrase means, "make your way," "go to."

396   *dentte.* P gives *dette*; emended by M.

435 ff.   The subject celebrated in the Carle's daughter's performance — the convergence of love and war in true courtesy — is typical of elite chivalric romance, as in the works of Chrétien de Troyes, in Wolfram von Eschenbach's *Parzifal*, or (with added tension) in *Sir Gawain and the Green Knight*. Popular chivalric romances typically present such idealized if improbable performances, simultaneously masking and making plain the contradictory impulses of the genre in this way. These tales almost never offer a detailed account of a performance event resembling the sort of production the romances themselves must have entailed; the closest one comes to such carnivalesque, interactive, kinetic events are the vague references to *fest*, *game*, *myrthe*, *playe*, and *mynstrellis* (lines 640 ff.).

465   *Therof Gawen toke the Carle goode hede.* K drops the scribe's abbreviation for *Gawen* (apparently taking it as a mistaken anticipation of the following line), and so emends to *Therof toke the Carle goode hede.*

         hede. P gives *hed*; M reads *hede.*

466   *far.* Now illegible in P, but so read by M.

500   *We.* M reads *Ne.*

508   *Maré, marcé.* A reads *Mare merci.*

514   *schall.* M reads *schalt.*

517 ff.   The Carle's "transformation" here consists in his confession to Gawain, and his vow to reform. *Carlisle* seems to omit at this point a scene of physical action — a beheading, like those in *Carle*, *Sir Gawain and the Green Knight*, *Greene*

Knight, and *Turke* — that would account for the sudden change. In shedding a former evil identity that was perhaps imposed on him by sorcery, the Carle resembles Ragnelle; compare the remark of the lady in *Marriage*, that her wicked stepmother had "witched my brother to a carlish" shape (line 179).

518   *maked*. A reads *make*.

524   *schulde*. A reads *schuld*.

535   *blody serke*. *Carlisle* seems here to preserve a snatch of popular verse, familiar through some lost narrative of desperate love. The phrase survives only in two adaptations to religious contexts. The English translation of the *Gesta Romanorum* tells of a knight who asks that, if he should die in battle, his lady "sette out my blody serke on a perch afore," so that she will think of him always. The story is then allegorized, so that the knight is Christ, and the bloody sark the emblem of his sacrifice. (See *Gesta Romanorum*, ed. Sidney J. H. Herrtage, EETS e.s. 33 [London, 1879], pp. 23–26, at p. 24.) Robert Henryson tells a similar story, with strong ballad emphases, of a "lusty lady ying [young]" rescued by a "knycht"; dying from his effort, the knight asks that she take "my sark that is bludy / And hing it forrow [before] yow" as a momento. Henryson allegorizes the story identically to the *Gesta*, and concludes, "Think on the bludy serk." (See *Robert Henryson: Poems*, ed. Charles Elliott [Oxford: Oxford University Press, 1963], pp. 115–18.) In this passage *Carlisle* imposes a similar religious moralization upon this emblem of heroic devotion.

537   *sene*. P gives *see*; I follow K's emendation for the sake of rhyme.

552   *Ikeverid*. M reads *koverid*.

553   *clere*. M reads *dere*.

570   *was non on molde*. P gives *was alle here molde*. The reading makes little sense, desperate philological arguments notwithstanding. I adopt what seems an obvious emendation, suggested in K's notes. The previous two lines repeat the formulaic description of the Carle's wife, at lines 370–71.

595 ff. The first two items mentioned here are brass instruments, and the remaining six are stringed. A *sawtry* was an ancestor of the zither; a *geteron* was a kind of guitar. Except for the bowed *fedylle*, all these instruments were plucked. *Men-*

strelcy here probably refers not to the players themselves, or their performance, but to a further group of instruments; compare Chaucer, Manciple's Tale, line 113: "Pleyen he kaude on every mynstralcie."

599   *menstrelcy*. P gives *merely*; K reads *menstracy*. I emend in accordance with scribal spelling (compare line 643).

600   *fett*. P gives *sett*; K emends to *halle hem fett*.

619   *seyde*. A reads *sayde*.

620   The Carle's understatement ironically reverses (and echoes) his earlier chastisements of Arthurian chivalry (see lines 193, 275 ff., 314 ff., and 329 ff.).

629   *gafe*. M reads *gefe*.

640   *idyght*. P gives *idygh*; M reads *idyght*, followed by K.

643   *geftys*. P gives *yeftys*.

650   *rede*. P gives *redee*; M reads *rede*, followed by K.

655   *monkys gray*. Monks of different orders were often referred to by the distinctive color of their habits; Benedictines were known as Black Monks, and Cistercians as White Monks or Gray Monks (as opposed to the Gray Friars, the title for the Franciscan mendicant order). The Cistercians, however, had no establishment in Carlisle, and the reference may be to the priory of Augustinian Canons (Black Canons), which became the site of the cathedral church after Carlisle was made a bishop's seat in 1133. K offers additional information in her notes.

659   *Jesu*. A reads *Ihu*.

The Avowyng of Arthur

Introduction

The Avowyng of Arthur takes as both its starting point and the substance of its story a series of knightly vows. In many romances, chivalric identity — worship and honor — turns upon a hero's living up to his own established reputation, or to the general ideals of knightly behavior, such as courtesy. In particular cases, a knight's renown may be established or tested in intimate circumstances, through his giving and keeping his private word, as in the "forwards" or agreements of *Sir Gawain and the Green Knight* and *Greene Knight,* or through a delicate pact like that entered into by Gawain in *Gologras.* But much more frequently, a knight's worship rests entirely upon a public utterance — an extravagant vow — and upon the fit between that formulaic self-description and his consequent actions. The "gabs" sworn in *Cornwall,* the oaths made before the court at the Christmas feast in *Sir Gawain and the Green Knight* and *Greene Knight,* or the ill-considered boasts of *Carlisle* all illustrate this pattern.

The Avowyng begins when Arthur, Kay, Gawain, and Baldwin leave the court at Carlisle in order to hunt a great boar in Inglewood Forest. Once there, they utter vows that determine the unfolding of the poem's plot. The first three propose to undertake some immediate adventure within the Forest: Arthur will hunt the marauding boar, Gawain will maintain a "wake" or watch at the Tarn Wathelene all night, and Kay will ride the Forest in search of battle (lines 114 ff.). Fulfilling these vows takes up precisely half of *Avowyng* — that is, thirty-six of the poem's seventy-two stanzas (though the eighteenth stanza lacks four lines following line 284). The vows that Baldwin swears differ from those of the other heroes in number and kind: while the three oaths he pronounces equal the total for the others, they commit him to no peremptory action. In fact, they more resemble prohibitions than promises of achievement, committing Baldwin to avoid certain reactive behaviors rather than to undertake risk or knightly deeds: he swears never to be jealous of a woman, never to refuse anyone his hospitality or food, and never to fear violent death. The testing out and explanation of Baldwin's vows take up the second half of *Avowyng.*

As in *Ragnelle,* Arthur goes off by himself on a hunt, but in *Avowyng* the emphasis falls upon his successful skills as a woodsman rather than upon any unanticipated adventure in Inglewood. After a strenuous pursuit, the King kills this "Satan" or "fiend" of a boar, and then expertly butchers him (lines 161 ff., 257 ff.). The episode ends almost as a dream-vision: the King falls asleep and remains in the Forest until dawn (line 468), though he has no visitors, supernatural or otherwise. In the meantime, Kay in his travels through Inglewood meets a knight who holds a maiden captive (lines 273 ff.). Heeding the calls of the woman, Kay challenges the knight to battle; he turns out to be Sir Menealfe of the Mountayn (line 307), a name (with its -*elf* component) that perhaps connects him to the enchanted realms of fairy. Despite his bold challenge, Kay is predictably defeated by the strange knight (lines 321 ff.), but he then asks that Menealfe seek ransom for him from Sir Gawain at the Tarn Wathelene.

Through Kay's petition, Gawain's encounter with Menealfe and the unnamed woman comes to constitute Gawain's adventure at the Tarn. He fulfills his vow by unseating his opponent twice, once for the ransoming of Kay and a second time for mastery over the fate of Menealfe and of the maiden as well (lines 381, 417 ff.). He swears Menealfe and the woman to abide by the judgment of Queen Guenevere. Accompanied by these two, Kay and Gawain then rejoin the King, and they return to Carlisle bringing "Bothe the birde and the brede" (i.e., "the woman and the meat," line 491). After a favorable interview with the King, Menealfe presents himself to the Queen, who resigns him to the King's power (lines 513 ff.); on the basis of his prowess in the combat with Gawain, he is made a Knight of the Round Table (lines 565 ff.). The first part ends with all parties reconciled and all vows fulfilled — except for Baldwin's.

The second half of *Avowyng* — precisely equal to part one, except for its missing quatrain — divides into two further sections, the testing out of Baldwin's vows and then the rationalization of their meaning. At Arthur's instigation, Kay gathers a force of a half dozen knights and blocks Baldwin's way on his return to Carlisle (lines 585 ff.). Baldwin, without hesitation, prepares to joust, unhorses each knight in his turn, and proceeds to dine with Arthur. When the King asks about his journey, he reports he encountered nothing "butte gode" (line 683); the King marvels all the more when he hears of the beating Kay and the others sustained (lines 689 ff.). Arthur next sends his minstrel as a spy to Baldwin's household, enjoining him to observe the nature of the knight's hospitality; the minstrel finds that all guests — "the grete and the smalle," "knygte, squyer, yoman, [and] knave" — are served without distinction and to their complete satisfaction (lines 717 ff.). Arthur marvels at Baldwin's largesse, and then devises a test for the remaining vow. Arthur sends Baldwin on a hunt, arranging for him to spend the night in the forest (lines 781 ff.); back at the manor house, the King orchestrates matters so that one of his retainers literally spends the night in bed next to, but completely apart from, Baldwin's wife (lines 813 ff.). When Baldwin is brought in to witness the scene and is told the facts of the case, he shows neither anger nor shame, accepting the propriety of the situation because it must have come about "atte hur awen wille" (line 897).

Arthur's expressed surprise at Baldwin's complete lack of reaction — not merely in this bedroom scene, but in the first two "tests" as well — leads Baldwin to explain how his vows stem from principles of his behavior. These explanations take the form of three further stories, all ostensibly based upon Baldwin's experience as a veteran of chivalric warfare. The anecdotes do not however add depth to Baldwin's character, or offer the audience insight into any deeper motives. Instead they work almost as sermon exempla, and offer the etiology for an unusual variety of chivalric pragmatism. Baldwin first tells a brutally misogynistic variant of Chaucer's Pardoner's Tale, in which three washerwomen plot to murder one another, though here one survives (lines 925–88). In this story, the focus of the women's desire is not the defeat of death or even a bushel of gold, but masculine attention, in the form of collective physical violation by five hundred men. Besides working as laundresses, the women service the sexual needs of an entire barracks, and successively kill one another out of jealousy for the men's desire. The lesson Baldwin draws from this incident is not altogether clear, but it seems to be that a man should stay clear of a woman's jealousy, for women are dangerous when they feel discontent. Versions of this story appear elsewhere in medieval literature, both in learned sources (John of Garland's Latin *Poetria*) and fabliau narrative, though the precise source used by the *Avowyng* poet remains uncertain.

Baldwin's second anecdote offers a rationalization for his not ever fearing for his life (lines 1013–45). While in charge of his castle, Baldwin and others sortie out into fierce combat; they return to find that one of their knights, who had hidden in a barrel to avoid the fighting, has been killed by a stray missile. Baldwin's final illustration resembles a story that recurs in a number of medieval chronicles (lines 1053–1126). Baldwin's besieged garrison, at the point of being starved out, welcomes an emissary from the opposing forces with a lavishness that exhausts their last bit of food and drink. Upon returning to his own troops, the emissary reports that the garrison's supplies remain so abundant that they will never surrender, and the siege is lifted.

Arthur's hunt and the chivalric combats of Kay and Gawain, together with the boasts that motivate them, operate as self-explanatory chivalric pursuits in the first part of *Avowyng*. Baldwin's boasts and behavior, on the other hand, insist on their need for explanation, and thus raise suspicions about their proper chivalric status. On the one hand, all three episodes unarguably address central virtues of chivalry: the first assays Baldwin's physical courage and prowess, and the other two prove his courtesy, both public (in the manor hall) and private (in his Lady's bedroom). Yet their unshakable, downright practicality appears far removed from the idealizations of knighthood associated with both aristocratic and popular celebrations of chivalry. The stimulating arguments of Burrow and Johnson that Baldwin's character represents the mature view of a seasoned knight perhaps credits *Avowyng* with a fuller chivalric ethos than it actually possesses; in tethering apparent daring and recklessness to rationality and calculation, the poem effects a transformation of knighthood that may have rendered it especially appealing to a bourgeois audience.

Burrow and Johnson have also properly and convincingly redirected readers' attention to the remarkable symmetries of *Avowyng*. Each half of the poem contains thirty-six tail-rhyme stanzas; moreover, the three vows of three heroes in the first part are countered by the three vows and three anecdotal explanations of a single hero in the second. Perhaps even more than *Awntyrs*, *Avowyng* structures itself as a diptych. In Burrow's view, the poem contrasts the boldly active life of youthful chivalry with the more sedate geniality of Baldwin's mid-elde existence; Johnson argues that the diptych more precisely opposes an impractical and idealistic chivalry to a "real-world, socially-grounded system of values" that reflects "the actuality of warfare" as a "flesh-and-blood fifteenth-century Englishman" would have known it. Yet, like Baldwin's explanations, the structure of *Avowyng* seems finally too rigid. The poem notably lacks the gothic spikiness that Spearing identifies in the framework of *Awntyrs*, and which in that poem and in *Gologras* excite so much readerly response. *Avowyng*, in providing so shapely a narrative, rounds off all its corners; its alignment of incident and explanation suggests that all mysteries have their reasons, and that, as in Baldwin's case, all motives are self-interested or at least justifiable.

Avowyng is composed in sixteen-line tail-rhyme stanzas, rhyming *aaabcccbdddbeeeb*. Its lines are made up not of regular metric feet, but contain varying numbers of stresses; the triplets contain from three to five beats, and the linking *b*-lines two or three stresses. Some of the individual stanzas are linked through verbal concatenation, but in a way that is much less consistent and structurally telling than in *Awntyrs* or *Pearl*. Alliteration is common throughout, but is not a structural feature of the verse, as in *Awntyrs* and *Gologras*. Though the surviving copy contains linguistic features associated with the Midlands, these appear to be scribal, and the original version was produced in the northwest of England, with Cumberland itself — the county in which Inglewood Forest and the Tarn Wathelene are located — a possible place of origin.

Text

Avowyng survives in a single manuscript, Ireland Blackburn, fols. 35r–59r; the manuscript is now in the Robert H. Taylor Collection at Princeton University. The

Introduction

extant version dates from about the third quarter of the fifteenth century, though *Avowyng* may have been composed as early as the last quarter of the fourteenth century. Like many other late Middle English texts, *Avowyng* is written in a hand that often does not distinguish decisively between letter forms (especially *a* and *ei*, and *e* and *o*), and that does not indicate clearly when strokes added to the middle or end of words are significant. Different readings in earlier editions often reflect this ambiguity. The present edition in general disregards scribal strokes and flourishes, rather than transcribing them as unstressed *-e*. Exceptions, differences from earlier editions, and puzzling cases are recorded in the notes.

Select Bibliography

Manuscript

Ireland Blackburn MS, Robert H. Taylor Collection, Princeton, New Jersey.

Editions (arranged chronologically)

Madden, Frederic. 1839. See Bibliography of Editions and Works Cited.

Robson, John. 1842. See Bibliography of Editions and Works Cited.

Smith, James A., ed. *"The Avowynge of King Arthur, Sir Gawan, Sir Kaye and Sir Bawdewyn of Bretan": A Middle English Romance from the Ireland MS.* Leeds University Master's Thesis, 1938.

French, Walter Hoyt, and Charles Brockway Hale, eds. *Middle English Metrical Romances.* New York: Prentice-Hall, 1930. Rpt. in two volumes, Russell and Russell, 1964. Pp. 605–46.

Brookhouse, Christopher, ed. *"Sir Amadace" and "The Avowing of Arthur," Two Romances from the Ireland MS.* Anglistica, 25. Copenhagen: Rosenkilde and Bagger, 1968.

Dahood, Roger, ed. *The Avowing of King Arthur.* New York: Garland, 1984.

Dass, Nirmal. *The Avowing of King Arthur: A Modern Verse Translation.* New York: University Press of America, 1987.

The Avowyng of Arthur

Criticism

Burrow, J. A. *"The Avowing of King Arthur."* In *Medieval Literature and Antiquities: Studies in Honor of Basil Cottle*. Ed. Myra Stokes and T. L. Burton. Woodbridge, Suffolk: D. S. Brewer, 1987. Pp. 99–109.

Greenlaw, E. A. "The Vows of Baldwin: A Study in Mediaeval Fiction." *PMLA* 21 (1906), 575–636.

Johnson, David. "The Real and the Ideal: Attitudes to Love and Chivalry in *The Avowing of King Arthur*." In *Companion to Middle English Romance*, eds. Henk Aertsen and Alasdair A. MacDonald. Amsterdam: VU University Press, 1990. Pp. 189–208.

Kittredge, George L. *"The Avowing of Arthur."* *Modern Language Notes* 8 (1893), 251–52.

The Avowyng of Arthur

	He that made us on the mulde,	*earth*
	And fair fourmet the folde,	*shaped the firmament*
	Atte His will, as He wold,	*would*
	The see and the sande,	
5	Giffe hom joy that will here	*Give them; hear*
	Of dughti men and of dere,	*doughty; fierce*
	Of haldurs that before us were,	*elders*
	That lifd in this londe.	*lived*
	One was Arther the Kinge,	
10	Wythowtun any letting;	*contradiction*
	Wyth him was mony lordinge	
	Hardi of honde.	*hand*
	Wice and war ofte thay were,	*Wise; wary*
	Bold undur banere,	
15	And wighte weppuns wold were,	*powerful weapons did bear*
	And stifly wold stond.	*staunchly*
	This is no fantum ne no fabull;	*fantasy*
	Ye wote wele of the Rowun Tabull,	*You know well*
	Of prest men and priveabull,	*ready; worthy*
20	Was holdun in prise:	*high esteem*
	Chevetan of chivalry,	*Paragons*
	Kyndenesse and curtesy,	
	Hunting full warly,	*expertly*
	As wayt men and wise.	*hardy*
25	To the forest thay fare	*go*
	To hunte atte buk and atte bare,	*buck; boar*
	To the herte and to the hare,	*hart*
	That bredus in the rise.	*breeds; woods*
	The King atte Carlele he lay;	*Carlisle; stopped*
30	The hunter cummys on a day —	*comes one day*
	Sayd, "Sir, ther walkes in my way	
	A well grim gryse.	*very formidable boar*

	"He is a balefull bare —	*frightening boar*
	Seche on segh I nevyr are:	*Such a one saw; before*
35	He hase wroghte me mycull care	*caused; great*
	And hurte of my howundes,	
	Slayn hom downe slely	*them; cunningly*
	Wyth feghting full furcely.	*fighting; fiercely*
	Wasse ther none so hardi	
40	Durste bide in his bandus.	*Dared linger; vicinity*
	On him spild I my spere	*lost*
	And mycull of my nothir gere.	*much of my other equipment*
	Ther moue no dintus him dere,	*may; blows; wound*
	Ne wurche him no wowundes.	*Nor cause*
45	He is masly made —	*hugely*
	All offellus that he bade.	*He destroys all that he has encountered*
	Ther is no bulle so brade	*broad*
	That in frith foundes.	*wood moves about*
	"He is hegher thenne a horse,	*higher*
50	That uncumly corse;	*ugly creature*
	In fayth, him faylis no force	*he lacks*
	Quen that he schalle feghte!	*When*
	And therto, blake as a bere,	*In addition; bear*
	Feye folk will he fere:	*Faint; scare off*
55	Ther may no dyntus him dere,	*blows him harm*
	Ne him to dethe dighte.	*bring*
	Quen he quettus his tusshes,	*When he whets; tusks*
	Thenne he betus on the busshes:	
	All he rives and he russhes,	*tears; breaks*
60	That the rote is unryghte.	*root; disturbed*
	He hase a laythelych luffe:	*hateful force*
	Quen he castus uppe his stuffe,	*tusk*
	Quo durst abide him a buffe,	*Who dares endure from him attack*
	Iwisse he were wighte."	*Indeed; strong*
65	He sais, "In Ingulwode is hee."	*Inglewood Forest*
	The tother biddus, "Lette him bee.	*other commands*
	We schall that Satnace see,	*Fiendish creature*
	Giffe that he be thare."	*If*
	The King callut on knyghtis thre:	*summoned*

70	Himselvun wold the fuyrthe be.	*fourth*
	He sayd, "There schalle no mo mené	*troop*
	Wynde to the bore."	*Go*
	Bothe Kay and Sir Gauan	
	And Bowdewynne of Bretan,	
75	The hunter and the howundus squayn	*keeper*
	Hase yarket hom yare.	*Readied themselves quickly*
	The Kinge hase armut him in hie,	*armed himself in haste*
	And tho thre buirnes hym bie;	*those three knights [are] by him*
	Now ar thay fawre alle redie,	*four*
80	And furthe conne thay fare.	*did they go*
	Unto the forest thay weynde	*traveled*
	That was hardy and heynde.	*Who were; gracious*
	The hunter atte the northe ende	
	His bugull con he blaw,	*bugle did*
85	Uncoupult kenettis as he couthe;	*[And] released dogs; knew how*
	Witturly thay soghte the southe —	*Without fail they headed*
	Raches wyth opon mouthe	*Dogs [yelping]*
	Rennyng on a raw	*in a pack*
	Funde fute of the bore,	*Discovered the track*
90	Faste folutte to him thore.	*Quickly were on to him there*
	Quen that he herd, he hade care;	*When; took fright*
	To the denne conne he draw:	*his den did*
	He sloghe hom downe slely	*struck them down cunningly*
	Wyth feghting full fuyrsly;	*fighting; fiercely*
95	But witte ye, sirs, witturly,	*understand; clearly*
	He stode butte litull awe.	*felt; fear*
	Thay held him fast in his hold;	*cornered; lair*
	He brittunt bercelettus bold,	*slashed hounds*
	Bothe the yunge and the old,	
100	And rafte hom the rest.	*stripped them of comfort*
	The raches comun rennyng him by,	*dogs came running up to him*
	And bayet him full boldely,	*brought him to bay*
	Butte ther was non so hardy	
	Durste on the fynde fast.	*Dared; fiend attack*
105	Thenne the hunter sayd, "Lo, him thare!	*Beware of him there*
	Yaw thar, such him no mare!	*You; seek*

	Now may ye sone to him fare;	*at once; go*
	Lette see quo dose beste.	*who performs*
	Yaw thar, such him nevyr more!	*You; seek*
110	Butte sette my hed opon a store	*set my head; stake*
	Butte giffe he flaey yo all fawre,	*If he doesn't flay; four*
	That griselich geste!"	*grisly ghost*
	Thenne the hunter turnes home agayn.	
	The King callut on Sir Gauan,	*called; Gawain*
115	On Bawdewin of Bretan,	
	And on kene Kay.	*bold*
	He sayd, "Sirs, in your cumpany,	
	Myne avow make I:	
	Were he nevyr so hardy,	
120	Yone Satenas to say —	*Fiend to assay*
	To brittun him and downe bringe,	*[I vow] to butcher him and bring him down*
	Wythoute any helpinge,	
	And I may have my levynge	*If; keep my life*
	Hen till tomorne atte day!	*From now until tomorrow morning*
125	And now, sirs, I cummaunde yo	
	To do as I have done nowe:	
	Ichone make your avowe."	*Each one*
	Gladdely grawuntutte thay.	*agreed*
	Then unsquarut Gauan	*answered*
130	And sayd godely agayn,	*in return*
	"I avowe, to Tarne Wathelan,	*at*
	To wake hit all nyghte."	*watch over it*
	"And I avow," sayd Kaye,	
	"To ride this forest or daye,	*[throughout]; before*
135	Quoso wernes me the waye,	*[And] whoever denies*
	Hym to dethe dighte."	*To fight him to the death*
	Quod Baudewyn, "To stynte owre strife,	*make end to; contest*
	I avow bi my life	
	Nevyr to be jelus of my wife,	*jealous*
140	Ne of no birde bryghte;	*attractive woman*
	Nere werne no mon my mete	*Nor to deny; person; food*
	Quen I gode may gete;	*When; goods; possess*
	Ne drede my dethe for no threte	*fear; threat*
	Nauthir of king ner knyghte."	*Neither; nor*

122

145	Butte now thay have thayre vowes made,	*now that*
	Thay buskutte hom and furth rade	*made themselves ready*
	To hold that thay heghte hade,	*promised*
	Ichone sere way.	*Each in a different*
	The King turnus to the bore;	*boar*
150	Gauan, wythoutun any more,	*without further ado*
	To the tarne con he fore,	*lake did he go*
	To wake hit to day.	*watch; until*
	Thenne Kay, as I conne roune,	*may relate*
	He rode the forest uppe and downe.	
155	Boudewynne turnes to toune	
	Sum that his gate lay,	*As his way (home) lay*
	And sethun to bed bownus he;	*then; goes*
	Butte carpe we now of ther othir thre,	*speak; those other three*
	How thay prevyd hor wedde-fee,	*pledge*
160	The sothe for to say.	*truth*
	Furst, to carpe of oure Kinge,	
	Hit is a kyndelich thinge —	*natural*
	Atte his begynnyng,	
	Howe he dedde his dede.	*did*
165	Till his houndus con he hold;	*To; did take his course*
	The bore, wyth his brode schilde,	*protective skin*
	Folut hom fast in the filde	*Followed them; field*
	And spillutte hom on gode spede.	*injured them quickly*
	Then the Kinge con crye,	
170	And carputte of venerie	*called out as a hunter*
	To make his howundus hardi —	*bold*
	Hovut on a stede.	*[He] remained on horseback*
	Als sone as he come thare,	
	Agaynus him rebowndet the bare:	*Against; charged*
175	He se nevyr no syghte are	*saw; before*
	So sore gerutte him to drede.	*caused; be afraid*
	He hade drede and doute	*worry*
	Of him that was stirrun and stowte;	*[the boar]; fierce; strong*
	He began to romy and rowte,	*roar; growl*
180	And gapes and gones.	*opens his mouth; bares teeth*
	Men myghte noghte his cowch kenne	*lair see clearly*

	For howundes and for slayn men	*Because of*
	That he hade draun to his denne	
	And brittunt all to bonus.	*ripped; bones*
185	Thenne his tusshes con he quette,	*tusks; whet*
	Opon the Kinge for to sette;	*attack*
	He liftis uppe, wythoutun lette,	*tosses aside; pause*
	Stokkes and stonis.	*Branches*
	Wyth wrathe he begynnus to wrote:	*fury; root*
190	He ruskes uppe mony a rote	*rips; root*
	Wyth tusshes of thre fote,	*tusks; three feet*
	So grisly he gronus.	*growls*
	Thenne the Kinge spanos his spere	*grasps*
	Opon that bore for to bere;	*to encounter*
195	Ther may no dyntus him dere,	*strokes; wound*
	So sekir was his schilde.	*strong; protective skin*
	The grete schafte that was longe	*spear-shaft*
	All to spildurs hit spronge;	*splinters*
	The gode stede that was stronge	*horse*
200	Was fallun in the filde.	*field*
	As the bore had mente,	*Just as; meant*
	He gave the King such a dinte,	*blow*
	Or he myghte his bridull hente,	*Before; get hold*
	That he myghte evyr hit fele.	*forever feel it*
205	His stede was stonet starke ded:	*stunned stone dead*
	He sturd nevyr owte of that sted.	*[The King] stirred; saddle*
	To Jhesu a bone he bede,	*favor; prayed*
	Fro wothes hym weylde.	*From sorrows; protect*
	Thenne the King in his sadul sete,	*straightened himself*
210	And wightely wan on his fete.	*agilely gained*
	He prays to Sayn Margarete	
	Fro wathes him ware;	*From harm to protect him*
	Did as a dughty knyghte —	*bold*
	Brayd oute a brand bryghte	*Drew; sword*
215	And heve his schild opon highte,	*raised; on high*
	For spild was his spere.	*destroyed*
	Sethun he buskette him yare,	*Then he readied himself quickly*
	Squithe, wythoutun any mare,	*Right away; more [delay]*

Agaynus the fynde for to fare *fiend; go*
220 That hedoes was of hiere. *hideous; pelt (hair)*
So thay cowunturt in the fild: *clashed*
For all the weppuns that he myghte weld, *Despite; wield*
The bore brittunt his schild *tore apart*
On brest he conne bere. *[Which] over his breast; did*

225 There downe knelus he *kneels*
And prayus till Him that was so fre: *God; gracious*
"Send me the victoré!
This Satanas me sekes." *harries*
All wroth wex that sqwyne, *furious became; swine*
230 Blu, and brayd uppe his bryne; *Snorted; raised; eyebrows*
As kylne other kechine, *furnace (kiln) or kitchen*
Thus rudely he rekes. *foully he reeks (smells)*
The Kynge myghte him noghte see, *could [the boar]*
Butte lenyt hym doune bi a tree, *leaned himself over by*
235 So nyghe discumford was hee *nearly undone was [the King]*
For smelle other smekis. *or fumes*
And as he neghet bi a noke, *[the boar] came near to an oak*
The King sturenly him stroke, *struck*
That both his brees con blake; *brows did darken*
240 His maistry he mekes. *prowess [the king] shows*

Thus his maistry mekes he
Wyth dyntus that werun dughté. *blows; doughty*
Were he nevyr so hardé,[1]
Thus bidus that brothe.
245 The Kinge, wyth a nobull brande, *sword*
He mette the bore comande: *met; straight on (coming)*
On his squrd, till his hande, *Against his sword; up to*
He rennes full rathe. *quickly*
He bare him inne atte the throte: *drove [the sword] in*
250 He hade no myrth of that mote — *[The boar]; encounter*
He began to dotur and dote *dodder; stagger*
Os he hade keghet scathe. *Since (as); caught great harm*

---

[1] Lines 243–44: *No matter how fierce he (the boar) might be, | The bold hunter waits him out*

Wyth sit siles he adowne.   *pain sinks*
To brittun him the King was bowne,   *butcher; eager*
255   And sundurt in that sesun   *divided (sundered); moment*
    His brode schildus bothe.   *shoulder quarters*

The King couthe of venery: *was expert in hunting lore*
Colurt him full kyndely.   *[He] collared; properly*
The hed of that hardy   *bold beast*
260   He sette on a stake.
Sethun brittuns he the best   *Then cuts up; beast*
As venesun in forest;   *slain deer*
Bothe the thonge and lees   *strips and slices*
    He hongus on a noke.   *hangs on an oak*
265   There downe knelys hee
That loves hur that is free;   *[the Virgin Mary]; gracious*
Sayd, "This socur thou hase send me   *help*
    For thi Sune sake!"   *Son's*
If he were in a dale depe,   *Not only was he; valley desolate*
270   He hade no knyghte him to kepe.   *accompany*
Forwerré, slidus he on slepe: *Completely worn out; slides*
    No lengur myghte he wake.

The King hase fillut his avowe.   *fulfilled*
Of Kay carpe we nowe —   *speak*
275   How that he come for his prowe   *fared with regard to his prowess*
    Ye schall here more.
Als he rode in the nyghte   *As; through*
In the forest he mette a knyghte
Ledand a birde bryghte;   *Leading a beautiful woman*
280   Ho wepputte wundur sore.   *She wept; sorrowfully*
Ho sayd, "Sayn Maré myghte me spede   *She; May Saint Mary help me*
And save me my madunhede,   *for me*
And giffe the knyghte for his dede   *grant; deed*
    Bothe soro and care!"

285   Thus ho talkes him tille   *she speaks; to*
Quille ho hade sayd all hur wille;   *Until; desire*
And Kay held him full stille,   *quietly*
    And in the holte hoves.   *wood lingers*

	He prekut oute prestely	*galloped; rapidly*
290	And aurehiet him radly,	*overtook; quickly*
	And on the knyghte conne cry,	*did call*
	And pertely him reproves,	*openly upbraids him*
	And sayd, "Recraiand knyghte,	*Renegade*
	Here I profur the to fighte	*challenge*
295	Be chesun of that biurde brighte!	*By reason; lovely woman*
	I bede the my glovus."	*offer; gloves (throw down the gauntlet)*
	The tother unsquarut him wyth skille	*other answered; in proper form*
	And sayd, "I am redy atte thi wille	
	That forward to fulfille	*challenge*
300	In alle that me behovus."	*is proper for me*
	"Now, quethen art thou?" quod Kay,	*from where*
	"Or quethur is thou on way?	*whither*
	Thi righte name thou me say!	*proper; tell*
	Quere wan thou that wighte?"	*Where captured; person*
305	The tother unsquarut him agayn:	*in turn*
	"Mi righte name is noghte to layn:	*to be concealed*
	Sir Menealfe of the Mountayn	
	My gode fadur highte.	*father was named*
	And this Lady sum I the telle:	*(of) this Lady something; you*
310	I fochet hur atte Ledelle,	*captured*
	Ther hur frindus con I felle	*Where; friends; did; defeat*
	As foes in a fighte.	
	So I talket hom tille	*In such ways I talked to them (egged them on)*
	That muche blode conne I spille,	
315	And all agaynus thayre awne wille	*against*
	There wan I this wighte."	*won; person*
	Quod Kay, "The batell I take	*undertake*
	Be chesun of the birdus sake,	*By reason; woman's*
	And I schalle wurch the wrake" —	*do you harm*
320	And sqwithely con squere.	*on the spot did swear his word*
	Thenne thay rode togedur ryghte	*jousted*
	As frekes redy to fighte	*bold men*
	Be chesun of that birde bryghte,	
	Gay in hor gere.	*Radiant in her gown*
325	Menealfe was the more myghty:	

	He stroke Kay stifly —	*struck; fiercely*
	Witte ye, sirs, witturly —	*Understand; clearly*
	Wyth a scharpe spere.	
	All toschildurt his schilde,	*[Menealfe] splintered [Kay's]*
330	And aure his sadull gerut him to held,	*over; caused; fall*
	And felle him flatte in the filde,	*knocked*
	And toke him uppeon werre.	*captured; by laws of war*
	Thus hase he wonun Kay on werre,	
	And all tospild is his spere,	*destroyed*
335	And mekill of his othir gere	*much; equipment*
	Is holden to the pees.	*lost because of the defeat*
	Thenne unsquarut Kay agayn	*answered*
	And sayd, "Sir, atte Tarne Wathelan	
	Bidus me Sir Gauan,	*Awaits*
340	Is derwurthe on dese;	*most worthy on dais (among other knights)*
	Wold ye thethur be bowne	*thither be bound*
	Or ye turnut to the towne,	*Before; go*
	He wold pay my rawunsone	
	Wythowtyn delees."	*delay*
345	He sayd, "Sir Kay, thi lyfe I the heghte	*promise you*
	For a cowrce of that knyghte!"	*tilt (course) with*
	Yette Menealfe, or the mydnyghte,	*But; before*
	Him ruet all his rees.	*regretted; haste*
	Thus thay turnut to the Torne	*traveled; Tarn (lake)*
350	Wyth the thrivand thorne.	*burgeoning thorn tree*
	Kay callut on Gauan yorne;	*eagerly*
	Asshes, "Quo is there?"	*[Gawain] asks, "Who*
	He sayd, "I, Kay, that thou knawes	*whom*
	That owte of tyme bostus and blawus;	*at the wrong times boasts and brags*
355	Butte thou me lese wyth thi lawes,	*Unless; release; courtesy*
	I lif nevyr more.	*I am dead*
	For as I rode in the nyghte,	
	In the forest I mette a knyghte	
	Ledand a birde bryghte;	*Leading a beautiful woman*
360	Ho wepput wundur sore.	*She*
	There togedur faghte we	*fought*
	Be chesun of that Lady free;	*For the sake of*

128

On werre thus hase he wonun me, *In combat; captured*
 Gif that me lothe ware. *Though [to] me hateful it were*

365 "This knyghte that is of renowun *honorable*
 Hase takyn me to presowun, *as prisoner*
 And thou mun pay my rawunsun, *must*
  Gawan, wyth thi leve." *by your leave*
 Then unsquarutte Gauan *answered*
370 And sayd godely agayn, *agreeably in return*
 "I wille, wundur fayne: *most gladly*
  Quatt schall I geve?" *What; do (to proceed)*
 "Quen thou art armut in thi gere, *When; armed; gear*
 Take thi schild and thi spere
375 And ride to him a course on werre; *with him; joust*
  Hit schall the noghte greve." *you not at all hurt*
 Gauan asshes, "Is hit soe?" — *asks, "Is that right?"*
 The tother knyght grauntus, "Yoe";
 He sayd, "Then togedur schull we goe *[Gawain]*
380 Howsumevyr hit cheve!" *Whatever happens*

 And these knyghtus kithun hor crafte, *demonstrate their [knightly] prowess*
 And aythir gripus a schafte *each one*
 Was als rude as a rafte; *large as a beam*
  So runnun thay togedur. *charged*
385 So somun conne thay hie *So (fiercely) did they charge together*
 That nauthir scaput forbye; *neither escaped at all*
 Gif Menealfe was the more myghtie, *If*
  Yette dyntus gerut him to dedur: *blows caused; dodder*
 He stroke him sadde and sore. *[Gawain] struck; grievously*
390 Squithe squonut he thore; *Quickly he passed out there*
 The blonke him aboute bore, *horse; carried*
  Wiste he nevyr quedur. *Knew; in what direction*
 Quod Kay, "Thou hase that thou hase soghte! *You got what you asked for*
 Mi raunnsun is all redy boghte; *completely paid*
395 Gif thou were ded, I ne roghte! *If you [Menealfe]; wouldn't care*
  Forthi come I hedur." *This is what I came for*

 Thus Kay scornus the knyghte,
 And Gauan rydus to him ryghte. *rides; directly*

	In his sadul sette him on highte,	*[Gawain] straightened him upright*
400	Speke gif he may.	*So that he might speak*
	Of his helme con he draw,	*Off*
	Lete the wynde on him blaw;	*Let*
	He speke wyth a vois law —	*low*
	"Delyveryt hase thou Kay.	*Rescued*
405	Wyth thi laa hase made him leyce,	*swordplay; free*
	Butte him is lothe to be in pece.	*Although to him it is hateful; peace*
	And thou was aye curtase	*were unfailingly courteous*
	And prins of ich play.	*chief in each combat*
	Wold thou here a stowunde bide,	*[If]; short time wait*
410	A nother course wold I ride;	*second*
	This that hoves by my side,	*This [woman] who remains*
	In wedde I wold hur lay."	*As pledge; offer*

	Thenne unsquarut Gauan,	*answered*
	Sayd godely agayn,	*agreeably in turn*
415	"I am wundur fayn	*glad*
	For hur for to fighte."	
	These knyghtus kithun thayre gere	*readied*
	And aythir gripus a spere;	
	Runnun togedur on werre	
420	Os hardy and wighte.	*As; powerful*
	So somen ther thay yode	*[violently] together; went*
	That Gauan bare him from his stede,	*thrust*
	That both his brees con blede	*brows did bleed*
	On growunde qwen he lighte.	*when he landed*
425	Thenne Kay con on him calle	
	And sayd, "Sir, thou hade a falle,	
	And thi wench lost wythalle,	*[you have] lost in addition*
	Mi trauthe I the plighte!"	*My trowth I pledge to you*

	Quod Kay, "Thi leve hase thou loste	*beloved*
430	For all thi brag or thi boste;	
	If thou have oghte on hur coste,	*spent*
	I telle hit for tente."	*consider; as lost*
	Thenne speke Gauan to Kay,	
	"A mons happe is notte ay;	*good fortune; everlasting*
435	Is none so sekur of asay	*sure of mettle*

	Butte he may harmes hente."	receive
	Gauan rydus to him ryghte	directly
	And toke uppe the tother knyghte	
	That was dilfully dyghte	sorrowfully dealt with
440	And stonet in that stynte.	stunned at that break (in combat)
	Kay wurdus tenut him mare	words grieved him more
	Thenne all the harmes that he hente thare;	Than; mischance; received
	He sayd, "And we allone ware,	If
	This stryf schuld I stynte."	spleen; stop

	"Ye, hardely," quod Kay;	scarcely
445	"Butte thou hast lost thi fayre may	maiden
	And thi liffe, I dar lay."	life; wager
	Thus talkes he him tille.	
	And Gauan sayd, "God forbede,	
450	For he is dughti in dede."	bold
	Prayes the knyghte gud spede	[He]; with good wishes
	To take hit to none ille	without offense
	If Kay speke wurdes kene.	sharp
	"Take thou this damesell schene;	beautiful
455	Lede hur to Gaynour the Quene,	Guenevere
	This forward to fulfille;	compact
	And say that Gawan, hur knyghte,	her
	Sende hur this byurde brighte;	beautiful woman
	And rawunsun the anon righte	yourself forthwith
460	Atte hur awne wille."	(Guenevere's) own

	Therto grawuntus the knyghte	agrees
	And truly his trauthe plighte,	troth pledges
	Inne saveward that byurde bryghte	As safeguard
	To Carlele to bringe.	
465	And as thay hovet and abode,	stood; waited
	He squere on the squrd brode.	swore; sword
	Be he his othe hade made,	Just at the moment
	Thenne waknut the King.	awakened
	Thenne the day beganne to daw;	dawn
470	The Kinge his bugull con blaw;	did
	His knyghtus couth hitte welle knaw,	could it easily recognize
	Hit was a sekur thinge.	a sure thing

	Sethun thay busket hom yare,	*Then; hastened quickly*
	Sqwith, wythowtun any mare,	*Immediately; more [time]*
475	To wete the Kingus welefare,	*ascertain*
	Wythowtun letting.	*delay*

PRIMUS PASSUS   *[End of] First Part*

	To the forest thay take the way —	
	Bothe Gawan and Kay,	
	Menealfe, and the fare may	*fair woman*
480	Comun to the Kinge.	*Came*
	The bore brittunt thay funde,	*butchered*
	Was colurt of the Kingus hande;	*carved by*
	If he wore lord of that londe,	*Even though he were*
	He hade no horsing.	*mount*
485	Downe thay take that birde bryghte,	*lovely woman*
	Sette hur one, behinde the knyghte;	*her upon [horseback]*
	Hur horse for the King was dyghte,	*made ready*
	Wythoutun letting;	*delay*
	Gave Kay the venesun to lede,	*meat to take charge of*
490	And hiet hamward, gode spede;	*hastened homeward, happily*
	Bothe the birde and the brede	*woman; meat*
	To Carlele thay bringe.	

	Now as thay rode atte the way,	*on*
	The Kynge himselvun con say	*did*
495	Bothe to Gauan and to Kay,	
	"Quere wan ye this wighte?"	*Where won; person*
	Thenne Kay to the King spake;	
	He sayd, "Sir, in the forest as I con wake	*watch*
	Atte the anturis hoke,	*marvelous oak*
500	Ther mette me this knyghte.	
	Ther togedur faghte we	*fought*
	Be chesun of this Lady fre;	*reason*
	On werre hase he thus wonun me,	*In just combat; defeated*
	Wyth mayn and wyth myghte.	
505	And Gawan hase my rawunsun made	
	For a course that he rode	*joust*

And felle him in the fild brode;
   He wanne this biurde bryghte.   *woman*

        "He toke him there to presunnere" —   *as prisoner*
510   Then loghe that damesell dere   *laughed*
And lovet wyth a mylde chere   *praised*
   God and Sir Gawan.
Thenne sayd the King opon highte,   *aloud*
All sqwithe to the knyghte,   *quickly*
515   "Quat is thi rawunsun, opon ryghte?   *What; lawfully*
   The soth thou me sayn."   *truth; to me*
The tothir unsquarut him wyth skille,   *answered*
"I conne notte say the thertille: *tell you about that*
Hit is atte the Quene wille;
520   Qwi schuld I layne?   *Why; lie*
Bothe my dethe and my lyfe
Is inne the wille of thi wife,
Quethur ho wulle stynte me of my strife *Whether she; make an end*
   Or putte me to payne."   *set me some penalty*

525   "Grete God," quod the King,
"Gif Gawan gode endinge,   *Give; happy*
For he is sekur in alle kynne thinge, *trustworthy; kinds of*
   To cowuntur wyth a knyghte!   *enter combat*
Of all playus he berus the prise,   *encounters; takes; honor*
530   Loos of ther ladise.   *Praise; these*
Menealfe, and thou be wise,   *if*
   Hold that thou beheghte,   *what; have promised*
And I schall helpe that I maye,"   *insofar as*
The King himselvun con saye.
535   To Carlele thay take the waye,
   And inne the courte is lighte.   *[the company] arrived*
He toke this damesell gente;   *[Menealfe]; noble*
Before the Quene is he wente,
And sayd, "Medame, I am hedur sente   *hither*
540   Fro Gawan, your knyghte."

He sayd, "Medame, Gawan, your knyghte,
On werre hase wonun me tonyghte,   *defeated*

	Be chesun of this birde brighte;	*For the sake of*
	Mi pride conne he spille,	*did; undo*
545	And gerut me squere squyftely	*caused; swear swiftly*
	To bringe the this Lady	*you*
	And my nowne body,	*my own*
	To do hit in thi wille.	*submit*
	And I have done as he me bade."	
550	Now quod the Quene, "And I am glad.	
	Sethun thou art in my wille stade,	*Since; placed*
	To spare or to spille,	*save; dispose of*
	I giffe the to my Lord the Kinge —	*give*
	For he hase mestur of such a thinge,	*sovereignty over*
555	Of knyghtus in a cowunturinge —	*combat*
	This forward to fullfille."	*compact*
	Now the Quene sayd, "God almyghte,	
	Save me Gawan, my knyghte,	*for me*
	That thus for wemen con fighte —	*Who; women does*
560	Fro wothus him were!"	*From harm protect him*
	Gawan sayd, "Medame, as God me spede,	
	He is dughti of dede,	*[Menealfe]*
	A blithe burne on a stede,	*warrior on horseback*
	And grayth in his gere."	*accomplished*
565	Thenne thay fochet furth a boke,	*fetched*
	All thayre laes for to loke;	*laws (customs); review*
	The Kinge sone his othe toke	*administered*
	And squithely gerut him squere;	*right away caused him to swear*
	And sekirly, wythouten fabull,	*surely, without lie*
570	Thus dwellus he atte the Rowun Tabull,	
	As prest knyghte and priveabull,	*ready; worthy*
	Wyth schild and wyth spere.	
	Nowe gode frindus ar thay.	*friends*
	Then carpus Sir Kay —	*says*
575	To the King con he say:	
	"Sire, a mervaell thinke me	*wonder it seems to me*
	Of Bowdewyns avouyng,	*vow*
	Yusturevyn in the evnyng,	*Yesterday*
	Wythowtun any lettyng,	*Without lie*

580	Wele more thenne we thre."	*Even*
	Quod the King, "Sothe to sayn,	
	I kepe no lengur for to layn:	*allow [it]; to [be] concealed*
	I wold wete wundur fayn	*know gladly*
	How best myghte be."	*[The nature of the oath] as fully as possible*
585	Quod Kay, "And ye wold gif me leve,	*If you; give; permission*
	And sithun take hit o no greve,	*after; not in insult*
	Now schuld I propurly preve,	*positively show*
	As evyr myghte I thee!"	*prosper*
	"Yisse," quod the King, "on that comande,	*provision*
590	That o payn on life and on londe	*on pain of*
	That ye do him no wrunge,	
	Butte save wele my knyghte.	
	As men monly him mete,	*As knights manly (chivalrously); accost*
	And sithun forsette him the strete:	*then bar the road*
595	Ye fynde him noghte on his fete!	*feet (i.e., he will mount and challenge)*
	Be warre, for he is wyghte.	*powerful*
	For he is horsutte full wele	*well-horsed*
	And clene clad in stele;	*armor*
	Is none of yo but that he mun fele	*you [excepted]; (may not) overcome*
600	That he may on lyghte.	*Whom; light upon*
	Ye wynnun him noghte owte of his way,"	*drive him not from his course*
	The King himselvun con say;	
	"Him is lefe, I dar lay,	*To him it is precious; bet*
	To hald that he heghte."	*hold to what he promised*
605	Thenne sex ar atte on assente,	*six are together in one compact*
	Hase armut hom and furthe wente,	*armed themselves*
	Brayd owte aure a bente	*Set out over a field*
	Bawdewyn to mete,	*encounter*
	Wyth scharpe weppun and schene,	*bright*
610	Gay gowuns of grene	*robes*
	To hold thayre armur clene,	*To keep; unstained*
	And were hitte fro the wete.	*protect it; wet (weather)*
	Thre was sette on ich side	*Three; each*
	To werne him the wayus wide —	*To deny [Baldwin]; roads*
615	Quere the knyghte schuld furth ride,	
	Forsette hym the strete.	*Bar*

	Wyth copus covert thay hom thenne,	*capes they covered themselves*
	Ryghte as thay hade bene uncowthe men,	*unknown (of no renown)*
	For that thay wold noghte be kennet —	*recognized*
620	Evyn downe to thayre fete.	
	Now as thay hovut and thay hyild,	*lingered; hid [themselves]*
	Thay se a schene undur schild	*bright [knight] armed*
	Come prekand fast aure the filde	*galloping; over*
	On a fayre stede;	
625	Wele armut, and dyghte	*equipped*
	As freke redy to fyghte,	*warrior*
	Toward Carlele ryghte	*directly*
	He hies gode spede.	*hastens with*
	He see ther sixe in his way;	*saw those six*
630	Thenne to thaymselvun con thay say,	*did*
	"Now he is ferd, I dar lay,	*frightened; bet*
	And of his lyfe adrede."	*for; worries*
	Then Kay crius opon heghte,	*aloud*
	All squyth to the knyghte:	*Right away*
635	"Othir flee or fighte:	*Either*
	The tone behovus the nede!"	*One of these you must needs do*
	Thenne thay kest thayre copus hom fro.	*threw; capes from them*
	Sir Bawdewyn se that hit wasse so,	*it was (as Kay said)*
	And sayd, "And ye were als mony mo,	*as many more [again]*
640	Ye gerutte me notte to flee.	*would not have caused me*
	I have my ways for to weynde	*travel*
	For to speke wyth a frynde;	*friend*
	As ye ar herdmen hinde —	*boorish shepherds*
	Ye marre notte me!"	*may not harm me*
645	Thenne the sex sembult hom in fere	*gathered themselves together*
	And squere by Him that boghte us dere,	*swore*
	"Thou passus nevyr away here	*passes; through*
	Butte gif thou dede be!"	*Except if*
	"Yisse, hardely," quod Kay,	*Yes, indeed*
650	"He may take anothir way —	*choose*
	And ther schall no mon do nere say	*And in that case; nor*
	That schall greve the!"	*[Anything]*

"Gode the foryilde," quod the knyghte,   *reward you; [Baldwin]*
"For I am in my wais righte;   *proper*
655 Yisturevyn I the King highte   *promised*
   To cumme to my mete.   *for dinner*
I warne yo, frekes, be ye bold,   *you, fighters, even if you are*
My ryghte ways wille I holde!"
A spere in fewtre he folde,   *its socket (for jousting); places*
660   A gode and a grete.
Kay stode nexte him in his way:
He jopput him aure on his play;   *toppled; over with his thrust*
That hevy horse on him lay —   *[Kay]*
   He squonet in that squete.   *swooned; struggle*
665 He rode to there othir fyve: *those*
Thayre schene schildus con he rive,   *handsome; did he shred*
And faure felle he belyve,   *four overcame; quickly*
   In hie in that hete.   *In haste; heat (mêlée)*

Hardely wythouten delay,   *With scarcely any pause*
670 The sex to hom hase takyn uppe Kay;   *six to themselves*
And thenne Sir Bawdewin con say,
   "Will ye any more?"   *Do you want any more*
The tother unsquarutte him thertille,   *other (sixth) answered*
Sayd, "Thou may weynd quere thou wille,   *go where*
675 For thou hase done us noghte butte skille,   *shown toward us; except mastery*
   Gif we be wowundut sore."   *Although*
He brayd aure to the Kinge,   *[Baldwin] hastened over*
Wythowtun any letting;   *hindrance*
He asshed if he hade herd any tithing   *[The king] asked; news*
680   In thayre holtus hore.   *woods bare*
The knyghte stedit and stode;   *paused*
Sayd, "Sir, as I come thro yondur wode,   *came*
I herd ne se butte gode   *[neither] heard nor saw*
   Quere I schuld furthe fare."   *go forth*

685 Thanne was the Kinge amervaylet thare   *astonished*
That he wold telle him no more.
Als squithur thay ar yare,   *As soon as; ready*
   To Masse ar thay wente.   *did they go*
By the Masse wasse done,   *By [the time]*

137

690   Kay come home sone,
       Told the King before none,   *in early afternoon*
         "We ar all schente   *done in*
       Of Sir Baudewyn, your knyghte: *By*
       He is nobull in the fighte,
695   Bold, hardy, and wighte   *powerful*
         To bide on a bente.   *deal with on the battlefield*
       Fle wille he nevyr more:
       Him is much levyr dee thore.   *To him; preferable to die there*
       I may banne hur that him bore,   *curse her*
700   Suche harmes have I hente!"   *received*

       Noue the King sayd, "Fle he ne can,   *Now; Flee*
       Ne werne his mete to no man;   *deny; food*
       Gife any buirne schuld him ban,   *If; fighter; curse*
         A mervail hit ware."   *it were*
705   Thenne the King cald his mynstrelle
       And told him holly his wille: *completely his wish*
       Bede him layne atte hit were stille,   *Bid him dissemble so that it were secret*
         That he schuld furth fare
       To Baudewins of Bretan: *Baldwin's [manor]*
710   "I cummawunde the, or thou cum agayne,   *command; before; return*
       Faurty days, o payne,   *Forty; upon penalty*
         Loke that thou duelle there,   *See*
       And wete me prevely to say   *inform; secretly*
       If any mon go meteles away;   *without food*
715   For thi wareson for ay,   *To ensure your well-being always*
         Do thou me nevyr more."   *for me nothing more [than this]*

       Then the mynstrell weyndus on his way
       Als fast as he may.
       Be none of the thryd day,   *none (about 3 p.m.)*
720   He funde thaym atte the mete,   *at table*
       The Lady and hur mené   *household*
       And gestus grete plenté.   *guests in great number*
       Butte porter none funde he   *met*
         To werne him the gate;   *turn him away*
725   Butte rayket into the halle   *he proceeded*
       Emunge the grete and the smalle,   *Among*

And loket aboute him aure alle. *overall (all around)*
   He herd of no threte, *constraint*
Butte riall servys and fyne: *royal service*
730 In bollus birlutte thay the wyne, *bowls poured*
And cocus in the kechine *cooks*
   Squytheli con squete. *Readily did sweat*

Then the Ladi conne he loute, *did he bow to*
And the biurdes all aboute; *women*
735 Both wythinne and wythoute,
   No faute he ther fonde.
Knygte, squyer, yoman, ne knave,
Hom lacket noghte that thay schuld have; *To them [there] lacked*
Thay nedut notte aftur hit to crave: *to make request*
740 Hit come to hor honde. *to their hand [unbidden]*
Thenne he wente to the dece, *dais*
Before the pruddust in prece. *most noble in the group*
That Lady was curtase,
   And bede him stille stonde.
745 He sayd he was knoun and couthe, *renowned and celebrated*
And was comun fro bi southe, *the south*
And ho had myrth of his mouthe, *she; joy*
   To here his tithand. *tales*

A sennyght duellut he thare. *A week stayed*
750 Ther was no spense for to spare: *luxury*
Burdes thay were nevyr bare, *Boards (tables)*
   Butte evyr covurt clene. *covered completely [with food]*
Bothe knyghte and squiere,
Mynstrelle and messyngere, *messenger*
755 Pilgreme and palmere *wayfarer*
   Was welcum, I wene. *understand*
Ther was plenty of fode:
Pore men hade thayre gode, *goods for themselves*
Mete and drinke or thay yode, *went off again*
760 To wete wythoutyn wene. *To understand; doubt*
The lord lenge wold noghte, *[Baldwin] linger [at Arthur's court]*
Butte come home qwen him gode thoghte, *when [to] him good [it] seemed*

139

And both he hase wyth him broghte
   The Kinge and the Quene.

   A FITTE   *Segment [i.e., end of second section]*

765	Now ther come fro the kechine	*kitchen*
	Riall service and fine;	*Royal*
	Ther was no wonting of wine	*lack*
	To lasse ne to mare.	*lower; greater [in rank]*
	Thay hade atte thayre sopere	
770	Riche metes and dere.	
	The King, wyth a blythe chere,	*glad look*
	Bade hom sle care.	*them slay anxiety*
	Than sayd the Kinge opon highte,	*aloud*
	All sqwithe to the knyghte:	*Right away*
775	"Such a service on a nyghte	*on a single night*
	Se I nevyr are."	*Saw; before*
	Thenne Bawdewyn smylit and on him logh;	*laughed to himself*
	Sayd, "Sir, God hase a gud plughe!	*plow [i.e., God provides well]*
	He may send us all enughe:	
780	Qwy schuld we spare?"	*Why*

	"Now I cummawunde the," quod the King,	*command*
	"Tomorne in the mornyng	
	That thou weynde on huntyng,	*go*
	To wynne us the dere.	*take for us*
785	Fare furthe to the fenne;	*Go directly; wilderness*
	Take wyth the howundus and men,	
	For thou conne hom best kenne:	*can best appraise them*
	Thou knoes best here.	*know; (in your own home)*
	For all day tomorne will I bide,	*await*
790	And no forthir will I ride,	
	Butte wyth the ladés of pride	*noble ladies*
	To make me gud chere."	
	To bed bownut thay that nyghte,	*went off*
	And atte the morun, atte days lighte,	
795	Thay blew hornys opon highte	*out loud*
	And ferd furthe in fere.	*went; together*

Thenne the Kynge cald his huntere,   *huntsman*
And sayd, "Felaw, come here!"
The tother, wyth a blithe chere,   *That one; good will*
800   Knelet on his kne: *Kneeled*
Dowun to the Kinge con he lowte.   *did; bow*
"I commawunde the to be all nyghte oute;   *out (on the hunt)*
Bawdewyn, that is sturun and stowte,   *bold and hardy*
    Wyth the schall he be.   *you*
805   Erly in the dawyng   *At daybreak*
Loke that ye come fro huntyng;
If ye no venesun bring,
    Full litill rechs me."   *does it trouble me*
The tother unsquarut him thertille,   *answered; in return*
810   Sayd, "Sir, that is atte your aune wille: *as you wish*
That hald I resun and skille,   *proper and right*
    As evyr myghte I the."   *prosper*

And atte evyn the King con him dyghte   *did make himself ready*
And callut to him a knyghte;
815   And to the chambur full ryghte   *directly*
    He hiees gode waye   *hastens along*
Qwere the Lady of the howse   *Where*
And maydyns ful beuteowse
Were, curtase and curiowse,   *[who] courteous and attentive*
820   Forsothe in bed lay.
The Kyng bede, "Undo!"   *Open the door*
The Lady asshes, "Querto?"   *asks, "For whom?"*
He sayd, "I am comun here, loe,
    In derne for to play."   *In secret to make love*
825   Ho sayd, "Have ye notte your aune Quene here,   *She; own*
And I my lord to my fere?   *as my mate*
Tonyghte more neghe ye me nere,   *nearer to me you should not be*
    In fayth, gif I may!"   *if*

"Undo the dur," quod the Kinge,   *door*
830   "For bi Him that made all thinge,
Thou schall have no harmynge
    Butte in thi none wille."   *But [all will be] at your own will*
Uppe rose a damesell squete,   *sweet*

	In the Kinge that ho lete.	*So that she might let in the King*
835	He sette him downe on hur beddus fete,	
	And talkes so hur tille,	*in this way to her*
	Sayd, "Medame, my knyghte	
	Mun lye wyth the all nyghte	*Must lie with you*
	Til tomorne atte days lighte —	
840	Take hit on non ille.	*in no bad way*
	For als evyr myghte I the,	*thrive (i.e., on my life)*
	Thou schall harmeles be:	*blameless*
	We do hit for a wedde fee,	*bet*
	The stryve for to stylle."	*contest; put an end to*

845	Thenne the Kyng sayd to his knyghte,	
	"Sone that thou were undyghte,	*[I command] immediately; undressed*
	And in yondur bedde ryghte!	
	Hie the gud spede!"	*Hasten with all speed*
	The knyghte did as he him bade,	
850	And qwenne ho se him unclad,	*when she saw*
	Then the Lady wex drede,	
	Worlyke in wede.	*Excellent among women (lit., "in clothes")*
	He sayd, "Lye downe prevely hur by,	*close by her*
	Butte neghe noghte thou that Lady;	*touch not*
855	For and thou do, thou schall dey	*if; die*
	For thi derfe dede;	*grievous*
	Ne noghte so hardy thou stur,	*Nor be so bold that you become aroused*
	Ne onus turne the to hur."	*Nor once make advances*
	The tother sayd, "Nay, sur!"	
860	For him hade he drede.	*Of him; awe*

	Thenne the Kyng asshet a chekkere,	*called for a chessboard*
	And cald a damesel dere;	
	Downe thay sette hom in fere	*themselves together*
	Opon the bedsyde.	
865	Torches was ther mony lighte,	*lighted*
	And laumpus brennyng full bryghte;	
	Butte notte so hardy was that knyghte	
	His hede onus to hide.	*once to get under the bedclothes*
	Butte fro thay began to play	*from the time*
870	Quyle on the morun that hit was day,	*Until; when it was daylight*

142

	Evyr he lokette as he lay,	*watched out*
	Baudewynne to byde.	*await*
	And erly in the dawyng	
	Come thay home from huntyng,	
875	And hertis conne thay home bring,	*did*
	And buckes of pride.	*outstanding*
	Thay toke this venesun fyne	
	And hade hit to kechine;	*had it brought*
	The Kinge sende aftur Bawdewine,	
880	And bede him cum see.	
	To the chaumbur he takes the way:	
	He fyndus the King atte his play;	*playing chess*
	A knyghte in his bedde lay	
	Wyth his Lady.	
885	Thenne sayd the King opon highte,	*aloud*
	"Tonyghte myssutte I my knyghte,	*missed*
	And hithir folut I him ryghte.	*trailed; directly*
	Here funden is hee;	*discovered*
	And here I held hom bothe stille	*in their places*
890	For to do hom in thi wille.	*with them according to*
	And gif thou take hit now till ille,	*if; badly (i.e., as an insult)*
	No selcouthe thinge me!"	*wonder [it would seem to]*
	Then the King asshed, "Art thou wroth?"	*asked; angry*
	"Nay, Sir," he sayd, "wythouten othe,	
895	Ne wille the Lady no lothe.	*wish; any injury*
	I telle yo as quy —	*the reason why*
	For hitte was atte hur awen wille:	*by her own*
	Els thurt no mon comun hur tille.	*Otherwise no man would dare; to her*
	And gif I take hitte thenne to ille,	
900	Muche maugreve have I.	*dishonor incur*
	For mony wyntur togedur we have bene,	
	And yette ho dyd me nevyr no tene:	*she; injury*
	And ich syn schall be sene	*For each offense must be examined*
	And sette full sorely."	*established; solemnly*
905	The King sayd, "And I hade thoghte	*Yet; curiosity*
	Quy that thou wrathis the noghte,	*[To know] why you are not angry*

And fyndus him in bed broghte
  By thi Laydy."

Quod Bawdewyn, "And ye will sitte,   *If; tarry*
910 I schall do yo wele to witte."   *make you understand fully*
"Yisse!" quod the King, "I the hete,   *promise you*
  And thou will noghte layne."   *If; dissemble*
"Hit befelle in your fadur tyme,   *time of your fathers (ancestors)*
That was the Kyng of Costantyne,   *by the name of*
915 Purvayed a grete oste and a fyne   *Assembled; army*
  And wente into Spayne.
We werrut on a sawdan   *made war; sultan*
And all his londus we wan,   *captured*
And himselvun, or we blan.   *before we left off*
920 Then were we full fayn.   *glad*
I wos so lufd wyth the King,   *honored by*
He gaf me to my leding —   *a command*
Lordus atte my bidding   *Knights*
  Was buxum and bayne.   *ready and eager*

925 "He gafe me a castell to gete,   *hold*
Wyth all the lordschippus grete.   *attached rights of lordship*
I hade men atte my mete,   *in my household*
  Fyve hundryth and mo,
And no wemen butte thre,
930 That owre servandis schild be.   *should*
One was bryghtur of ble   *handsomer in looks*
  Then ther othir toe.   *those; two*
Toe were atte one assente: *Two were of a single will*
The thrid felow have thay hente;   *third companion; seized*
935 Unto a well ar thay wente,   *did they go*
  And says hur allso: *as follows*
'Sithin all the loce in the lise,   *praise in you lies*
Thou schall tyne thine aprise.'   *lose your renown*
And wurchun as the unwise,   *[they] acted foolishly*
940 And tite conne hur sloe.   *quickly did her slay*

"And for tho werkes were we wo,   *because of those acts; aggrieved*
Gart threte tho othir for to slo.   *[And] made a threat; to put to death*

144

Thenne sayd the tone of tho,   *the one*
  'Lette us have oure life,
945 And we schall atte your bidding be   *be at your pleasure*
As mycull as we all thre;   *As much; [were before]*
Is none of yaw in preveté   *None of you in the privacy of your bed*
  Schall have wontyng of wyfe.'   *sexual deprivation*
Thay held us wele that thay heghte,   *carried out for us; promised*
950 And dighte us on the daylighte,   *served*
And thayre body uch nyghte,   *[gave] each*
  Wythoutun any stryve.   *complaint*
The tone was more lovely   *The one*
That the tother hade envy: *So that*
955 Hur throte in sundur prevely   *asunder in secret*
  Ho cutte hitte wyth a knyfe.   *She; it*

"Muche besenes hade we   *Many pains*
How that best myghte be;   *be resolved*
Thay asshed cowuncell atte me   *asked advice*
960 To do hur to dede.   *To put her to death*
And I unsquarut and sayd, 'Nay!   *answered*
Loke furst qwatt hurselvun will say,   *what she herself*
Quether ho may serve us all to pay;   *Whether she; with satisfaction*
  That is a bettur rede.'   *plan*
965 Ther ho hette us in that halle   *promised*
To do all that a woman schild fall,   *be proper to*
Wele for to serve us all
  That stode in that stede.   *place*
Ho held us wele that ho heghte,   *She performed for us; promised*
970 And dighte us on the daylighte,   *served*
And hur body ich nyghte   *each night*
  Intill oure bed beed.   *[she] offered*

"And bi this tale I understode,
Wemen that is of mylde mode   *pleasant disposition*
975 And syne giffes hom to gode,   *then occupy themselves with*
  Mecull may ho mende;   *Much; she improve*
And tho that giffus hom to the ille,   *those; occupy themselves*
And sithin thayre folis will fullfill,   *then; faults; carry out*
I telle yo wele, be propur skille,   *with full assurance*

145

980	No luffe will inne hom lende.	*linger*
	Wyth gode wille grathely hom gete, [1]	
	Meke and mylde atte hor mete,	
	And thryvandly, wythoutun threte,	*happily; without distress*
	Joy atte iche ende.	*[There will be] joy at all events*
985	Forthi jelius schall I never be	*Therefore jealous*
	For no sighte that I see,	
	Ne no biurdes brighte of ble;	*Nor for no woman with good looks*
	Ich ertheli thinke hase ende."	*Each; thing*
	The King sayd, "Thou says wele.	
990	Sir," he sayd, "as have I sele,	*good luck*
	I will thou wote hit iche dele.	*I wish you to understand each detail*
	Therfore come I,	*Then, [when] I came*
	Thi Lady gret me to squere squyftelé,	*implored; swear immediately*
	Or I myghte gete entré,	*Before*
995	That ho schuld harmeles be,	*untouched*
	And all hur cumpany.	
	Then gerut I my knyghte	*made*
	To go in bed wyth the biurde bryghte,	*woman*
	On the fur syde of the lighte,	*(i.e., a distance from her)*
1000	And lay hur dowun by.	*beside her*
	I sette me doune hom besyde,	*them*
	Here the for to abide;	*you to await*
	He neghit nevyr no naked syde	*got near*
	Of thi Lady.	
1005	"Forthi, of jelusnes, be thou bold, [2]	
	Thine avow may thou hold.	
	Butte of tho othir thinges that thou me told	
	I wold wete more:	*know*
	Quy thou dredus notte thi dede	*Why; fear; death*
1010	Ne non that bitus on thi brede?	*Nor none who eat*
	As evyr brok I my hede,	*As ever I keep my head (i.e., on my life)*

---

[1] Lines 981–82: *With good will, keep them firmly under supervision, / Meek and mild at home (at their meals)*

[2] *Therefore, as far as jealousy is concerned, be assured*

Thi yatis are evyr yare!"   *Your gates; ready [for guests]*
Quod Bawdewyn, "I schall yo telle:
Atte the same castell
1015   Quere this antur befelle,   *Where this adventure*
       Besegitte we ware.   *Beseiged*
On a day we usshet oute   *One day; issued*
And toke presonerus stoute;
The tone of owre feloys hade doute,   *one; companions became fearful*
1020   And durst notte furthe fare.   *forth*

"The caytef crope into a tunne   *coward crept; barrel*
That was sette therowte in the sunne.   *outside*
And there come fliand a gunne,   *flying a missile*
       And lemet as the levyn,   *gleamed; lightning*
1025   Lyghte opon hitte, atte the last,   *[And] landed on it*
       That was fastnut so fast;   *closed up*
All in sundur hit brast,
       In six or in sevyn.
And there hit sluye him als —   *killed; as well*
1030   And his hert was so fals!
Sone the hed fro the hals,   *Immediately; neck*
       Hit lyputt full evyn.   *jumped right off*
And we come fro the feghting
Sowunde, wythoutun hurting,   *Uninjured*
1035   And then we lovyd the King   *praised*
       That heghhest was in hevyn.

"Then owre feloys con say,   *companions did*
'Schall no mon dee or his day,   *die before*
Butte he cast himselfe away   *Except; throw*
1040   Throgh wontyng of witte.'   *lack*
And there myne avow made I —   *resolution*
So dyd all that cumpany —
For dede nevyr to be drery: *death; anxious*
       Welcum is hit —
1045   Hit is a kyndely thing."   *It; natural*
"Thou says soth," quod the King,
"Butte of thi thryd avowyng
       Telle me quych is hit,   *how is it*

147

Quy thi mete thou will notte warne | *Why; food; deny*
1050 To no levand barne?" | *living person*
"Ther is no man that may hit tharne — | *lose (miss the point)*
Lord, ye schall wele wete. | *understand*

"For the sege aboute us lay stille; | *siege; remained yet*
We hade notte all atte oure wille [1]
1055 Mete and drinke us to fille:
Us wontutte the fode. | *For us food was lacking*
So come in a messyngere,
Bade, 'Yild uppe all that is here!' | *[And] commanded, "Yield*
And speke wyth a sturun schere [2]
1060 'I nyll, by the Rode!'
I gerutte him bide to none, | *had him wait till afternoon*
Callud the stuard sone, | *[I]; steward immediately*
Told him all as he schuld done, | *that he should do*
As counsell is gud;
1065 Gerutte trumpe on the wall, | *[I] staged a fanfare*
And coverd burdes in the hall; | *had tables set*
And I myself emunge hom all | *among them*
As a king stode.

"I gerut hom wasshe; to mete wente. | *had them wash up; to the meal [we] went*
1070 Aftur the stuard then I sente:
I bede that he schuld take entente | *commanded; care*
That all schuld well fare — | *eat well*
Bede bringe bred plenté, | *roast meat*
And wine in bollus of tre, | *wood*
1075 That no wontyng schuld be | *lack*
To lasse ne to mare. | *less*
We hade no mete butte for on day — | *food; one*
Hit come in a nobull aray. | *came (was served)*
The messyngere lokit ay | *was ever watchful*
1080 And se hom sle care. | *saw them put care aside*
He toke his leve atte mete. | *at (after) the meal*

---

[1] Lines 1054–55: *By no means were we able to fulfill / Our need for meat and drink*
[2] Lines 1059–60: *And [I] replied in a stern manner, / 'I will not, by the Cross!'*

We gerutte him drinke atte the gate,   *insisted he*
And gafe him giftus grete,
 And furthe con he fare.   *did; go*

1085 "But quen the messyngere was gone,   *when*
These officers ichone   *each one*
To me made thay grete mone,   *complaint*
 And drerely con say —   *gloomily did*
Sayd, 'In this howse is no bred,
1090 No quyte wine nyf red;   *white; nor*
Yo behoves yild uppe this stid   *You must yield; castle*
 And for oure lyvys pray.'   *lives*
Yette God helpus ay his man!   *always*
The messyngere come agayn than   *returned then*
1095 Wythoute to the chevytan,   *Outside to his captain*
 And sone conne he say: *immediately did*
'Thoghe ye sege this sevyn yere,   *lay siege*
Castell gete ye none here,
For thay make als mury chere   *as merry festivity*
1100 Als hit were Yole Day!'   *As if; Yule*

"Then the messyngere con say,   *did*
'I rede yo, hie yo hethin away, *advise; hasten you from here*
For in your oste is no play, *your own army; abundance*
 Butte hongur and thurst.'
1105 Thenne the king con his knyghtis calle.   *did*
Sethin to cowunsell wente thay all —   *Then*
'Sythin no bettur may befall, *[He said] Since nothing better may come*
 This hald I the best.'   *This [course]*
Evyn atte the mydnyghte,   *Just*
1110 Hor lordis sembelet to a syghte, *Their; assembled at a place*
That were hardy and wighte: *Who; powerful*
 Thay remuyt of hor rest. *moved from their resting place*
Mete laynes mony lakke: *Food covers over many a lack*
And there mete hor sege brake, *broke down their siege*
1115 And gerut hom to giffe us the bake; *caused them to turn their backs on us*
 To preke thay were full preste. *To gallop off; eager*

149

	"And then we lokit were thay lay	*where they had been*
	And see oure enmeys away.	
	And then oure felawis con say,	*did*
1120	The lasse and the mare,	
	'He that gode may gete	*who goods may possess*
	And wernys men of his mete,	*denies*
	Gud Gode that is grete	
	Gif him sory care!	
1125	For the mete of the messyngere,	*feeding*
	Hit mendutte all oure chere.'"	*made better; outlook*
	Then sayd the King, that thay myghte here,	
	And sqwythely con square,	*vehemently did swear*
	"In the conne we fynde no fabull;	*In you do we; falsehood*
1130	Thine avowes arne profetabull."	*well taken*
	And thus recordus the Rownde Tabull,	*bears witness*
	The lasse and the more.	
	Thenne the Kinge and his knyghtis all,	
	Thay madun myrthe in that halle.	
1135	And then the Lady conne thay calle,	*did*
	The fayrist to fold;	*embrace*
	Sayde Bawdewyn, "And thou be wise,	*[The King] said [to]; If*
	Take thou this Lady of price —	*worthy*
	For muche love in hur lyce —	*lies*
1140	To thine hert hold.	*bind [her]*
	Ho is a biurde full bryghte,	*She; woman; handsome*
	And therto semely to thy sighte.	
	And thou hase holdin all that thou highte,	*carried out; promised*
	As a knighte schulde!"	
1145	Now Jhesu Lord, Hevyn Kynge,	
	He graunt us all His blessynge,	*[May] He*
	And gife us all gode endinge,	
	That made us on the mulde.	*earth*

Amen.

150

Notes

Abbreviations: Ir = Ireland MS; R = Robson's edition; FH = French and Hale's edition; B = Brookhouse's edition; D = Dahood's edition. See Select Bibliography for these editions.

1   *He that made us on the mulde.* This first line of *Avowyng* virtually repeats the final line of the poem (*That made us on the mulde*), linking its beginning to its ending and emphasizing the symmetries of structure. Such echoic repetition occurs as well in *Awntyrs* (see lines 1 and 714–15 and notes), *Sir Gawain and the Green Knight*, *Pearl*, and *Patience*.

2   *fair.* FH: *fare.*

13   *wice.* R, B: *wite.*

22   *Kyndenesse and.* Ir: *Kyndenesse of*; I emend for sense.

24   *wayt men and wise.* D emends to *waythmen* (i.e., "hunters") *wise.*

25   *thay.* Ir: *tha*; FH, B emend to *thay*; D retains Ir's reading.

29   *Carlele.* Many of the Arthurian verse romances, and especially those involving Gawain, name Carlisle as a habitual northern court for the Knights of the Round Table. The mention of Inglewood Forest (line 65) and Gawain's vow to keep watch at the Tarn Wathelene (line 132) further localize the action in Cumberland. *Ragnelle, Carlisle, Awntyrs, Greene Knight*, as well as the ballad versions of the first two, all mention Carlisle as the seat of Arthur's court, as do Malory, *Lancelot of the Laik*, and the two poems on Arthur's death, the *Stanzaic Morte Arthur* and the *Alliterative Morte Arthure.*

40   *bandus.* D emends to *boundus* for sake of rhyme.

43   *moue*. R, FH, B: *mone*. The letter formation makes either "u" or "n" plausible; I follow D's reading.

46   *offellus*. Ir: *of fellus*; D reads the latter as one word, and so makes sense of the line.

48   *frith*. R, B read *frithe*. R and B frequently read final scribal stroke as "e"; I have usually indicated such readings only where at least one other edition agrees.

54   *he*. B prints *be* without explanation.

61   *luffe*. D emends to *lusse* in this line, and to *tusse* and *busse* in lines 62 and 63. While his emendations are ingenious and to a large degree persuasive, they are not necessary. The manuscript readings make more than minimal sense, and the position of the three words as rhymes gives their forms additional authority.

74   *Bowdewynne of Bretan*. I assume that the popular romances mean this character to be identical with the "Byschope Bawdewyn" who appears in *Carlisle*, in the same way that Malory seems to understand Sir Baudwen of Bretayne and "the ermyte [hermit], sir Bawdewyn of Bretayne" as the same person. See line 914 and note below, and notes at *Carlisle*, line 28 and *Turke*, line 54.

78   *buirnes*. The three strokes that make up "ui" can be read as several possible letter combinations; R, B give *biurnes* here and at 703. The spelling at line 563 (*burne*) confirms the present reading.

79   *alle*. B, D read *all*.

83   *hunter*. Here and at line 105 the word ending is abbreviated; at line 113 the full form is given as *hunter*. Though the usual scribal spelling for this termination is *-ur* (as in *undur*, *sekur*, *wyntur*, and so on), I follow D in expanding the word as *hunter*.

100   *rafte*. Ir: *raste*, so R, B; I follow emendation of FH, which D prints without comment.

101   *rennyng*. Ir: *rengnyng*, with a mark under the first *g* to indicate excision.

110   *Butte sette my hed.* FH emends to *I sette my hed.* The hunter uses an emphatic phrase, similar to "I'll stake my neck on it."

118   *Myne avow make I.* Arthur's vow and the subsequent hunt apparently have no specific sources in other romances, though boar hunts occur in *Sir Gawain and the Green Knight* and other popular narratives.

127   *make your avowe.* The act of making a public vow (or boast, or "gab"), often in competition with other knights, occurs in twelfth-century *chansons de geste* such as *Le Pelerinage de Charlemagne* (perhaps imitated in *Cornwall*), as well as in a well-known scene in Jacques de Longuyon's *Les Voeux du Paön* [*The Vows of the Peacock*], an early fourteenth-century romance. On the connection of vows to chivalric practice and literary portrayals, see Gail Orgelfinger, "The Vows of the Pheasant and Late Chivalric Ritual," pp. 611–43 in *The Study of Chivalry*, ed. Howell Chickering and Thomas H. Seiler, TEAMS publications (Kalamazoo: Medieval Institute, 1988); Orgelfinger provides translations of vows made by actual and fictional knights, as well as a full discussion of their contexts.

131   *Tarne Wathelan.* The Tarn Wathelene was a lake within Englewood Forest; see line 29 above and note, and *Awntyrs*, line 2 and note.

132   *To wake hit all nyghte.* Gawain's vow to watch, or carry out an all-night "wake," at the Tarn implies a willingness to encounter supernatural forces. The ghost of Guenevere's mother rises to meet Gawain and Guenevere from the Tarn in *Awntyrs*. Gawain meets strange foes at water crossings in other romances, such as *Sir Gawain and the Green Knight* and Chrétien's *Yvain* (and in the Middle English version, *Ywain and Gawain*).

133 ff.   Kay's windy recklessness, and his seemingly inevitable humiliation, are a stock motif in popular Arthurian romances; in the present volume, this pattern occurs in *Carlisle*, *Carle*, *Gologras*, *Turke*, and *Marriage*.

135   *Quoso.* Ir, D: *Quose.* I emend the form since it is inconsistent with scribal spelling, though it is at times difficult to distinguish scribal *e* from *o*; compare note at line 160.

137 ff.   Baldwin's vows, offered merely to close off the exchange, have a proverbial ring, and recall a number of literary and folk traditions; D (p. 33) connects them

specifically to the cycle of the Three Wise Counsels, a widespread motif of three oaths or admonitions.

143   *Ne.* R, FH, B read Ir as *Ne*; D gives *Ore* without comment.

149   *bore.* FH: *bare.*

150   *wythoutun any.* Ir: *wyth any*; FH, B, D all emend for sense. I follow D's scribal spelling.

151   *fore.* D emends to *fare.*

156   *Sum that.* FH emends to *Quer that.*

160   *The* Ir: *Tho*; so R, B; FH emends for sense. D reads apparent *o* here and elsewhere as *e.*

165   *hold.* D, arguing that scribal *e* and *o* are difficult to distinguish from one another, reads *held*, which fits the rhyme slightly better.

168   *spillutte hom on gode spede.* Ir: *spillutte on hom gode spede.* I emend the word order on the basis of sense and syntax since *spill* almost never occurs as a verbal phrase with a preposition, and *on* (or *in*) (*good*) *speed* is a common phrase (see OED, *speed* sb. 7a).

193   *spanos.* D: *spanes.*

196   *sekir.* FH reads *seker.*

204   *he myghte evyr hit fele.* D, following suggestion of FH, emends to *he evyr hit feld*, for the sake of rhyme and meter.

206   *He sturd.* I understand the subject here to be Arthur, caught in his saddle as his horse falls to the ground. It would be possible, however, to take *He* as referring to the mount, with the implication that the horse never returned from the hunt.

207   *Jhesu.* Here and at line 1145 D reads *Iesu.*

212   *ware.* D emends to *were.*

Notes

218   *Squithe*. D reads *Squith*.

227   *victoré*. R, B read *vittore*.

229   *wroth*. B: *wrote*.

231   Medieval religious exposition and popular narrative both connect the devil (and the eternal fires of hell) with kitchens and cooking.

243   *nevyr*. B: *hevyr*.

250   *hade*. Ir: *hade*, though unclear (so R, FH); B: *made*; D: *had* (without comment).

254 ff.   Arthur's eagerness to *brittun him* corresponds to the "assay" or breaking of the deer, described in detail in *Ragnelle* (lines 46 ff., and line 48 and note), *Carlisle* (line 31 and note), and *Sir Gawain and the Green Knight* (lines 1325 ff.). The ritual of butchering is not simply a matter of technical knowledge, but a display of the rule-bound nature of the hunt that makes it a hallmark of aristocratic identity; Arthur's performance here, within the precincts of the royal forests, is an exemplary demonstration of his kingly demeanor.

258   *Colurt*. B: *Tholurt*. The precise meaning of this verb is not clear, though it would appear to describe some feature of the ritual butchering — perhaps the removal of the head, or the carving of the shoulders; the word occurs again (*colurt*) at line 482.

263   *thonge*. Ir: *yonge*; so R, FH, B, D. D's long discussion of the crux reaches no conclusion, and I emend (according to suggestion in FH) to *thonge* as offering the best sense.

266   *hur*. R, B read *her*.

267   *Sayd*. FH reads *Says*.

273 ff.   This stanza clearly lacks one quatrain, with the consequence that the *Avowyng*'s perfectly symmetrical division into two parts (lines 1–572, and lines 573–1048) is off by four lines. Spearing, Burrow, and Johnson have drawn attention to this feature of the poem's structural meaning.

275 *for*. Ir: *fro*; I follow emendation of FH.

279 *birde*. FH: *brede*.

280 *Ho*. R, FH, B read *Ho*; D reads *He* and emends to *Ho*.

286 *all*. R, FH read *alle*.

295 *biurde*. D: *buirde*, but scribal spelling at lines 458, 463 (*byurde*) makes *biurde* preferable here (so R, FH, B) and in other occurrences at lines 508, 734, 987, 998, and 1141.

297 *skille*. B, D: *skill*. Here and elsewhere D reads the characteristic final flourish by the scribe as without significance, and so prints *skill*; the flourish here differs very little from other cases — e.g., *tille* (line 285) and its rhymes, or *Quille* (line 286) — and so I follow earlier editors in retaining final *e* in some cases where D has rejected it. Compare also lines 966, 967, where omission of final *e* seems scribal.

298 *atte thi wille*. Scribal letter forms and strokes are especially hard to distinguish in the final phrase; R: *at thi wille*; FH: *atte thi wille*; B: *at the will*; D: *atte thi will*.

300 *that*. Ir: *the*; so R, B, D. FH emends to *that*.

305 *tother*. FH reads *tothur*.

307 ff. *Sir Menealfe of the Mountayn / My gode fadur highte*. No other character, knightly or otherwise, named Menealfe occurs in medieval Arthurian literature. D notes the possible components (*man + elf*), and this resonant hybrid connects Menealfe with other Arthurian opponents, like Sir Gromer Somer Jour in *Ragnelle* and *Turke*, who seem to have preternatural or folk antecedents. D also points out that the encounter at the Tarn or lake resembles Celtic ford combats, though these proliferate in chivalric romance, as when Gawain faces strange opponents at almost every water crossing in *Sir Gawain and the Green Knight*: "At uche warthe other water ther the wyghe passed, / He fonde a foo hym byfore, bot ferly it were" (lines 715–16: At each ford or stream where he passed, it was a wonder if he did not face a foe in front of him). See also note on line 132 above. The syntax and word formation leave the meaning of line

308 unclear: it can mean "Menealfe my godfather named [me]" (as D interprets the line), or "Menealfe my good father was named," implying an hereditary title of sorts and an identical name for the present speaker (as understood here).

310   *Ledelle.* D identifies this with Liddel Strength (or Liddel Mote), a fortification about ten miles north of Carlisle, on the Liddel River, at the border of Scotland and England.

311   *I felle.* Ir: *he felle*, corrected from *hur selle*; R, FH, D, give the former, B the latter. I emend to *I* to maintain the first-person character of the statement and the continuity of the speech (which D repunctuates).

313 ff. Menealfe's "talk," which leads to fighting and bloodshed, is itself another clear instance of the knightly speech acts that are at the center of *Avowyng.* Menealfe's words deliberately offended the honor of the woman's kin, leading to combat and the "capture" of the woman.

319   *wurch.* R, B: *wurche.*

333   *wonun.* So Ir, followed by R, B, D; FH: *wonnen.*

335   *of his othir.* Ir: *of othir*; I follow emendation suggested by FH.

349   *Torne.* D: *Terne*, for the sake of rhyme and phonology.

350   *thorne.* D reads *therne.*

351   *yorne.* D reads *yerne.*

352   *there.* D emends to *thare.*

355   *lawes.* This word has presented problems to readers, since its conventional meaning does not seem appropriate here. The form does not invite emendation because of its position in the rhyme. FH suggests the meaning "surety," or it might be possible to construe it as a reference to Gawain's reputation as "fyne fader of nurture" (*Sir Gawain and the Green Knight*, line 919), the father or source of the laws of courtesy. D's solution is to see *lawes* as a plural of *laa* (line 405).

378 *The tother*. Ir: *To tother*, so R, FH, B; I follow D's emendation, reflecting scribal phrasing at lines 517 and 799.

380 *hit cheve*. Ir: *hit chevis*, so R, FH, B; I follow D in emending for rhyme.

381 *kithun*. Ir: *kithum*; so R, B, D. FH reads *kithiun*. I emend to normalized form, as in line 417.

382 *aythir*. B: *authir*.

385 *thay*. Ir: *tha*, so R, D; FH, B emend.

390 *Squithe*. D reads *Squith*.

394 *raunnsun*. R, B, D read the ambiguous set of minims as *rauunsun*; FH gives *raunnsum*. I offer what seems the more likely scribal spelling.

417 *kithun*. Ir: *kithum*; I emend as in line 381.

  thayre. Ir: *thay*, so R; FH, B, D emend.

419 *togedur*. So R, B, D; FH adds final *e* which is not legible.

421 *ther*. Ir: *that*, so R, B; FH, D emend.

422 *from*. R, B read *fro*.

425 ff. Kay's taunting of Menealfe here, earlier at lines 393 ff., and later at lines 429 ff. and 445 ff., constitutes a vivid if ungracious example of the linkage between knightly honor and speech acts. Kay "talkes . . . him tille" with "wurdes kene" (lines 448, 453) in order to assert his superiority over the fallen knight, if only through Gawain's agency. Gawain's own reserve and his implicit rebuke of Kay (lines 433 ff. and 449 ff.) demonstrate his own understated courtesy. See lines 313 ff. and note.

432 *for tente*. B glosses as "intent," which seems not at all to fit the context. D reads the two words as one, *fortente*, and glosses as "utterly lost." I understand *tente* as from the same root (meaning "lost"), but as past participle used as adjective; see OED, *tine* v.2, and *tint* p.pl.a.

442   *harmes*. FH reads *hapnes* (i.e., "chances").

472   *Hit*. Ir: *His*; so R, FH, B, D. I emend for the sake of sense and idiom.

477   Next to this line at the right margin the scribe has written *Primus Passus*, and then left a gap of two lines to indicate a break. A similar rubric occurs at line 765 (see note). These markers divide *Avowyng* into sections of 476, 288, and 384 lines, perhaps indicating convenient performance sessions. They do not, however, correspond to the striking structural divisions of the poem, in particular to the decisive break at the precise mid-point (line 573). See introduction and lines 273 ff. and note.

481   *funde*. So Ir, R, B, D; FH emends to *fande* for rhyme.

482   *hande*. Ir: *hunde*, so R, B; FH, D emend.

489   *Kay the venesun*. Ir: *Kay to the venesun*, with *to* marked for excision.

491 ff. The conjunction here of *the birde* and *the brede* that *To Carlele thay bringe* as trophies suggests clearly the status of this nameless woman as a marker of chivalric honor among famous men. Menealfe first told Kay how he had "wan" her (line 316), provoking Kay to try to win her for himself. After ransoming Kay, Gawain gladly agrees to a second course "For hur for to fighte" (line 416); when he wins, he consigns the woman's fate to the judgment of Queen Guenevere (lines 454 ff.), though she remains in Menealfe's custody. As the prize of Kay's and Gawain's forest adventures, she is bracketed here with the dead meat of the King's hunt. Though noble and a "fayre may" (line 446), she stands as a direct counterpart to the laundress exchanged among the five hundred soldiers in Baldwin's barracks story (lines 909 ff.).

499   *anturis*. The scribe's letter combinations are sometimes ambiguous, especially *-rus* and *-ris* (e.g., *berus*, line 529); here, however, the compression of the writing seems to indicate *anturis*, though FH gives *anturus*.

503   *wonun*. FH: *wonnen*.

511   *wyth a mylde chere*. B: *wyth mylde chere*, omitting the article.

159

516   *thou me sayn.* D emends to *thou mon sayn* (i.e., "you must say"), for the sake of sense.

529   *berus.* FH reads *beris.*

530   *ladise.* B: *ladies.*

537 ff.   Menealfe's submission to the judgment of Queen Guenevere recalls the situation of the knight-rapist of Chaucer's Wife of Bath's Tale (a version of the *Ragnelle* story), whose fate is determined by Arthur's Queen and her ladies.

542   *werre.* B: *were.*

567   *The.* FH reads *Tho.*

571   *priveabull.* The scribe abbreviates the prefix, and the indistinct scribal spelling has produced a variety of editorial readings. R: *preuabulle*; D: *preueabull*; FH: *priueabull*; B: *preuabull*. I follow FH in expanding according to the scribal spelling at line 19.

573   *ar.* FH reads *are.*

573 ff.   The first test of Baldwin's vows, the ambush devised by Kay, parallels episodes in Malory and other popular romances.

584   *How best myghte be.* Just what Arthur wishes for here is unclear: how he might best find out the meaning of Baldwin's oath, or what plan would be most satisfactory, or how things might be arranged for the best in general, are all plausible readings for the line.

589   *comande.* R, B read *couande.*

591   *no wrunge.* D emends to *no schande* (i.e., "shame") to preserve the rhyme.

599   *fele.* I take this as a form of *fellen*, "to overcome or kill," as in line 311, *felle*, rather than as a form of *fele*, "to feel or perceive." The constraints of the rhyme help to account for the unusual spelling, and what amounts to a double negative in *none . . . but* complicates the lines' meaning. The import is, "Any

one of you, no one excepted, he may overcome, whom he happens to light upon."

610   *gowuns*. R, B: *gownus*.

610 ff.   The decision by Kay and his five accomplices to wear *Gay gowuns of grene* in setting up the ambush of Baldwin suggests that they intend to disguise themselves; their further attempt to cover themselves with capes, as *uncowthe men*, confirms this. The choice of green costumes may correspond to the conventional garb of highwaymen and forest outlaws like Robin Hood, who are said to dress in green. In any case, the unchivalrous assault in uneven numbers, the attempt to hide (line 621), and the assumption of an ignoble identity (*uncowthe men*) make clear that this is not, like the combats between Kay and Menealfe and Gawain and Menealfe, a knightly encounter; see also line 643 and note.

622   *se*. R, FH, B: *so*; D reads *se* (FH's suggested emendation).

623   *Come*. B: *Thome*, mistaking (as at line 258) the scribe's initial *C*.

632   *adrede*. Ir: *dredus*, so R, FH, B. D emends to *drede*; I follow FH's suggested emendation.

643   *herdmen hinde*. FH glosses as "gentle retainers"; B glosses neither word; D's separate glosses give "valiant knights." This seems not a compliment, but fighting words on Baldwin's part as he prepares to fight six antagonists; as an insult, it strips these disguised knights who far outnumber him of any claim to noble status, and deprives them of any possible honor in the combat that ensues. Baldwin's affront is an instance of the specialized insult to honor that precipitates and defines chivalric conflict; Sir Menealfe refers to this earlier (line 313 f.): "So I talket hom tille / That muche blode conne I spille." MED, *hine* n., gives only one instance of the spelling *hind* (in a Chaucer text); by the sixteenth century this was the common spelling, and the contemptuous phrase *hired hines*, often in association with *herdis* or herdsmen, was common in Middle English.

659   *folde*. Ir: *foldes*. I follow D in emending to *folde* for the sake of rhyme.

668   *In hie in*. B: *In his in*.

671   *Bawdewin.* Ir: *Bawewin*; R, B: *Bawdewin* without note; FH, D emend to *Bawdewin*.

687   *Als squithur.* D emends to *Als squith as* for the sake of grammatical convention.

691   *before none.* Here and at lines 719 and 1061, I take *none* to mean not "noon," but "none," one of the seven canonical hours (or prescribed times of daily prayer), often used colloquially to designate a time of day. None was the ninth hour (counting from matins at 6 a.m.), or 3 p.m., so that *before none* would indicate early afternoon rather than late morning.

701 ff. The test of Baldwin's largesse resembles the spectacle of public courtesy portrayed in *Sir Gawain and the Green Knight, Carlisle,* and the two episodes of *Gologras,* though these other romances make the event as much a test of the guest's courtesy as of the host's.

703   *buirne.* R, B: *biurne.*

710   *cummawunde.* D reads *commawunde.*

712   *there.* D emends to *thare* for the sake of rhyme.

715   *For thi wareson.* FH glosses as "on your eternal welfare"; Arthur's injunction here seems to be much more limited, referring to his own favor.

765   The scribe again indicates a division in the narrative; "fitte" occurs in popular narratives as the equivalent of "passus" (see line 477 and note). It marks a division or apportioning of the story, though whether it signals a less decisive turn than "passus" (as D remarks, line 476 and note) seems unclear.

777   *on him logh.* In a chivalric shame culture, any public gesture constitutes socially meaningful behavior. To laugh aloud might therefore either be an act of gracious inclusiveness (as in the recurrent laughter of *Sir Gawain and the Green Knight*), or of scornful exclusion. That Baldwin laughs *on him* — privately — removes his act from the public forum of chivalric honor; this stands in contrast, for example, to the spectacle of the speech act Arthur has just performed, "wyth a blythe chere" and "opon highte."

781 ff. The far-fetched prank that Arthur devises to test Baldwin's private courtesy appears to be an inversion of the bed trick. Rather than secretly introducing a substitute for the anticipated lover on the wedding night (as when Isolde induces Brangane to take her place in bed with King Mark), Arthur's trick consists in an overt supplanting of the husband in the marital act. Though the retainer has spent the entire night in Baldwin's wife's bed, rendering her technically unfaithful, there are no sexual relations. The situation resembles the test imposed by the Carle of Carlisle, who puts Gawain in bed with his own wife (*Carlisle*, lines 445 ff.), and to a lesser extent Lady Bertilak's "capture" of Gawain in bed in *Sir Gawain and the Green Knight*, which takes place while her lord (like Baldwin) is off on a hunt.

787 *best*. D reads *beste*.

808 *litill rechs*. FH reads *litille reche*.

818 *ful*. B: *full*.

821 *Undo*. Ir: *Unto*; emended as in the present text by all editors.

827 ff. This statement by Baldwin's wife combines her wish and determination; reversing the lines, she says in effect, "In faith, if I have any sway in the matter, tonight you should not be (any) more near to me (than you are right now)."

829 *dur*. FH reads *dore*.

830 B misnumbers line 831, so that from here to end his numeration is off by one line; references to B in these notes are to actual (not misnumbered) lines.

837 *Sayd*. D reads *Sayde*.

856 *dede*. B: *ded*.

876 *And buckes*. FH: *And x buckes* (ten bucks), indicating in a note that the Roman numeral is uncertain.

879 *sende*. Ir: *sonde*, so R, FH, B. D claims this is an ambiguous letter form, and reads as *sende*. I emend for sense.

     aftur. R, B: *after*.

895   Baldwin's remark implies that he sees here no obligation to redress an insult to his honor. Arthur's elaborately staged "infidelity" — in which the wife literally spends the night in bed with another man — attempts to compromise Baldwin's manly honor as a husband. Baldwin rejects the public character of the act — in which his wife's conduct would be an extension of his own social identity — insisting instead that it is a private matter, where she acts as a free agent on her own behalf. This seeming rejection of the values associated with a chivalric honor culture turns out not to be an assertion of women's autonomy, but (in the brutally misogynistic anecdote that follows) an assertion of women's ungovernable treachery.

900   *I. Ir: Y.* I have similarly normalized the first-person singular pronoun at line 992.

903   *And ich syn schall be sene.* I take this to be a statement of anti-feminist domestic prudence on Baldwin's part, not a moralizing claim for eternal justice (as FH, D).

909   *sitte.* D emends to *sette* on phonological grounds.

909 ff.   Versions of Baldwin's anecdote of the murderous laundresses occur in a fabliau, and in John of Garland's *Parisiana poetria* (ed. Traugott Lawler [New Haven and London: Yale University Press, 1974]). John (c. 1195 – c. 1258) was born in England and taught at Paris and Toulouse; the *Poetria* apparently dates from between 1220 and 1235. John provides a twelve-line summary of the story in prose, and then uses this plot to compose what he designates a representative instance of tragedy in verse, running one hundred twenty-six lines in hexameters (Lawler, pp. 136–43, with facing translation and notes).

914   *Costantyne.* There are two notable Constantines in Arthurian legend: one is Arthur's grandfather, the other the son of Sir Cador. I assume Baldwin's remark does not confuse Constantine with Arthur's father, but simply means "a generation or two ago." In Malory, before leaving for the campaign against Lucius, Arthur appoints as his two regents "Sir Baudwen of Bretayne, an auncient and an honorable knyght" and "Sir Cadore," father of "Sir Constantyne that aftir was kynge, aftir Arthurs dayes" (*Works*, p. 195). This link between Baldwin and Constantine's father in one version of Arthurian chronicle may account for the association between Baldwin and the other

Constantine (Arthur's grandfather) mentioned here. *Carlisle* also mentions a "Syr Costantyn" among its roster of Arthurian knights (line 44 and note).

922   *leding.* See OED, *leading* sb.1, 2, for the technical sense of this word as "command" in a martial context.

943   *sayd.* FH reads *says.*

944   *oure.* D reads *our.*

951   *uch.* R, FH, B: *uche.*

956   *Ho.* D reads *He* and emends to *Ho,* the reading of R, FH, B.

965   *that.* Ir: *ther,* so R; B: *the;* FH, D emend to *that.*

966   *fall.* R, FH read *falle.*

967   *all.* R, FH read *alle.*

971   *ich.* R, FH, B read *iche.*

976   *ho.* D emends to *tha* to preserve consistency of number.

980   *lende.* Ir: *lenge;* so R, FH, B. I follow D's emendation, for the sake of rhyme.

982   *atte hor mete.* R, B read *atte her mete.*

983   *And thryvandly.* Ir: *Thryvandly.* I follow FH in adding the conjunction to preserve continuity. See note on line 984.

984   *Joy.* Ir: *And joy.* I follow FH in removing *and* to beginning of previous line. See note on line 983.

985   *jelius.* FH: *jeluis.*

996   *hur.* FH reads *hire.*

998   *bryghte.* D prints *brighte* without comment.

999   *fur.* FH reads *far.*

1003   The double negative seems here to underscore that the nameless knight was neither in proximity to the wife's naked body, nor anywhere near any particular part (*naked syde*) of her body.

1007   *thinges.* FH reads *thingus.*

1009   *thou.* B: *u*, apparently missing the initial letters.

1010   *Ne.* FH reads *No.*

1011   *evyr.* FH, B indicate that the first two letters are indecipherable (as they are on microfilm), and emend; D states that the letter impressions are visible on the parchment, and gives this as his reading.

1013 ff.   This moralizing story on the fate of the timid apparently has no specific source.

1019   *feloys.* D reads *feloys*; R, FH, B read *foloys* and emend.

1040   *Throgh.* R, FH, B read *Throghe*; I follow D in not reading final *e.*

1051   D punctuates to make this line part of Arthur's speech. My punctuation makes it the beginning of Baldwin's reply to the king.

1051 ff.   The episode of the duped emissary has many parallels; D (p. 33) points out examples from classical history and poetry, and from medieval chronicles and tales.

1057   *come in a. in* appears inserted above line in Ir; R, B: *come a.*

1077   *for on day.* B reads *for one day.*

1079   *messyngere.* FH: *messungere.*

1081   *mete.* Ir, FH: *me*; R, B, D emend for sense to *mete.* D offers a phonological justification for the seeming off-rhyme.

1090   *nyf red.* FH emends to *ner red* (i.e., "nor red"), a more common form of the phrase.

1098   *Castell.* R, FH: *Castelle*; though again the scribe's final flourish is ambiguous, I follow the reading of B and D.

1099   *mury.* R, B: *mirry.*

1102   *hethin.* R, B: *hethinne*; FH reads *hethinn.* I follow D's reading.

1105   *calle.* D reads *call* without comment.

1106   *Sethin.* Here, and in the following line, editors differ in their reading of *sethin* and *sythin* as in *hethin* (line 1102).

          all. R, FH read *alle.*

1107   *befall.* R, FH read *befalle.*

1110   *to a syghte.* FH, B, D take this phrase to mean "in plain view"; I take it to mean "on a site." Lydgate uses a similar spelling; see OED *site* sb.2, 1.a.

1113   *Mete laynes mony lakke.* A proverbial line (noted also by D); see B. J. and J. W. Whiting, *Proverbs, Sentences, and Proverbial Phrases from English Writings Mainly before 1500* (Cambridge, Massachusetts: Harvard University Press, 1968), M472.

1126   *all.* R, FH read *alle.*

1128   *con square.* Ir: *con squere*, so R, FH, B. I follow D in emending to *square* for the sake of rhyme, though not in dropping *con.*

1131   *Tabull.* R, FH read *Tabulle.*

1133   *all.* R, FH read *alle.*

1134   *myrthe.* D: *myrth*, without comment.

1137   *Sayde.* FH: *Sayd.*

1139   *muche.* D: *much*, without comment.

1143   *holdin.* Editors differ in their readings here; see lines 1102, 1106 and notes, as well as scribal and editorial confusion at lines 333, 381, 417, and so on.

1146   *all.* R reads *alle.*

1147   *all.* R, FH read *alle.*

1148   This final line substantively repeats the first line of *Avowyng*, giving the poem a circular structure; see line 1 and note.

The Awntyrs off Arthur

Introduction

The Awntyrs off Arthur survives complete in four separate medieval manuscripts, none of which is based upon any of the other extant copies. Though its language and meter indisputably indicate northern composition — perhaps in Cumberland, whose seat is Carlisle — the four copies were made in different parts of England, including Yorkshire, the Midlands, and the London area. The number and pattern of surviving copies constitute material evidence that *Awntyrs* enjoyed a remarkable popularity outside (and also presumably within) the region in which it originated. Such popularity seems even more extraordinary since the poem did not begin as an oral tale, like *Ragnelle, Carlisle, Turke,* or the ballads. While its supernatural and chivalric storylines have affinities with popular tales, the complex rhyme scheme, narrative structure, written sources, allusions, and content demonstrate that *Awntyrs* was a distinctively literary effort. *Awntyrs* emerges from a transitional cultural context, in which a literate author has fully exploited oral stylistics and techniques.

Until fairly recently, editors and critics have regarded *Awntyrs* (meaning "adventures") as deficient in structural and thematic unity. The poem divides neatly — almost perfectly, according to Spearing's arguments — into two halves: the first part (lines 1–338) transforms a popular legend associated with Pope Gregory the Great — the Mass or Trental of Saint Gregory — into a chivalric episode. *Awntyrs* begins with the standard opening for a Gawain romance: as in *Ragnelle, Carlisle, Avowyng,* and other tales, Arthur and his companions go off to hunt in Inglewood Forest. The "adventure" of *Awntyrs,* its encounter with the alien, takes the form of a gothic fantasy: a ghost, described in screeching and grotesque detail, appears to Gawain and Guenevere at the Tarn Wathelene. The specter turns out to be the tormented soul of Guenevere's mother, who suffers now for the hidden sins of the flesh she committed on earth. The ghost laments the split within her own life, between a brilliant, splendid appearance and a fetid inner corruption, and then goes on to commend her own condition as a general warning to the entire court. She cautions Gawain and Guenevere, as representatives of the Round Table, that the conduct of knights and ladies must conform to Christian precept, and that the court must narrow the chasm between its excessive consumption and the desperate poverty that besets others in

169

the community: material and spiritual concerns must coincide. Her own visitation typifies this link, in her ghostly intervention into the worldly life of the court, and, perhaps more strikingly, in her requesting Masses for her soul, making clear that those still in the flesh may affect the fate of those in the spirit world.

The apparition passes and the hunt ends, and the second part (lines 339–702) follows a scenario familiar in chivalric romance: as Arthur and the Round Table are seated at dinner in Rondoles Halle, a strange knight enters, accuses Arthur and Gawain of being in false possession of his lands, and demands an honorable combat. Sir Galeron of Galloway's challenge falls to Sir Gawain — a fitting outcome, given Gawain's popular title as the Lord of Galloway during the Middle Ages and after. The narrative lingers over the courage, skill, and ferocity of the fight; neither knight can gain early victory, and each does great damage to his opponent. Just as Gawain seems at the point of a lethal triumph, Galeron's lady and then Guenevere intervene, and Arthur halts the combat. Galeron submits to Gawain's prowess (and to Arthur's lordship), but the king composes the dispute by assigning other lands to Gawain, and having his nephew restore lands to Galeron. Galeron marries his lady and becomes a knight of the Round Table. In the last stanza of *Awntyrs*, Guenevere arranges the Masses for her mother, and the poem ends with a verbal repetition of its opening line.

Though each part of *Awntyrs* presents a self-contained episode, they can be read not as autonomous, unconnected units, artificially or arbitrarily joined, but as narrative elements thematically linked by contrast and complementarity. Spearing has elegantly compared *Awntyrs* to a diptych — a conventional medieval form, in which two separate framed subjects are physically joined into a unity by a hinge; in such a doubled structure, meaning is produced not simply through a continuous harmony of parts, but through the collision this manifestly split structure sets up. A dialogic vision of this sort produces no rigidly moralized or single meaning, but "a potentiality for meaning," "a creative gesture in which the spectator or reader himself participates. Sparks leap across the gap between the two parts, and the on-looker's mind is set alight by them" (Spearing 1981, pp. 186–87).

The interactive reading strategy necessitated by this doubled structure locates the coherence of *Awntyrs* in the first part's unresolved conflicts of value, and in the way these conflicts then suffuse the battle of the second part. The physical grandeur of chivalric prowess and display appears projected through the filter of the spiritual imperatives stipulated by the ghost of Guenevere's mother. The first part exemplifies this allusive and contrastive dynamic even in its treatment of sources, for it recasts a popular tale of religious devotion (in which a monk-pope rescues his mother's soul from eternal torment) as a critique of the ideals and practice of the highest secular aristocracy. This dialogic process of meaning within the poem's structure and sources plays out at the thematic level as well: in both its halves, *Awntyrs* presents a view of social and spiritual interdependency that reflects common medieval notions of society as a unified political and sacred body. *Awntyrs* assumes, and gives vital expression to, a sense of corporate religiosity, in which the living and the dead are directly in touch with each other, so that those in heaven, on earth, and in hell (or limbo) act together in securing their mutual welfare. The care of the rich for the poor, of the living for the "very special dead" — and the converse, the powerful claims of the poor on the propertied, and of the ghost world on the flesh — define the contours of a cosmic community; within this framework matter and spirit are features of a single, continuous spectrum, and the individual's life can have final meaning only inside this corporate identity.

The ethos of chivalry participates in a similar corporate sensibility. The knight's honor exists only as it is publicly ratified by a community. First and foremost, of course, this consists in the medieval world of the elite caste of other knights, who can best judge chivalric worth and extend fellowship. But in principle it includes the entire Christian community (represented in this instance by the broad audience for chivalric romance), and *Awntyrs* throws a searching light on this larger set of connections. With astonishing bluntness, Gawain raises the question of chivalry as a sponsor of violence, rather than a protection against it:

> "How shal we fare," quod the freke, "that fonden to fight,
> And thus defoulen the folke on fele kinges londes,
> And riches over reymes withouten eny right,
> Wynnen worshipp in werre thorgh wightnesse of hondes?"
>
> (lines 261–64)

The ghost answers with her allusive but frightening and peremptory prophesy of the downfall of the Round Table (lines 265–312). The shortcomings of golden-age chivalry should in consequence seem distressingly obvious for Gawain, let alone for a late medieval and decidedly post-Arthurian audience, and they are all the more thrilling and portentous for coming from beyond the grave. Yet this narrow vision of chivalry from hell applies to knighthood not the general community standards of late medieval christendom, but the austere strictures typical of Christianity's most other-worldly-strain. Moreover, the almost certainly clerical composer embeds these ghostly condemnations within a lavish expenditure of sound and phrase, so that even at the level of its most fundamental units *Awntyrs* insists upon the compound nature of its meaning.

One of the remarkable achievements of *Awntyrs'* doubled and dialogic style is its capacity to move from a consciousness of the contradictions within the ethos of knighthood and the fatal history of Arthur's court to a celebration of the magnificence of chivalric ideals and practices. The antagonism of Galeron and Gawain begins as a quarrel over proper title to lands, but from the outset it is clear that even chivalric "enemies" are bound by a framework of forms and values that transcend individual hostilities. The plot and themes of *Awntyrs*' second episode strongly resemble the subtle and striking twist that controls the second part of *Gologras*; the poem manages their combat so that the outcome increases the honor of each knight, and thereby still further exalts the worship of chivalry. Through the daunting prowess and courtesy of Gawain, and the magnanimity of Arthur and the Round Table, Galeron — the intruder of the second part — is accorded a proper identity within the fellowship at Carlisle. He reconciles with Gawain, marries his lady, and becomes one with the other knights. This romance ending has as both its cause and effect the harmonious affirmation of Arthur's lordship at the head of a peaceable pan-Britannic community. The particular instance — the integration of the initially truculent Scots knight Galeron — sets out the fundamental pattern within the Gawain romances, whereby outlying Celtic territories are assimilated to a centralizing English perspective; Arthur's kingship consists in his power to control and redistribute the lands — Scotland, Wales, Brittany, perhaps Ireland — that mark the borders of the body politic. The final stanza of *Awntyrs* projects this romance drive towards restored identity and inclusiveness onto the communion of the saints: the Masses arranged for the soul of Guenevere's mother bring heaven and earth together, and promise her full reconciliation with God.

Awntyrs is composed in one of the most demanding and richly echoic verse forms in the English language. Each stanza contains thirteen lines, rhymed *abababababcdddc*. The first nine verses are alliterative long lines, structurally bound by four stresses in addition to the end rhyme. The last four verses of each stanza form a "wheel"; each line contains two (sometimes three) stresses, while the first three rhyme on the same sound, and the last (often the shortest) line rhymes with the long ninth line. The density of alliteration in *Awntyrs* is higher than that of any other Middle English poem, with almost half its long lines containing four alliterating stresses. Moreover, more than half the stanzas begin with a couplet bound by identical alliteration (and six stanzas extend this identical alliteration through the first three couplets). In addition to this bonding within the stanza through repeated sound patterns, each stanza is linked to the preceding and following stanza through verbal concatenation: the first line of every stanza incorporates a word or phrase from the last line of the previous stanza. (In some stanzas the ninth line additionally repeats a phrase from earlier in the stanza, further linking these words with the last line of the wheel.) Finally, the last lines of *Awntyrs* repeat the first line, linking these two stanzas and thereby imposing a circular, iterative structure on the entire poem.

Introduction

The features fundamental to *Awntyrs*'s distinctive achievement have baffled readers in precisely opposite ways, producing complaints of deficiency — its discontinuity of plot, its lack of thematic unity — and excess — its proliferation of throw-away phrases, its formulaic and metric gymnastics. The spectacle that *Awntyrs* makes through its story and its language differs in kind from the qualities we associate with learned, high literate forms — for example, a Shakespearian sonnet or Dante's *terza rima*. The effects achieved by these latter forms are directed almost exclusively to readers — often solitary, non-vocalizing readers — and they solicit from such readers a highly intellectualized, intertextually informed, reflective response. The lapidary brilliance and density of poems like *Awntyrs* put formal manipulation of language to a different use: the cloisonné surface gives preeminence to pattern, to exteriority as meaning. The poem's profligate consumption of formulaic phrases and type scenes, of nearly fetishized objects like tapestries, dress, swords, helmets, shields, or coats of arms, urges an audience not to a extract a unique, internalized meaning, but to take delight in the structural, narrative, thematic, and stylistic variations that constitute the substance of such a performance.

Such delight is a special taste, and grows from the intersection of popular interests in chivalric ideals, the remnants of an aristocratic ethos or aesthetic available to a wider audience, and the talents of a learned (clerical) writer who could bring these together in a work like *Awntyrs*. The profligate quality that marks the poem does not simply use up words, but functionally extends the poem's cultural contacts at several levels: for a full appreciation, *Awntyrs* assumes on the part of its audience unthinking access to a long-absorbed store of words and phrases, and (on the model of the diptych structure) a continuously interactive response. Like *Sir Gawain and the Green Knight* and other alliterative poems, *Awntyrs* relies upon a remarkably literate improvisation, activating what is already inside the audience through its established formulas; devoted listeners to such poetry — whether literate or not, like those for improvisational jazz, opera and romantic lieder, or MTV — imperceptibly become attuned to conventions, cues, and repeats that themselves turn into the source of pleasure in such performances. The repetitions within *Awntyrs* at the level of phrase, line, stanza, and episode are calculated not to appear novel, but to resonate with what the audience brings to the poem, at the level of conscious memory and of a cultural unconscious.

The fusion of popular and learned, native and Latin, oral and literate in *Awntyrs* accurately conveys the transitional context in which a mixed chivalric romance of this sort participated and was performed. To view the jewel-like surface of *Awntyrs* as superficial misses, then, the compacted quality of the poem's language and its narrative. Just as we need to abandon expectations of narrative unity in favor of the contingent understandings produced by a diptych structure, so in unpacking the

173

meanings and effects the romance might have had in its own time, we need to abandon surface/depth or exterior/interior metaphors, which apply to exegesis, allegory, and other traditional high literate interpretive strategies. The decorated qualities of *Awntyrs* ask to be understood as a cultural event for listeners and readers already stocked with phrases and themes. In its place between literate and oral traditions, its surface *is* its substance, and performance — whether religious ritual, chivalric courtesy and prowess, or poetic composition — is a crucial part of its meaning.

Text

The survival of *Awntyrs* in four transcriptions, all of which contain distinctive features (and defects) ensures that any edition misrepresents the "original." The poem's sources, its subtlety of structure and thought, and the complexity of its verse forms make almost certain that *Awntyrs* was a written, rather than an oral, composition. This means that there may actually have been an "original" on which (at various removes) the surviving copies are based. Yet a modern editorial search for "authentic" or even "correct" readings based on such a lost "original" would not necessarily reflect the expectations or experience of the original audiences. The practice of medieval scribes and amateur copyists/readers, in routinely and consciously altering, editing, and adding to their texts, suggests that (to rephrase a cliché of postmodernism) in the Middle Ages there were no "copies," only originals. Allen has recently argued the corollary of this proposition, that there can be no "final" edition, in relation to *Awntyrs*. Faced with these multiple transcriptions, an editor may choose to offer a "synthetic" or eclectic text, that makes best use (in the editor's own judgment) of the surviving variants or that even reconstructs the lost readings of the hypothetical undefective version, based on the witness of these variants. (Hanna's edition largely attempts this, and produces a text that is satisfyingly coherent; its readings are exceptionally learned, occasionally ingenious and sometimes inspired, and often convincing.) At the other extreme, an editor might simply transcribe without alteration one (or all) of the four existing manuscripts; this would present a text (or texts) that would at times be puzzling or nonsensical (especially to inexperienced readers), but that would give an accurate sense of a medieval reader's situation. The present edition offers what may seem an unsatisfying compromise: I have given the text as it reads in the Douce MS, though in those instances where it is defective — either because lines are clearly missing or repeated, or because the passage makes no sense to me — I have emended, usually basing my changes on the readings of the other manuscripts. (These emendations generally rely on the copy in the Ireland MS.) What I have aimed to produce is a text of *Awntyrs* that accurately reflects what has survived for us from the Middle Ages, and that nonetheless tells a coherent and enjoyable story, even for a reader new to Middle English.

Oxford MS Douce 324 (Bodleian MS 21898) dates from the third quarter of the fifteenth century. Its scribe wrote in a northwest Midlands dialect, though linguistic traces in the four surviving transcriptions locate the poem's area of composition on the northwest border of England and Scotland; given the setting of the action in Carlisle, Cumberland seems a likely place of origin. In its present form, the Douce MS contains only *Awntyrs*; formerly, however, it was part of a collection that included poetical excerpts from Gower, Hoccleve, Lydgate, and others, and prose digests of *Mandeville's Travels* and the stories of Thebes and Troy (see Kathleen Smith, "A Fifteenth-Century Vernacular Manuscript Reconstructed," *Bodleian Library Record* 7 [1966], pp. 234–41; also Hanna, pp. 8–9). I have regularized orthography, so that *u/v/w* and *i/j* appear according to modern usage; abbreviations have been expanded, numerals spelled out, and modern punctuation and capitalization added. I have followed Hanna in his decision not to transcribe flourishes as medial or final *e*, though I have inconsistently taken this scribal notation as signifying a vowel where common practice indicates its presence (e.g., lines 489, 566, 591).

Select Bibliography

Manuscripts

Oxford, Bodleian Library, MS Douce 324.

Lambeth Palace Library, MS 491.B.

Thornton MS, Lincoln Cathedral Library, MS 91.

Ireland Blackburn MS, Robert H. Taylor Collection, Princeton, New Jersey.

Editions (arranged chronologically)

Madden, Frederic. 1839. See Bibliography of Editions and Works Cited.

Robson, John. 1842. See Bibliography of Editions and Works Cited.

Amours, F. J. 1897. See Bibliography of Editions and Works Cited.

The Awntyrs off Arthur

Gates, Robert J., ed. *The Awntyrs off Arthure at the Terne Wathelyne: A Critical Edition*. Philadelphia: University of Pennsylvania Press, 1969.

Hanna, Ralph, III, ed. *The Awntyrs off Arthure at the Terne Wathelyn: An Edition Based on Bodleian Library MS. Douce 324*. Manchester: Manchester University Press, 1974.

Phillips, H., ed. *The Awntyrs of Arthure*. Lancaster Modern Spelling Texts, 1. Lancaster: Lancaster University Department of English, 1988. [I have not been able to examine a copy of this edition.]

Mills, Maldwyn, ed. *Ywain and Gawain, Sir Percyvell of Gales, The Anturs of Arther*. Everyman's Library. London: J. M. Dent Ltd.; Rutland, Vermont: Charles E. Tuttle, 1992. Pp. 161–82.

Shepherd, Stephen H. A., ed. *Middle English Romances*. New York: Norton, 1995. Pp. 219–42. [I have not been able to examine a copy of this edition.]

Criticism

Allen, Rosamund. "Some Sceptical Observations on the Editing of *The Awntyrs off Arthure*." In *Manuscripts and Texts: Editorial Problems in Later Middle English Literature: Essays from the 1985 Conference at the University of York*. Ed. Derek Pearsall. Cambridge: D. S. Brewer, 1987. Pp. 5–25.

Eadie, John. "Two Notes on *The Awntyrs of Arthure*." *English Language Notes* 21.2 (1983), 3–7.

Fichte, J. O. "*The Awyntyrs off Arthure*: An Unconscious Change of the Paradigm of Adventure." In *The Living Middle Ages: Studies in Mediaeval English Literature and Its Tradition: A Festschrift for Karl Heinz Göller*. Ed. Uwe Böker, Manfred Markus, and Rainer Schöwerling. Belser Stuttgart: Mittelbayerische Druckerei- und Verlags-Gesellschaft, 1989. Pp 129–36.

Hanna, Ralph, III. "*The Awntyrs off Arthure*: An Interpretation." *Modern Language Quarterly* 31 (1970), 275–97.

——. "À la Recherche du temps bien perdu: The Text of *The Awntyrs off Arthure*." *Text* 4 (1988), 189–205.

Introduction

Klausner, David N. "Exempla and *The Awntyrs of Arthure*." *Medieval Studies* 34 (1972), 307–25.

Lowe, Virginia A. P. "Folklore as Unifying Factor in *The Awntyrs off Arthure*." *Folklore Forum* 13 (1980), 199–223.

Mathewson, Jeanne T. "Displacement of the Feminine in *Golagros and Gawane* and *The Awntyrs off Arthure*." *Arthurian Interpretations* 1.2 (1987), 23–28.

Spearing, A. C. "*The Awntyrs off Arthure*." In *The Alliterative Tradition in the Fourteenth Century*. Ed. Bernard S. Levy and Paul E. Szarmach. Kent, Ohio: Kent State University Press, 1981. Pp. 183–202.

———. "Central and Displaced Sovereignty in Three Medieval Poems." *Review of English Studies* 33 (1982), 247–61, esp. 248–52.

———. *Medieval to Renaissance in English Poetry*. Cambridge: Cambridge University Press, 1985. Pp. 121–42.

The Awntyrs off Arthur

In the tyme of Arthur an aunter bytydde,	*adventure occurred*
By the Turne Wathelan, as the boke telles,	*relates*
Whan he to Carlele was comen, that conquerour kydde,	*famous*
With dukes and dussiperes that with the dere dwelles.	*companions; beloved [king]*
5 To hunte at the herdes that longe had ben hydde,	*hidden (i.e., in the wild)*
On a day thei hem dight to the depe delles,	*themselves went off; valleys*
To fall of the femailes in forest were frydde,	*slay; does; enclosed*
Fayre by the fermesones in frithes and felles. [1]	
Thus to wode arn thei went, the wlonkest in wedes,	*most splendid in apparel*
10 Bothe the Kyng and the Quene,	
And al the doughti bydene.	*brave ones together*
Sir Gawayn, gayest on grene,	*the most polished of all*
Dame Gaynour he ledes.	*Guenevere*

Thus Sir Gawayn the gay Gaynour he ledes,	
15 In a gleterand gide that glemed full gay —	*glittering gown*
With riche ribaynes reversset, ho so right redes, [2]	
Rayled with rybees of riall array;	*Ornamented; rubies; royal*
Her hode of a hawe huwe, ho that here hede hedes,	
Of pillour, of palwerk, of perré to pay; [3]	
20 Schurde in a short cloke that the rayne shedes,	*Clothed; repels*
Set over with saffres sothely to say,	*sapphires truly*
With saffres and seladynes set by the sides;	*celedonies studded at*
Here sadel sette of that ilke,	*Her; same*
Saude with sambutes of silke;	*Covered; saddle-clothes*
25 On a mule as the mylke,	*as [white as] milk*
Gaili she glides.	

---

[1] *Thriving because of the close season in the woods and hills*

[2] *With rich strands of material reversed to show their colors, whoever takes proper notice*

[3] Lines 18–19: *Her hood [is] a shade of aqua, [as] anyone who pays attention to her head [will note], / With fur, rich cloth, and jewels most pleasingly arranged*

The Awntyrs off Arthur

	Al in gleterand golde, gayly ho glides	*she passes [along]*
	The gates with Sir Gawayn, bi the grene welle.	*paths*
	And that burne on his blonke with the Quene bides	*knight; horse; stays*
30	That borne was in Borgoyne, by boke and by belle. [1]	
	He ladde that Lady so longe by the lawe sides;	*along; hill sides*
	Under a lorre they light, loghe by a felle.	*laurel; low; ridge*
	And Arthur with his erles ernestly rides,	
	To teche hem to her tristres, the trouthe for to telle. [2]	
35	To here tristres he hem taught, ho the trouthe trowes.	*stations; who; believes*
	Eche lorde withouten lette	*hesitation*
	To an oke he hem sette,	*At an oak*
	With bowe and with barselette,	*bow; hound*
	Under the bowes.	*boughs*

40	Under the bowes thei bode, thes burnes so bolde,	*wait; warriors*
	To byker at thes baraynes in bonkes so bare.	*shoot; fawnless does; hills*
	There might hatheles in high herdes beholde,	*nobles in haste; espy*
	Herken huntyng in hast, in holtes so hare.	*Take note; haste; woods; frosty*
	Thei kest of here couples in cliffes so colde,	*cast off their [dogs'] leashes*
45	Conforte her kenettes to kele hem of care.	*their hounds; cool them of agitation*
	Thei fel of the femayles ful thikfolde;	*killed; manyfold*
	With fressh houndes and fele, thei folowen her fare.	*many; pursue their trail*
	. . . .	
	With gret questes and quelles,	*assaults; kills*
50	Both in frethes and felles.	*woods; ridges*
	All the dure in the delles,	*deer; valleys*
	Thei durken and dare.	*hide; cringe*

	Then durken the dere in the dymme skuwes,	*cower; dark woods*
	That for drede of the deth droupes the do.	*[So] that; goes to ground; doe*
55	And by the stremys so strange that swftly swoghes	*rapids so strong; rush*
	Thai werray the wilde and worchen hem wo.	*make war on; cause them woe*
	The huntes thei halowe, in hurstes and huwes,	*hunters; shout; hillsides; cliffs*
	And till thaire riste raches relyes on the ro. [3]	

---

[1] *Who was born in Burgundy, [I swear] by book and by bell*

[2] *To assign them to their hunting stations, to tell the truth*

[3] *And at their hiding places the hounds set on the deer*

The Awntyrs off Arthur

	They gaf to no gamon grythe that on grounde gruwes.	*game quarter; lives*
60	The grete greundes in the greves so glady thei go;	*greyhounds; thickets*
	So gladly thei gon in greves so grene.	*thickets*
	The King blowe rechas	*blows "rechase" (see note)*
	And folowed fast on the tras	*track*
	With many sergeant of mas,	*mace*
65	That solas to sene.	*That pleasant sight to [go] see*
	With solas thei semble, the pruddest in palle,	*pleasure; gather; noblest; dress*
	And suwen to the Soverayne within schaghes schene.	*meet up with; woods bright*
	Al but Sir Gawayn, gayest of all,	*[knight] most gracious*
	Beleves with Dame Gaynour in greves so grene.	*[Who] stays behind; groves*
70	By a lorer ho was light, undur a lefesale	*laurel she remained; arbor*
	Of box and of berber bigged ful bene.	*box trees; barberry amply made*
	Fast byfore undre this ferly con fall	*Just; mid-morning; marvel did occur*
	And this mekel mervaile that I shal of mene.	*great; tell*
	Now wol I of this mervaile mele, if I mote.	*speak; might*
75	The day wex als dirke	*became as dark*
	As hit were mydnight myrke;	*murky*
	Thereof the King was irke	*distressed*
	And light on his fote.	*alighted [from his horse]*
	Thus to fote ar thei faren, the frekes unfayn,	*have proceeded the troubled knights*
80	And fleen fro the forest to the fawe felle.	*mottled hill*
	Thay ranne faste to the roches, for reddoure of the raynne	*rocks; severity; rain*
	For the sneterand snawe snartly hem snelles.	*driving hail keenly them stings*
	There come a lowe one the loughe — in londe is not to layne —[1]	
	In the lyknes of Lucyfere, laytheste in Helle,	*most hateful*
85	And glides to Sir Gawayn the gates to gayne,	*path to block*
	Yauland and yomerand, with many loude yelle.	*Howling and wailing*
	Hit yaules, hit yameres, with waymynges wete,	*cries out; lamentations tearful*
	And seid, with siking sare,	*sighing sore*
	"I ban the body me bare!	*curse; [that] me bore*
90	Alas! Now kindeles my care;	*kindles*
	I gloppen and I grete!"	*despair; wail*

---

[1] *There appeared a fire in the lake — not to conceal a word*

The Awntyrs off Arthur

	Then gloppenet and grete Gaynour the gay	*became fearful and wailed*
	And seid to Sir Gawen, "What is thi good rede?"	*best advice*
	"Hit ar the clippes of the son, I herd a clerk say,"	*It is an eclipse of the sun*
95	And thus he confortes the Quene for his knighthede.	*chivalrously*
	"Sir Cadour, Sir Clegis, Sir Costardyne, Sir Cay —	
	Thes knyghtes arn uncurtays, by Crosse and by Crede,	*are ungallant*
	That thus oonly have me laft on my dethday	*all alone; left (abandoned)*
	With the grisselist goost that ever herd I grede."	*grisliest; moan*
100	"Of the goost," quod the grome, "greve you no mare,	*knight; worry; more*
	For I shal speke with the sprete.	*sprite*
	And of the wayes I shall wete,	*its pains; inquire*
	What may the bales bete	*torments relieve*
	Of the bodi bare."	*body bare*
105	Bare was the body and blak to the bone,	
	Al biclagged in clay uncomly cladde.	*clotted with earth foully covered*
	Hit waried, hit wayment as a woman,	*cursed; wailed*
	But on hide ne on huwe no heling hit hadde.	*skin; complexion; cover*
	Hit stemered, hit stonayde, hit stode as a stone,	*stammered; was stunned*
110	Hit marred, hit memered, hit mused for madde. [1]	
	Agayn the grisly goost Sir Gawayn is gone;	*Towards*
	He rayked oute at a res, for he was never drad.	*moved; in a rush; frightened*
	Drad was he never, ho so right redes.	*whoever correctly understands*
	On the chef of the cholle,	*top; neck*
115	A pade pikes on the polle,	*toad bites into the skull*
	With eighen holked ful holle	*eyes sunken; hollow*
	That gloed as the gledes.	*glowed; coals*
	Al glowed as a glede the goste there ho glides,	*she*
	Umbeclipped in a cloude of clethyng unclere,	*Enclosed; shrouds unfathomable*
120	Serkeled with serpentes all aboute the sides —	*Encircled; on all sides*
	To tell the todes theron my tonge wer full tere. [2]	
	The burne braides oute the bronde, and the body bides; [3]	
	Therefor the chevalrous knight changed no chere.	*At that; expression*

---

[1] *It grieved, it murmered, it groaned as a mad person*

[2] *To account [the number of] the toads clinging to her would be too tedious for my tongue*

[3] *The knight pulls out his sword and the corpse stands still*

	The houndes highen to the holtes, and her hede hides,	*hasten; their heads hide*
125	For the grisly goost made a grym bere.	*outcry*
	The grete greundes wer agast of the grym bere.	*greyhounds; corpse*
	The birdes in the bowes,	*branches*
	That on the goost glowes,	*stare*
	Thei skryke in the skowes	*screech; woods*
130	That hatheles may here.	*noble men may hear*

	Hathelese might here, the hendeste in halle,	*Nobles; hear; handsomest*
	How chatered the cholle, the chaftis and the chynne.	*jowls; jaws; chin*
	Then conjured the knight — on Crist con he calle:	*implored; did*
	"As thou was crucifiged on Croys to clanse us of syn:	*cleanse*
135	That thou sei me the sothe whether thou shalle, [1]	
	And whi thou walkest thes wayes the wodes within."	*on these paths*
	"I was of figure and face fairest of alle,	*appearance*
	Cristened and knowen with kinges in my kynne;	*Baptized and renowned; family*
	I have kinges in my kyn knowen for kene.	*celebrated for bold deeds*
140	God has me geven of his grace	
	To dre my paynes in this place.	*suffer through*
	I am comen in this cace	*at this time*
	To speke with your Quene.	

	"Quene was I somwile, brighter of browes	*formerly; in looks*
145	Then Berell or Brangwayn, thes burdes so bolde;	*those women*
	Of al gamen or gle that on grounde growes	*pleasures or mirth; occurs on earth*
	Gretter then Dame Gaynour, of garson and golde,	*More [I enjoyed] than; treasure*
	Of palaies, of parkes, of pondes, of plowes,	*enclosures; estates*
	Of townes, of toures, of tresour untolde,	*strongholds*
150	Of castelles, of contreyes, of cragges, of clowes.	*lands; mountains; valleys*
	Now am I caught oute of kide to cares so colde;	*snared without kin in*
	Into care am I caught and couched in clay.	*laid out*
	Lo, sir curtays kniyght,	
	How delfulle deth has me dight!	*doleful; treated*
155	Lete me onys have a sight	*once*
	Of Gaynour the gay."	

---

[1] *[I demand] that you tell me the truth [about] where you intend to go*

The Awntyrs off Arthur

After Gaynour the gay Sir Gawyn is gon,
And to the body he her brought, the burde bright.   *ghostly corpse; woman*
"Welcom, Waynour, iwis, worthi in won.   *indeed, among your people*
160   Lo, how delful deth has thi dame dight!   *Behold; grievous; your mother left*
I was radder of rode then rose in the ron,   *ruddier of complexion; branch*
My ler as the lelé lonched on hight.   *face; lily bloomed*
Now am I a graceles gost, and grisly I gron;
With Lucyfer in a lake logh am I light.   *deep; sunk*
165   Thus am I lyke to Lucefere: takis witnes by mee!   *take warning*
For al thi fressh foroure,   *fur garments*
Muse on my mirrour;   *Think*
For, king and emperour,
Thus dight shul ye be.   *so treated*

170   "Thus dethe wil you dight, thare you not doute;   *treat you, of that*
Thereon hertly take hede while thou art here.   *heartily; still alive*
Whan thou art richest arraied and ridest in thi route,   *decked out; company*
Have pité on the poer — thou art of power. [1]
Burnes and burdes that ben the aboute,   *Servants and women; you*
175   When thi body is bamed and brought on a ber,   *embalmed; borne on a bier*
Then lite wyn the light that now wil the loute, [2]
For then the helpes no thing but holy praier.   *nothing helps you*
The praier of poer may purchas the pes —   *for you peace*
Of that thou yeves at the yete, [3]
180   Whan thou art set in thi sete,   *seat of honor*
With al merthes at mete   *joys; meal*
And dayntés on des.   *delicacies; dais*

"With riche dayntés on des thi diotes ar dight,   *feasts are furnished*
And I, in danger and doel, in dongone I dwelle,   *sorrow, in bondage I languish*
185   Naxté and nedefull, naked on night.   *Nasty*
Ther folo me a ferde of fendes of helle;   *follow; troop*
They hurle me unhendely; thei harme me in hight;   *rudely; lacerate me violently*
In bras and in brymston I bren as a belle.   *brass (cauldron); burn; bonfire*

---

[1] *Have pity on the poor — you have the power [to do so]*

[2] *Then little wish [they] to comfort you, who now will flatter you*

[3] *According to what you distribute [to the poor] at your gate*

Was never wrought in this world a wofuller wight.   *a more woeful person*
190   Hit were ful tore any tonge my turment to telle;   *tedious; torment*
Nowe wil Y of my turment tel or I go.   *I; before*
Thenk hertly on this —   *intently*
Fonde to mende thi mys.   *Try to amend your misdoing*
Thou art warned ywys: *for sure*
195   Be war be my wo."   *by my woe*

"Wo is me for thi wo," quod Waynour, "ywys!   *Guenevere*
But one thing wold I wite, if thi wil ware: *know, if it were your will*
If auther matens or Mas might mende thi mys,   *either liturgy or Mass; hardship*
Or eny meble on molde? My merthe were the mare   *goods on earth; joy; more*
200   If bedis of bisshopps might bring the to blisse,   *prayers*
Or coventes in cloistre might kere the of care.   *clergy; deliver you from*
If thou be my moder, grete mervaile hit is
That al thi burly body is broughte to be so bare!"   *fine; has lost color*
"I bare the of my body; what bote is hit I layn?   *bore; profit; conceal it*
205   I brak a solempne avowe,   *broke; vow*
And no man wist hit but thowe;   *knows; you*
By that token thou trowe,   *believe*
That sothely I sayn."   *truthfully; speak*

"Say sothely what may the saven of thi sytis   *you save; troubles*
210   And I shal make sere men to singe for thi sake.   *several (priests)*
But the baleful bestes that on thi body bites   *beasts; your*
Al blendis my ble — thi bones arn so blake!" [1]
"That is luf paramour, listes and delites   *[The cause] is sexual love; pleasure*
That has me light and laft logh in a lake.   *brought me low and left me deep*
215   Al the welth of the world, that awey witis   *that [wealth] completely vanishes*
With the wilde wormes that worche me wrake;   *work me pain*
Wrake thei me worchen, Waynour, iwys.   *Pain*
Were thritty trentales don   *thirty series of masses said*
Bytwene under and non,   *morning and afternoon (in one day)*
220   Mi soule were socoured with son   *aided immediately*
And brought to the blys."

---

[1] *All blanches (i.e., whitens) my countenance — [because] your skeleton is so black*

The Awntyrs off Arthur

"To blisse bring the the Barne that bought the on Rode, [1]
That was crucifiged on Croys and crowned with thorne.
As thou was cristened and crisomed with candel and code,   *chrism cloth*
225 Folowed in fontestone on frely byforne —   *Baptized at font openly when young*
Mary the mighti, myldest of mode,   *in spirit*
Of whom the blisful barne in Bedlem was borne,   *child; Bethlehem*
Lene me grace that I may grete the with gode   *Grant; commemorate you properly*
And mynge the with matens and Masses on morne."   *remember you; each morning*
230 "To mende us with Masses, grete myster hit were.   *remember; need*
For Him that rest on the Rode,   *For [the sake of] Him who hung; Cross*
Gyf fast of thi goode   *energetically*
To folke that failen the fode   *lack food*
While thou art here."   *alive*

235 "Here hertly my honde thes hestes to holde,   *[I promise] these vows to keep*
With a myllion of Masses to make the mynnyng.   *multitude; you remembrance*
Bot one word," quod Waynour, "yit weten I wolde: *But; know about*
What wrathed God most, at thi weting?"   *angered; according to your understanding*
"Pride with the appurtenaunce, as prophetez han tolde   *excess; have*
240 Bifore the peple, apertly in her preching.   *openly; their*
Hit beres bowes bitter: therof be thou bolde;   *sprouts branches; vigilant*
That makes burnes so boune to breke his bidding.   *people ready; commandment*
But ho his bidding brekes, bare thei ben of blys;   *whoever; deprived; heaven*
But thei be salved of that sare,   *Unless; absolved; wound*
245 Er they hethen fare,   *go hence from this world*
They mon weten of care,   *must endure woe*
Waynour, ywys."   *indeed*

"Wysse me," quod Waynour, "som wey, if thou wost,   *Teach; know*
What bedis might me best to the blisse bring?"   *prayers; best lead me*
250 "Mekenesse and mercy, thes arn the moost;   *are the greatest*
And sithen have pité on the poer, that pleses Heven king.
Sithen charité is chef, and then is chaste,   *Accordingly; paramount; chastity*
And then almessedede aure al other thing.   *next almsgiving above*
Thes arn the graceful giftes of the Holy Goste
255 That enspires iche sprete withoute speling.   *inspires each soul; instruction*

---

[1] *May the hero who redeemed you on the Cross bring you to bliss*

185

Of this spiritual thing spute thou no mare.   *doctrine dispute no further*
Als thou art Quene in thi quert,   *court*
Hold thes wordes in hert.   *Keep*
Thou shal leve but a stert;   *live; fit (i.e., a short time)*
260   Hethen shal thou fare."   *Hence*

"How shal we fare," quod the freke, "that fonden to fight,   *warrior; undertake*
And thus defoulen the folke on fele kinges londes,   *put down; diverse; countries*
And riches over reymes withouten eny right,   *enter; realms; any*
Wynnen worshipp in werre thorgh wightnesse of hondes?"[1]
265   "Your King is to covetous, I warne the sir knight.   *too*
May no man stry him with strenght while his whele stondes.[2]
Whan he is in his magesté, moost in his might,   *[Just at the point] when*
He shal light ful lowe on the sesondes.   *fall full low; seashore*
And this chivalrous Kinge chef shall a chaunce: *shall receive his fate*
270   Falsely Fortune in fight,   *strife*
That wonderfull wheelwryght,
Shall make lordes to light —   *to fall*
Take witnesse by Fraunce.

"Fraunce haf ye frely with your fight wonnen;   *completely; conquered*
275   Freol and his folke, fey ar they leved.   *Frollo; troop, dead; left*
Bretayne and Burgoyne al to you bowen,   *Brittany and Burgundy; have yielded*
And al the Dussiperes of Fraunce with your dyn deved.   *warcry are stunned*
Gyan may grete the werre was bigonen;   *Aquitaine; rue that war*
There ar no lordes on lyve in that londe leved.   *no warriors alive; left*
280   Yet shal the riche Romans with you be aurronen,   *by you be overrun*
And with the Rounde Table the rentes be reved;   *And by; incomes be taken over*
Then shal a Tyber untrue tymber you tene.[3]
Gete the, Sir Gawayn: *Take heed*
Turne the to Tuskayn.   *Go quickly*
285   For ye shul lese Bretayn   *lose*
With a knight kene.   *Through; bold*

---

[1] *Achieve renown in warfare through prowess of arms*
[2] *No man may overthrow him by force while Fortune holds him high on her wheel*
[3] *Then shall the treacherous Tiber (Rome) cause you woe*

"This knight shal kenely croyse the crowne,   *boldly sieze office of king*
And at Carlele shal that comly be crowned as king.   *nobleman*
That sege shal be sesede at a sesone   *knight; empowered; time*
290   That myche baret and bale to Bretayn shal bring.   *strife; sorrow*
Hit shal in Tuskan be tolde of the treson,   *announced*
And ye shullen turne ayen for the tydynge.   *come back; news*
Ther shal the Rounde Table lese the renoune: *lose its renown*
Beside Ramsey ful rad at a riding   *suddenly; battle*
295   In Dorsetshire shal dy the doughtest of alle.   *die; boldest*
Gete the, Sir Gawayn,   *Take heed*
The boldest of Bretayne;
In a slake thou shal be slayne,   *valley*
Sich ferlyes shull falle.   *Such wonders; occur*

300   "Suche ferlies shull fal, withoute eny fable,   *wonders; befall; falsehood*
Uppon Cornewayle coost with a knight kene.   *coast because of a knight fierce*
Sir Arthur the honest, avenant and able,   *honorable, gracious and powerful*
He shal be wounded, iwys — wothely, I wene.   *indeed; lethally, I trust*
And al the rial rowte of the Rounde Table,   *royal company*
305   Thei shullen dye on a day, the doughty bydene,   *one day the brave ones together*
Suppriset with a suget: he beris hit in sable,[1]
With a sauter engreled of silver full shene.   *cross showing a notched edge; bright*
He beris hit of sable, sothely to say;   *black, truly*
In riche Arthures halle,
310   The barne playes at the balle   *child; with*
That outray shall you alle,   *undo*
Delfully that day.   *Sorrowfully*

"Have gode day, Gaynour, and Gawayn the gode;
I have no lenger tome tidinges to telle.   *more time to give information*
315   I mot walke on my wey thorgh this wilde wode   *must; wood*
In my wonyngstid in wo for to welle.   *dwelling place; woe; seethe*
Fore Him that rightwisly rose and rest on the Rode,   *righteously; hung; Cross*
Thenke on the danger and the dole that I yn dwell.   *peril; sorrow; in*
Fede folke for my sake that failen the fode   *who lack food*
320   And menge me with matens and Masse in melle.   *remember; services; besides*

---

[1] *Overcome by a subject (i.e., one of the King's retainers): he bears a black coat of arms*

	Masses arn medecynes to us that bale bides;	*who torment endure*
	Us thenke a Masse as swete	*We think (i.e., to us seems)*
	As eny spice that ever ye yete."	*ate*
	With a grisly grete	*groan*
325	The goste awey glides.	
	With a grisly grete the goost awey glides	
	And goes with gronyng sore thorgh the greves grene.	*groves green*
	The wyndes, the weders, the welken unhides —	*weathers; sky clears*
	Then unclosed the cloudes, the son con shene.	*parted; sun did*
330	The King his bugle has blowen and on the bent bides;	*field waits*
	His fare folke in the frith, thei flokken bydene,	*wood; flock together*
	And al the riall route to the Quene rides;	*royal company*
	She sayes hem the selcouthes that thei hadde ther seen.	*tells them of the wonders*
	The wise of the weder, forwondred they were.	*learned; utterly bewildered*
335	Prince proudest in palle,	*robes*
	Dame Gaynour and alle,	*every one [else]*
	Went to Rondoles Halle	
	To the suppere.	
	The King to souper is set, served in sale,	*seated; hall*
340	Under a siller of silke dayntly dight	*canopy*
	With al worshipp and wele, innewith the walle,	
	Briddes brauden and brad in bankers bright. [1]	
	There come in a soteler with a symballe,	*musician; cymbal*
	A lady lufsom of lote ledand a knight;	*lovely of face leading*
345	Ho raykes up in a res bifor the Rialle	*She moves quickly; King*
	And halsed Sir Arthur hendly on hight.	*saluted; courteously aloud*
	Ho said to the Soverayne, wlonkest in wede,	*She; most radiant in clothing*
	"Mon makeles of might,	*Sire without equal*
	Here commes an errant knight.	*questing*
350	Do him reson and right	*Treat him with consideration and justice*
	For thi manhede."	*manhood*

---

[1] Lines 340–42: *Under a canopy of silk, daintily wrought / With distinction and splendor, [a canopy located] up against the wall, / [With] birds embroidered and displayed on its brilliant panels*

	The mon in his mantell sittes at his mete	*man [King]; meal*
	In pal pured to pay, prodly pight,	*cloth trimmed handsomely, richly displayed*
	Trofelyte and traverste with trewloves in trete; [1]	
355	The tasses were of topas that wer thereto tight.	*topaz; to that affixed*
	He gliffed up with his eighen that grey wer and grete,	*glanced; eyes*
	With his beveren berde, on that burde bright.	*reddish beard, at that woman fair*
	He was the soveraynest of al sitting in sete	*lordliest; in his proper place*
	That ever segge had sen with his eye sight.	*person had seen*
360	King crowned in kith carpes hir tille:	*among his household speaks to her*
	"Welcom, worthely wight —	*honorable woman*
	He shal have reson and right!	
	Whethen is the comli knight,	*From where*
	If hit be thi wille?"	*If it pleases you [to say]*

365	Ho was the worthiest wight that eny wy welde wolde; [2]	
	Here gide was glorious and gay, of a gresse grene.	*Her dress; grass-green*
	Here belle was of blunket, with birdes ful bolde,	*cloak; wool, [embroidered]*
	Brauded with brende gold, and bokeled ful bene. [3]	
	Here fax in fyne perré was fretted in folde,	*Her hair; jewels; arranged in pleats*
370	Contrefelet and kelle coloured full clene,	*Ribbon and head-dress; brightly*
	With a crowne craftly al of clene golde.	*finely [wrought]*
	Here kercheves were curiouse with many proude prene,	
	Her perré was praysed with prise men of might: [4]	
	Bright birdes and bolde	*women*
375	Had ynoghe to beholde	*enough*
	Of that frely to folde,	*that [woman] gracious to embrace*
	And on the hende knight.	*courteous*

	The knight in his colours was armed ful clene,	*heraldic dress; armed to perfection*
	With his comly crest clere to beholde,	*handsome plume*
380	His brené and his basnet burneshed ful bene,	*armor; headpiece; well*
	With a bordur abought al of brende golde.	*about; burnished*

---

[1] *Decorated and crisscrossed with love-knots in a row*

[2] *She was the most worthy person that anyone might wish to have governance of*

[3] *Embroidered with burnished gold and fashioned most attractively*

[4] Lines 372–73: *Her head-scarves were remarkable with many noble brooches, / Her clothing was admired by renowned warriors*

His mayles were mylke white, enclawet ful clene;   *[coat of] mail; fastened*

His horse trapped of that ilke, as true men me tolde;   *in trappings of the same*

His shelde on his shulder of silver so shene,   *bright*

385   With bere hedes of blake browed ful bolde;   *bear heads; with brows*

His horse in fyne sandel was trapped to the hele.   *silk; draped; feet*

And, in his cheveron biforne,   *horse's head armor*

Stode as an unicorne,

Als sharp as a thorne,

390   An anlas of stele.   *dagger*

In stele he was stuffed, that stourne uppon stede,   *armor; warrior [mounted]*

Al of sternes of golde, that stanseld was one straye;   *stars; patterned at random*

His gloves, his gamesons glowed as a glede   *outer coat; coal*

With graynes of rebé that graithed ben gay.   *beads of ruby; fashioned; graciously*

395   And his schene schynbaudes, that sharp wer to shrede,

His poleinus with pelydodis were poudred to pay.

With a launce on loft that lovely con lede; [1]

A freke on a freson him folowed, in fay.   *squire; Friesland horse; in truth*

The freson was afered for drede of that fare,   *spooked with fear of those goings on*

400   For he was selden wonte to se   *seldom accustomed*

The tablet fluré: *table so decorated with fleurs-de-lis*

Siche gamen ne gle   *Such games or festivities*

Sagh he never are.   *Saw; ere (i.e., before)*

Arthur asked on hight, herand him alle: *aloud all hearing him*

405   "What woldes thou, wee, if hit be thi wille? [2]

Tel me what thou seches and whether thou shalle,   *seek; wither you intend to go*

And whi thou, sturne on thi stede, stondes so stille?" [3]

He wayved up his viser fro his ventalle;   *lifted; visor; helmet*

With a knightly contenaunce, he carpes him tille: *chivalric manner; speaks to him*

410   "Whether thou be cayser or king, her I the becalle   *emperor; challenge*

Fore to finde me a freke to fight with my fille.   *an opponent; to my satisfaction*

---

[1] Lines 395–97: *And his handsome greaves (shin guards), that were sharp for slashing, / His knee guards with gems were pleasingly spangled. / With his lance at rest that worthy [knight] presented himself*

[2] *What do you desire, knight, if you please*

[3] *And why you, fearsome on your horse (i.e., mounted for combat), abide here so silently?*

Fighting to fraist I fonded fro home." [1]

Then seid the King uppon hight,   *said; aloud*

"If thou be curteys knight,   *courteous*

415   Late and lenge al nyght,   *Stay; tarry*

And tel me thi nome."   *name*

"Mi name is Sir Galaron, withouten eny gile,   *guile*

The grettest of Galwey of greves and gyllis,   *greatest [knight]; thickets; ravines*

Of Connok, of Conyngham, and also Kyle,   *[places in Scotland?]*

420   Of Lomond, of Losex, of Loyan hilles.

Thou has wonen hem in werre with a wrange wile   *taken; war; unjust trick*

And geven hem to Sir Gawayn — that my hert grylles.   *angers*

But he shal wring his honde and warry the wyle,   *hand(s); curse the time*

Er he weld hem, ywys, agayn myn unwylles. [2]

425   Bi al the welth of the worlde, he shal hem never welde,   *them never rule*

While I the hede may bere,   *my head*

But if he wyn hem in were,   *Unless; combat*

With a shelde and a spere,

On a faire felde.   *fair field (i.e., in equitable combat)*

430   "I wol fight on a felde — thereto I make feith —   *will; oath*

With eny freke uppon folde that frely is borne.   *warrior; earth; nobly*

To lese suche a lordshipp me wolde thenke laith, [3]

And iche lede opon lyve wold lagh me to scorne."

"We ar in the wode went to walke on oure waith, [4]

435   To hunte at the hertes with hounde and with horne.   *deer*

We ar in oure gamen; we have no gome graithe, [5]

But yet thou shalt be mached be mydday tomorne.

Forthi I rede the, thenke rest al night."   *Therefore I advise you take care to*

Gawayn, grathest of all,   *most accomplished*

---

[1] *Fighting to demand (i.e., seeking combat) I set out from home*

[2] *Before he wield them, indeed, over my resistance*

[3] Lines 432–33: *To lose such lordship (i.e., dominion over those lands) to me would seem hateful, / And every warrior alive would laugh me to scorn*

[4] *We have come to the forest to proceed on our hunt (i.e., we are unprepared for combat)*

[5] Lines 435–36: *We are at our games (i.e., fitted out for the hunt); we have no champion ready, / Though nonetheless you shall be matched [with an opponent] by noon tomorrow*

440	Ledes him oute of the hall	
	Into a pavilion of pall	*rich cloth*
	That prodly was pight.	*proudly made up*
	Pight was it prodly with purpour and palle,	*Adorned; purple; rich cloth*
	Birdes brauden above, in brend gold bright.	*Birds embroidered; burnished*
445	Inwith was a chapell, a chambour, a halle, [1]	
	A chymné with charcole to chaufe the knight.	*chimney; coals; warm*
	His stede was stabled and led to the stalle;	
	Hay hertly he had in haches on hight.	*plentifully; fodder-racks*
	Sithen thei braide up a borde, and clothes thei calle,	*set up a table; call for*
450	Sanapes and salers, semly to sight,	*Table-cloths; salt-cellars*
	Torches and brochetes and stondardes bitwene. [2]	
	Thus thei served that knight	
	And his worthely wight,	*worthy companion*
	With rich dayntes dight	*delicacies prepared*
455	In silver so shene.	*bright*
	In silver so semely thei served of the best,	
	With vernage in veres and cuppes ful clene.	*wine in glasses; brim full*
	And thus Sir Gawayn the good glades hour gest,	*entertains their guest*
	With riche dayntees endored in disshes bydene.	*glazed; in succession*
460	Whan the riall renke was gone to his rest,	*princely warrior had gone*
	The King to counsaile has called his knightes so kene.	
	"Loke nowe, lordes, oure lose be not lost. [3]	
	Ho shal encontre with the knight? Kestes you bitwene."	
	Then seid Gawayn the goode, "Shal hit not greve.	*grieve*
465	Here my honde I you hight,	*[with] my hand; promise*
	I woll fight with the knight	
	In defence of my right,	
	Lorde, by your leve."	

---

[1] *Therein was a chapel, a chamber (i.e., a private room), [and] a hall (i.e., a public space)*

[2] *Candles and candleholders and tapers in the middle*

[3] *Lines 462–63: Look [to it] now (i.e., take care), lords, [that] our honor (reputation) is not lost. / Who shall join battle with the knight? Decide between yourselves*

"I leve wel," quod the King. "Thi lates ar light, [1]

470 But I nolde for no lordeshipp se thi life lorne."   *would not for any; lost*

"Let go!" quod Sir Gawayn. "God stond with the right! [2]

If he skape skathlesse, hit were a foule skorne."   *escape unscathed; insult*

In the daying of the day, the doughti were dight,   *dawning; bold men; outfitted*

And herden matens and Masse erly on morne.   *matins (i.e., early service)*

475 By that on Plumton Land a palais was pight,   *Right after that; enclosure; pitched*

Were never freke opon folde had foughten biforne.   *Where; warrior on earth*

Thei setten listes bylyve on the logh lande. [3]

Thre soppes demayn   *Three pieces of fine bread soaked in wine*

Thei brought to Sir Gawayn

480 For to confort his brayn,

The King gared commaunde.   *[As]; did*

The King commaunded kindeli the Erlis son of Kent: *Earl of Kent's son*

"Curtaysly in this case, take kepe to the knight." [4]

With riche dayntees or day he dyned in his tente;   *before daylight he (i.e., Galeron)*

485 After buskes him in a brené that burneshed was bright. [5]

Sithen to Waynour wisly he went;   *Afterwards to Guenevere prudently*

He laft in here warde his worthly wight.   *left in her keeping his noble lady*

After aither in high hour horses thei hent,   *Then both hastily their horses seized*

And at the listes on the lande lordely done light   *barriers onto; nobly did alight*

490 Alle bot thes two burnes, baldest of blode.   *warriors; boldest; blood (i.e., in spirit)*

The Kinges chaier is set   *throne*

Abowve on a chacelet;   *dais*

Many galiard gret   *Many a hardy [knight] called out*

For Gawayn the gode.

495 Gawayn and Galerone gurden her stedes;   *gird (i.e., ready)*

Al in gleterand golde, gay was here gere.   *glittering; equipment*

The lordes bylyve hom to list ledes,   *promptly move to the barrier*

---

[1] *"I believe [that] easily," said the King. "Your sense of honor is quick*

[2] *"Don't worry!" said Sir Gawain. "May God stand with (uphold) the right"*

[3] *They set [up] lists (i.e., jousting barriers) quickly on the level field*

[4] *With all courtesy proper to the circumstances [of the impending combat], see to [preparing] the knight (i.e., Galeron)*

[5] *Afterwards, he goes off in his armor that burnished was brightly*

The Awntyrs off Arthur

With many serjant of mace, as was the manere. [1]
The burnes broched the blonkes that the side bledis; *spurred the horses so that*
500 Ayther freke opon folde has fastned his spere. *Each warrior on the turf; fixed*
Shaftes in shide wode thei shindre in shedes, *split wood; splinter in shards*
So jolilé thes gentil justed on were! *spiritedly; nobles jousted in combat*
Shaftes thei shindre in sheldes so shene, *splinter upon; bright*
And sithen, with brondes bright, *after; swords*
505 Riche mayles thei right. *armor; strike*
There encontres the knight *enters combat; (i.e., Galeron)*
With Gawayn on grene. *on [the] grass*

Gawayn was gaily grathed in grene, *splendidly equipped*
With his griffons of golde engreled full gay, *engraved*
510 Trifeled with tranes and trueloves bitwene; *Adorned with devices; love-knots*
On a startand stede he strikes on stray. *rearing; hammers away*
That other in his turnaying, he talkes in tene: *jousting; speaks in anger*
"Whi drawes thou the on dregh and makes siche deray?" [2]
He swapped him yn at the swyre with a swerde kene; *struck; neck; sharp*
515 That greved Sir Gawayn to his dethday.
The dyntes of that doughty were doutwis bydene; *blows; absolutely dreadful*
Fifté mayles and mo *mail-links and more*
The swerde swapt in two, *snapped*
The canelbone also, *collar bone*
520 And clef his shelde shene. *cleft (i.e., cut through)*

He clef thorgh the cantell that covered the knight, *shield-cover; protected*
Thorgh the shinand shelde a shaftmon and mare. *shining; hand's-breadth; more*
And then the lathely lord lowe uppon hight, *fierce; laughed out loud*
And Gawayn greches therwith and gremed ful sare: *seethed at that; felt deep anger*
525 "I shal rewarde the thi route, if I con rede right." [3]
He folowed in on the freke with a fressh fare; *moved in; new thrust*
Thorgh blason and brené, that burneshed wer bright, *shield; mail coat*
With a burlich bronde thorgh him he bare. *stout sword into him he cut*

---

[1] *With many a sergeant-at-arms (i.e., mace bearer), as was the custom*
[2] *Why do you draw yourself back so far and make such a fuss?*
[3] *I shall pay you back [for] your stroke, if I have anything to say [about it]*

The bronde was blody that burneshed was bright. [1]

530 Then gloppened that gay —   *was stunned that knight [Galeron]*
    Hit was no ferly, in fay.   *marvel, in truth*
    The sturne strikes on stray   *hardy [knight] (Galeron) hammers away*
    In stiropes stright.   *[Standing] in his stirrups upright*

    Streyte in his steroppes, stoutely he strikes,
535 And waynes at Sir Wawayn als he were wode.   *rushes; mad*
    Then his lemman on lowde skirles and skrikes, [2]
    When that burly burne blenket on blode.   *goodly knight shone with*
    Lordes and ladies of that laike likes   *with that turnabout are pleased*
    And thonked God of his grace for Gawayn the gode.
540 With a swap of a swerde, that swithely him swykes;
    He stroke of the stede hede streite there he stode. [3]
    The faire fole fondred and fel, bi the Rode.   *foal (i.e., horse) stumbled; Cross*
    Gawayn gloppened in hert;   *was stunned*
    He was swithely smert.   *intensely angry*
545 Oute of sterops he stert   *jumped*
    Fro Grissell the goode.   *[his horse]*

    "Grissell," quod Gawayn, "gon is, God wote!   *God knows*
    He was the burlokest blonke that ever bote brede.   *hardiest horse; took food*
    By Him that in Bedeleem was borne ever to ben our bote,   *Bethlehem; remedy*
550 I shall venge the today, if I con right rede."   *avenge [myself on] you*
    "Go fecche me my freson, fairest on fote;   *Frisian [horse]; afoot*
    He may stonde the in stoure in as mekle stede."   *serve you in combat just as well*
    "No more for the faire fole then for a risshrote.   *[I'll take] no more; weed*
    But for doel of the dombe best that thus shuld be dede, [4]
555 I mourne for no montur, for I may gete mare."   *grieve for; mount; more*
    Als he stode by his stede,   *As*
    That was so goode at nede,
    Ner Gawayn wax wede,   *Nearly; went mad*
    So wepputte he sare.   *sorrowfully*

---

[1] *The sword was bloody that polished had been brightly*

[2] *Then his beloved screams aloud and shrieks*

[3] Lines 540–41: *With a stroke of a sword, that knight (Galeron) promptly calls him up short; / He struck off the horse's head right where it stood*

[4] *Except for the sadness over the dumb beast that died so [disgracefully]*

560	Thus wepus for wo Wowayn the wight,	*weeps; hardy*
	And wenys him to quyte, that wonded is sare.	*intends to get revenge; sorely*
	That other drogh him on dreght for drede of the knight [1]	
	And boldely broched his blonk on the bent bare.	*spurred his horse; field open*
	"Thus may thou dryve forthe the day to the derk night!"	*throw away (pass)*
565	The son was passed by that mydday and mare. [2]	
	Within the listes the lede lordly done light;	*warrior (i.e., Galeron); did dismount*
	Touard the burne with his bronde he busked him yare. [3]	
	To bataile they bowe with brondes so bright.	*move*
	Shene sheldes wer shred,	*Bright; shredded*
570	Bright brenés bybled;	*mail-coats stained with blood*
	Many doughti were adred,	*brave [warriors]; afraid*
	So fersely thei fight.	*fiercely*

	Thus thei feght on fote on that fair felde	
	As fressh as a lyon that fautes the fille.	*fierce; lacks its fill*
575	Wilelé thes wight men thair wepenes they welde;	*Adroitly; wield their weapons*
	Wyte ye wele, Sir Gawayn wantis no will.	*Believe me; lacks no determination*
	He brouched him yn with his bronde under the brode shelde	*stabbed into him*
	Thorgh the waast of the body and wonded him ille.	*waist; seriously*
	The swerd stent for no stuf — hit was so wel steled.	*stopped; equipment; forged*
580	That other startis on bak and stondis stonstille. [4]	
	Though he were stonayed that stonde, he strikes ful sare —	*stunned; moment*
	He gurdes to Sir Gawayn	*pierces*
	Thorgh ventaile and pesayn;	*face and neck armor*
	He wanted noght to be slayn [5]	
585	The brede of an hare.	

| | Hardely then thes hathelese on helmes they hewe. | *Fiercely; warriors; helmets* |
| | Thei beten downe beriles and bourdures bright; | *knock off beryls (gems) and trim* |

---

[1] *The other (i.e., Galeron) drew himself away because of uncertainty about the knight (i.e., about the proper response to Gawain's want of a horse)*

[2] *The sun had passed by that [time] midday and more (i.e., it was after noon)*

[3] *Towards the knight (i.e., Gawain) with his [drawn] sword he (i.e., Galeron) moved quickly*

[4] *That other (i.e., Galeron) falls back and stands still as a stone*

[5] Lines 584–85: *He (i.e., Gawain) lacked nothing to be slain / [Only] the breadth of a hair (i.e., Gawain escaped death by a hair's breadth)*

The Awntyrs off Arthur

	Shildes on shildres that shene were to shewe,	*Shields on shoulders; bright; look on*
	Fretted were in fyne golde, thei failen in fight.	*[Which] adorned were; fail*
590	Stones of iral thay strenkel and strewe;	*rainbow colors; scatter*
	Stithe stapeles of stele they strike done stright.	*Strong clasps; right off*
	Burnes bannen the tyme the bargan was brewe,	*People curse; brewed (made)*
	The doughti with dyntes so delfully were dight.	*strokes so grievously were covered*
	The dyntis of tho doghty were doutous bydene.	*absolutely terrible*
595	Bothe Sir Lete and Sir Lake	
	Miche mornyng thei make.	*Much*
	Gaynor gret for her sake	*lamented for their*
	With her grey eyen.	

	Thus gretis Gaynour with bothe her grey yene	*weeps; eyes*
600	For gref of Sir Gawayn, grisly was wound.	*Out of distress for; [who]*
	The knight of corage was cruel and kene,	*[Gawain]*
	And, with a stele bronde, that sturne oft stound;	*the bold [Galeron] often stunned*
	Al the cost of the knyght he carf downe clene.	*side; carved through cleanly*
	Thorgh the riche mailes that ronke were and rounde	*strong; round*
605	With a teneful touche he taght him in tene,	*hurtful stroke; attacked him in anger*
	He gurdes Sir Galeron groveling on gronde.	*strikes; writhing to the ground*
	Grisly on gronde, he groned on grene.	*Horribly; on [the] grass*
	Als wounded as he was,	
	Sone unredely he ras	*rashly he arose*
610	And folowed fast on his tras	*pursued [Gawain] fast in his tracks*
	With a swerde kene.	

	Kenely that cruel kevered on hight, [1]	
	And with a cast of the carhonde in cantil he strikes,	*left hand; shield corner*
	And waynes at Sir Wawyn, that worthely wight.	*rushes; worthy warrior*
615	But him lymped the worse, and that me wel likes. [2]	
	He atteled with a slenk haf slayn him in slight; [3]	
	The swerd swapped on his swange and on the mayle slikes,	*struck; thigh; slides*
	And Gawayn bi the coler keppes the knight.	*by the collar takes captive*
	Then his lemman on loft skrilles and skrikes —	*lover; screams and shrieks*

---

[1] *Boldly that fierce [knight] (i.e., Galeron) defended [himself] (i.e., retaliated) in haste*

[2] *But something worse befell him (i.e., Galeron), and that well pleases me*

[3] *He undertook a blow that would have slain him (i.e., Gawain) through its skill*

197

620   Ho gretes on Gaynour with gronyng grylle: *She beseeches; groaning bitter*
      "Lady makeles of might,   *matchless in*
      Haf mercy on yondre knight
      That is so delfull dight,   *woefully set upon*
      If hit be thi wille."

625   Than wilfully Dame Waynour to the King went;
      Ho caught of her coronall and kneled him tille: *removed her crown; to him*
      "As thou art Roye roial, richest of rent,   *King majestic; most powerful overlord*
      And I thi wife wedded at thi owne wille —
      Thes burnes in the bataile so blede on the bent,   *knights; field*
630   They arn wery, iwis, and wonded full ille.   *weary, surely; wounded grievously*
      Thorgh her shene sheldes, her shuldres ar shent;   *Through their; destroyed*
      The grones of Sir Gawayn dos my hert grille.   *torment*
      The grones of Sir Gawayne greven me sare.   *grieve*
      Wodest thou leve, Lorde,   *If you please*
635   Make thes knightes accorde,
      Hit were a grete conforde   *comfort*
      For all that here ware."   *here were*

      Then spak Sir Galeron to Gawayn the good: *spoke*
      "I wende never wee in this world had ben half so wight. [1]
640   Here I make the releyse, renke, by the Rode,   *grant you quit-claim, sir; Cross*
      And, byfore thiese ryalle, resynge the my ryghte; [2]
      And sithen make the monraden with a mylde mode   *after; homage; good will*
      As man of medlert makeles of might." [3]
      He talkes touard the King on hie ther he stode,   *aloud from where*
645   And bede that burly his bronde that burneshed was bright: [4]
      "Of rentes and richesse I make the releyse."
      Downe kneled the knight
      And carped wordes on hight;   *aloud*

---

[1] *I never imagined [there was a] knight in the world [who] was half so powerful [as you are]*

[2] *And, before these royal [persons], [I] resign [to] you my right (i.e., all claims to lands and entitlements)*

[3] *[Insofar] as [you are a] man of middle earth matchless in strength (i.e., as a man without equal in this world)*

[4] *And offered that good [man] his sword that was brightly polished*

The King stode upright
650 And commaunded pes.   *peace (i.e., silence)*

The King commaunded pes and cried on hight,
And Gawayn was goodly and laft for his sake.   *gracious; left [off]*
Then lordes to listes they lopen ful light —   *barriers; leapt*
Sir Ewayn Fiz Uryayn and Arrak Fiz Lake,
655 Marrake and Moylard, that most wer of might —
Bothe thes travayled men they truly up take.   *wearied; gave support*
Unneth might tho sturne stonde upright —   *Scarcely; those bold [knights]*
What, for buffetes and blode, her blees wex blak; [1]
Her blees were brosed, for beting of brondes.   *faces were bruised*
660 Withouten more lettyng,   *goings on (delay)*
Dight was here saghtlyng;   *Prepared; reconciliation*
Bifore the comly King,
Thei held up her hondes.   *[in sign of agreement]*

"Here I gif Sir Gawayn, with gerson and golde,   *together with treasure*
665 Al the Glamergan londe with greves so grene,   *Glamorganshire; groves*
The worship of Wales at wil and at wolde,   *lordship; at his command*
With Criffones Castelles curnelled ful clene;   *crenellated*
Eke Ulstur Halle to hafe and to holde,   *Also*
Wayford and Waterforde, wallede I wene;   *fortified [towns] I guess*
670 Two baronrees in Bretayne with burghes so bolde,   *fortified cities*
That arn batailed abought and bigged ful bene. [2]
I shal doue the a duke and dubbe the with honde,   *endow (invest)*
Withthi thou saghtil with the knight   *On condition you accord*
That is so hardi and wight,   *bold and strong*
675 And relese him his right,   *give freely to*
And graunte him his londe."

"Here I gif Sir Galeron," quod Gawayn, "withouten any gile,
Al the londes and the lithes fro Lauer to Layre,   *vassals*
Connoke and Carlele, Conyngham and Kile;
680 Yet, if he of chevalry chalange ham for aire,   *In addition; claims them as heir*

---

[1] *What with the beatings and bleeding, their faces waxed black (i.e., had become darkened)*

[2] *That have surrounding battlements and have been very well built*

The Lother, the Lemmok, the Loynak, the Lile,
With frethis and forestes and fosses so faire. *woods; moats*
Withthi under our lordeship thou lenge here a while, *If then; you [will] abide*
And to the Round Table make thy repaire, *(i.e., join in the fellowship)*
685   I shal refeff the in felde in forestes so fair." *reinvest you on this field with*
Bothe the King and the Quene
And al the doughti bydene, *together*
Thorgh the greves so grene, *Through; groves*
To Carlele thei cair. *travel*

690   The King to Carlele is comen with knightes so kene,
And al the Rounde Table on rial aray. *royal*
The wees that weren wounded so wothely, I wene, *knights; lethally*
Surgenes sone saned, sothely to say; *Surgeons swiftly made [them] whole*
Bothe confortes the knightes, the King and the Quene. [1]
695   Thei were dubbed dukes both on a day. *a [single] day*
There he wedded his wife, wlonkest I wene, *most beautiful*
With giftes and garsons, Sir Galeron the gay; *treasures*
Thus that hathel in high withholdes that hende. [2]
Whan he was saned sonde, *cured wholly*
700   Thei made Sir Galeron that stonde *They (i.e., the court); at that point*
A knight of the Table Ronde
To his lyves ende.

Waynour gared wisely write into the west [3]
To al the religious to rede and to singe;
705   Prestes with procession to pray were prest, *urged*
With a mylion of Masses to make the mynnynge. *perform the memorials*
Bokelered men, bisshops the best, *Book-learned*
Thorgh al Bretayne belles the burde gared rynge. [4]
This ferely bifelle in Ingulwud Forest, *marvel occurred; Inglewood*
710   Under a holte so hore at a huntyng — *wood so bare*

---

[1] *Both (royal persons) comfort the knights, the King and the Queen*

[2] *Thus that knight quickly takes to himself that gracious [woman]*

[3] Lines 703–04: *Guenevere commanded, wisely, [that] written messages be sent into the west (i.e., had word sent throughout the land) / To all the clergy to read and to sing (i.e. to celebrate masses)*

[4] *Throughout all Britain the Queen had [them] ring [church] bells*

Suche a huntyng in holtis is noght to be hide.   *left untold*
Thus to forest they fore,   *went*
Thes sterne knightes in store.   *brave; in battle*
In the tyme of Arthore
715 This anter betide.   *adventure occurred*

Notes

Unlike Hanna's edition, this text does not try to indicate the shape or intention of an author or original; and unlike Gates' edition, it does not attempt to document all variants and manuscript evidence. What I offer here is a conservative reading text, conservative in that it reproduces the readings of the Douce MS insofar as these make sense (or can be argued to make sense). I emend only when lexical, grammatical, metrical, or contextual lapses seem to demand it.

Abbreviations: D = Douce MS; Ir = Ireland MS; L = Lambeth MS; T = Thornton MS; A = Amours' edition; G = Gates' edition; H = Hanna's edition. See Select Bibliography for these selections.

1   *In the tyme of Arthur.* This is the classic characterization for the setting of a Gawain narrative. Compare the first line of *Gologras*: "In the tyme of Arthur, as trew men me tald"; *Ragnelle,* line 4: "In the tyme of Arthoure thys adventure betyd"; and *Sir Gawain and the Green Knight,* line 2522 (nine lines from the end): "Thus in Arthurus day this aunter bitidde." The last line of *Awntyrs* repeats this first line almost verbatim (see note).

2   *By the Turne Wathelan. Tarne* or *terne* was a northern ME word for a small lake. The Tarn Wathelene (I adopt this spelling as common among local historians of Cumberland) was renowned out of all proportion to its size as a site for Arthurian adventure. It is mentioned in *Avowyng* ("Tarne Wathelan," lines 131 and 338, and notes at lines 29, 131, and 132), and in *Marriage* ("Tearne Wadling," line 32 and note), and its setting in Inglewood Forest is alluded to in *Ragnelle* (line 16 and note); *Greene Knight* may also invoke the Tarn (line 493 and note). The lake's name is given further variants in the colophon at the end of *Awntyrs* (see line 715 and note), and in the titles of editions by G and H.

        as the boke telles. A conventional alliterative formula, though *Awntyrs* clearly draws upon literary sources.

3   *that.* D: *and*; Ir, T: *that,* so emended by A, G, and H.

4   *dussiperes*. The legendary twelve companions of Charlemagne. See line 277, and compare *Gologras* line 1334 and note at line 1313.

7   *were*. D: *and*; L: *were*, so emended by G and H.

8   *fermesones*. D: *firmysthamis*; Ir: *fermesones*; T: *ferysone tyme*; emended to *fermysone tyme* by A and G; to *fermyson* by H.

    by the fermesones. A technical term for the closed season (approximately September to June), when hunting male deer was prohibited. In *Sir Gawain and the Green Knight*, the first day's hunt for deer takes place "in fermysoun tyme," when the lord has forbidden the taking of "the male dere" (lines 1156–57). Arthur serves the Roman senators "Flesch fluriste of fermysone" (*Alliterative Morte Arthure*, line 180), apparently fatted does taken in the closed season.

13   *Dame Gaynour*. In his novel *The Lyre of Orpheus* (recounting the production of a rediscovered opera, *Arthur of Britain, or The Magnanimous Cuckold*), Robertson Davies suggests that in Welsh Guenevere's name signifies "white ghost" — which would give peculiar resonance to the queen's encounter with the blackened ghost of her mother. See *The Lyre of Orpheus* (New York: Viking, 1989), p. 137. Kenneth G. T. Webster, in his *Guinevere: A Study of Her Abductions* (Milton, Massachusetts: Turtle Press, 1951), notes that "the name in Welsh is Gwenhwfar, which may mean white ghost, or enchantress" (pp. 2–3).

18   *hawe*. D: *herde*; Ir, T: *hawe*, so emended by A, G, and H. H inserts *ho* to regularize *hedes*.

22   *set by*. Ir, L: *serclet on*, followed by G and H. See phrase in line 120.

30   *Borgoyne*. Neither Gawain nor Guenevere have connections with Burgundy. Madden and A somewhat desperately suggest that Gawain's horse (called Grissell at line 546) may have been born in France. H suggests that *Borgoyne* is a corrupted reading of "Orkney," connected to Gawain's birth.

    by boke and by belle. A conventional phrase indicating an oath sworn by the Holy Sacrament (celebrated by reading the sacred text and ringing bells at the elevation), or by the rite of excommunication, which entailed the ritual use of bell, book, and candle.

48   The rhyme scheme makes clear that a line is lacking here in all surviving manuscripts.

51   *dure*. D: *durere*, with *er* abbreviated; *dure* given provisionally by G, unconditionally by H (disregarding G's note); emended to *dere* by A; I follow G's provisional reading of D as *dure*.

55   This line is omitted in D; supplied from T (following G).

56   *wilde*. D follows this word with *swyne* (agreeing with Ir, L, T); *swyne* is omitted by A, G, and H.

58   *And till thaire riste raches relyes on the ro*. D: *And bluwe reches ryally, they ran to the ro*, which repeats line 62; like A, G, and H, I follow T, though I substitute D's *on the ro* for T's final phrase, *on thaire ray*.

59   *grythe*. Omitted by D, though it occurs in the other three manuscripts (spelling from T).

60   *greundes*. D: *grendes*; I follow G's emendation (adopted by H).

62   *rechas*. This is a technical hunting term for the horn note that signals hounds and hunters to reassemble. Gawain and Guenevere ignore the call (lines 68 ff.).

70   *By*. D: *Under*; *By* inserted from Ir, L, T.

       undur a lefesale substituted from Ir (following G and H), for D, *that lady so small*, which seems a nonsensical tag rhyme (though it occurs in L and T as well).

74   *mele*. D: *meve*; Ir, L: *mele*, followed by G and H.

80   *fawe felle*. D: *fewe felles*; I follow emendation suggested by A, accepted by G and H.

81   This line omitted by D; supplied from T (following G).

82   *sneterand snawe*. This is a notable instance (among many) where *Awntyrs* directly imitates a memorable passage from *Sir Gawain and the Green Knight*:

The snawe snitered ful snart, that snayped the wylde;
The werbelande wynde wapped fro the hyghe,
And drof uche dale ful of dryftes ful grete.
(lines 2003–05)

83 *a lowe one the loughe.* D: *a lede of the lawe*; I follow T (with A).

84 This line omitted by D; I follow T (as do A, G, and H).

85 *glides to Sir Gawayn.* Ir, L, and T all have the ghost first approach *Dame Gaynoure*, and the opening of the next stanza, in giving Guenevere's horrified reaction, perhaps supports an initial address to the Queen by the apparition.

86 *yelle.* D: *yelles*; L, T: *yelle*, so emended by A, G, and H.

    The participles and verbs of this and the next line vividly recall the second day's hunt in *Sir Gawain and the Green Knight*, when the hounds "Ful yomerly yaule and yelle" (line 1453).

91 *I gloppen and I grete.* Guenevere's reaction here echoes the description of the fright Morgan Le Faye intended for the Queen in *Sir Gawain and the Green Knight*: she hoped "to haf greved Gaynour and gart hir to dyghe / With glop-nyng of that ilke gome that gostlyche speked / With his hede in his honde bifore the hyghe table" (She hoped to have grieved Guenevere and caused her to die from fright of that being that, like a ghost, spoke with his head in his hand before the high table; lines 2460–62).

94 *clippes of the son.* Gawain's quick-witted and protective rationalization of the horrible apparition (like his resilient efforts in his exchanges with Lady Bertilak in *Sir Gawain and the Green Knight*, where "he defended hym so fayr that no faut semed" line 1531) expresses the unfailing courtesy that upholds his "knighthede."

96 *Sir Cadour, Sir Clegis, Sir Costardyne, Sir Cay.* What these four knights, all familiar figures in Arthurian romance, have here in common seems mainly to be their alliterating names; see *Carlisle*, lines 35, 44, and notes. *Costardyne* seems to be a variant spelling of "Constantine," perhaps the son of *Sir Cadour* who succeeded Arthur as king; see also *Avowyng* line 914 and note.

112   *he.* Omitted by D; included by other manuscripts and editors.

114   *cholle.* D: *clolle*; clearly a misspelling, corrected by A, G, and H, according to Ir, L, and T.

119   *Umbeclipped in a cloude of clethyng unclere.* D: *Umbeclipped him with a cloude of cleyng*; A, G, and H follow Ir and T in substituting *in* and expanding to *clethyng.*

120   *Serkeled.* D: *skeled*; T: *serkeled*, followed by A, G, and H.

124   *holtes.* D: *wode*; alliteration demands *h* (as in Ir, L, and T). I follow Ir (with G).

131   *the hendeste in halle.* D: *so fer into halle*; A, G, and H substitute *hendeste in* from T.

132   *the chaftis and the chynne.* D: *the chalus on the chynne*; A, G, and H correct reduplication of *cholle* by substituting *chaftis and* from T (H spells *chaftes*).

134 ff.   The syntax here is confusing because of the repeated *thou* (lines 134, 135 twice, 136). Gawain begins by calling upon Christ for aid, but then addresses the ghost in the same second-person singular. Having uttered his prayer directly to Christ, Gawain seems to feel authorized to make the demand of the ghost that follows (paraphrased in the footnote).

138   *knowen.* L agrees in this reading, while Ir and T read *krysommede*, adopted by A, G, and H to eliminate reduplication in the following line.

145 456X *Berell or Brangwayn.* I capitalize *Berell*, assuming that the phrase names two women (rather than comparing the speaker's brows to beryl). *Berell* is otherwise unknown in ME romance, and H suggests the line originally named the enchantress Brusen (see Malory, *Works*, pp. 794 ff.). *Brangwayn* is Isolde's servant in the Tristan stories, a look-alike who substitutes for the Queen on her wedding night.

158   *the burde bright.* D: *and to the burde*; I omit *and to* as intrusive.

162   *lonched.* D: *louched* (so A and G read); H reads *lonched*, which I follow, though I retain *on hight* from D, in place of *so light* (G, H).

165   *Thus am I lyke to Lucefere: takis witnes by mee!* D: *Take truly tent tight nowe by me.* The repetition of a key word, usual in the ninth line of each stanza, fails in D. I follow A and G (and H, with modification) in substituting T's line.

167   *Muse on my mirrour.* Ir: *your*; L: *thy*, followed by H; T: *thir*. D's reading makes good sense within the tradition of the three living and the three dead, where the supernatural apparition forms a mirror of the ultimate fate of the living. In *Gologras*, the latter hero offers a commentary on his defeat by Gawain, and Gawain's pretense of submission, in which he invokes in passing Fortune and the Nine Worthy; in the course of the speech, Gologras suggests that each person, "Baith knyght, king and empriour . . . [may] muse in his myrrour" (lines 1230–31; see note). The recommendation of grisly, gruesome, and morbid subjects as useful mirrors of moral understanding to those in the midst of life occurs widely in ME poetry; in *The Parlement of the Thre Ages*, Elde admonishes (just before launching into a lengthy exposition of the Nine Worthy), "Makes youre mirrours bi me, men, bi youre trouthe" (line 290; see M. Y. Offord's edition [EETS 246 (Oxford, 1959)], with note at line 290, and Introduction, pp. xl–xlii).

169   *dight.* This word is inserted from L, following H, for stanza linking.

170   *Thus dethe wil.* D: *Thus dight wil*; *dethe* inserted from Ir, L, and T (following G and H).

173   *thou art of power.* Ir, L add *whil*, and T adds *for* before this phrase.

174   *that ben the aboute.* Ir, L, T present variants of *are besye the aboute.*

179   *at the yete.* D: *at the thete*; Ir, L, T: *yate*; emended for rhyme by G and H.

183   *ar.* D: *art.*

199   *meble on molde.* Guenevere's spontaneous question — whether possessions on earth can aid those beyond the grave — and the ghost's grateful, affirmative reply underscores the profound bond in *Awntyrs* of material with spiritual, living with dead; in doctrinal terms, this is epitomized by the communion of the saints, which allows grace and merit to be redistributed among the saved. Communal prayer — *matens* or *Mas* — may thus undo temporal punishment (in some legends, even eternal punishment) due an individual's sinful acts, and the

individual's fate is beyond her own control. The phrase itself is a distinctive alliterative formula, occurring only here and in *Gologras*, line 807; compare line 499.

202   *mervaile*. D: *wonder*; alliteration demands *mervaile* (from T, though I take spelling from lines 73 and 74); so emended by A, G, and H (note).

209   *the saven of thi sytis*. D: *the sauen ywys*; I emend with L's phrase for the sake of alliteration and rhyme, following A and G.

211   *body bites*. D: *body is*; rhyme demands *bites*, as in Ir, L, and T (so emended by A, G, and H).

212   *blendis*. D: *bledis*; L, T: *blendis*, followed by A, G, and H.

218   *thritty tentales*. A trental is a series of thirty Masses in memory of the dead; Guenevere's mother therefore requests that nine hundred Masses be said for her soul. The merit earned by these Masses (in the form of indulgences) frees her from the torment of *Helle* (line 84), which may actually mean Purgatory. See line 236 and note.

220   *were*. This word is inserted from Ir, L, following G, H.

227   *barne*. D: *barme*, an apparent misspelling; correctly given in Ir and L; emended by A (glossary) and H.

228   *grete*. This form seems to draw upon a collapsed sense of *greten*, "greet, give honor" (MED, 2) and a different verb with identical form, *greten*, "lament, cry out" (MED, 3), which can be transitive, as here. The variant in D of *the* for *thi soule* indicates that the verb takes an object, and is seen as salutation by the D scribe. Yet the passage suggests that *grete* here takes in both the formal features of honor and the personal dimension of lament in referring to the liturgical remembrance and intercession of the Trental of Masses. It seems then to mean "commemorate, mourn for"; this meaning is reinforced by *mynge* in the next line, which also refers to the formal commemoration of the soul through Masses for the dead.

236   *a myllion of Masses*. Guenevere's promise here encompasses a huge number of Masses, though not literally a million. Lollards and their sympathizers, who

openly criticized the ritual observances of the Church, were particularly out-
raged by the assumption (implied, for example, by trentals) that the eternal
merit and satisfaction of Christ's sacrifice in the Mass might be improved by
multiplication. The *thritty trentales* requested by the ghost (line 218 and note)
would comprise nine hundred Masses, and *myllion* may here (and at line 706)
simply round this number to one thousand. Archbishop Henry Bowet of York,
who died in 1421, designated in his will that money be given "pro mille missis
celebrandis more trentale Sancti Gregorii . . ." (for a thousand Masses to be
celebrated in the form of St. Gregory's trental); see *Speculum* 49 (1974), 89.
Such a request was therefore not so unusual for late medieval Christians.

237   *Bot one word, quod Waynour.* D: *A quod Waynour iwis*; alliteration requires
word, which appears in L and T (so emended by A, G, and H); I omit *iwis* for
the sake of meter.

239   *Pride.* While pride is here designated the greatest of the seven deadly sins,
Awntyrs places a corresponding emphasis on the sin which, during the high and
later Middle Ages, came to rival pride as the worst — avarice. The ghost's
concern for charity to the poor (see lines 232 ff., 251 ff., and her final exhorta-
tion at line 319) suggests that the remedy for aristocratic excess is acceptance
of responsibility for the material support of all in the Christian community.
The ghost's instructions reinforce the corporate identity that marks late medi-
eval chivalry and religion by linking the spiritual treasury of merit (*trentales*,
line 218) with the distribution of earthly goods (*almessedede*, line 253).

240   *apertly.* D: *apt*; L: *apertly*, T: *appertly*, so emended by A and G; H: *apert*.

242   *boune.* D: *bly*; Ir: *boune* (adopted by G) makes contextual sense.

253   *aure.* D: *cure.* To make sense and complete alliteration, I follow Ir's reading
(adopted by A and G; modified by H).

255   *withoute speling.* H gives "destruction, waste" (from OE *spillan*); G gives
"sparing" (from OE *spelian*). The context implies, however, that these gifts are
infused in each soul — *graceful, enspires iche sprete* — and that *speling* therefore
means "formal training, instruction," which conscience does not require in
order to act charitably. *Awntyrs* here offers the view that the moral under-
standing prerequisite for salvation — the Golden Rule or the two great com-
mandments — is implanted in each person *withoute speling.* The reference in the

next line to *spiritual thing* about which a lay woman should dispute no further links the passage yet more closely to formal theological discourse. Similar issues, concerning intuitive knowledge or "kinde knowing" versus the need for explicit dogmatic or sacramental understanding, are explored in contemporary poems like *St. Erkenwald* and *Piers Plowman*.

261 ff. Gawain's question to the ghost, had it originated with an actual medieval knight, would demonstrate a remarkable degree of self-consciousness and self-criticism. Other chivalric narratives offer similar chastisement of territorial avarice that renders a king *to covetous*; in particular, Arthur's downfall in the *Alliterative Morte Arthure* follows upon his desire to spread his rule across Europe to Jerusalem (see lines 3216–17).

266 *while his whele stondes*. The ghost here refers to the traditional image of Fortune's wheel, which commonly shows four kings moving through various phases of rule (about to rule, ruling, falling from power, out of power) as the wheel turns; Arthur is momentarily at the top of the wheel, and cannot be overthrown while Fortune keeps him there. But the ghost also prophesies that the *wonderfull wheelwryght* will give the king *a chaunce*, and he will suffer a fall from high estate (lines 267–68). The *Alliterative Morte Arthure* provides an elaborate dream, complete with interpretation, of Fortune's Wheel; as a prophecy of Arthur's eventual downfall, and the disintegration of the Round Table, it serves as a commentary and explanation for the end of the Arthurian fellowship. *Gologras* also employs the image of Fortune's Wheel, together with the Nine Worthy, but uses these to pinpoint the nature of knightly honor, rather than to underscore its transitoriness; see *Gologras*, lines 1220 ff. and notes.

269 *Kinge*. D: *knight*; Ir, T: *kynge*, followed by A, G, and H.

   a. D: *thorgh*; Ir, L, T: *a*, followed by A, G, and H.

270 *Falsely Fortune*. D: *Falsely fordone*; L, T: *False Fortune*, followed by A, G, and H.

271 *That wonderfull wheelwryght*. D: *With a wonderfull wight*; Ir, T (followed by A, G, and H) give the present reading.

273 *Take witnesse by Fraunce*. This line and the next stanza to which it links allusively encompass the entire career of Arthur's European adventures, and in a version that closely resembles that told in the *Alliterative Morte Arthure*. The

ghost's account of the Round Table's exploits, though they are presented as if already accomplished (at least through line 280, which moves to future tense), must be taken as a prophetic prologue to Arthur's downfall.

275   *Freol and his folke.* In the *Alliterative Morte Arthure* and other versions of Arthur's career (beginning with Geoffrey of Monmouth), Arthur initiates his continental conquests by defeating Frollo, the tribune in charge of Roman forces in France (Gaul). Fortune tells Arthur that she has "fellid downe Sir Frolle" (*Alliterative Morte Arthure*, line 3345), and the interpreters of Arthur's dream link "Froille" with "Ferawnt" (line 3404). T's reading, *Freol and his farnaghe*, would appear to be a confused reminiscence, one of many signs of borrowing from the *Alliterative Morte Arthure* in *Awntyrs*.

276   *and.* D: *in*; Ir, L, T: *and,* followed by A, G, and H.

280   *Romans.* D: *remayns*; Ir, L, T: *Romans,* followed by A, G, and H.

       you. D: *one*; Ir, L, T: *you,* followed by A, G, and H.

280 ff.   Arthur's campaign against the Romans, the culmination in the *Alliterative Morte Arthure* of his continental wars, takes him to Tuscany (lines 284, 291), but is aborted before he can reach Rome and receive the Emperor's crown; the dream of Fortune, and the news of Mordred's treachery in Britain, cause him to lead his fellowship back to England for the final battles, as the ghost here prophesies (lines 291 ff.).

282   *Then.* D: *thus*; *then,* suggested for sense by A, followed by G.

       you. D: *with*; T: *you,* supported by A.

286   *knight.* D: *King*; Ir, L, T: *knyghte* (followed by A, G); here as elsewhere, I adopt an emendation (as does H) to reflect D's usual scribal spelling.

       knight kene. The phrase refers to Mordred, Arthur's son-nephew, as the oblique and ominous prediction of the fall of the Round Table in the following twenty-five lines indicates. The ghost makes clear the inevitability of Arthur's death (line 302), Gawain's death (line 298), and the disintegration of the fellowship (line 293), all through *treson* (line 291). As H and William Matthews (*The Tragedy of Arthur: A Study of the Alliterative "Morte Arthure"* [Berkeley and Los

Angeles: University of California Press, 1960], pp. 156–61) point out, many details and verbal echoes connect this passage to the *Alliterative Morte Arthure* and its descriptions of Mordred's arms, his actions, Gawain's death, and the fall of the Round Table. The ghost's striking vision of the destruction of Arthurian chivalry through a little child who even now "playes at the balle" (line 310), nursed in the household of the powerful Arthur, epitomizes the emphasis in *Awntyrs* on the tensions inherent in Christian knighthood.

287   *shal kenely croyse the crowne.* D: *shal be clanly enclosed with a crowne.* To have Mordred decisively crowned makes less sense than Ir's reading of Mordred's treason, which I adopt. In accepting the reading of Ir, *croyse,* I follow the MED in taking this as a form of *crushen,* used figuratively to mean "acquire by conquest" (though this is the only instance cited where such a meaning is possible). H ingeniously inserts *encroche the crowne.*

288   *at Carlele.* The adventures of *Awntyrs* start when Arthur comes to Carlisle (line 3), and the poem concludes with the entire court assembled again at Carlisle (lines 689, 690). In making Carlisle the seat of the Round Table, *Awntyrs* resembles *Ragnelle, Avowyng, Greene Knight,* and so on, which place Arthur's court there. This explains the precise appropriateness of Mordred's overthrowing his uncle/father by being crowned at the very center of power. No other romance stages the rebellion in this way.

289   *That sege shal be sesede at a sesone.* D: *A sege shal he seche with a cession.* All editors reject D's line as "meaningless" (A); I substitute T's reading (with slightly modified spelling).

292   *tydynge.* D: *tying;* Ir, L, T: *tydynge,* followed by A, G, and H.

293 ff.   The ghost here foretells to Gawain his own death — *In Dorsetshire shal dy the doughtest of alle* — though it remains unclear whether Gawain understands her indirection. By muffling this prophecy of Gawain's death and the fall of the Round Table, *Awntyrs* potentially magnifies its shattering impact; this effect, however, depends upon the audience's familiarity with the vivid description of Gawain's final combat in the *Alliterative Morte Arthure,* when after a sea battle he wades ashore and is slain by Mordred (lines 3706–3863). Both Mordred and Arthur offer moving laments on his death (lines 3875 ff., 3956 ff.). In the *Alliterative Morte Arthure,* Arthur moves his force "to Dorsett" (line 4052) for the confrontation with Mordred only after Gawain's death.

294   *Ramsey*. Matthews argues that this is Romsey in Hampshire, next to Dorset, and that the line therefore refers to the place of Arthur's last battle in the *Alliterative Morte Arthure*.

        riding. This word must mean "battle" or "encounter" rather than "region," "area." It has the latter meaning only when applied to one of the three "ridings" (i.e., "thridings," thirds) of Yorkshire.

298   Matthews (following A's note) argues that the precision of this prophecy, involving as it does the relatively unusual word *slake*, proves direct borrowing from the *Alliterative Morte Arthure*, where Gawain impetuously wades ashore at a "slyke" only to meet death at Mordred's hand (line 3719).

306   *suget*. D: *surget*; I follow G's emended spelling.

306 ff.   Any description of Mordred's arms is exceptional in Arthurian literature; in this case, the details are unmistakably taken from the *Alliterative Morte Arthure*, where Mordred disguises himself by putting aside "the sawturoure engrelede" (line 4182).

314   *to*. Omitted from D, this word is supplied from Ir, L, and T (followed by A, G, and H).

316   *welle*. D: *dwelle*; alliteration requires *welle*, as in Ir and T (followed by A, G, and H).

318   *and*. D: *that*; Ir, L, T: *and the dole* (with variants), which meter requires (so emended by A, G, and H).

337   *Rondoles Halle*. The other manuscripts read "Rondallsete" (Ir, L) and "Randolfesett" (T). A, following a nineteenth-century local historian, connects this with Randalholme, "an ancient manor house near the junction of the Ale with the Tyne" in Cumberland.

339   *sale*. D: *halle*; Ir, L, T: *sale*, which alliteration requires (followed by A, G, and H).

341   *innewith*. D: *menewith the walle* (so A, G read MS); as A notes, the abbreviation strokes are not clear, and H ingeniously reads (without comment) *innewith*, which I adopt.

342   *brauden*. A reads *branden*, G concurs, offering "(? for *braudene*)"; my reading
        agrees with H.

352   *The mon in his mantell sittes at his mete*. D: *Mon, in thy mantell, that sittes at thi*
        mete; G adopts T's reading, and H emends using T, a decision I follow.

354   This line is omitted in D; supplied from T, following A, G, and H. This line
        may have been omitted in exemplars of the other copies as well, and supplied
        by scribal copying from line 510, with which it is nearly identical. The descrip-
        tions here, and of the tapestries above and the lady's cloak and Galeron's
        pavilion below (lines 340 ff., 367 ff., and 443 ff.) echo the elaborately embroi-
        dered materials associated in *Sir Gawain and the Green Knight* with the Green
        Knight's appearance (lines 165–66), the arming of Sir Gawain (lines 609 ff.),
        and the dress of Morgan (lines 959–60).

357   *his beveren berde*. Bertilak's beard is "bever-hwed" in *Sir Gawain and the Green*
        Knight (line 845), and in the *Alliterative Morte Arthure* (in a scene reminiscent
        of Froissart's description of King Edward III's wearing a beaverskin hat in his
        ship before the battle of Winchelsea, 1350) Arthur is described "with beveryne
        lokkes" (line 3630).

360   *carpes*. D: *talkes*; Ir, T: *carpis*, which alliteration requires (followed by A, G,
        and H).

363   *Whethen*. D: *Whelen*; emended from Ir and T (followed by A, G, and H).

365   *eny wy welde wolde*. D: *eny wede wolde*; present emendation adapts T, *wy myghte*
        welde, following G.

372   *prene*. D: *pene*; Ir, L: *prene*, followed by A, G, and H.

375   *ynoghe*. D: *Had I nore*; Ir, T: *ynoghe*, followed by G, H.

381   *bordur*. D: *brandur*; Ir, L, T: *bordur*, followed by A, G, and H.

382   *enclawet ful clene*. D: *white many hit seen*; reading from Ir adopted for allitera-
        tion (also by A, G, and H).

385   *blake*. D: *brake*; emended for sense by A, G, and H.

387 ff. The suggestion that the *cheveron* — ME *chaumfrein*, from French *chaufrein*, the top or front of the horse's head-armor — makes Gawain's horse resemble a unicorn is not simply a literary fantasy. In the later Middle Ages armor for both knight and mount became ever more elaborate and decorative, and visual evidence affirms the use of dagger-like horns such as that described here.

392 *that stanseld was one straye.* D: *golde his pencell displaied*; the manuscripts show much confusion here, though Ir, L, T show vague agreement in their description. I adopt T's phrasing, though I insert Ir's *stanseld*; A, G, and H make other modifications.

394 *graithed.* D: *graied*; L, T: *graythede*; emended for sense (following A, G, and H).

396 *poleinus.* A and G read D as *polemus*; I follow H's astute reading of D and his gloss.

  pelydodis. D: *pelicocus*; Ir: *pelidoddes*, L: *pelydodis* (emended variously by A, G, and H).

397 *that lovely con lede.* Variants show that scribes thought the phrase should be taken as "the knight accompanies or leads in that lovely woman": *that lady gane he lede* (T), *that lovely he ledus he ludus* (Ir, with obvious scribal error). MED, *loveli*, 4a, interprets the line similarly, reediting "Thus, launce opon lofte, that lovely [T: *lady*] he ledus" (which agrees with no manuscript reading, but follows Robson's edition, stanza XXI). But *loveli*, as adjective and substantive, is used of men as well as women; given that the lady has preceded Galeron into the hall and moved to the dais, it makes no sense that he would be said to be leading her. In this case, *lede* would mean either procede — "that worthy knight did go forward with his lance at rest" — or, better, conduct himself (see OED, *lead*, v.1, 9, 12, and so on) — "that worthy knight did present himself." See also line 497, where "lordes . . . hom . . . ledes" is used reflexively, meaning "the lords move."

398 *A freke on a freson.* A Frisian horse was apparently not an appropriate chivalric mount, but a workhorse; when Galeron offers Gawain his "freson, fairest on fote" (line 551) as a substitute steed, the latter refuses with scorn. The phrase recalls the *Alliterative Morte Arthure*, where a Roman warrior pursuing Gawain and his band is described (perhaps contemptuously) as a "freke alle in fyne golde . . . [who did] Come forthermaste on a fresone" (lines 1364–65).

404   *herand him alle.* All four manuscripts read *hem alle,* which may refer to the lady and Galeron, to whom Arthur will give a hearing. But the context of public speech engaging the interest of the entire court suggests the line specifies that the assembled nobility stand as witnesses for the formal exchanges and compact that follow. The phrase is equivalent to "in their hearing"; I therefore emend *hem* to *him,* reading the phrase as "with all hearing him (Arthur)." Here and in many other details the narrative emphasizes that the public, festive nature of the occasion intensifies how much of the court's reputation as the font of chivalric values is at stake in Galeron's challenge.

410   *be.* D lacks this word, which is supplied from Ir, L, and T (followed by A, G, and H).

412   *Fighting to fraist.* Galeron's statement of his desire for combat with a champion of the Round Table recalls the Green Knight's disavowal of any such interest: "Nay, frayst I no fyght, in fayth I the telle . . . Here is no mon me to mach, for myghtez so wayke" (*Sir Gawain and the Green Knight,* lines 279–81: "Nay, I seek no fight, in faith I tell you . . . There is no man here to match me, for want of might").

415   *and.* D lacks this word, which occurs in Ir, L, and T.

417   *Sir Galaron. Carlisle* mentions "Syr Galerowne" in its roster of knights of the Round Table (line 43), and "Galyran" appears (together with Gawain) in the *Alliterative Morte Arthure* (line 3636). As Sir Galeron of Galloway he makes one of the twelve knights (all "of Scotlonde" or connected to Gawain's affinity) who in Malory align themselves with Mordred and Aggravayne in the ambush of Lancelot at the Castle of Carlisle (*Works,* p. 1164). Sir Gyngalyne, clearly the same knight as the son of Ragnelle and Gawain (*Ragnelle,* line 799) and identical in other romances with the Fair Unknown (Libeaus Desconus; see *Carlisle,* line 55 and note), is also among this group, as is Sir Gromore Somyr Joure (see *Ragnelle,* line 62 and note, and *Turke,* line 320 and note).

418   *gyllis.* D: *grylles;* Ir, L, T: *gyllis* (followed by A and G); H: *gylles.*

       Galwey. Galloway is the southwesternmost territory of Scotland, northwest of Carlisle and the Solway Firth, and north of the Isle of Man (the setting of *Turke*). In his note (p. xli), Madden points out that from the Middle Ages

216

Gawain was popularly known as Lord of Galloway, making Galeron's challenge to Arthur's sovereignty particularly pointed.

419 ff. Galeron's territorial possessions — the source of identity for a knight, as a member of the landed aristocracy — are all presumably in Scotland, though scribal corruption of proper names makes some difficult to locate precisely. The claim by a Scots lord that the English king had illegitimately taken his lands resonates with the continuous hostilities between England and Scotland in the fourteenth and fifteenth centuries. It reflects also a pattern common to the Gawain romances, whereby the Arthurian court (often set in its familiar seat at Carlisle, near the northern border) gains possession or control of far-flung, sometimes exotic or magical (and often Celtic) territories and provinces. At the point when Galeron accepts Arthur's lordship and joins the Round Table, he has some of the lands mentioned in these lines restored to him by Gawain (lines 677 ff. and note).

424 *unwylles*. D: *umwylles*; Ir, L: *unwilles*, followed by A, G, and H.

433 What motivates Galeron is less an internalized sense of righteousness than his public identity derived from the honor of his lordship, and the desire to avoid the shame of public derision for non-action.

434 ff. Arthur's remarks here point up the intrusive character of Sir Galeron's combat-ready status. He sits upon his charger in battle armor, facing a court that is on holiday and unready for the rites of chivalric violence. The scene precisely repeats the opening confrontations of *Sir Gawain and the Green Knight* and *Greene Knight*, where a mounted knight challenges the court. It also resembles the opening of *Ragnelle*, where Arthur, in the midst of a hunt, is approached by the armed Sir Gromer Somer Joure, who unchivalrously coerces the King's agreement in a compact. Galeron has demonstrated his own knightly honor by insisting that he wishes to fight by the laws of war, "On a faire felde" (line 429). In its adherence to the codes of chivalric combat, promoting honor through ritualized but unrestrained violence, the fight between the two heroes in the present poem resembles that between Gawain and Gologras, even down to the description of particular details and the use of verbal formulas; see line 499 below, with note, and *Gologras*, lines 586, 754, 807, and notes.

438 H emends ingeniously to *I rede the, renke, rest the al night*, which suits the alliterative pattern; A and G adopt readings from T. I have left D unemended.

443 *it.* D lacks this word, which is supplied from L and T (followed by A, G, and H).

450 *Sanapes and salers.* D: *sanape and saler*; Ir, L, T: *sanapes and salers*, followed by A, G, and H.

471 *God stond with the right.* Gawain's assertion here is not simply equivalent to "May the best man win," but a statement of an honor code's fundamental commitment to the display or vindication of worship through violence. The public and ritualized combat of the joust or duel, like an ordeal, assumes that God's honor is at stake as well, or at least that divine justice supports the rightness of the outcome. *Awntyrs* itself creates a showcase for the display of chivalric honor, even as it raises questions (through Guenevere's mother, Galeron's complaints, or the references to the poor) about the self-evident rightness of traditional aristocratic values.

475 *Plumton Land.* Plumpton and Plumpton Head are villages in Cumberland, south of Carlisle, along the Roman road that passes alongside Inglewood Forest and the Tarn Wathelene.

477 *Thei setten listes.* Here and at lines 489 and 497 *listes* refers to the barriers that enclose the area set off for the joust between the two knights, and perhaps as well to a central barrier or palisade serving to keep the mounted knights apart but on course as they rush at each other with lances. The rule-bound and spectacular nature of the chivalric ethos emerges clearly in the care given to organizing this combat, including the installation of viewing places for the King and other noble witnesses (line 492). Two further examples from Malory (*Works*, pp. 518, 1233, cited by H), and Chaucer's description of Theseus' seat in the *Knight's Tale*, equally emphasize the essential role of display and judgment in chivalric combat.

 bylyve. I agree with H, where A and G read *by lyne*.

482 *kindeli.* D: *krudely*; Ir: *kindeli* (followed by G, whose reading I adopt); H takes *krudely* as a garbled proper name.

490 *Alle bot.* D: *bothe*, without *Alle*; Ir, L, T: *Alle bot*, followed by A, G, and H.

492 *Abowve.* D: *Quene*; Ir, L, T: *Abowve*, followed by A, G, and H.

495 ff.   The single combat that follows underscores Gawain's role as the preeminent champion of the Round Table. It strikingly resembles Gawain's part as representative of the Round Table in *Sir Gawain and the Green Knight*, and his comparably bloody duels with Sir Gologras (see note at lines 434 ff., above) and with Sir Piramus in the *Alliterative Morte Arthure* (lines 2513 ff.).

499   *The burnes broched the blonkes that the side bledis.* *Gologras* offers almost identical phrasing of this distinctive alliterative formula; see lines 306, 754.

509   *griffons of golde engreled.* In *Sir Gawain and the Green Knight,* Gawain's heraldic device is the pentangle; in the *Alliterative Morte Arthure*, Kyng Froderike of Frisia asks Mordred about the knight "with the gaye armes, / With this gryffoune of golde" (lines 3868–69). In *Carlisle* (lines 80 ff.), the arms of Sir Ironside (son of the Knyght of Armus Grene) consist of a golden griffin on a field of blue, surrounded by fleurs-de-lis. In *Carle* (lines 55 ff.; see note), Ironside bears similar arms, though apparently with several griffins, which are said to be those of his father (the Knight of Green Arms) with a difference. In one fifteenth-century album of arms, Gawain's device is said to be three golden lions' heads on an azure field, or, alternatively, three golden griffins on a green field (see General Introduction, note 21). It may be that the arms of Gawain or his kin have been mistakenly transferred to Ironside; see the notes accompanying the lines in *Carlisle* and *Carle* mentioned above.

511   *startand.* D: *staryand*; Ir, T: *startand*, followed by A, G, and H.

       he. D: *that*; Ir, L, T: *he,* followed by A, G, and H.

521–22   These lines echo the description in the *Alliterative Morte Arthure* of the blows Arthur strikes against Mordred:

> The cantelle of the clere schelde he kerfes in sondyre,
> Into the schuldyre of the schalke a schaftmonde large.
> (lines 4231–32)

    A further variation of line 521 occurs in *Gologras*: "And claif throw the cantell of the clene schelde"; see line 937 and note.

522   *shinand.* D: *shiand*; I emend spelling for sense.

523   *the lathely lord.* D: *the lady loude*; L: *lothely that lord*, adopted by G; H: *lathely*.

536   *skrikes.* D: *skirkes*; I emend spelling for sense, following G and H.

539   *of his grace.* D: *fele sithe*; Ir, L: *of his grace*, followed by A, G, and H.

540   *swithely.* D: *swathel*; G: *swithely*.

542   *bi the Rode.* D: *o the grounde*; Ir: *bi the Rode,* followed by A, G, and H for the sake of rhyme.

544   *He was swithely smert.* D: *Of he were hasty and smert*; line supplied from L (following G), for the sake of sense.

546   *Grissell.* Gawain's horse bears this name (meaning "gray") in no other romance; in *Sir Gawain and the Green Knight* (as in Chrétien and other French romances) Gawain's horse is Gryngolet (line 597 and elsewhere).

559   *wepputte.* D: *siked*; I emend to Ir's reading (following A, G, and H) for the sake of concatenation with the first line of the following stanza.

562 ff.   The action of these lines is so compacted that it is hard to follow. With the killing of Gawain's horse and his refusal of another mount, Galeron feels *drede* — doubt, not fear — about how the combat should properly continue. He *boldely* — vigorously — spurs his horse across the field, so that he can dismount and continue the fight fairly, on foot (lines 566–67); but first he taunts Gawain for his want of action (line 564) in the wake of Grissell's death. A and H take line 564 as spoken by Gawain, not Galeron.

565   Other editors place quotation marks at the end of this line, making it part of the direct discourse of the preceding line. As a marker of time on the part of the narrator, the line seems to recall Gawain's mythic associations with the sun god, whereby his strength increased until noon and diminished afterward (see *Stanzaic Morte Arthur* lines 2802–07, and Malory, *Works*, pp. 1216–17).

567   *yare.* D: *thare*; Ir, L: *yare,* followed by A, G, and H.

576   D omits this line; I follow H in substituting L's line.

577   *brouched.* A, G read *bronched*, which A glosses as "pierced" and G glosses as "crouched"; I follow H in my reading of the manuscript.

591   *stright.* D: *stight*; Ir: *streghte*, followed by A and G; H: *stright*, emended for rhyme.

594–98 D gives the following for these lines:

> Then gretes Gaynour, with bothe her gray ene,
> For tho doughti that fight,
> Were manly mached of might
> Withoute reson or right,
> As al men sene.

The nonsensical use of rhyming tags and the lack of concatenation with the following stanza indicate the lines are corrupt; A, G, and H emend. I follow G in adopting L for these lines.

595   *Sir Lete and Sir Lake.* A and H follow Ir, where the first name reads *Lote*, no doubt King Lot of Lothian and Orkney, Gawain's father; A and H identify *Lake* as the father of Erec, King Lac. Medieval forms of address almost never make use of the last term (derived from a place or family name) in a knight's title, so that an allusion to Lancelot de Lake or to Arrak Fiz Lake (that is Erec, son of King Lac, line 654) could not be intended here.

600   *wound.* D: *wounded*; I follow A, G, and H for the sake of rhyme.

602   *stound.* D: *stonded*; A, H: *stound.*

603   *the knyght.* D lacks the article, which is supplied from Ir and L (so emended by A, G, and H).

609   *unredely.* I follow H's reading of D.

610   *on his tras.* I retain the reading of D, which makes adequate sense. A, G, and H emend to Ir's *on his face* (T: *faas*). All three editors seem to take this literally as specifying the place where Galeron attacks Gawain. The immense array of words for "face," "visage," "countenance," "look," "gaze," "glance," and so on, which occurs throughout *Awntyrs*, *Gologras*, and other martial chivalric romances,

may indicate that this should be taken as an adverbial phrase of manner: Galeron, wounded and exhausted, makes his last desperate attack "in Gawain's face" — that is, without any care for self-protection, in full view of others and especially of one's adversary, and therefore in the face of ultimate threat. Such a usage resembles phrases appropriated by American English from African-American dialects: "in your face," "in your face disgrace," "get out of my face." As in chivalric romances, such contemporary phrases contain traces of orality and oral contest, and insist that the ultimate point of self-display in an honor society is to command the attention of others. In such situations, success does not depend upon physical victory, for dying gloriously (as Galeron seems about to do) can be a vindication of honor; success instead consists in making a spectacle of honor and prowess and of forcing others — in particular, the adversary — to witness and assent to it, as the court and Gawain do here.

613 *a cast of the carhonde.* D: *a scas of care*; Ir: *a cast of the carhonde*, followed by A, G, and H.

   cantil. I follow H's reading, where A and G give *cautil* ("craft," "deceit").

618 *bi the coler.* Gawain takes hold of Galeron by his *coler*, the part of his armor that protects his neck and throat (the gorget). The idiomatic use of "collar" as a verb does not seem implied here, and is not recorded in English until the sixteenth century.

625 *Than wilfully.* D: *wisly*, without *than*; T: *Than wilfully*, followed by A, G, and H for concatenation.

625 ff. The Queen's plea for mercy, on bended knee before her sovereign, seeking the life of a captive knight, is a stylized scene in chronicle and romance. A notable instance occurs in Froissart, when six citizens of Calais, stripped to their undergarments with nooses around their necks, present themselves to Edward III and offer him the keys to their city. When Edward orders them put to death, "the noble Queen of England, pregnant as she was, humbly threw herself on her knees before the King and said, weeping: 'Ah, my dear lord, since I crossed the sea at great danger to myself, you know that I have never asked a single favour from you. But now I ask you in all humility, in the name of the Son of the Blessed Mary and by the love you bear me, to have mercy on these six men.' The King remained silent for a time, looking at his gentle wife as she knelt in tears before him. His heart was softened . . . , and at last he said: 'My lady, I

could wish you were anywhere else but here. Your appeal has so touched me that I cannot refuse it. So, although I do this against my will, here, take them. They are yours to do what you like with'" (*Froissart: Chronicles*, trans. Geoffrey Bereton, Harmondsworth: Penguin, 1969, p. 109). Similar scenes of queenly intervention occur in Chaucer's Knight's Tale and Wife of Bath's Tale. In the morality play *Pride of Life*, the Queen of Life attempts to warn her mate against deadly arrogance; in the romance *Athelston*, the pregnant Queen kneels and begs mercy for the King's sworn brother, though he strikes her and thereby kills their unborn heir. These poetical and dramatic scenes underscore the conventionality of Froissart's anecdote, discussed by Paul Strohm in "Queens as Intercessors," *Hochon's Arrow: The Social Imagination of Fourteenth-Century Texts* (Princeton, New Jersey: Princeton University Press, 1992), pp. 95–119.

627   *Roye.* D: *ioy*; L, T: *roye*, followed by A, G, and H.

634   I follow H's punctuation, which makes *leve* not an adjective ("dear lord"), but a subjunctive verb form ("if you would allow").

637   *here.* D: *ther*; L, T: *here*, followed by A, G, and H.

640   *releyse.* Galeron here uses a quasi-technical term in giving a quitclaim on Gawain's estates; since he makes it *byfore thiese ryalle* — in the royal presence — it stands as a legally binding agreement. A knight's word delivered in public, oral performance thus becomes the ultimate example and guarantee of his honor.

641   *byfore thiese ryalle, resynge.* D: *by rial reyson relese*; I adopt T's reading, following A, G, and H.

654   *Ewayn Fiz Uryayn.* D: *Ewayn Fiz Grian*; the other manuscripts contain different variants, and I adapt the spelling "Uryayn" [Urian] from Ir's *Fusuryayn*.

654–55   The names of the knights specified here appear muddled because of scribal transmission. *Carlisle* includes in its roster of the Round Table Syr Eweyne the Uyttryan (line 40 — Ywain fitz Urien) and Syr Mewreke (line 34). Before the final battle with Mordred in the *Alliterative Morte Arthure*, Arthur arrays his troops so that

The Awntyrs off Arthur

Sir Ewayne, and Sir Errake, and othire gret lordes
Demenys the medilwarde menskefully thareaftyre,
With Merrake and Meneduke, myghtty of strenghes

(lines 4075–77).

The group that runs to the lists in *Awntyrs* clearly seems to be drawn from this passage.

655   *Marrake and Moylard.* D: *Sir Drurelat and Moylard*; Ir, L, T mention *Marrake*, and all three garble a second alliterating name (*Melidule, Marcaduk, Menegalle*). A, G, H emend to *Meneduke* (as found in the *Alliterative Morte Arthure*; see previous note). I follow the other editors in substituting *Marrake* for the non-alliterating *Drurelat*, but retain D's *Moylard* as metrically appropriate (if otherwise unknown).

664 ff.   Arthur seems here to bestow upon Gawain, in compensation for the territories he is about to restore to Galeron, the lordship of Wales together with a collection of individual lands. Glamorganshire occupies the southeast portion of Wales, with its major towns Cardiff and Swansea on the Bristol Channel. *Bretayne* likely refers to Brittany, an area of northwestern France with strong Celtic links. The other place names cannot be precisely identified; A and H assume they refer to towns in Wales or northern England. *Ulstur Halle* and *Waterforde* might as easily refer to Ireland; the English crown was actively involved in holding and developing its possessions in these two areas of Ireland during the fourteenth and fifteenth centuries. The vagueness and interchangeability of reference to these fringe territories underscores their function in the Gawain romances as tokens of Arthur's kingly power; such scenes suggest that the English king can give away to his vassals (and thus retain control of) the entire Celtic world. In granting Gawain *The worship of Wales* Arthur seems close to endowing Gawain with the principality of Wales. From the time of Edward III (fourteenth century, a generation or so before the composition of *Awntyrs*), the eldest son of the king was created Prince of Wales by the monarch to signify his status as heir to the throne. Given that he has no son (except Mordred), Arthur's bestowal here of *The worship of Wales* upon Gawain seems to hint at the possibility that the King intends his sister's son to be his successor; in any case, the title given here would have special resonance for a medieval audience.

666   *at wolde.* D: *al wolde*; I follow emendation of A, G, and H.

667 *Criffones Castelles.* Ir: *kirfre castell;* T: *Gryffones castelle.* I take this as another garbled place name, though (as the scribe of T suggests in his rationalized reading) one might stretch the line to mean "crenelated castles with griffins." The latter symbols are associated with Gawain in romance heraldry; see *Carlisle,* lines 80 ff. and note, and *Carle,* lines 55 ff. and note.

669 *wallede.* D: *in Wales;* Ir, L, T: *wallede,* followed by A, G, and H.

672 *doue.* D: *dight;* Ir: *doue;* T: *endewe;* A, G: *endowe* (misreading T); H: *dowe,* emending spelling.

677 *Gawayn.* D: *G.;* I expand abbreviation, with G.

678 ff. Gawain's gift returns to Galeron some of those territories Arthur had bestowed upon Gawain (though not Galloway; compare lines 418, 419 ff. and notes). Except for the names repeated from this earlier passage, none of the place names can be identified with certainty, and equally garbled names appear in the other manuscripts. Though some invite guesses (*Lother,* the Lowther Hills?; *Carlele* itself), they seem mainly to serve as empty markers of Arthur's power to exercise dominion over border territories; indeed, Galeron seems positioned — as a lord with holdings in both Scotland and England — as a marcher lord, entrusted with resolving differences between emergent national identities.

680 There are several erasures and additions to the line in D, and the other manuscripts show more confusion than usual. I follow G in simply retaining D with its inserted corrections.

683 *Withthi.* I follow H in supplying this word from Ir as a connective.

 our. D: *your;* Ir, L: *our,* followed by H.

 thou. D: *to;* Ir: *thou,* followed by H.

684 *make thy.* D: *to make* (corrected in MS); L: *make thy,* followed by H.

685 *the.* D: *him;* Ir, L: *the,* followed by H.

693 *saned.* A and G read D as *saved;* I follow H's equally plausible reading of the MS (here and in line 699) since it seems more appropriate.

696   *wlonkest.* D: *slonkest*; Ir: *wlonkest,* so emended by G and H.

703   *into.* D: *in*; Ir, L, T: *into,* followed by A, G, and H.

708   *belles the burde.* D: *besely the burde*; G: *belles the burde,* followed by H. The ringing of church bells usually signals public celebration, and in particular marks the passage of a soul from Purgatory; *St. Erkenwald* (which, like *Awntyrs*, has connections to the *Trental of St. Gregory*) ends on this same note.

709   *Ingulwud.* D: *Englond*; Ir: *Ingulwud,* followed by G and emended for spelling by H.

711   *holtis.* D: *haast*; Ir, T: *holtis,* followed by A, G, and H (with modification).

714–15   In having these last lines almost precisely repeat the opening lines, *Awntyrs* creates a final stanzaic concatenation that links the whole poem in a circular structure. A number of other alliterative poems, most of them nearly contemporary with *Awntyrs*, employ this structural device; these include *Avowyng, Sir Gawain and the Green Knight, Pearl,* and *Patience.* T provides a colophon in couplets following the final line: "This ferly byfelle, full sothely to sayne, / In Yggillwode Foreste at the Tern Wathelayne." For this location, see line 2 and note.

The Knightly Tale of Gologras and Gawain

Introduction

The Knightly Tale of Gologras and Gawain rivals the *Alliterative Morte Arthure* as the single richest and most impressive romance of arms and battle that survives from late medieval Britain. In its passionate attention to the details and motives of combat and its dedication to the honor of individual knights and the glory of chivalry, *Gologras* offers a vigorous celebration of rule-bound yet unrestrained violence. The poem reads and resonates as a literary counterpart of the lavish ornamentation and conspicuous consumption that mark the chivalry it describes: specialized terms proliferate for knightly livery, armor, swordplay, combat, horsemanship, landscape, and for the coded behaviors that define aristocratic courtesy and honor. This huge and difficult vocabulary, the poem's exceptionally demanding rhyme scheme and alliteration, and the formidable Scots dialect in which it survives (together with the general unavailability of the text) have given *Gawain and Gologras* many fewer readers than the energy and excitement of the poem otherwise would claim.

The plot of *Gologras* consists of two distinct episodes, the second almost four times the first in length. The two separate parts work together to produce a unified meaning, though not, as in *Awntyrs*, through a diptych-style, contrastive structure; in *Gologras* the two parts relate almost as orders of architecture, in which the larger structure both repeats and supports the smaller unit. The poem's second episode in this way recapitulates, and greatly elaborates, the pattern of action and meaning in the first part. In view of *Gologras'* density and unfamiliarity, a summary of its action may prove helpful. As in the *Alliterative Morte Arthure*, Arthur and his knights undertake an expedition to Italy; in *Gologras*, however, his purpose is pilgrimage rather than conquest, and his ultimate destination is the Holy Land. Just at the point when the supplies and strength of the Arthurian entourage are exhausted, they come upon "ane cieté . . . With torris and turatis" (lines 41–42). The location is ostensibly France west of the Rhone, though the descriptions of landscapes and fortifications, here and in the second part, conform strikingly to the border areas between Scotland and England, where the poem originates. Sir Kay (as he does in *Carlisle*) attempts simply to expropriate the goods needed by the army, and suffers a humiliating

227

thrashing; Gawain then asks courteously for assistance from the unnamed lord, who puts all of his people and possessions at the disposal of the Round Table. Arthur and his knights refresh themselves, offer proper thanks, and then continue on their way (line 221).

En route to Jerusalem, Arthur notes a handsome and well-fortified castle, "the seymliast sicht that ever couth I se" (line 255). The text locates this castle "On the riche river of Rone" (line 1345; see line 310 and note), though again descriptions resonate with northern Britain. Sir Spynagros (who serves as commentator throughout the second episode) explains that the seigneur of this castle, who turns out to be Sir Gologras, owes allegiance to no lord. This news appalls the King, who vows to gain lordship over Gologras at any cost. After completing their pilgrimage to the Holy Land, Arthur and his knights besiege Gologras, and the poem recounts in detail a series of ringing but costly combats, which culminate in a hand-to-hand encounter between Sir Gawain and Sir Gologras. Like Sir Galeron in *Awntyrs*, this opponent nearly prevails through his knightly skill and endurance, but in the end Arthur's nephew triumphs. In defeat, Gologras demands to die honorably by Gawain's hand. At Gawain's urgent beseeching, he finally agrees to keep his life, but on one condition: Gawain must give the appearance of defeat at Gologras' hand, and, at the risk of his life, return with the apparent victor to face Gologras' vassals in the castle. In accord with his own perfect courtesy and his conviction of Gologras' impeccable honor, Gawain agrees. Faced with this extraordinary display of knightly troth, Gologras' people accept fealty to their lord's conqueror, Gawain, and implicitly to their new lord's lord, Arthur. The progress of Gawain, Gologras, and his knights to Arthur's camp at first gives the King a fright, but the poem ends with Gologras pledging his loyalty to the King, and with Arthur in turn courteously releasing his allegiance in the last lines.

The reduplicating plots of *Gologras* set up an economy of chivalric honor that produces all gains and no losses. Despite Kay's humiliation, Gologras' defeat, and even deaths on both sides during the siege, the honor of all involved (except perhaps for Kay) increases. The reciprocity of honor emerges clearly in the initial episode: first the anonymous knight establishes his rightful lordship within his own domain, as Gawain acknowledges (lines 146–47). Then, by freely and courteously receiving Arthur — returning to him "his awin" (line 153) — he implicitly concedes the King's sovereignty, while he also enlarges his own worship. In such scenes, *Gologras* presents courtesy as a rich and subtle ritual of cultural communication; self-control operates not as an internal discipline alone, but paradoxically as a *spectacle* of restraint. As in *Carlisle*, Gawain demonstrates his knightly superiority to Kay by refusing to do, or even claim, all he might, in the presence of an inferior; he makes a show of his physical and moral force not through coercion, but through honorable submission, which directly produces more honor and more submission.

The representation of chivalry in *Gologras* thus makes courtesy an infinitely subtle concoction of repression and assertion. This emerges most explicitly in the "devis" or charade by which Gawain allows Gologras to save face (lines 1090 ff.), putting aside the immediate opportunity to kill his opponent for the chance of a more willing and complete submission by Gologras later. Both knights' show of composure, or even of a passionate insouciance, in the face of deeply felt disappointment or terrible danger, provides an index of their extraordinary honor and courtesy. This comes through as well in Gologras' grim determination that he *appear* "mery" (lines 769 ff.), whatever anyone thinks. Gologras' resolve recalls Gawain's own remarkable performance in *Sir Gawain and the Green Knight* when, on the last night before his fateful appointment with the Green Knight, he seems to all at Bertilak's castle merrier than ever before. The entrenchment of chivalric values, within art and life equally, is strikingly conveyed by Froissart's anecdote of Edward III asking Sir John Chandos to join the minstrels in singing a dance song just as he was about to join battle with the Spanish at Winchelsea. Such behaviors advertise not the loss of senses or extreme frivolity, but quite the opposite: an unwavering show of disregard of danger, a conspicuous consumption of valuable time, a commitment to the pleasurable and admiring gaze of others. As Froissart says, Edward "was in a gayer mood than he had ever been seen before . . . his knights were cheerful at seeing him so cheerful" (*Froissart: Chronicles*, trans. Geoffrey Brereton [Harmondsworth: Penguin, 1968], p. 115). *Gologras'* chivalry thus insists upon both the extraordinary character of such a gesture towards ordinariness, and upon the fact that above all it is a gesture — a social communication from which others may take heart.

In *Gologras*, as at Winchelsea, such flagrant restraint takes its full meaning by being set against the extraordinary violence surrounding it. Where even the show of composure — the refusal of reaction — is a revealing action, a knight *is* what he does. Accordingly, the narrative gives little space to psychology or internal reflection. Indeed, calculation is, in a chivalric context, a bad thing: Gawain's immediate acceptance of Gologras' unorthodox terms (he pauses just long enough to spell out to the audience precisely how high the stakes are, lines 1103 ff.) enacts his peculiar courtesy, unhesitating and almost reckless. As Arthur later says, with a mix of fatherly worry and knightly exultation, "This is ane soveranefull thing, be Jhesu, think I, / To leif in sic perell, and in sa grete plight" (lines 1304–05). Through this action, Gawain stands to lose nothing, except his life, and as both title characters have pointed out earlier (lines 808 ff. and 1073 ff.), loving one's life is a major impediment to chivalric renown. What Gawain stands to gain, for himself and for all his companions and opponents, is honor: his risk allows Gologras to save face in the immediate situation, before his own vassals, and, what is more, he gives Gologras the chance to reciprocate and so increase his own honor by sparing Gawain in turn when he has the physical force to crush him. Gologras' submission to Gawain, not under constraint on the battlefield, but freely in his own stronghold, reprises Gawain's own gracious and unconstrained deference, and foreshadows Gologras' consequent obeisance to Gawain's lord, Arthur. Such narrative patterning makes the final ripple in this sequence of reciprocal honor seem inevitable: Arthur freely returns to Gologras his own lordship. This edict, issued in the last stanza of the poem, leaves Gologras outside the Arthurian fellowship, and so creates a failure of inclusion that is unusual in popular romance. *Gologras* more than compensates for this slight gap in political cohesion through the unrelieved masculinity of the poem's world; the almost complete absence of women from the action, and the emphasis on violence and direct confrontation, carry through a process of generalized male identification and bonding that far surpass any overt breaks in allegiance.

In *Gologras* then, if honor and courtesy contain violence, violence no less contains courtesy. *Gologras'* superb and profoundly disturbing celebration of the mutual implication of courtesy and violence, of the simultaneous containment and production of these apparent opposites within chivalry, stands out, appropriately and most strikingly, at the narrative center of the poem — in the long, gritty, ritualized combat between the title characters (lines 778–1129). The blunt materiality of this diehard performance — the stress and pain endured by the horses, the lavishness of war gear, the bodily hurt the knights expertly wreak on each other, the effort of moving in armor (ever greater as the fight proceeds) — hammers home the prodigal expense of spirit at the heart of chivalry. Only knights with so much to lose, and whose worth and valor depend not just on accepting but on seeking such loss, can make manifest, to the spectators in the poem as to its listeners and readers, at what cost chivalry purchases its glory.

Because honor is constrained in this way, raw violence and risk form the substance of *Gologras* only insofar as they are able to be transformed by chivalric codes and appreciated by an informed audience. Within the poem, this appreciation consists mainly in spectatorship — the expert yet emotionally engaged scrutiny of the action by Arthur and his knights, by Gologras and his vassals and ladies, and, especially by Sir Spynagros. This knight — whose invented name distinctly recalls that of Gologras, and who thus links the two opposing camps — appears in no other Arthurian romance, and seems to have been created expressly to serve as narrator and advisor within *Gologras*. His continual interventions and elucidations of the action underscore the ways in which external appearance, speech events, and social rituals demand interpretation. His running commentary — on political relations, the protocols of combat, the demeanor of knights in battle, the meaning of ringing bells and torchlit processions — has a double effect. It explains particular goings on, but implies as well the necessity everywhere of cultural explication — technical, moral, political — for those within the poem, as well as for its listeners and readers. A typical instance occurs towards the end of the poem, when Spynagros calms the king and his knights by reading the clothing and demeanor of Gologras and his company, as they proceed towards the Arthurian camp:

> "Yone riche cummis arait in riche robbing . . .
> Betwix Schir Gologras and he
> Gude contenance I se."
>
> (lines 1265–69)

This sense of a person's look, dress, or actions as a form of display available at all times to the gaze of others — and thereby the core of identity, and the potential source of shame or honor conferred by others — underlies all the lavish description and versification of *Gologras*.

The two episodes that make up *Gologras* are drawn from a French romance, the *First Continuation* of Chrétien de Troyes' *Percival*. The second of these tells of the siege of Chastel Orguellous; Gologras, who appears in no other Arthurian romance, thus possesses what might seem a quasi-allegorical name (akin to Edmund Spenser's Orgoglio), derived from the Castle of Pride. Gologras acts out of an idealized chivalric honor, yet he is hardly an emblem of pride, for he embodies an ethos of knightly action rooted in broad social sympathies and concrete description. *Gologras* seems to have been written not long before the Scots printers, Andrew Chepman and David Myllar, published the poem at Edinburgh in 1508. It is among the first half dozen books to be issued from the press in Scotland, and is written in a Middle Scots dialect that has much in common with the vocabulary and forms of *Awntyrs*, *Sir Gawain and the Green Knight*, and other northern Middle English alliterative poems. Its thirteen-line stanza form, identical to that of *Awntyrs*, is among the most complicated in English: the first nine lines are alliterative long lines, using traditional concatenating patterns of sound and formulaic phrases with a density surpassed by only two or three other Middle English poems. The last four lines of each stanza are short, two-stress lines forming a separate quatrain (a "wheel"), though linked by final rhyme to the ninth line. The rhyme scheme is *abababababcdddc*. The form of *Gologras*, therefore, and its very words, phrases, and formulas, give further expression to the ostentatious display its narrative describes. In all these respects, *Gologras* occupies an extraordinary cultural moment, when oral narrative traditions, the aristocratic shame culture of chivalry, high literary sensibility, the cult of Arthur and his nephew Gawain, and the mass production of print culture come together.

The Knightly Tale of Gologras and Gawain

The Text

Gologras was printed by Chepman and Myllar in 1508; only one copy of this edition remains, in the National Library of Scotland (Advocates Library H.30.a). The text was published again by J. Pinkerton in 1792. In 1827 David Laing created a facsimile of Chepman and Myllar's type, and issued what is thus a type facsimile of the black letter edition; Laing edited and corrected the text, however, so it is by no means identical to Chepman and Myllar. Madden based his edition upon the 1827 type facsimile reprint, not upon the Chepman-Myllar print. The facsimile of Chepman-Myllar edited by Beattie in 1950 makes the original print available to all readers, and I have worked from that. Amours' astonishingly learned and careful Scottish Text Society edition (1897) has been of enormous help in preparing the present edition. In transcribing the print, I have regularized orthography, so that *u / v / w* and *i / j* appear according to modern usage; abbreviations have been expanded, numerals spelled out, and modern punctuation and capitalization added. I have also adjusted word breaks to conform with modern usage, both joining and separating forms from the printed text. This policy transforms the characteristic form *our* (representing a monosyllabic pronunciation of "over," "o'er") to *ovr* (and so *ovrcum* and other compounds); though this spelling looks a bit odd, I have decided to stay with it, rather than adding another letter (*over*) or going back to the original form, which would appear at least as odd to modern readers.

Select Bibliography

Manuscript

No manuscript version survives.

Editions (arranged chronologically)

The Knightly Tale of Golagros and Gawane. Edinburgh: W. Chepman and A. Myllar, 8 April 1508.

Facsimile Edition of Chepman and Myllar, 1508. Edinburgh: D. Laing, 1827. [This is a version of 76 copies produced from facsimile type; it is not a facsimile of the original Chepman and Myllar print.]

Introduction

Madden, Frederic. 1839. See Bibliography of Editions and Works Cited.

Trautman, Moritz, ed. *"Golagrus and Gawain." Anglia* 2 (1879), 395–440.

Amours, F. J. 1897. See Bibliography of Editions and Works Cited.

Stevenson, George, ed. *The Knightly Tale of Golagros and Gawane.* In *Pieces from the Makulloch and the Gray MSS. Together with the Chepman and Myllar Prints.* Scottish Text Society, no. 65. Edinburgh and London: William Blackwood and Sons, 1918. Pp. 67–110.

Beattie, William, ed. *The Chepman and Myllar Prints: Nine Tracts from the First Scottish Press, Edinburgh 1508: A Facsimile.* Edinburgh Bibliographical Society. Oxford: Oxford University Press, 1950. Pp. 7–51.

Criticism

Barron, W. R. J. *"Golagros and Gawain*: A Creative Redaction." *Bibliographical Bulletin of the International Arthurian Society* 26 (1974), 173–85.

Ketrick, Paul J. *The Relation of Golagros and Gawane to the Old French Perceval.* Washington, D.C.: Catholic University of America, 1931.

Mathewson, Jeanne T. "Displacement of the Feminine in *Golagros and Gawane* and *The Awntyrs off Arthure.*" *Arthurian Interpretations* 1.2 (1987), 23–28.

The Knightly Tale of Gologras and Gawain

	In the tyme of Arthur, as trew men me tald,	*told*
	The King turnit on ane tyde towart Tuskane,	*journeyed; time; Tuscany*
	Hym to seik ovr the sey, that saiklese wes sald,	*seek over the sea; guiltless; sold*
	The syre that sendis all seill, suthly to sane;	*wholesomeness, truly to say*
5	With banrentis, barounis, and bernis full bald,	*bannerets, barons; fighting men; bold*
	Biggast of bane and blude bred in Britane.	*bone; blood*
	Thai walit out werryouris with wapinnis to wald,	*They chose warriors; weapons; wield*
	The gayest grumys on grund, with geir that myght gane;[1]	
	Dukis and digne lordis, douchty and deir,	*Dukes; worthy; bold and outstanding*
10	Sembillit to his summoune,	*Assembled; summons*
	Renkis of grete renoune,	*Nobles*
	Cumly kingis with croune	*Handsome; crown(s)*
	Of gold that wes cleir.	*was bright*
	Thus the Royale can remove, with his Round Tabill,	*King did set out*
15	Of all riches maist rike, in riall array.	*nobles most kingly; royal*
	Wes never fundun on fold, but fenyeing or fabill,[2]	
	Ane farayr floure on ane feild of fresch men, in fay;[3]	
	Farand on thair stedis, stout men and stabill,	*Traveling; steeds; unwavering*
	Mony sterne ovr the streit stertis on stray.	*Many a bold one on the way starts out*
20	Thair baneris schane with the sone, of silver and sabill,	*banners shone; sun; sable*
	And uthir glemyt as gold and gowlis so gay;	*other [gear] gleamed; gules (i.e., red)*
	Of silver and saphir schirly thai schane;	*sapphire (i.e., blue) brightly*
	Ane fair battell on breid	*troop in breadth*
	Merkit ovr ane fair meid;	*Marched over; field*
25	With spurris spedely thai speid,	*quickly; moved*
	Ovr fellis, in fane.	*Over moors, with joy*

---

[1] *The most splendid warriors on earth, with gear who might go*

[2] *Was never known in the world, but in make-believe or story*

[3] *A fairer crop [of warriors] on any field of hardy men, in faith*

234

The Knightly Tale of Gologras and Gawain

The King faris with his folk, ovr firthis and fellis,	*travels; forest; moors*
Feill dais or he fand of flynd or of fyre;	*Many days before he came upon flint*
Bot deip dalis bedene, dounis and dellis, [1]	
30 Montains and marresse, with mony rank myre;	*morass; swollen bogs*
Birkin bewis about, boggis and wellis,	*Birch trees; swamps and streams*
Withoutin beilding of blis, of bern or of byre;	*building; comfort; barn; shed*
Bot torris and tene wais, teirfull quha tellis. [2]	
Tuglit and travalit thus trew men can tyre, [3]	
35 Sa wundir wait wes the way, wit ye but wene;	*fantastically harsh was; know; without doubt*
And all thair vittalis war gone,	*supplies*
That thay weildit in wone;	*carried as usual*
Resset couth thai find none	*Welcome could*
That suld thair bute bene.	*should; safe-keeping be*

40 As thay walkit be the syde of ane fair well,	*by; spring*
Throu the schynyng of the son ane cieté thai se,	*shining; sun; walled city; see*
With torris and turatis, teirfull to tell,	*towers; turrets; toilsome to tell [fully]*
Bigly batollit about with wallis sa he.	*Greatly fortified; so [very] high*
The yettis war clenely kepit with ane castell;	*gates were fully guarded by*
45 Myght none fang it with force, bot foullis to fle.	*take; except birds that fly*
Than carpit King Arthur, kene and cruell:	*spoke out; bold and fierce*
"I rede we send furth ane seynd to yone cieté,	*advise; a messenger; city*
And ask leif at the lord yone landis suld leid, [4]	
That we myght entir in his toune,	*manor*
50 For his hie renoune,	*high*
To by us vittale boune,	*buy provisions right away*
For money to meid."	*as compensation*

Schir Kay carpit to the King, courtes and cleir:	*Sir; spoke; courteously*
"Grant me, lord, on yone gait graithly to gay;	*way quickly to go*
55 And I sall boidword, but abaid, bring to you heir,	*shall a message, just wait; here*
Gif he be freik on the fold, your freynd or your fay."	*Whatever person he be on earth; foe*

---

[1] *But deep valleys continuously, uplands and [wooded] vales*

[2] *[There was nothing] but mounds and grievous ways, toilsome [to] who[ever] tells [about it]*

[3] *Dragged about and travel-worn thus true men did become tired*

[4] *And [have the messenger] ask leave of the lord [who] those lands has governance over (i.e., who governs there)*

"Sen thi will is to wend, wy, now in weir,   *Since; go, man; cautiously*

Luke that wisly thow wirk, Criste were the fra wa!"   *behave; keep you from woe*

The berne bounit to the burgh with ane blith cheir, *warrior advanced; in good spirits*

60 Fand the yettis unclosit, and thrang in full thra.   *gates; went in boldly*

His hors he tyit to ane tre, treuly that tyde;   *tied; time*

Syne hynt to ane hie hall   *Afterwards [he] went to a tall building*

That wes astalit with pall;   *set out with rich cloth*

Weill wroght wes the wall,   *Beautifully decorated*

65 And payntit with pride.   *splendidly*

The sylour deir of the deise dayntely wes dent *canopy rich; dais gracefully was adorned*

With the doughtyest in thair dais dyntis couth dele; [1]

Bright letteris of gold blith unto blent,   *delightful to the glance*

Makand mencioune quha maist of manhede couth mele. [2]

70 He saw nane levand leid upone loft lent, [3]

Nouthir lord na lad, leif ye the lele.   *believe; truth*

The renk raikit in the saill, riale and gent, *warrior moved ahead; hall, royal and lavish*

That wondir wisly wes wroght with wourschip and wele. [4]

The berne besely and bane blenkit hym about; *warrior attentively and quickly glanced*

75 He saw throu ane entré   *doorway*

Charcole in ane chymné;

Ane bright fyre couth he se

Birnand full stout.   *Burning*

Ane duergh braydit about, besily and bane,   *dwarf bustled; deftly*

80 Small birdis on broche be ane bright fyre.   *skewer by*

Schir Kay ruschit to the roist, and reft fra the swane, *roast and wrested [it]; servant*

Lightly claught, throu lust, the lym fra the lyre. [5]

To feid hym of that fyne fude the freik wes full fane. *feed himself; food; man; eager*

Than dynnyt the duergh, in angir and yre,   *clamored the dwarf*

85 With raris, quhil the rude hall reirdit agane. *roars while; great; resounded back*

---

[1] *With [images of] the stoutest heroes who dealt blows in their days*

[2] *Making mention of who, greatest in their manhood, could fight*

[3] *He saw no living person up above [on the dais] settled*

[4] *That with wondrous subtlety was decorated, with grandeur and riches*

[5] *Quickly snatched because of hunger the drumstick from the body*

	With that come girdand in greif ane woundir grym sire;	*bounding in anger; fierce lord*
	With stout contenance and sture he stude thame beforne,	*ferocious*
	With vesage lufly and lang,	*face; full*
	Body stalwart and strang;	
90	That sege wald sit with none wrang	*warrior would suffer*
	Of berne that wes borne.	*From [any] person*

	The knyght carpit to Schir Kay, cruel and kene:	*spoke out*
	"Me think thow fedis the unfair, freik, be my fay!	*feed yourself wrongfully man*
	Suppose thi birny be bright, as bachiler suld ben,	*Even if; armor; knight's should be*
95	Yhit ar thi latis unlufsum and ladlike, I lay.	*Yet; manners offensive and ignoble; declare*
	Quhy has thow marrit my man, with maistri to mene?[1]	
	Bot thow mend hym that mys, be Mary, mylde may,	
	Thow sall rew in thi ruse, wit thow but wene,	
	Or thow wend of this wane wemeles away!"	*Before; depart; castle unharmed*
100	Schir Kay wes haisty and hate, and of ane hie will;	*hot[-headed]; strong will*
	Spedely to hym spak:	*Directly*
	"Schort amendis will I mak;	
	Thi schore compt I noght ane caik,	*threat count; cake*
	Traist wele thair till."	*Trust well thereto*

105	Thairwith the grume, in his grief, leit gird to Schir Kay,	*lord; anger, did approach*
	Fellit the freke with his fist flat in the flure.	*on the floor*
	He wes sa astonayt with the straik, in stede quhare he lay	*astonished; stroke; spot where*
	Stok still as ane stane, the sterne wes sa sture!	*Stock-still; stone; angry [lord]; so ferocious*
	The freik na forthir he faris, bot foundis away.	*warrior; goes, but strides*
110	The tothir drew hym on dreigh in derne to the dure,[2]	
	Hyit hym hard throu the hall to his haiknay,	*Hastened him fast; hackney (horse)*
	And sped hym on spedely on the spare mure.	*to the barren moor*
	The renk restles he raid to Arthour the King;	*warrior breathless; rode*
	Said: "Lord, wendis on your way,	*go*
115	Yone berne nykis yow with nay;	*knight rebuffs*

---

[1] Lines 96–98: *Why have you hurt my man, trying to assert your superiority? / Unless you make amends to him for that wrong, by Mary [the] gracious virgin, / You shall grieve (rue) for your honor, understand (know you) without doubt*

[2] *The other (i.e., Kay) made his way at a distance stealthily toward the door*

To prise hym forthir to pray,   *To attempt; to beseech*
It helpis na thing."

Than spak Schir Gawane the gay, gratious and gude: *gracious*
"Schir, ye knaw that Schir Kay is crabbit of kynde;   *irritable by nature*
120 I rede ye mak furth ane man, mekar of mude, [1]
That will with fairnes fraist frendschip to fynd.   *fairness attempt; to seek [out]*
Your folk ar febill and faynt for falt of thair fude;   *people (i.e., army); lack of food*
Sum better boidword to abide, undir wod lynd."   *message to await; lindenwood*
"Schir Gawyne, graith ye that gait, for the gude Rude!   *take you this mission; holy Cross*
125 Is nane sa bowsum ane berne, brith for to bynd."   *amiable a person anger; quell*
The heynd knight at his haist held to the toune.   *gentle; behest made for*
The yettis wappit war wyde;   *gates were flung wide [open]*
The knyght can raithly in ryde,   *did quickly*
Reynit his palfray of pryde,   *Reined; handsome*
130 Quhen he wes lightit doune.   *When; alighted*

Schir Gawyne gais furth the gait, that graithit wes gay, [2]
The quhilk that held to the hall, heyndly to se;   *which; led; pleasing*
Than wes the syre in the saill, with renkis of array,   *lord; hall; warriors in order*
And blith birdis hym about, that bright wes of ble.   *pleasant women; countenance*
135 Wourthy Schir Gawyne went on his way;
Sobirly the soverane salust has he: *Politely; saluted (i.e., greeted)*
"I am send to your self, ane charge for to say,   *message*
Fra cumly Arthur, the King, cortesse and fre;   *courteous*
Quhilk prays for his saik and your gentrice,   *Who; sake; courtesy*
140 That he might cum this toun till   *into*
To by vittale at will,   *purchase supplies*
Alse deir as segis will sell,   *As dear as people*
Payand the price."   *Paying*

Than said the syre of the saill and the soverane: *hall*
145 "I will na vittale be sauld your senyeour untill."   *will [allow]; lord*
"That is at your aune will," said wourthy Gawane;   *own*

---

[1] *I advise [that] you send forth some man, more deferential (meeker) in demeanor*

[2] *Sir Gawain goes on the path, who dressed was handsomely*

"To mak you lord of your aune, me think it grete skill."   *act as; own; quite reasonable*

Than right gudly that grome answerit agane: *lord answered in return*

"Quhy I tell the this taill, tak tent now thair till:[1]

150   Pase on thi purpos furth to the plane.   *Continue; mission*

For all the wyis I weild ar at his aune will,   *people I rule; (i.e., Arthur's) own*

How to luge and to leynd, and in my land lent.   *lodge; linger; remain*

Gif I sauld hym his awin,   *If I sold*

It war wrang to be knawin;[2]

155   Than war I wourthy to be drawin   *drawn (i.e., punished for treason)*

Baldly on bent.   *Openly on ground (i.e., among people)*

"Thare come ane laithles leid air to this place,   *discourteous "boy" (i.e., Kay) earlier*

With ane girdill ovrgilt, and uthir light gere;   *gilded-over; trifling gear*

It kythit be his cognisance ane knight that he wes,   *appeared by his heraldic dress*

160   Bot he wes ladlike of laitis, and light of his fere.   *ignoble; manners; silly; behavior*

The verray cause of his come I knew noght the cace,   *actual; visit; circumstances*

Bot wondirly wraithly he wroght, and all as of were.   *hostile he acted; war*

Yit wait I noght quhat he is, be Goddis grete grace!   *Yet know*

Bot gif it happin that he be ane knyght of youris here,   *But if*

165   Has done my lord to displeise, that I hym said ryght,[3]

And his presence plane,   *Or his majesty offended*

I say yow in certane,   *tell*

He salbe set agane,   *shall be compensated*

As I am trew knight!"

170   Schir Gawyne gettis his leif, and grathis to his steid,   *obtains his leave; goes; steed*

And broght to the bauld King boidword of blis: *bold; message*

"Weill gretis yow, Lord, yone lusty in leid,   *yon powerful [one] with his people*

And says hym likis in land your langour to lis;   *it pleases him; distress to lessen*

All the wyis and welth he weildis in theid   *subjects; possesses in his land*

175   Sall halely be at your will, all that is his."   *Shall wholly*

Than he merkit with myrth ovr ane grene meid   *marched; over; meadow*

With all the best, to the burgh, of lordis, I wis.   *city; surely*

---

[1] *Why I tell you this tale, take heed now thereto (i.e., the reason I spoke to you in this manner I will now explain)*

[2] *It would be wrong [for it] to be known (i.e., it would be a misdeed that would cause great shame)*

[3] *And if what I said plainly to him has made my lord (Arthur) displeased*

The Knightly Tale of Gologras and Gawain

The knight kepit the King, cumly and cleir;   *met; comely and fresh*
With lordis and ladyis of estate,
180 Met hym furth on the gate,   *on the way*
Syne tuke him in at yate   *Afterwards; the gate*
With ane blith cheir.   *cheerful regard*

He had that heynd to ane hall, hiely on hight,[1]
With dukis and digne lordis, doughty in deid.   *worthy; deed*
185 "Ye ar welcum, cumly King," said the kene knyght,   *powerful*
"Ay, quhil you likis and list to luge in this leid.   *Always while; wish to lodge; land*
Heir I mak yow of myne maister of myght,   *Here; in my domain sovereign complete*
Of all the wyis and welth I weild in this steid.   *people; territory*
Thair is na ridand roy, be resoun and right,   *knightly prince*
190 Sa deir welcum this day, doutles but dreid.   *without any doubt*
I am your cousing of kyn, I mak to yow knawin;   *cousin (i.e., relation) by birth*
This kyth and this castell,   *country*
Firth, forest, and fell,   *Wood; meadow*
Ay, quhill yow likis to dwell,   *while*
195 Ressave as your awin.   *Receive*

"I may refresch yow with folk, to feght gif you nedis,   *refresh (i.e., provide); to fight*
With thretty thousand tald, and traistfully tight,   *[all] told; reliably equipped*
Of wise, wourthy, and wight, in thair were wedis,   *powerful; war gear*
Baith with birny and brand to strenth you ful stright,[2]
200 Weill stuffit in steill, on thair stout stedis."   *dressed out in steel*
Than said King Arthur hymself, seymly be sight: *to sight*
"Sic frendschip I hald fair, that forssis thair dedis;   *Such; hold; that shows forth*
Thi kyndnes salbe quyt, as I am trew knight."   *kindness shall be requited*
Than thay buskit to the bynke, beirnis of the best.   *moved off; bench, warriors*
205 The King crownit with gold,
Dukis deir to behold,   *worthy*
Allyns the banrent bold   *In all ways the banneret (powerful knight)*
Gladit his gest.   *Welcomed*

---

[1] *He (the lord) had that fair man (Arthur) [escorted] to a hall, [and seated] above on a high [dais]*

[2] *Both with armor and sword to support you completely*

	Thair myght service be sene, with segis in saill,	*hospitality; warriors in hall*
210	Thoght all selcought war soght fra the son to the see. [1]	
	Wynis went within that wane, maist wourthy to vaill,	*Wines were passed; castle; enjoy*
	In coupis of cleir gold, brichtest of blee.	*cups; brightest of surface*
	It war full teir for to tell treuly in taill	*toilsome; tale*
	The seir courssis that war set in that semblee.	*many courses; company*
215	The meriest war menskit on mete, at the maill,	*honored at dinner during the meal*
	With menstralis myrthfully makand thame glee.	*minstrels; making [for] them*
	Thus thay solaist thameselvin, suthly to say,	*enjoyed; truly*
	Al thay four dais to end;	*those four days in full*
	The King thankit the heynd,	*handsome [lord]*
220	Syne tuke his leve for to wend,	*Then; to go*
	And went on his way.	

	Thus refreschit he his folk in grete fusioun,	*abundance*
	Withoutin wanting in waill, wastell or wyne.	*lack of choice items [of] bread or wine*
	Thai turssit up tentis and turnit of toun,	*packed; departed from*
225	The Roy with his Round Tabill, richest of ryne.	*King; lands*
	Thay drive on the da deir be dalis and doun,	*pursue the doe deer by dales*
	And of the nobillest bename, noumerit of nyne.	*[took in] number nine*
	Quhen it drew to the dirk nycht, and the day yeid doun,	*When; dark; went*
	Thai plantit doun pavillonis, proudly fra thine.	*pavilions; thence*
230	Thus journait gentilly thyr chevalrouse knichtis,	*journeyed; these*
	Ithandly ilk day,	*Continuously each*
	Throu mony fer contray,	*far*
	Ovr the montains gay,	
	Holtis and hillis.	*Woods*

	Thai passit in thare pilgramage, the proudest in pall,	*passed on; robes*
235	The prince provit in prese, that prise wes and deir.	*proven in battle; renowned*
	Syne war thai war of ane wane, wrocht with ane wal,	*Then were; aware; building, fortified*
	Reirdit on ane riche roche, beside ane riveir,	*Erected; magnificent*
	With doubill dykis bedene drawin ovr all;	*moats together set*
240	Micht nane thame note with invy, nor nygh thame to neir. [2]	

---

[1] *Though all variety [of food] was sought from the sun to the sea*

[2] *No one might get power over them through malice, nor approach too near to them*

The land wes likand in large and lufsum to call; *pleasing in extent; handsome to describe*
Propir schene schane the son, seymly and feir. *[With] special splendor shone the sun*
The King stude vesiand the wall, maist vailyeand to se: *viewing; valiant*
On that river he saw
245 Cumly towris to knaw; *behold*
The Roy rekinnit on raw *counted on row*
Thretty and thre.

Apone that riche river, randonit full evin *arranged symmetrically*
The sidewallis war set, sad to the see; *firm against the sea*
250 Scippis saland thame by, sexty and sevyn, *[There were] ships sailing*
To send, quhen thameself list, in seir cuntré, [1]
That al thai that ar wrocht undir the hie hevin *[Such] that; made*
Micht nocht warne thame at wil to ische nor entré. *prevent; to issue or enter*
Than carpit the cumly King, with ane lowd stevin: *Then spoke out; voice*
255 "Yone is the seymliast sicht that ever couth I se. *most beautiful*
Gif thair be ony keyne knycht that can tell it, *keen*
Quha is lord of yone land, *Who*
Lusty and likand, *Vigorous and handsome*
Or quham of is he haldand, *Or from whom is he holding [his lordship]*
260 Fayne wald I wit." *Happily; know*

Than Schir Spynagrose with speche spak to the King:
"Yone lord haldis of nane leid, that yone land aw, *holds [power] through no lord; governs*
Bot everlesting but legiance, to his leving, [2]
As his eldaris has done, enduring his daw." *elders (i.e., ancestors); to his day*
265 "Hevinly God!" said the heynd, "how happynis this thing? *handsome [King]*
Herd thair ever ony sage sa selcouth ane saw! *any wise [person] so marvelous a saying*
Sal never myne hart be in saill na in liking, *health; happiness*
Bot gif I loissing my life, or be laid law, *Unless; lose; low*
Be the pilgramage compleit I pas for saull prow, [3]
270 Bot dede be my destenyng, *Unless death; destiny*
He sall at my agane cumyng *return*

---

[1] *[Available] for dispatch, when them [it] pleased, into diverse countries*

[2] *But [holds it] forever without [owing] service [to a superior lord], until his death*

[3] *When the pigrimage is completed [which] I pass (i.e., undertake) for my soul's welfare*

Mak homage and oblissing,   *homage and obeisance*
I mak myne avow!"

"A! Lord, sparis of sic speche, quhill ye speir more,   *cease from such; until; inquire*
275   For abandonit will he noght be to berne that is borne.   *subjugated; knight*
Or he be strenyeit with strenth, yone sterne for to schore, [1]
Mony ledis salbe loissit, and liffis forlorne.   *men shall be lost; forfeited*
Spekis na succeudry, for Goddis sone deir!   *Speak no false pride*
Yone knicht to scar with skaitht, ye chaip nocht but scorne. [2]
280   It is full fair for to be fallow and feir   *fellow (i.e., equal) and companion*
To the best that has bene brevit you beforne.   *praised*
The myghty king of Massidone, wourthiest but wene, [3]
Thair gat he nane homage,   *got*
For all his hie parage,   *high rank*
285   Of lord of yone lynage,   *lineage*
Nor never none sene.   *since*

"The wy that wendis for to were quhen he wenys best,   *person; (make) war; knows better*
All his will in this warld, with welthis I wys,   *power; resources indeed*
Yit sall be licht as leif of the lynd lest, [4]
290   That welteris doun with the wynd, sa waverand it is.   *flutters; so insecure*

. . . .

Your mycht and your majesté mesure but mys."   *majesty add up only to trouble*
"In faith," said the cumly King, "trou ye full traist,   *believe you securely*
My hecht sall haldin be, for baill or for blis: *promise; woe*
Sall never my likame be laid unlaissit to sleip,   *body; unlaced [i.e., without armor]*
295   Quhill I have gart yone berne bow,   *Until; made yon knight bow down*
As I have maid myne avow —
Or ellis mony wedou   *a widow*
Ful wraithly sal weip."   *wrenchingly shall weep*

---

[1] *Before he [may] be constrained by force, as concerns threatening yonder fierce (warrior)*

[2] *[If] you threaten yonder knight with harm, you will not escape without shame*

[3] *The powerful king of Macedon (i.e., Alexander the Great), the most worshipful without doubt*

[4] *Shall nonetheless be as light (i.e., ineffectual) as the least leaf of the linden tree*

	Thair wes na man that durst mel to the King	*speak*
300	Quhan thai saw that mighty sa movit in his mude.	*powerful [one]; mood*
	The Roy rial raid withoutin resting,	*royal rode*
	And socht to the cieté of Criste, ovr the salt flude.	*sought for; flood (i.e., sea)*
	With mekil honour in erd he maid his offering,	*much; earth*
	Syne buskit hame the samyne way that he before yude.	*Then hastened home; went*
305	Thayr wes na spurris to spair, spedely thai spring;	*spurs to spare; rushed [off]*
	Thai brochit blonkis to thair sidis brist of rede blude.	*spurred horses till; burst; blood*
	Thus the Roy and his rout restles thai raid	
	Ithandly ilk day,	*Steadily each*
	Ovr the montains gay,	
310	To Rone tuke the reddy way,	*[the] Rhone [valley]*
	Withoutin mare abaid.	*more delay*
	Thai plantit doun ane pailyeoun, upone ane plane lee,	*set out; pavilion; plain sheltered*
	Of pall and of pillour that proudly wes picht,	*rich cloth; fur; constructed*
	With rapis of rede gold, riale to see,	*tassels*
315	And grete ensenyes of the samyne, semly by sicht;	*heraldic bearings; same [material]*
	Bordouris about, that bricht war of ble,	*bright; appearance*
	Betin with brint gold, burely and bricht;	*Beaten; burnished gold, noble*
	Frenyeis of fyne silk, fretit ful fre	*Fringes; crisscrossed*
	With deir dyamonthis bedene, that dayntely wes dicht. [1]	
320	The King cumly in kith, coverit with croune,	*with his household*
	Callit knichtis sa kene,	
	Dukis douchty bedene:	*together*
	"I rede we cast us betwene,	*advise we take counsel*
	How best is to done."	*do*
325	Than spak ane wight weriour, wourthy and wise:	*powerful*
	"I rede ane sayndis man ye send to yone senyeour,	*messenger; lord*
	Of the proudest in pall, and haldin of prise, [2]	
	Wise, vailyeing, and moist of valour.	*valiant and most*
	Gif yone douchty in deid wil do your devise,	*If; request*
330	Be boune at your bidding in burgh and in bour,	*compliant; city; private room*

---

[1] *With costly diamonds grouped together, that subtly were crafted*

[2] *[One] of the most impressive in appearance, and [someone] held in highest esteem*

Ressave him reverendly, as resoun in lyis;   Receive; honorably; as lies within reason

. . . .

And gif he nykis you with nay, yow worthis on neid   scorns you [it] becomes you

For to assege yone castel   assault

With cant men and cruel,   bold; fierce

335 Durandly for to duel   Stoutly; fight

Ever quhill ye speid."   flourish

Than Shir Gawane the gay, grete of degre,

And Shir Lancelot de Lake, without lesing,   lying

And avenand Schir Ewin, thai ordanit that thre   courteous; dispatched

340 To the schore chiftane, chargit fra the Kyng.   fearsome; instructed

Spynagros than spekis, said, "Lordingis in le,   on earth [i.e., right here]

I rede ye tent treuly to my teching,   advise; attend

For I knaw yone bauld berne better than ye,   bold warrior

His land, and his lordschip, and his leving.   living (i.e., income)

345 And ye ar thre in this thede, thrivand oft in thrang, Though; company; triumphing; combat

War al your strenthis in ane,   Were; [combined] into one

In his grippis and ye gane,   if you go

He wald ovrcum yow ilkane,   each one

Yone sterne is sa strang.

350 "And he is maid on mold meik as ane child,   made (i.e., conducts himself) on earth

Blith and bousum that berne as byrd in hir bour,   gracious; bride in her own room

Fayr of fell and of face as flour unfild,   skin; unspoiled

Wondir stalwart and strang to strive in ane stour.   battle

Thairfore meikly with mouth mel to that myld,   speak

355 And mak him na manance, bot al mesoure. [1]

Thus with trety ye cast yon trew undre tyld,

And faynd his frendschip to fang with fyne favour.   seek; to obtain

It hynderis never for to be heyndly of speche;   pleasing

He is ane lord riale,

360 Ane seymly soverane in sale,   hall

---

[1] Lines 355–56: *And make no threat against him, but [show] complete moderation. / Thus with diplomacy (i.e., entreaty) [should] you act [toward] that true [knight] in his castle (i.e., under his protection)*

Ane wourthy wy for to wale, *person to exalt*
Throu all this warld reche." *world magnificent*

"Thi counsale is convenabill, kynd and courtese; *appropriate*
Forthi us likis thi lair listin and leir."[1]
365 Thai wyis, wourthy in weid, wend on thair ways, *Those men; dress, move*
And caryis to the castell, cumly and cleir; *go [off] to*
Sent ane saynd to the soverane sone, and hym sais, *[They]; messenger; right away; [to] him*
Thre knichtis fra court cum thay weir. *were*
Than the ledis belife the lokkis unlaissis; *servants quickly the locks unlatch*
370 On fute freschly thai frekis foundis but feir; *foot; men proceed without doubt*
The renkis raithly can raik into the round hald. *men directly do advance; hold (i.e., castle)*
Thair met thame at the entré
Ladys likand to se, *ladies pleasing to see*
Thretty knichtis and thre,
375 That blith war and bald.

Thai war courtes and couth thair knyghthed to kyth, *courteous and polished; to display*
Athir uthir wele gret in gretly degré; *Each [the] other; saluted*
Thai bowit to the bernys, that bright war and blith, *bowed (i.e., showed deference)*
Fair in armys to fang, of figure sa fre. *embrace, in appearance so noble*
380 Syne thay sought to the chalmer, swiftly and swith, *Then; sought out the chamber; briskly*
The gait to the grete lord semely to se, *path*
And salust the soverane sone, in ane sith, *greet; immediately, [all] at one time*
Courtesly inclinand, and kneland on kne. *bowing*
Ane blithar wes never borne of bane nor of blude; *A more noble [knight]; bone*
385 All thre in certane
Salust the soverane, *Greet*
And he inclynand agane, *acknowledging in return*
Hatles, but hude. *Hatless, but [for] his hood*

Than Schir Gawyne the gay, gude and gracius,
390 That ever wes beildit in blis, and bounté embrasit, *anchored; [with] largesse filled*
Joly and gentill, and full chevailrus,
That never poynt of his prise wes fundin defasit, *detail; honor was found deficient*

---

[1] *Therefore it pleases us [to] listen and learn [from] your lore*

Egir and ertand, and ryght anterus, *Eager and lively; adventurous*

Illuminat with lawté, and with lufe lasit, *Radiant with loyalty; love bound up*

395 Melis of the message to Schir Golagrus. *Speaks*

Before the riale on raw the renk wes noght rasit; *in his place the knight; discomposed*

With ane clene contenance, cumly to knaw, *a candid look; behold*

Said: "Our soverane, Arthour,

Gretis the with honour,

400 Has maid us thre as mediatour,

His message to schaw. *show (i.e., make known)*

"He is the raillest Roy, reverend and rike, *kingliest King; powerful*

Of all the rentaris to ryme or rekin on raw. *lords to make note of or reckon in order*

Thare is na leid on life of lordschip hym like, *lord*

405 Na nane sa doughty of deid, induring his daw. *during his day (i.e., life)*

Mony burgh, mony bour, mony big bike, *Many [a] city; dwelling; swarm of men*

Mony kynrik to his clame, cumly to knaw, *kingdom; control*

Maneris full menskfull, with mony deip dike; *Manors; noble; deep moats*

Selcouth war the sevint part to say at saw. *Wondrous were the seventh; in words*

410 Thare anerdis to our Nobill, to note quhen hym nedis, [1]

Twelf crownit kingis in feir,

With all thair strang poweir,

And mony wight weryer, *many [a] powerful warrior*

Worthy in wedis. *gear*

415 "It has bene tauld hym with tong, trow ye full traist, *tongue*

Your dedis, your dignité and your doughtynes,

Brevit throu bounté for ane of the best *Renowned for largesse; one*

That now is namyt neir of all nobilnes, [2]

Sa wyde quhare wourscip walkis be west.

420 Our seymly Soverane hymself, forsuth, will noght cese *truly; cease*

Quhill he have frely fangit your frendschip to fest; *Until; accepted; in hand*

Gif pament or praier mught mak that purchese, *If gift or prayer; agreement*

For na largese my Lord noght wil he never let, *riches; let [up]*

---

[1] Lines 410–11: *There answer to our Lord, for service when he needs [them], / Twelve crowned kings together*

[2] Lines 418–19: *Who now is reputed to be virtually the paragon of all nobility / So widely (i.e., in every place) where honor walks by the west (i.e., where honor spreads widely among the people)*

	Na for na riches to rigne. [1]	
425	I mak you na lesing,	*lie*
	It war his maist yarnyng	*yearning*
	Your grant for to get."	*[feudal] submission to receive*

	Than said the syre of the sail, with sad sembland:	*lord of the hall with solemn look*
	"I thank your gracious grete lord and his gude wil;	
430	Had ever leid of this land, that had bene levand,	*lord; living*
	Maid ony feuté before, freik, to fulfil,	*Made any fealty; sir*
	I suld sickirly myself be consentand,	*surely; agreeable*
	And seik to your soverane, seymly on syll.	*on throne*
	Sen hail our doughty elderis has bene endurand, [2]	
435	Thrivandly in this thede, unchargit as thril,	
	If I, for obeisance or boist, to bondage me bynde,	
	I war wourthy to be	*[Then] I were*
	Hingit heigh on ane tre,	*Hanged*
	That ilk creature might se,	*each*
440	To waif with the wynd.	*wave*

	"Bot savand my senyeoury fra subjectioun,	*keeping [safe] my sovereignty*
	And my lordscip unlamyt, withoutin legiance,	*unimpaired; service*
	All that I can to yone King, cumly with croun,	
	I sall preif all my pane to do hym plesance,	*prove (take) every pain*
445	Baith with body and beild, bowsum and boun,	*possessions friendly and eager*
	Hym to mensk on mold, withoutin manance.	*to honor; hostility*
	Bot nowthir for his senyeoury, nor for his summoun,	*neither; lordship; command*
	Na for dreid of na dede, na for na distance,	*no strife*
	I will noght bow me ane bak for berne that is borne.	*bow my back one time*
450	Quhill I may my wit wald,	*wield (i.e., possess)*
	I think my fredome to hald,	*intend my [own] lordship*
	As my eldaris of ald	
	Has done me beforne."	

---

[1] *Not for any riches (i.e., thing) to reign (i.e., within his power)*

[2] Lines 434–36: *Since (i.e., because) [as] free [men] our ancestors have always lived, / Prosperously among this people, not bound as vassals [to anyone], / Were I, through [either] submissiveness or threat, in homage [to another to] bind (i.e., obligate) myself*

Thai lufly ledis at that lord thair levis has laught;   *Those; their leaves have taken*

455 Bounit to the bauld King, and boidword him broght.   *Went; message*

Than thai schupe for to assege segis unsaught,   *prepared to assault warriors unyielding*

Ay the manlyest on mold, that maist of myght moght.

Thair wes restling and reling but rest that raught.   *tumult and confusion without; went on*

Mony sege ovr the sey to the cité socht;   *fighter; made way*

460 Schipmen ovr the streme thai stithil full straught,   *hasten straightaway*

With alkin wappyns, I wys, that wes for were wroght.   *all kinds of weapons; war*

Thai bend bowis of bras braithly within;   *furiously*

Pellokis paisand to pase,   *Cannonballs heavy to [set in] place*

Gapand gunnys of brase,   *Huge*

465 Grundin ganyeis thair wase,   *Sharpened darts there were*

That maid ful gret dyn.   *din*

Thair wes blawing of bemys, braging and beir;   *trumpets, racket and blare*

Bretynit doune braid wod, maid bewis full bair;   *Chopped; broad branches; boughs*

Wrightis welterand doune treis, wit ye but weir,   *Carpenters hacking; without doubt*

470 Ordanit hurdys ful hie in holtis sa haire,   *Set up hurdles; woods so bare*

To gar the gayest on grund grayne undir geir.   *To cause; (to) groan in their gear*

For to greif thair gomys, gramest that wer,   *enemies, most hostile*

Thus thai schupe for ane salt, ilk sege seir;   *prepared; assault, each and every warrior*

Ilka soverane his enseyne shewin has thair;   *commander his heraldic sign displayed*

475 Ferly fayr wes the feild, flekerit and faw   *Marvelously; sparkling and dappled*

With gold and goulis in greyne,   *gules (i.e., red) dyed fast*

Schynand scheirly and scheyne;   *brightly; beautiful*

The sone, as cristall sa cleyne,

In scheildis thai schaw.   *reflect*

480 Be it wes mydmorne and mare, merkit on the day,   *By [the time] it; as the day goes*

Schir Golagros mery men, menskful of myght,   *Gologras' hearty; proud*

In greis and garatouris, grathit full gay,   *greaves and sashes, fitted out*

Sevyne score of scheildis thai schew at ane sicht.   *show at one sight*

Ane helme set to ilk scheild, siker of assay,   *tried and true*

485 With fel lans on loft, lemand ful light.   *lethal lances aloft, gleaming*

Thus flourit thai the forefront, thair fays to fray,   *deployed; foes to frighten*

The frekis, that war fundin ferse and forssy in fight.   *warriors; proven fierce and stalwart*

Ilk knyght his cunysance kithit full cleir;   *[heraldic] device displayed*

Thair names writtin all thare,

490	Quhat berne that it bare,	*Which knight*
	That ilk freke quhare he fare	*wherever*
	Might wit quaht he weir.	*make known who he was*
	"Yone is the warliest wane," said the wise King,	*most formidable stronghold*
	"That ever I wist in my walk, in all this warld wyde;	*saw in my travels*
495	And the straitest of stuf, with richese to ring,	*soundest built; with power to reign*
	With unabasit bernys bergane to abide;	*undaunted warriors conflict to endure*
	May nane do thame na deir with undoyng;	*harm with open attack*
	Yone house is sa huge hie, fra harme thame to hide.	
	Yit sal I mak thame unrufe, foroutin resting,	*[for] them strife without*
500	And reve thame thair rentis, with routis full ride,	*deprive; [feudal] rents; pillaging fierce*
	Thoght I suld fynd thame new notis for this nine yeir;[1]	
	And in his aune presence	*territory*
	Heir sall I mak residence,	
	Bot he with force mak defence,	*Unless*
505	With strenth me to steir."	*[And]; drive off*
	"Quhat nedis," said Spinagrus, "sic notis to nevin,	*such words to say*
	Or ony termis be turnit, I tell you treuly?	*Before; exchanged*
	For thair is segis in yone saill wil set upone sevin[2]	
	Or thay be wrangit, I wis, I warne you ilk wy.[3]	
510	Nane hardiar of hertis undir the hevin:	
	Or thay be dantit with dreid, erar will thai de;	*daunted; sooner; die*
	And thai with men upone mold be machit full evin,	*If; earth are matched up evenly*
	Thai salbe fundin right ferse, and full of chevalrie.	*found*
	Schir, ye ar in your majesté, your mayne and your myght,	
515	Yit within thir dais thre,	*these days three*
	The sicker suth sall ye se,	*unshakable truth*
	Quhat kin men that thai be,	*What kind [of]*
	And how thai dar fight."	

---

[1] *Though I should find them (i.e., the people on the lands) new occupation for these nine years*

[2] *For there are warriors in this hall [who] will take a great risk* (see note)

[3] *Before they [will] be wronged (i.e., crossed), indeed, I assure you [concerning] each man*

	As the reverend Roy wes reknand upone raw,	*considering [each point] in a row*
520	With the rout of the Round Tabill, that wes richest,	*company; most powerful*
	The King crounit with gold, cumly to knaw,	
	With reverend baronis and beirnis of the best,	
	He hard ane bugill blast brym and ane loud blaw,	*loudly; trump*
	As the seymly sone silit to the rest.	*sank to its*
525	A gome gais to ane garet, glisnand to schaw,	*turret, sparkling to behold*
	Turnit to ane hie toure, that tight wes full trest;	*Went; constructed was soundly*
	Ane helme of hard steill in hand has he hynt,	*grasped*
	Ane scheld wroght all of weir,	*[gold] wire*
	Semyt wele upone feir;	*[Which] seemed well together*
530	He grippit to ane grete speir,	
	And furth his wais wynt.	

	"Quhat signifyis yone schene scheild?" said the Senyeour.	*Lord*
	"The lufly helme and the lance, all ar away,	*are gone [now]*
	The brym blast that he blew with ane stevin stour?"	*fierce; powerful sound*
535	Than said Spynagrus with speche: "The suth sall I say.	*truth*
	Yone is ane freik in his force, and fresch in his flour.	*warrior in his prime*
	To se that his schire weid be sicker of assay,	*To test; handsome gear; sure against attack*
	He thinkis prouese to preve for his paramour,	*his prowess to show; beloved*
	And prik in your presence to purchese his pray.	*ride (joust); earn his reputation*
540	Forthi makis furth ane man, to mach hym in feild,	*Therefore put forth*
	That knawin is for cruel,	*fierce*
	Doughty dyntis to dell,	*strokes to strike*
	That for the maistry dar mell	*engage*
	With schaft and with scheild."	

545	Than wes the King wondir glaid, and callit Gaudifeir;	
	Quhilum in Britane that berne had baronyis braid.	*Once; sired*
	And he gudly furth gais, and graithit his geir,	*readies*
	And buskit hym to battell, without mair abaid.	*hastened; delay*
	That wy walit, I wis, all wedis of weir	*warrior picked out; garments of war*
550	That nedit hym to note gif he nane had.	*it was necessary for him to use*

. . . .

	Bery broune wes the blonk, burely and braid,	*Berry-brown; horse, burly and huge*
	Upone the mold, quhare thai met, before the mydday.	
	With lufly lancis and lang,	

	Ane faire feild can thai fang,	*did they take*
555	On stedis stalwart and strang,	
	Baith blanchart and bay.	*white and reddish-brown*

	Gaudifeir and Galiot, in glemand steil wedis,	*steel armor*
	As glavis glowand on gleid, grymly thai ride.	*blades; on live coals*
	Wondir sternly thai steir on thair stent stedis:	*they advance; unflinching*
560	Athir berne fra his blonk borne wes that tide. [1]	
	Thai ruschit up rudly, quhasa right redis;	*furiously, whoso rightly understands*
	Out with swerdis thai swang fra thair schalk side.	*noble*
	Thairwith wraithly thai wirk, thai wourthy in wedis, [2]	
	Hewit on the hard steil, and hurt thame in the hide.	*skin*
565	Sa wondir freschly thai frekis fruschit in feir,	*struggled together*
	Throw all the harnes thai hade,	*armor*
	Baith birny and breistplade,	*Both cuirass and breastplate*
	Thairin wappynis couth wade,	*Where; penetrate*
	Wit ye but weir.	*You may be certain*

570	Thus thai faught upone fold, with ane fel fair,	*lethal onslaught*
	Quhill athir berne in that breth bokit in blude.	*strife moved about through blood*
	Thus thai mellit on mold, ane myle way and maire,	*struggled; for about half an hour*
	Wraithly wroht, as thei war witlese and wode.	*Furiously; reckless and mad*
	Baith thai segis, forsuth, sadly and sair, [3]	
575	Thoght thai war astonait, in that stour stithly thai stude.	
	The feght sa felly thai fang, with ane fresch fair, [4]	
	Quhil Gaudifeir and Galiot baith to grund yhude.	*Until; fell*
	Gaudifeir gat up agane, throu Goddis grete mightis —	
	Abone him wichtely he wan,	*Over him (i.e., Galiot) powerfully he prevailed*
580	With the craft that he can.	*skill; could [muster]*
	Thai lovit God and Sanct An,	*praised; Saint Anne*
	The King and his knightis.	

---

[1] *Either warrior was overthrown from his horse in that [first] pass*

[2] *With that furiously they work (i.e., fight), those worthy [fighters] in armor*

[3] Lines 574–75: *Both those warriors, indeed, stoutly and eagerly, / Though they were stunned, in that conflict valiantly stood [their ground]*

[4] *The fight so lethally they engaged, with each fresh attack*

Than wes Galiot the gome hynt in till ane hald.   *knight taken into a stronghold*

Golagrus grew in greif, grymly in hart,

585 And callit Schir Rigal of Rone, ane renk that wes bald: *bold*

"Quhill this querrell be quyt, I cover never in quert. [1]

With wailit wapnis of were, evin on yone wald,   *choice (i.e., valuable); war; field*

On ane sterand steid that sternly will stert   *lively; boldly will move*

I pray the, for my saik, that it be deir sald;   *dear bought*

590 Was never sa unsound set to my hert."   *such trouble*

That gome gudly furth gays and graithit his gere,   *warrior; goes and readies*

Blew ane blast of ane horne,

As wes the maner beforne;

Scheld and helm has he borne

595 Away with his spere.

The King crownit with gold this cumpas wele knew,   *pattern*

And callit Schir Raunald, cruell and kene: *fierce and eager*

"Gif ony pressis to this place, for prowes to persew,   *hastens; prowess to pursue*

Schaip the evin to the schalk, in thi schroud schene." [2]

600 The deir dight him to the deid, be the day dew: [3]

His birny and his basnet, burnist full bene;   *armor; helmet polished well are*

Baith his horse and his geir wes of ane hale hew,   *a single color*

With gold and goulis sa gay graithit in grene;   *red; adorned*

Ane schene scheild and ane schaft, that scharply was sched.   *honed*

605 Thre ber hedis he bair,   *bear heads [as heraldic device]*

As his eldaris did air,   *ancestors did before*

Quhilk beirnis in Britane wair   *Which warriors*

Of his blude bred.

Quhen the day can daw, deirly on hight,   *did dawn*

610 And the sone in the sky wes schynyng so schir,   *bright*

Fra the castell thair come cariand ane knight,   *riding*

Closit in clene steill, upone ane coursyr.   *Enclosed; warhorse*

Schir Rannald to his riche steid raikit full right;   *proceeded*

---

[1] *Until this insult is answered, I [will] never recover in court*

[2] *Present yourself directly to the knight, in your bright gear*

[3] *The worthy (knight) readied himself for the deed (i.e., the encounter), at the day appointed*

Lightly lap he on loft, that lufly of lyre.   *leaped he aloft; appearance*

615   Athir laught has thair lance, that lemyt so light;   *Each [warrior] grasped; sparkled*

On twa stedis thai straid, with ane sterne schiere.   *advanced; look*

Togiddir freschly thai frekis fruschit, in fay;   *struggled in faith*

Thair speris in splendris sprent   *splinters shattered*

On scheldis, schonkit and schent,   *shivered and ruined*

620   Evin ovr thair hedis went

In feild fir away.   *far*

Thai lufly ledis belife lightit on the land,   *fighters quickly dismounted*

And laught out swerdis, lufly and lang.   *snatched*

Thair stedis stakkerit in the stour, and stude stummerand, [1]

625   Al tostiffillit and stonayt, the strakis war sa strang!   *All strained and stunned the strokes*

Athir berne braithly bet with ane bright brand;   *fiercely beat (i.e., laid on)*

On fute freschly thai frekis feghtin thai fang;   *combat they engaged*

Thai hewit on hard steil, hartly with hand,   *heartily*

Quhil the spalis and the sparkis spedely out sprang.   *splinters*

630   Schir Rannald raught to the renk ane rout wes unryde;   *dealt to his foe a blow; grievous*

Clenely in the collair,   *collar*

Fifty mailyeis and mair   *chainlinks*

Evin of the schuldir he schair,   *Cleanly from; sheared*

Ane wound that wes wyde.

635   Thus thai faucht on fute, on the fair feild.

The blude famyt thame fra, on feild quhare thai found;   *foamed; they proved [each other]*

All the bernys on the bent about that beheild,   *on the field*

For pure sorow of that sight thai sighit unsound.   *sighed sorely*

Schire teris schot fra schalkis, schene undir scheild,   *Bright tears; knights; handsome*

640   Quhen thai foundrit and fel fey to the grund;   *lurched and fell dead*

Baith thair hartis can brist braithly, but beild.   *did burst violently without life*

Thair wes na stalwart unstonait, so sterne wes the stound!   *unshaken so terrible; shock*

Schir Rannaldis body wes broght to the bright tent;

Syne to the castel of stone   *Then*

645   Thai had Schir Regal of Rone;

With mekil murnyng and mone   *much mourning*

Away with him went.

---

[1] *Their steeds staggered on the battleground, and stood nickering*

	Thus endit the avynantis with mekil honour;	*died the courteous [knights]; much*
	Yit has men thame in mynd for thair manhede. [1]	
650	Thair bodeis wes beryit baith in ane hour;	*buried both in the same hour*
	Set segis for thair saullis to syng and to reid.	*[There were] appointed men (i.e., priests)*
	Than Gologrus graithit of his men in glisnand armour	*readied; gleaming*
	And Schir Louys the lele, ane lord of that leid;	*loyal; people*
	Ane uthir heght Edmond, that provit paramour; [2]	
655	The thrid heght Schir Bantellas, the batal to leid;	*called; lead*
	The ferd wes ane weryour worthy and wight,	*fourth*
	His name wes Schir Sanguel,	
	Cumly and cruel;	*fierce*
	Thir four, treuly to tell,	*Those*
660	Foundis to the feght.	*Set out*

	Schir Lyonel to Schir Louys wes levit with ane lance;	*left (i.e., paired) [each] with*
	Schir Ewin to Shir Edmond, athir ful evin;	*each equally matched*
	Schir Bedwar to Schir Bantellas, to enschew his chance,	*to follow his fate*
	That baith war nemmyt in neid, nobil to nevin;	*summoned; name*
665	To Schir Sangwel soght gude Gyromalance.	
	Thus thai mellit and met with ane stout stevin,	*struggled; tummult*
	Thir lufly ledis on the land, without legiance.	*fighters; submission*
	With seymely scheildis to schew, thai set upone sevin,	*took great risks*
	Thir cumly knightis to kyth ane cruel course maid. [3]	
670	The frekis felloune in feir	*fierce together*
	Wondir stoutly can steir,	*did conduct [themselves]*
	With geir grundin ful cleir	*burnished*
	Rudly thai raid.	*Violently they rode*

	Than thair hors with thair hochis sic harmis couth hint,	*leg joints such; did sustain*
675	As trasit in unquart quakand thai stand.	*harnessed [horses that have been] spooked*
	The frekis freschly thai fure, as fyre out of flynt;	*fought on*

---

[1] *And still have men kept them in mind because of their manhood (i.e., their spectacular courage)*

[2] *A second was named Edmond, that tried-and-true lover*

[3] *Those knights renowned as gracious began a savage joust*

Thair lufly lancis thai loissit, and lichtit on the land. — *destroyed; got down*

Right styth, stuffit in steill, thai stotit na stynt, — *stalwart, enclosed; hesitated nor ceased*

Bot buskit to battaille with birny and brand. — *hastened*

680 Thair riche birnys thai bet derfly with dynt, — *savagely*

Hewis doun in grete haist, hartly with hand.

Thai mighty men upon mold ane riale course maid, — *on earth; tilt*

Quhill clowis of clene maill — *Until scraps*

Hoppit out as the haill,

685 Thay beirnys in the bataill — *These warriors*

Sa bauldly thai baid! — *endured*

Thai bet on sa brymly, thai beirnys on the bent, — *fiercely; field*

Bristis birneis with brandis burnist full bene. — *Burst; polished full well*

Throu thair schene scheildis thair schuldiris war schent; — *shoulders were shattered*

690 Fra schalkis schot schire blude ovr scheildis so schene. — *bright blood*

Ryngis of rank steill rattillit and rent, — *hard steel rattled and gave way*

Gomys grisly on the grund grams on the grene. — *Felled knights grieve terribly on the field*

The Roy ramyt for reuth, richist of rent, — *cried out for pity; lordship*

For cair of his knightis cruel and kene, — *care; fierce*

695 Sa wondir freschly thair force thai frest on the feildis! — *vigorously; put to proof*

Sa huge wes the mellé, — *melee*

Wes nane sa sutell couth se — *acute*

Quhilk gome suld govern the gre, — *have the victory*

Bot God that al weildis.

700 The wyis wrocht uthir grete wandreth and weuch, — *warriors; each other; distress and sorrow*

Wirkand woundis full wyde with wapnis of were. — *war*

Helmys of hard steill thai hatterit and heuch; — *battered and hewed*

In that hailsing thai hynt grete harmys and here, — *encounter they sustained; loss*

All toturvit thair entyre, traistly and tewch. — *repulsed; charge stoutly; unyielding*

705 Burnist bladis of steill throw birneis thai bere. — *wield*

Schort swerdis of scheith smertly thai dreuch, — *from sheaths nimbly they drew*

Athir freik to his fallow, with fellonne affere; — *opponent, with fearsome war frenzy*

Throw platis of polist steill thair poyntis can pase. — *polished; did pass*

All thus thai threw in that thrang — *dealt; throng*

710 Stalwart strakis and strang; — *strokes*

With daggaris derfly thai dang, — *grievously they struck*

Thai doughtyis on dase. — *days [i.e., in their time]*

	Schir Lyonell Schir Lowes laught has in hand,	*taken*
	And sesit is Sangwell with Giromalans the gude.	*seized; by*
715	Schir Evin has Schir Edmond laid on the land,	
	Braithly bartynit with baill, bullerand in blude.	*Fiercely felled with woe, rolling*
	Schir Bedwar to Schir Bantellas yaldis up his brand,	*yields*
	In that stalwart stour thay styth men in stude.	*fierce battle those unyielding men*
	Wes nane forssy on fold that wes feghtand —[1]	
720	Unmanglit and marrit — myghtles in mude;	
	Wes nane sa proud of his part, that prisit quhen he yeid.	*earned worship; was taken*
	Bedwer and Lyonell	
	War led to the castell;	
	The cumly knight Sangwell	
725	To Arthour thay led.	

	Schir Edmond loissit has his life, and laid is full law;	*low*
	Schir Evin hurtis has hynt hidwise and sair.	*suffered hideous*
	Knightis caryis to the corse, wes cumly to knaw,	*proceed; corpse; decorous to see*
	And had hym to the castell with mekill hard cair;	*much deep sorrow*
730	Thai did to that doughty as the dede aw.	*dead deserve*
	Uthir four of the folk foundis to the fair,	*Another; gracious [lord] (i.e., Gologras)*
	That wes dight to the dede, be the day can daw;	*prepared; action, as soon as*
	Than said bernys bald, brym as bair:	*fierce as [a] bear*
	"We sal evin that is od, or end in the pane!"	*odd (unanswered); die*
735	Thai stuffit helmys in hy,	*in haste*
	Breistplait and birny;	
	Thay renkis maid reddy	
	All geir that mycht gane.	

	Schir Agalus, Schir Ewmond, honest and habill,	*able*
740	Schir Mychin, Schir Meligor, men of grete estait;	
	Than stertis out ane sterne knyght, stalwart and stabill,	*Then advances; solid*
	Ane berne that heght Schir Hew, hardy and hait.	*was named; hot[-tempered]*
	Now wil I rekkin the renkis of the Round Tabill,	*mention the knights*
	That has traistly thame tight to governe that gait.[2]	

---

[1] Lines 719–20: *[There] was not one [of those knights] who fiercely on the field was fighting— / [Whether] unscathed or wounded — [who was] infirm in spirit*

[2] *Who have faithfully prepared themselves to control the course [of action]*

745	Furth faris the folk, but fenyeing or fabill,	*without feigning or fable*
	That bemyt war be the lord, lufsum of lait:	*chosen were by; countenance*
	Schir Cador of Cornwel, cumly and cleir,	
	Schir Owales, Schir Iwell,	
	Schir Myreot, mighty emell;	*in their midst*
750	Thir four, treuly to tell,	*These*
	Foundis in feir.	*Set out together*

	Thair wes na trety of treux, trow ye full traist,	*truce, believe you [me]*
	Quhen thai myghty can mach, on mold quhair thai met.	*those; did join battle on ground*
	Thai brochit blonkis to thair sydis out of blude braist,	*spurred horses until*
755	Thair lufly lancis thai loissit, and lightit but let;	*destroyed, and alighted without pause*
	Sadillis thai temyt tyt, thir trew men and traist,	*emptied right off*
	Braidit out brandis, on birnys thai bet.	*Whipped; beat*
	As fyre that fleis fra the flynt, thay fechtin sa fast,	*flies; fought so hard*
	With vengeand wapnis of were throu wedis thai wet.	*pitiless weapons; strike [blows]*
760	It war teirfull to tell treuly the tend	*hard; outcome*
	Of thair strife sa strang,	
	The feght so fellely thai fang.	*fiercely they engaged*
	Thoght it lestit never so lang,	*lasted*
	Yit laught it ane end.	*found*

765	Schir Owiles, Schir Iwill, in handis war hynt,	*in hand-to-hand; taken*
	And to the lufly castell war led in ane lyng.	*column*
	Thairwith the stalwartis in stour can stotin and stynt,	*battle did stop and stint*
	And baith Schir Agalus and Schir Hew wes led to the Kyng.	
	Than Schir Golograse for greif his gray ene brynt,	*eyes burned*
770	Wod wraith as the wynd, his handis can wryng.	*Violently angry; did*
	Yit makis he mery, magry quhasa mynt —	*despite [what] anyone might think*
	Said: "I sal bargane abyde, and ane end bryng;	*conflict engage*
	Tomorne, sickirly, my self sall seik to the feild."	*Tomorrow indeed*
	He buskit to ane barfray —	*withdrew to a belfry*
775	Twa smal bellis rang thay;	
	Than seymly Arthur can say,	*did*
	Wes schene undir scheild:	

	"Quhat signifyis yone rynging?" said the Ryale.	*Royal (i.e., the King)*
	Than said Spynagros with speche: "Schir sens peir,	*Lord without peer*
780	That sall I tell yow with tong, treuly in taill.	

The wy that weildis yone wane, I warn you but weir, [1]

He thinkis his aune self shall do for his dail;   *own; estates*

Is nane sa provit in this part of pyth is his peir. [2]

Yow worthis wisly to wirk, ane wy for to wail,   *It profits you; fighter; choose*

785   That sal duchtely his deid do with yone deir.   *valiantly; worthy [lord]*

He is the forsiest freik, be fortoune his freynd,   *most powerful man, if fortune be*

That I wait levand this day."   *know living*

Than Schir Gawine the gay

Prayt for the journay,   *Entreated; mission*

790   That he myght furth weynd.   *go*

The King grantit the gait to Schir Gawane,   *mission*

And prayt to the grete God to grant him his grace,

Him to save and to salf, that is our soverane,   *preserve*

As he is makar of man, and alkyn myght haise.   *infinite power has*

795   Than Schir Spynagros, the freik, wox ferly unfane,   *became wondrously upset*

Murnyt for Schir Gawyne, and mekil mayne maise,   *Mourned; much lament makes*

And said: "For His saik, that saiklese wes slane,   *guiltless*

Tak nocht yone keyne knight to countir, in this hard cais — [3]

Is nane sa stalwart in stour, with stoutnes to stand.   *in combat; to withstand*

800   Of al that langis to the King,   *all [those] that are in service*

The mair is my murnyng,   *more*

Ye suld this fell fechting   *[That] you should; lethal fight*

Hynt upone hand.   *Take in hand*

"Sen ye ar sa wourschipfull, and wourthy in were,   *Since; war*

805   Demyt with the derrest, maist doughty in deid,   *Honored with the worthy*

Yone berne in the battale wil ye noght forbere,   *spare*

For al the mobil on the mold, merkit to meid."   *ransom; designated as recompense*

"Gif I de doughtely, the les is my dere,   *I [Gawain] die; hurt*

Thoght he war Sampsone himself, sa me Criste reid!   *help*

810   I forsaik noght to feght, for al his grete feir,   *refuse; fearsomeness*

I do the weill for to wit, doutlese but dreid."   *want you to understand, without any doubt*

Than said Schir Spynagrose: "Sen ye will of neid   *of necessity*

---

[1] *The lord who rules yonder stronghold, I advise you without doubt*

[2] *There is none so tried and true in these parts who is his peer in strength*

[3] *Do not take on this fierce knight in single combat in this tight spot*

	Be boun to the battale,	*Hasten*
	Wirkis with counsale —	*Act with counsel*
815	It sall right gret avale,	*shall very greatly help*
	And do it in deid.	*If [you]; for sure*

	"Quhen ye mach hym on mold, merk to hym evin,	*encounter; attack him straight on*
	And bere ye your bright lance in myddis his scheild;	
	Mak that course cruel, for Crystis lufe of hevin!	*fierce for love of Christ*
820	And syne wirk as I wise, your wappins to weild.	*afterwards work as I advise*
	Be he stonayt, yone sterne, stout beis his stevin;	*[If] he is stunned; will be his outcry*
	He wourdis brym as ane bair, that bydis na beild. [1]	
	Noy you noght at his note, that nobill is to nevin.	*Worry; voice; grand; sound*
	Suppose his dyntis be deip dentit in your scheild,	*Even if his strokes*
825	Tak na haist upone hand, quhat happunys may hynt;	*haste; whatever chances may occur*
	Bot lat the riche man rage,	*strong*
	And fecht in his curage,	*fight; strength*
	To swyng with swerd quhil he suage;	*until he lets up*
	Syne dele ye your dynt.	*Then*

830	"Quhen he is stuffit, thair strike, and hald hym on steir: [2]	
	Sa sal ye stonay yone stowt, suppose he be strang.	*stun that stout [knight], even if*
	Thus may ye lippin on the lake, throu lair that I leir; [3]	
	Bot gif ye wirk as wise, you worthis that wrang."	*Unless; deserve that misfortune*
	The King and his knihtis, cumly and cleir,	
835	In armour dewly hym dight, be the day sprang.	*properly him readied; sunrise*
	Than wes Schir Kay wondir wo, wit ye but weir,	*without doubt*
	In defalt of ane freik the feghting to fang. [4]	
	That gome gudely furth gais, and graithit his geir;	*[Kay] splendidly forth goes; prepares*
	Evin to the castell he raid,	*Right; rode*
840	Huvit in ane dern slaid;	*Pulled up in a secluded vale*
	Sa come ane knight as he baid,	*waited*
	Anairmit of weir.	*Armed for war*

---

[1] *He becomes fierce as a bear, that looks for no quarter*

[2] *When he is winded, there (i.e., at that point) strike, and keep him in action*

[3] *In this way may you succeed in the game (i.e., swordplay), through the lore that I teach*

[4] *At the lack of an [opposing] knight to engage in the fighting.*

That knight buskit to Schir Kay one ane steid broune,   *hastened toward*
Braissit in birneis and basnet full bene;   *Clad in mail; helmet; excellent*
845 He cryis his ensenye and conteris hym full soune,   *battle cry; assails*
And maid ane course curagiouse, cruell and kene.   *And ran a tilt*
Thair lufly lancis thai loissit, and lightit baith doune,   *splintered*
And girdit out swerdis on the grund grene,
And hewit on hard steill hartlie but houne.   *vigorously without pause*
850 Rude reknyng raise thair renkis betwene.   *Savage conflict arose those; between*
Thair mailyeis with melle thay merkit in the medis;   *armor; onslaught; dent; middle*
The blude of thair bodeis
Throw breistplait and birneis,
As roise ragit on rise,   *Like [a red] rose on thorny branch*
855 Ovrran thair riche wedis.   *Ran over; armor*

Thus thai faught upone fute, without fenyeing.   *in truth*
The sparkis flaw in the feild, as fyre out of flynt.   *flew*
Thai lufly ledis in lyke, thai layid on in ane ling,   *fighters handsome in body; laid on; moor*
Delis thair full doughtely mony derf dynt.   *Deal out there; many a strong blow*
860 Duschand on deir wedis, dourly thai dyng; [1]
Hidwise hurtis and huge haistely thai hynt.   *Hideous; immediately they sustain*
That knight carpit to Schir Kay, of discomforting: *[out] of perplexity*
"Of this stonayand stour I rede that ye stynt.   *numbing battle I urge; cease*
I will yeild the my brand, sen na better may bene.   *sword, since [it] no*
865 Quhair that fortoune will faill,   *Wherever; fall short*
Thair may na besynes availl."   *no busy-ness (i.e., efforts)*
He braidit up his ventaill   *threw; visor*
That closit wes clene.

For to ressave the brand the berne wes full blith,   *receive the sword the knight (i.e., Kay)*
870 For he wes byrsit and beft, and braithly bledand.   *bruised and buffeted; severely bleeding*
Thoght he wes myghtles, his mercy can he thair myth,   *weakened; did; show*
And wald that he nane harm hynt with hart and with hand. [2]
Thai caryit baith to the Kynge, cumly to kyth;   *moved off; of repute*
Thair lancis war loissit and left on the land.   *ruined*

---

[1] *Battering on rich armor, fiercely they strike*

[2] *And took care with heart and hand that he (i.e., Kay's opponent) suffered no harm*

261

875	Than said he loud upone loft: "Lord, will ye lyth: [1]	
	Ye sall nane torfeir betyde, I tak upone hand.	*[To] you; no injury befall; give my hand*
	Na mysliking have in hart, nor have ye na dout.	*misgiving; fear*
	Oft in romanis I reid:	*romance*
	Airly sporne, late speid."	*Early spurred; arrived*
880	The King to the pailyeoun gart leid	*pavilion had conducted*
	The knight that wes stout.	

	Thai hynt of his harnese, to helyn his wound;	*took off; heal*
	Lechis war noght to lait, with sawis sa sle.	*Physicians; too late; salves so subtle*
	With that, mony fresch freik can to the feild found,	*did; go*
885	With Gologras in his geir, grete of degre;	
	Armyt in rede gold, and rubeis sa round,	*rubies*
	With mony riche relikis, riale to se.	*heirlooms, royal*
	Thair wes on Gologras, quhair he glaid on the ground,	*advanced*
	Frenyeis of fine silk, fratit full fre.	*Fringes; decorated most lavishly*
890	Apone sterand stedis, trappit to the heill,	*lively; with trappings to the heel*
	Sexty schalkis full schene	*[Were] sixty knights*
	Cled in armour sa clene;	
	No wy wantit, I wene,	*No one was missing [of sixty]*
	All stuffit in steill.	

895	That berne raid on ane blonk of ane ble quhite,	*warhorse with forehead white*
	Blyndit all with bright gold and beriallis bright —	*Studded; beryls*
	To tell of his deir weid war doutles delite,	*costly gear were doubtless a joy*
	And alse ter for to tell the travalis war tight.	*as tedious; pains that were taken*
	His name and his nobillay wes noght for to nyte;	*reputation and his nobility; deny*
900	Thair wes na hathill sa heich, be half ane fute hicht.	*knight so high; foot's height*
	He lansit out ovr ane land, and drew noght ane lyte,	*rushed; drew [up] not a bit*
	Quhair he suld frastyn his force, and fangin his fight.	*make trial of his strength; join*
	Be that Schir Gawyne the gay wes graithit in his gere;	*By that [time]*
	Cummyng on the ta syde,	*the one side*
905	Hovand, battale to abyde,	*Halting; to engage*
	All reddy samyne to ryde,	*together*
	With schelde and with spere.	

---

[1] *Then said he [the King] for all to hear: "Sir (i.e., Kay's opponent), you are well-off*

Thir lufly ledis on the land left be thame allane,   *went off by themselves alone*

Tuke nowthir fremmyt nor freyndis, bot found thame fra; *foe nor friends; went [away]*

910 Twa rynnyng renkis raith the riolyse has tane,[1]

Ilk freik to his feir, to frestin his fa.

Thai gird one twa grete horse, on grund quhil thai grane.[2]

The trew helmys and traist in tathis thai ta; *sturdy in tatters they leave*

The rochis reirdit with the rasch, quhen thai samyne rane.[3]

915 Thair speris in the feild in flendris gart ga; *splinters are made to go*

The stedis stakerit in the stour, for strekyng on stray.[4]

The bernys bowit abak,   *drew*

Sa woundir rude wes the rak;   *fierce; crash*

Quhilk that happynnit the lak,   *Which [one] suffered the worse*

920 Couth na leid say!

Thai brayd fra thair blonkis, besely and bane. *jumped from; lively and quick*

Syne laught out swerdis, lang and lufly,   *Then grabbed*

And hewit on hard steill, wondir hawtane.   *courageously*

Baith war thai haldin of hartis heynd and hardy. *possessed of hearts noble*

925 Gologras grew in greif at Schir Gawane;   *anger*

On the hight of the hard steill he hyt hym in hy, *top; in haste*

Pertly put with his pith at his pesane,[5]

And fulyeit of the fyne maill ma than fyfty. *destroyed; more [links]*

The knight stakrit with the straik, all stonayt in stound,[6]

930 Sa woundir scharply he schair,   *keenly he hewed*

The berne that the brand bair.   *who the sword wielded*

Schir Gawyne, with ane fell fair,   *lethal thrust*

Can to his faa found.   *Did at his foe move*

With ane bitand brand, burly and braid, *biting sword, stout and broad*

935 Quhilk oft in battale had bene his bute and his belde, *Which; aid; protection*

---

[1] Lines 910–11: *Two rushing courses (i.e., tilts) the princely [knights] have vehemently taken, / Each man against his opposite, to try out his foe*

[2] *They spur on two great horses over the ground until they groan [as they gallop]*

[3] *The rocks resounded with (the sound of) the charge, when they ran together*

[4] *The steeds stagger in the battleplace, from the thrusting about*

[5] *Skillfully aimed with his strength at his gorget (i.e., neck-armor)*

[6] *The knight staggered with the stroke, all stunned in the encounter*

	He leit gird to the grome, with greif that he had,	*made to assault; anger*
	And claif throw the cantell of the clene schelde.	*cut through the corner*
	Throw birny and breistplait and bordour it baid;	*sank*
	The fulye of the fyne gold fell in the feild.	*foil (i.e., plating)*
940	The rede blude with the rout folowit the blaid,	*blow; blade*
	For all the wedis, I wise, that the wy weild,	*Through all the armor indeed; had on*
	Throw claspis of clene gold, and clowis sa cleir.	*ornaments*
	Thair with Schir Gologras the syre,	*At that; lord*
	In mekill angir and ire,	
945	Alse ferse as the fyre,	*As fierce*
	Leit fle to his feir.	*Did rush at his fellow knight (Gawain)*

	Sic dintis he delt to that doughty,	*Such blows he (Gologras) dealt*
	Leit hym destanyt to danger and dreid;	*Made him subject; fear*
	Thus wes he handillit full hait, that hawtane, in hy.	*manhandled so hotly; that noble*
950	The scheld in countir he kest ovr his cleir weid,	*in defense; shining armor*
	Hewit on hard steill woundir haistely;	
	Gart beryallis hop of the hathill about hym on breid. [1]	
	Than the King unto Criste kest up ane cry,	
	Said: "Lord, as Thow life lent to levand in leid,	*the living among [your] people*
955	As Thou formit all frute to foster our fude,	*created all living things; nourishment*
	Grant me confort this day,	
	As Thow art God verray!"	
	Thus prais the King in affray,	*anxiety*
	For Gawyne the gude.	

	Golagras at Gawyne in sic ane grief grew	*rage*
960	As lyoune, for falt of fude, faught on the fold.	*lion for lack; fought; earth*
	With baith his handis in haist that haltane couth hew,	*suddenly that warrior did*
	Gart stanys hop of the hathill, that haltane war hold, [2]	
	Birny and breistplait, bright for to schew;	
965	Mony mailye and plait war marrit on the mold.	*plate-armor*
	Knichtis ramyt for reuth; Schir Gawyne thai rew,	*cried out for pity; sorrow [for]*
	That doughty delit with hym sa, for dout he war defold,	*[Because]; handled; fear; shamed*
	Sa wondir scharply he schare throu his schene schroud.	*sliced; bright armor*

---

[1] *Caused the beryls (i.e., gems) [to] hop off the knight [all] around him on [the] field*

[2] *Caused precious stones to hop off the knight, who was held [to be] fierce*

His scheild he chopit hym fra
970 In twenty pecis and ma.
Schir Wawane writhit for wa,   *Gawain writhed for woe*
Witlese and woud.   *Reckless and enraged*

Thus wourthit Schir Gawyne wraith and wepand,   *became; angry to tears*
And straik to that stern knight but stynt.   *made for; without let-up*
975 All engrevit the grome, with ane bright brand,   *[Gawain] made grief for*
And delt thairwith doughtely mony derf dynt.   *many [a] bold blow*
Throw byrny and breistplait, bordour and band,   *edge*
He leit fle to the freke, as fyre out of flynt.   *let fly*
He hewit on with grete haist, hartly with hand,   *laid on*
980 Hakkit throw the hard weid, to the hede hynt;   *Hacked; struck*
Throw the stuf with the straik, stapalis and stanis, [1]
Schir Wawine, wourthy in wail,   *among the best*
Half ane span at ane spail,   *[From] half a span (nine inches) to a splinter*
Quhare his harnes wes hail,   *Where; had been unbroken*
985 He hewit attanis.   *at once*

Thus raithly the riche berne rassit his array.   *suddenly; destroys [Gologras'] armor*
The tothir stertis ane bak, the sterne that wes stout,   *[i.e., Gologras]*
Hit Schir Gawayne on the gere quhil grevit wes the gay,   *until*
Betit doune the bright gold and beryallis about;
990 Scheddit his schire wedis scharply away: *Sliced*
That lufly lappit war on loft, he gart thame law lout. [2]
The sterne stakrit with the straik, and stertis on stray,   *[Gawain] staggered; stroke; astray*
Quhill neir his resoune wes tynt, sa rude wes the rout!   *Until; lost; fierce*
The beryallis on the land of bratheris gart light,   *from bracers (arm protector); fall*
995 Rubeis and sapheir,   *rubies*
Precious stanis that weir;   *were*
Thus drese thai wedis sa deir,   *fares this gear so costly*
That dantely wes dight.   *delicately was decorated*

Thai gyrd on sa grymly, in ane grete ire,   *struggle*
1000 Baith Schir Gawine the grome, and Gologras the knight.

---

[1] *Through the gear with that stroke, through fastenings and gems*

[2] *[Those ornaments] that [so] beautifully were set out above (i.e., on the surface), he made fall low (i.e., off)*

The Knightly Tale of Gologras and Gawain

The sparkis flew in the feild, as fagottis of fire, *kindling*
Sa wondir frely thai frekis fangis the fight. *engage*
Thai luschit and laid on, thai luflyis of lyre. *struck out; in looks*
King Arthur Jhesu besoght, seymly with sight: *beseeched, seemly*
1005   "As Thow art Soverane God, sickerly, and syre, *truly, and lord*
At Thow wald warys fra wo Wawane the wight,[1]
And grant the frekis on fold farar to fall,
Baith thair honouris to saif."
At Crist with credence thai craif, *To; faith they pray*
1010   Knight, squyar and knaif; *squire and knave*
And thus pray thay all.

Thai mellit on with malice, thay myghtyis in mude,[2]
Mankit throu mailyeis, and maid thame to mer;[3]
Wraithly wroght, as thai war witlese and wod. *Angrily reckless; heedless and enraged*
1015   Be that Schir Wawane the wy likit the wer;[4]
The ble of his bright weid wes bullerand in blude. *surface; billowing*
Thair with the nobill in neid nyghit hym ner,[5]
Straik hym with ane steill brand, in stede quhare he stude. *in [the] spot where*
The scheld in fardellis can fle, in feild away fer; *splinters did fly*
1020   The tothir hyt hym agane with ane hard swerd. *other (i.e., Gologras); again (i.e., in return)*
As he loutit ovr ane bra, *bent; slope*
His feit founderit hym fra; *feet foundered*
Schir Gologras graithly can ga *immediately did go*
Grulingis to erd. *Groveling to earth*

1025   Or ever he gat up agane, gude Schir Gawane *Before*
Grippit to Schir Gologras on the grund grene. *Took hold of*
Thairof gromys wes glaid, gudly and gane, *For that; quickly*
Lovit Criste of that case with hartis sa clene. *[They] praised Christ for that outcome*
Ane daggar dayntely dight that doughty has drawne; *delicately made*

---

[1] Lines 1006–08: *[I pray] that Thou would keep from woe Gawain the powerful, / And grant that a more favorable fate may befall the knights on the field, / [In order] to keep safe the honor of both*

[2] *These (fighters) struggled on with violence, those mighty in spirit*

[3] *Maimed through (i.e., in spite of) mail (i.e., chain-links), and caused them to break*

[4] *At that point the warrior (i.e., Gologras) liked Gawain the worse*

[5] *With that, the hero at need (i.e., Gawain, the hero when things are worst) moved nearer to him (i.e., Gologras)*

1030	Than he carpit to the knight, cruel and kene:	*cried; fierce*
	"Gif thou luffis thi life, lelely noght to layne,	*in truth not to conceal [anything]*
	Yeld me thi bright brand, burnist sa bene;	*Surrender; polished so splendidly*
	I rede thow wirk as I wise, or war the betide." [1]	
	The tothir answerit schortly:	
1035	"Me think farar to dee,	*more worshipful to die*
	Than schamyt be, verralie,	*shamed (to) be truly*
	And sclander to byde.	*slander to endure*

	"Wes I never yit defoullit, nor fylit in fame,	*dishonored nor defiled*
	Nor nane of my eldaris, that ever I hard nevin.	*ancestors; heard named (talked of)*
1040	Bot ilk berne has bene unbundin with blame,	*each; unbesmirched*
	Ringand in rialté, and reullit thameself evin.	*Reigning; governed themselves wholly*
	Sall never sege undir son se me with schame,	
	Na luke on my lekame with light nor with levin,	*Nor look; body; scorn; contempt*
	Na nane of the nynt degré have noy of my name, [2]	
1045	I swere be suthfast God, that settis all on sevin!	*made all in seven [days of creation]*
	Bot gif that wourschip of were win me away,	*Unless honor in combat takes*
	I trete for na favour.	*negotiate*
	Do furth thi devoir —	*Do what you must*
	Of me gettis thou na more,	
1050	Doutles this day."	

	Lordingis and ladyis in the castell on loft,	
	Quhen thai saw thair liege lord laid on the landis,	*ground*
	Mony sweit thing of sware swownit full oft,	*sweet thing with lovely neck swooned*
	Wyis wourthit for wo to wringin thair handis.	*Nobles began*
1055	Wes nowthir solace nor sang thair sorow to soft —	*soften*
	Ane sayr stonayand stour at thair hartis standis.	*sore stunning strife*
	On Criste cumly thay cry: "On Croce as Thou coft,	*You redeemed [us]*
	With Thi blissit blude to bring us out of bandis,	*bondage*
	Lat never our soverane his cause with schame to encheif!	*his enterprise; to conclude*
1060	Mary, farest of face,	
	Beseik thi sone in this cace,	*Beseech; cause*

---

[1] *I urge [to] do as I advise, or worse [to] you [may] happen*

[2] *Nor none to the ninth degree (even my most distant kin) have dishonor through my name*

Ane drop of His grete grace
He grant us to geif!"   *give*

Thus the ledis on loft in langour war lent.   *were sunk*
1065   The lordis on the tothir side for likyng thay leugh.   *for pleasure they laugh*
Schir Gawyne tretit the knight to turn his entent,   *entreated; change his intention*
For he wes wondir wa to wirk hym mare wugh.   *reluctant; more harm*
"Schir, say for thiself, thow seis thou art schent;   *see; you say; lost*
It may nocht mend the ane myte to mak it so teugh.   *help you a bit; tough*
1070   Rise, and raik to our Roy, richest of rent;   *go*
Thow salbe newit at neid with nobillay eneuch,   *restored; honor enough*
And dukit in our duchery, all the duelling."   *[made a] duke; kingdom, all your life*
"Than war I woundir unwis,
To purchese proffit for pris,   *advantage [at the cost] of honor*
1075   Quhare schame ay ever lyis,   *always [would] prevail*
All my leving.   *life*

"The sege that schrenkis for na schame, the schent might hym schend, [1]
That mare luffis his life than lois upone erd.
Sal never freik on fold, fremmyt nor freynde,   *foe nor friend*
1080   Gar me lurk for ane luke, lawit nor lerd. [2]
For quhasa with wourschip sall of this warld wende,   *whoever; shall [out] of*
Thair wil nane wyis, that ar wis, wary the werd. [3]
For ony trety may tyde, I tell the the teynd,   *For any deal [that] might [be] arranged; shortly*
I wil noght turn myn entent, for all this warld brerd,   *change my intention; world entire*
1085   Or I pair of pris ane penny-worth in this place,   *Before I impair my honor*
For besandis or beryell;   *money or gems*
I knaw my aune quarrell —   *own affair (i.e., the rules of honor)*
I dreid not the pereill   *danger*
To dee in this cace!"   *To die under these conditions*

1090   Schir Gawyne rewit the renk, that wes riale,   *sorrowed [for] the knight*
And said to the reverend, riche and rightwis: *praiseworthy [man]; honor-bound*

---

[1] Lines 1077–78: *The knight who shrinks from no dishonor (i.e., who does not reject what is shameful) disgrace may well undo him, / Since he loves his life more than his renown here on earth (among the living)*

[2] *Make me hesitate in public, [neither] unlearned nor educated* (see note)

[3] *There (i.e., because of that) will no knights, who are courteous (wise), lament his fate*

"How may I succour the sound, semely in sale,   *keep you alive, handsome in hall*

Before this pepill in plane, and pair noght thy pris?"   *in plain [view]; impair; honor*

"That sall I tel the with tong, trewly in tale,   *tongue*

1095   Wald yow denye the in deid to do my devis: *put yourself at risk; plan*

Lat it worth at my wil the wourschip to wale,   *happen; have*

As I had wonnyn the of were, wourthy and wis;   *As [if]; overcome you in combat*

Syne cary to the castel, quhare I have maist cure.   *Then go [off] to; prerogative*

Thus may yow saif me fra syte;   *from disgrace*

1100   As I am cristynit perfite,   *baptized truly*

I sall thi kyndnes quyte,   *repay*

And sauf thyn honoure."   *And keep safe*

"That war hard," said that heynd, "sa have I gude hele!   *noble; health (i.e., on my life)*

Ane wounder peralous poynt, partenyng grete plight,   *dangerous spot, involving*

1105   To souer in thi gentrice, but signete or sele, [1]

And I before saw the never, sickerly, with sight.

To leif in thi lauté, and thow war unlele, [2]

Than had I cassin in cair mony kene knight.

Bot I knaw thou art kene, and alse cruell;   *valiant; fierce*

1110   Or thow be fulyeit fey, freke, in the fight,   *Before you are done [to] death*

I do me in thi gentrice, be Drightin sa deir!" [3]

He leynt up in the place;   *straightened*

The tothir raithly upraise.   *quickly got up*

Gat never grome sic ane grace,

1115   In feild of his feir!   *In combat from his fellow [knight]*

Than thei nobillis at neid yeid to thair note new — [4]

Freschly foundis to feght, all fenyeand thair fair.   *Newly proceed; staging their violence*

Tua schort swerdis of scheith smertly thai drew,   *Two*

Than thai mellit on mold, ane myle way and mare.   *tangled; a half-hour*

1120   Wes newthir casar nor king thair quentance that knew; [5]

---

[1] *To rest within your sense of honor, without signet or seal (i.e., formal agreement)*

[2] *Lines 1107–08: [If I were] to live (i.e, make my life depend) on your loyalty, and you should prove untrue, / Then had I encased in care many a brave knight [who depend on me as their champion]*

[3] *I do [entrust] myself to your honor, by [the] Lord so beloved*

[4] *Then those noble [knights] consequently moved to their new plan of action*

[5] *There was neither emperor nor king (who) their pact suspected*

It semyt be thair contenance that kendillit wes care.   *kindled was hostility*
Syne thai traist in that feild, throu trety of trew, [1]
Put up thair brandis sa braid, burly and bair.   *swords; brawny and naked*
Gologras and Gawyne, gracious and gude,
1125   Yeid to the castel of stane,   *Went*
       As he war yoldin and tane.   *As [if] he (Gawain) were subdued and taken [prisoner]*
       The King precious in pane   *in cloth*
       Sair murnand in mude.   *[Was] sorely mourning in spirit*

       The Roy ramand ful raith, that reuth wes to se,   *bursting out suddenly; pity*
1130   And raikit full redles to his riche tent;   *went off fully inconsolable*
       The watter wet his chekis, that schalkis myght se,   *water (i.e., tears); cheeks; fighters*
       As all his welthis in warld had bene away went,   *As [if]*
       And othir bernys for barrat blakynnit thair ble,   *grief darkened in their looks*
       Braithly bundin in baill, thair breistis war blent.   *Harshly bound in sorrow; troubled*
1135   "The flour of knighthede is caught throu his cruelté!   *boldness*
       Now is the Round Tabil rebutit, richest of rent,   *rebuked*
       Quhen wourschipfull Wawane, the wit of our were,   *spirit of our warfare*
       Is led to ane presoune;
       Now failyeis gude fortoune!"   *fails*
1140   The King, cumly with croune,
       Grat mony salt tere.   *Wept*

       Quhen that Gawyne the gay, grete of degre,
       Wes cummyn to the castel, cumly and cleir,
       Gromys of that garisoune maid gamyn and gle,   *stronghold; sport and celebration*
1145   And ledis lofit thair lord, lufly of lyere;   *[the] people praised; of appearance*
       Beirdis beildit in blise, brightest of ble.   *Women basked in bliss; looks*
       The tothir knightis maid care of Arthuris here; [2]
       Al thus with murnyng and myrth thai maid melle. [3]
       Ay, quhil the segis war set to the suppere,   *when*
1150   The seymly soverane of the sail marschel he wes;   *hall chief officer he was*
       He gart Schir Gawyne upga,   *had; go up*
       His wife, his doghter alsua,   *also*

---

[1] *Then they made compact in that field, through agreement in [good] faith*

[2] *The other knights [captured earlier] of Arthur's force lost heart*

[3] *All [of them], thus, with mourning and mirth made [a] mixed [sound]*

And, of that mighty, na ma   *of that magnificent [company], no more*
War set at that des.   *seated; dais*

1155   He gart at ane sete burd the strangearis begin;   *had; begin the board (i.e., do the honors)*
     The maist seymly in sale ordanit thame sete,   *arranged [for] them seats*
     Ilk knyght ane cumly lady, that cleir wes of kyn. [1]
     With kynde contenance the renk couth thame rehete,   *knight; cheer*
     Quhen thai war machit at mete, the mare and the myn,   *matched; greater; lesser*
1160   And ay the meryest on mold marschalit at mete.   *presided*
     Than said he lowd upone loft, the lord of that in,   *inn (i.e., castle)*
     To al the beirnys about, of gré that wes grete: *of degree (i.e., status)*
     "Lufly ledis in land, lythis me til!"   *listen*
     He straik the burd with ane wand,   *struck the table; scepter*
1165   The quhilk he held in hand.   *which*
     Thair wes na word muvand,   *stirring*
     Sa war thai all stil.

     "Heir ye ar gaderit in grosse, al the gretest   *gathered all together*
     Of gomys that grip has, undir my governyng,   *power; lordship*
1170   Of baronis and burowis, of braid land the best,   *baronies and towns; broad*
     And alse the meryest on mold has intrometting.   *[the chance to] take part*
     Cumly knightis, in this cace I mak you request,   *on this occasion*
     Freyndfully, but falsset, or ony fenyeing,   *Candidly, without falsehood; deceit*
     That ye wald to me, treuly and traist,   *would; faithfully*
1175   Tell your entent, as tuiching this thing   *touching this matter*
     That now hingis on my hart, sa have I gude hele!   *weighs; on my soul*
     It tuichis myne honour sa neir,
     Ye mak me plane answeir;   *[That] you; full*
     Thairof I you requeir —   *This I [of] you demand*
1180   I may noght concele.   *I make no attempt to hide it*

     "Say me ane chois, the tane of thir twa,   *Tell; one of these two*
     Quhethir ye like me lord, laught in the feild,   *Whether you prefer; [having been] captured*
     Or ellis my life at the lest lelely forga,   *at the least loyally forfeit*
     And boune yow to sum berne, that myght be your beild?" [2]

---

[1] *Each knight with a comely lady, who was distinguished of lineage*

[2] *And you bind yourselves to another lord, who might be your protection*

1185	The wourthy wyis at that word wox woundir wa,	*became deeply sorrowful*
	Than thai wist thair soverane wes schent undir scheild.	*When they knew; defeated*
	"We wil na favour here fenye to frende nor to fa.	*attachment here pretend*
	We like yow ay as our lord, to were and to weild;	*[make] war; govern*
	Your lordschip we may noght forga, alse lang as we leif.	*disavow; live*
1190	Ye sal be our governour,	
	Quhil your dais may endure,	
	In eise and honour,	*ease (i.e., well being)*
	For chance that may cheif."	*occur*

	Quhen this avenand and honest had maid this answer,	*these courteous [nobles]*
1195	And had tald thair entent trewly him till,	
	Than Schir Gologras the gay, in gudly maneir,	
	Said to thai segis, semely on syll,	*on [the] floor*
	How wourschipful Wawane had wonnin him on weir,	*captured him in combat*
	To wirk him wandreth or wough, quhilk war his wil;	*shame or sorrow, whichever*
1200	How fair him fell in feght, syne how he couth forbere. [1]	
	"In sight of his soverane, this did the gentill:	
	He has me savit fra syte throw his gentrice.	*from dishonor; nobility*
	It war syn, but recure,	*loss without remedy*
	The knightis honour suld smure, [2]	
1205	That did me this honoure,	*Who*
	Quhilk maist is of price.	*worth*

	"I aught as prynce him to prise for his prowese,	*praise*
	That wanyt noght my wourschip, as he that al wan;	*diminished; honor; won*
	And at his bidding full bane, blith to obeise	*eager, glad to serve*
1210	This berne full of bewté, that all my baill blan,	*nobleness; trouble relieved*
	I mak that knawin and kend, his grete kyndnes, [3]	
	The countirpas to kyth to him, gif I can."	
	He raikit to Schir Gawine, right in ane race,	*went; rush*
	Said: "Schir, I knaw be conquest thow art ane kynd man;	*by [your] conquest*
1215	Quhen my lyfe and my dede wes baith at thi will,	*death were both*

---

[1] *How fortune had befallen him in combat [and] after how he undertook to restrain [himself]*

[2] *[Anything which] that knight's honor should besmirch*

[3] Lines 1211–12: *I make known and affirm [in view of] his great kindness / The counterpart (i.e., same) to show him if I can*

Thy frendschip frely I fand;   *found*
Now wil I be obeyand,   *submissive*
And make the manrent with hand,   *do you homage*
As right is, and skill.   *and reasonable*

1220   "Sen Fortoune cachis the cours, throu hir quentys,   *As; directs; devices*
           I did it noght for nane dreid that I had to de,   *die*
           Na for na fauting of hart, na for na fantise.   *default of courage; cowardice*
           Quhare Criste cachis the cours, it rynnis quently —[1]
           May nowthir power nor pith put him to prise.   *strength make him to swerve*
1225   Quhan onfortone quhelmys the quheil, thair gais grace by;[2]
           Quha may his danger endure or destanye dispise,
           That led men in langour ay lestand inly,
           The date na langar may endure na Drightin devinis.
           Ilk man may kyth be his cure,   *make [himself] known by his hardship*
1230   Baith knyght, king and empriour,
           And muse in his myrrour;   *[may] reflect upon his own example*
           And mater maist mine is.   *[this] theme most [applies to] my own [situation]*

           "Hectour and Alexander, and Julius Cesar,
           David and Josué, and Judas the gent,   *Judas [Maccabeus]*
1235   Sampsone and Salamon, that wise and wourthy war,
           And that ryngis on erd, richest of rent: *And who reigned*
           Quhen thai met at the merk, than might thai na mair,[3]
           To speid thame ovr the sperefeild — enspringing thai sprent;
           Quhen Fortune worthis unfrende, than failieis welefair —
1240   Thair ma na tresour ovrtak nor twyn hir entent.
           All erdly riches and ruse is noght in thair garde;   *earthly; fame; keeping*
           Quhat menis Fortoune be skill,   *Whatever may mean Fortune by [her] devices*
           Ane gude chance or ane ill,

---

[1] *Whereas [in truth] Christ controls the course [of events], [and therefore] it runs smoothly*

[2] Lines 1225–28: *When misfortune overwhelms the wheel, there goes success away (i.e., then success is lost); / Whoever [has the spirit] to withstand peril and take no care about his [mortal] fate — / [Cares] that have pushed men to a faintheartedness that lasts forever within [them] — / [For those strong in spirit] their lot will endure no longer than the Lord decrees*

[3] Lines 1237–40: *When they had reached the mark (i.e., their set limit), then might they [do] no more / To advance themselves on the battlefield — [though] vaulting, they fell; / When Fortune becomes hostile, then fails prosperity / There [in such cases] may no [amount of] treasure overcome [Fortune] nor divert her course*

273

	Ilkane be werk and be will	*Each person by deed and by intention*
1245	Is worth his rewarde.	*Attains*
	"Schir Hallolkis, Schir Hewis, heynd and hardy,	*noble*
	Schir Lyonel lufly, and alse Schir Bedwere,	
	Schir Wawane the wise knight, wicht and wourthy —	*powerful*
	Carys furth to the King, cumly and clere;	*Go forth*
1250	Alse my self sall pase with yow reddy,	
	My kyth and my castel compt his conquere."	*[shall be] reckoned as his conquest*
	Thai war arait ful raith, that ryale cumpany,	*arrayed most quickly*
	Of lordis and ladis, lufsum to lere,	*describe*
	With grete lightis on loft, that gaif grete leime —	*lights on high; radiance*
1255	Sexty torcheis ful bright,	
	Before Schir Gologras the knyght;	
	That wes ane semely syght,	
	In ony riche reime.	*realm*
	All effrayt of that fair wes the fresch King,	*taken back by that commotion*
1260	Wend the wyis had bene wroght all for the weir.	*Thought; gathered; warfare*
	Lordis laught thair lancis, and went in ane lyng,	*caught up; formed; column*
	And graithit thame to the gait, in thair greif geir.	*readied themselves; gate; heavy gear*
	Spynok spekis with speche, said: "Move you na thing —	*Spynagros; Attempt*
	It semys saughtnyng thai seik, I se be thair feir.	*peaceful terms; fire*
1265	Yone riche cummis arait in riche robbing:	*lord (i.e., Gologras); arrayed; attire*
	I trow this devore be done, I dout for na deir.	*campaign; fear no harm*
	I wait Schir Gawane the gay has graithit this gait;	*perceive; made possible this outcome*
	Betwix Schir Gologras and he	*himself*
	Gude contenance I se,	*Mutual respect*
1270	And uthir knightis so fre,	*other*
	Lufsum of lait."	*appearance*
	The renk raikit to the Roy, with his riche rout —	*[Gologras] approached; company*
	Sexty schalkis that schene, seymly to schaw,	*warriors who gleamed, fair to view*
	Of banrenttis and baronis bauld hym about,	*bannerets*
1275	In clathis of cleyne gold, cumly to knaw.	*clothes*
	To that lordly on loft that lufly can lout,	*(i.e., Arthur); (i.e., Gologras) did bow*
	Before the riale renkis, richest on raw;	*in order*
	Salust the bauld berne, with ane blith wout,	*Greets; look*
	Ane furlenth before his folk, on feildis so faw.	*furlong in front of; dappled*

1280	The King crochit with croune, cumly and cleir,	*inclined [towards him]*
	Tuke him up by the hand,	
	With ane fair sembland;	*look*
	Grete honour that avenand	*noble [king]*
	Did to the deir.	*that worthy*

1285	Than that seymly be sight said to the gent,	*[one] handsome to look upon (i.e., Gologras)*
	Wes vailyeand and verteous, foroutin ony vice:	*[Who]; valiant; free from any*
	"Heir am I cumyn at this tyme to your present,	*presence*
	As to the wourschipfullest in warld, wourthy and wise,	
	Of al that ryngis in erd richest of rent,	*reigns on earth*
1290	Of pyth and of prowes, peirles of prise.	*might; unequaled in honor*
	Heir I mak yow ane grant, with gudly entent,	
	Ay to your presence to persew, with al my service;	*Ever; majesty to attend*
	Quhare ever ye found or fair, be firth or be fell,	*travel or fare, by wood or by hill*
	I sal be reddy at your will	
1295	In alkin resoune and skill,	*every cause and situation*
	As I am haldin thairtill,	*bound thereto*
	Treuly to tell."	

	He did the Conquerour to knaw all the cause quhy,	*He made; reason why*
	That all his hathillis in that heir, hailly on hight —[1]	
1300	How he wes wonnyn of wer with Wawane the wy,	*made prisoner*
	And al the fortoune the freke befell in the fight;	*events [that to] the knight (i.e., Gawain)*
	The dout and the danger he tauld him quently.	*peril; graciously*
	Than said Arthur himselvin, semely by sight:	
	"This is ane soveranefull thing, be Jhesu, think I,	*masterful (noble)*
1305	To leif in sic perell, and in sa grete plight.	*live in (go through) such*
	Had ony prejudice apperit in the partyce,	*small-mindedness; [opposing] party*
	It had bene grete perell.	
	Bot sen thi lawté is lell,	*loyalty is true*
	That thow my kyndnes wil heill,	*[So] that; acknowledge*
1310	The mare is thi price.	*your honor*

---

[1] *[So] that all of his warriors of that (i.e., Gawain's behavior) hear, wholly out loud (i.e., give ear to his public account)*

"I thank the mekill, Schir Knight," said the Ryall.

"It makis me blythar to be than all thi braid landis,   *to feel gladder*

Or all the renttis fra thyne unto Ronsiwall,   *yours unto Roncevaux*

Thoght I mycht reif thame with right, rath to my handis."   *[Even] though; seize; abruptly*

1315   Than said the senyeour in syth, semely in saill: *lord at once*

"Because of yone bald berne, that broght me of bandis, [1]

All that I have undir hevyne, I hald of you haill,   *exclusively*

In firth, forest and fell, quhare ever that it standis.   *woods; moor*

Sen wourschipfull Wawane has wonnyn to your handis   *Because*

1320   The senyory in governyng,   *lordship*

Cumly Conquerour and Kyng,

Heir mak I yow obeising,   *obeisance (homage)*

As liege lord of landis.   *sovereign*

"And syne fewté I yow fest, without fenyeing, [2]

1325   Sa that the cause may be kend, and knawin throw skill,

Blithly bow and obeise to your bidding,   *Gladly [I] bow and submit*

As I am haldin, to tell treuly, thairtill."   *bound; thereto*

Of Schir Gologras grant blith wes the King, [3]

And thoght the fordward wes fair, freyndschip to fulfil.   *pact*

1330   Thair Schir Gawane the gay, throu requiring,   *beseeching*

Gart the Soverane himself, semely on syll,   *Had; handsome on floor*

Cary to the castel, cleirly to behald —   *Go off*

With all the wourthy that were,   *were [there]*

Erll, duke and douchspere,   *douzeperes (companion knights)*

1335   Baith banrent and bachilere,   *banneret and bachelor [knights]*

That blyth war and bald.

Quhen the semely Soverane wes set in the saill,

It wes selcouth to se the seir service.   *wonderful; various courses*

Wynis wisly in wane went full grete waill [4]

---

[1] *Because of that bold knight who brought me in bonds (i.e., made me his prisoner)*

[2] Lines 1324–25: *Therefore fealty I to you [make] fast, without [any] deceit, / So that the compact may be [openly] shown, and known through signs*

[3] *By Sir Gologras' submission the King was delighted*

[4] Lines 1339–40: *Wines fittingly in (i.e., around) the hall went (i.e., circulated) [in] very great abundance / Among the princes at table, unequaled in honor*

1340	Amang the pryncis in place, peirles to price.
	It war teir for to tel, treuly in tail,
	To ony wy in this warld, wourthy, I wise,
	With revaling and revay all the oulk hale,
	Also rachis can ryn undir the wod rise;
1345	On the riche river of Rone ryot thai maid.
	And syne, on the nynte day,
	The renkis rial of array
	Bownyt hame thair way,
	Withoutin mare baid.

hardship; detail
in appropriate style, indeed
reveling and celebration all the week entire
As small hounds did run; forest boughs
Rhone festival
after; ninth

Set off
stay

1350	Quhen the ryal Roy, maist of renoune,
	With al his reverend rout wes reddy to ryde,
	The King, cumly with kith, wes crochit with croune.
	To Schir Gologras the gay said gudly that tyde:
	"Heir mak I the reward, as I have resoune,
1355	Before thir senyeouris in sight, semely beside,
	As tuiching thi temporalité, in toure and in toune,
	In firth, forest, and fell, and woddis so wide:
	I mak releisching of thin allegiance.
	But dreid I sall the warand,
1360	Baith be sey and be land,
	Fre as I the first fand,
	Withoutin distance."

greatest of renown
company
household was furnished
time

these lords in public
your estates

give release
Without doubt; declare
Both by sea

Absolutely

Explicit.

The end

Heir endis the Knightly Tale of Golagros and Gawane
[for sale] in the south gait of Edinburgh
be [by] Walter Chepman and Androw Millar,
the viii day of Aprile,
the yhere of God, M.CCCCC. and viii. yheris

Notes

I have normalized the orthography of the Chepman-Myllar print (giving "th" for thorn; "gh," "g," or "y" for yogh as appropriate; "j" [note quot. marks] for "i"; "u" for "v" and "w," "v" for "u" and "w," and "w" for "u" and "v") to accord with modern usage. I have expanded numerals and abbreviations ("&" as "and," and so on). Punctuation (including capitalization) is editorial, and word division reflects current standard use. I have recorded (and corrected) obvious compositor's errors, such as turned letters ("u" for "n," "c" for "t," "f" for long medial "s," and so on); in such cases I have only indicated those instances where Amours' edition differs. On the other hand, in those instances where errors in the print require a substantive emendation, I have tried to indicate the relationship of the present text to Amours' edition. Differentiating between corrections and emendations is not, however, always a straightforward process; I have tried nonetheless to give notice where decisions to change the text follow Amours' lead.

Abbreviations: CM = Beattie's facsimile of the Chepman-Myllar print (1508); A = Amours' edition; M = Madden's edition. See Select Bibliography for these editions.

Title   *Gologras*. I elect the spelling *Gologras* for the title as the representative one from the print; this occurs thirteen times, with *Golagras* and *Golograse* once each. Golagros occurs twice and in the colophon, and *Golagrus* and *Gologrus* once each. Editions and allusions have virtually exhausted the possible forms for the poem's title; Pinkerton (1792) used *Gologras*; David Laing's facsimile reprint (1827), *Golagrus*; Trautmann (*Anglia*, 1879), *Golagrus*; Madden and Amours use *Golagros*. The Asloan MS (c. 1515) refers to "The buke of Syr Gologruss and Syr Gawane"; in the *Complaynt of Scotland* (1543), one of the shepherds tells of *Gollogras*; and Sir David Lyndsay's "Squire Meldrum" (1548) alludes to *Golibras*. These latter references certainly demonstrate the romance was well known in the earlier sixteenth century.

2   *towart Tuskane*. In the French source, these adventures of the Round Table take place not on a pilgrimage to the Holy Land, but when Arthur and his company set out to release the imprisoned Girflet from the Chateau Orgueilleux. The specification of Tuscany (in northern Italy) as a part of Arthur's route to Jerusalem directly recalls one of the major narrative sections

of the *Alliterative Morte Arthure*; here Arthur rejects Rome's claims for tribute, and wages devastating war across France and Italy, until, in the last phase of the campaign, "into Tuskane he tournez" (line 3150). *Gologras* differs decisively from the other Gawain romances by altering its setting from the regional — Carlisle and its environs — to the international; in moving Arthurian adventure *ovr the sey* (line 3), *Gologras* places the Round Table in the context of what the *Alliterative Morte Arthure* calls "Ewrope the large" (line 574).

5   *barounis.* CM: *baroⁿs.*

9   *douchty.* CM: *donchty.*

16   *fenyeing.* CM: *senȝeing.*

17   *fresch.* CM: *fresth.*

18   *stout.* CM: *stont.*

19   *on stray.* This prepositional phrase is an ancestor of modern English "astray," though in alliterative poetry its meaning varies to the point, as A notes in his glossary, of being "often meaningless." In *Awntyrs*, lines 511, 532 (as below at line 916), it seems to mean to hammer "away" at an opponent, rather than to strike an errant blow. In *Jeaste*, line 207, *out of straye* seems to mean aside, off the path. Here it certainly does not imply "astray," but simply to be off and away; at line 992 below, which repeats the same phrase from this line, the meaning seems ambiguous, either "start off" or "go astray."

22   *silver.* CM: *silner.*

46   *Arthur.* CM: *Arthnr.*

47   *ane seynd.* CM: *ane send*; A: *ane saynd.*

49   *toune.* CM: *tonne.*

51   *boune.* CM: *bonne.*

66 ff. This description of the embroidered or engraved canopy, recording in pictures and words the most memorable deeds of heroic legend, parallels the passage on

the Nine Worthy (see lines 1233 ff. and note) or indeed *Gologras* itself as a mirror of honor bound together by alliteration and rhyme.

67   *doughtyest.* CM: *donghtyest.*

69   *couth.* CM: *couh.*

77   *couth.* CM: *conth.*

80   *broche . . . bright.* CM: *brothe . . . brigh.*

82   *claught.* CM: *clanght.*

84   *angir.* CM: *augir.*

86   *ane woundir grym sire. Gologras* maintains the anonymity of this protagonist, though in the source, the *Roman de Perceval*, the knight identifies himself as Ydier le Bel, a knight of the Round Table about whom there is a separate thirteenth-century French verse romance.

98   *Thow.* The first two letters of the first word of this line are lacking because of a missing piece of the leaf in the printed text. A provides *Thow*, which I follow.

99   *thow.* A emends to *thou.*

103   *noght.* CM: *noghr.*

112   *mure.* CM: *mnre.*

115   *nykis yow with nay.* This vivid alliterative formula occurs with some frequency, as below in line 332. When Gawain asks after the whereabouts of the Greene Knight, "al nykked hym wyth nay" (*Sir Gawain and the Green Knight,* line 706, and see line 2471); see also *The Pistel of Swete Susan,* line 148, in *Heroic Women From the Old Testament,* ed. Russell A. Peck, TEAMS Middle English Texts Series (Kalamazoo: Medieval Institute Publications, 1991).

122   *folk.* CM: *fosk.*

Notes

122–23 I punctuate as if line 123 were elliptical, meaning, "Let us await some better word." A suggests emending *faynt* to "fayn," which would give, "Your folk are feeble, and for lack of food are glad to await (or anticipate) some better word."

125 *nane.* CM: *naue.*

129 *Reynit.* CM: *Reymt.*

130 *lightit doune.* CM: *lighit dou̅n.*

133 *saill.* CM: *faill.*

145 The lord's response — I will allow no supplies to be sold — is calculated to mislead Gawain, and thereby to test his courtesy. When Gawain sidesteps the temptation to appropriation by force, the lord reveals that — in keeping with the gift economy of an idealized honor culture — payment or sale are not possible since he will freely give all he has.

147 *your.* CM: *yonr.*

148 *answerit.* CM: *ansnerit.*

151 *weild ar.* CM: *weildar.*

159 *cognisance.* A quasi-technical term designating the arms, colors, and dress distinctive to a knight; the lord here emphasizes the gap between Kay's unmistakable chivalric appearance, and his unknightly behavior. Moreover, by asserting "wait I noght quhut he is" (line 163) the lord reduces Kay to a nobody, stripping him of his chivalric identity and all claims to honor.

162 *wraithly.* CM: *wraighly.*

166 *And his presence plane.* The phrase seems to mean "before the king and court," where *presence* means "royal presence," and *plane* means "full" (from French *plein*, Latin *plenus*); see *A Dictionary of the Older Scotish Tongue*, presence, n.2.b.

167 *certane.* CM: *tertane.*

174   *and welth.* CM: *in welth.* I follow A's emendation.

176   *with.* CM: *witht.*

182   *blith.* CM: *bligh.*

189   *resoun.* CM: *resonn.*

191   *cousing.* CM: *consing.* Just who this anonymous knight is, or what relation he claims to Arthur, remains unknown; see line 86 and note.

195   *Ressave.* CM: *Ressane.*

196   *nedis.* CM: *uedis.*

203   *knight.* CM: *kinght.*

205   *crownit.* CM: *crovint*; A: *crovnit.*

209   *service . . . sene.* CM: *sernite . . . seue.*

211   *to vaill.* In this and analogous phrases — *in waill* (line 223), *to wale* (line 361) — *wale* means "to choose," "to be chosen," and suggests those things that are choicest, most honored and honorable, of greatest pleasure or abundance.

215   *war.* CM: *wai.*

217   *suthly.* CM: *futhly.*

218   *dais.* A reads *days.*

226 ff.   This cursory reference to a royal hunt signals the nearly obligatory nature of such episodes in Arthurian romance, and their function as narrative cues for impending events. *Ragnelle, Carlisle, Avowyng*, and *Awntyrs* all employ the royal hunt in this way. See also line 1344.

229   *pavillonis, proudly.* CM: *pauilloms prondly.*

230   *knichtis*. This rhyme, at the turning point of the stanza, is clearly a misprint or corrupt reading; "hathills" or some similar word is needed.

233   *montains gay*. CM: *montains pay*; A reads *mountains*. The original reading is rejected by all editors, who substitute *gay*; A suggests "graye" as an alternative.

237 ff.   The details of Gologras' castle, which stirs both admiration and hostility in Arthur, strikingly resemble those of the massive strongholds at the center of struggles between monarchs and local lords in the fifteenth and sixteenth centuries. Its location on a high rock by a river, with a long curtain wall and defensive towers, recalls, for example, the magnificent Bothwell Castle, built above the steep sides of the River Clyde, south of Glasgow. Bothwell was captured twice by Edward I, lost by Edward II, occupied by Edward III's forces, then captured again and destroyed by the Scots in 1337. It passed to the Douglas family who rebuilt it, and then lost it to King James II of Scotland in 1445. Both Spynagros (lines 274 ff.) and King Arthur (lines 493 ff.) hint at the terrible destructiveness characteristic of siege warfare and castle assault in the fifteenth and sixteenth centuries; within the narrative of *Gologras*, on the other hand, such wholesale destruction becomes transformed into idealized chivalric combat between individual champions. Other castles in the south of Scotland associated with great families and enmeshed in strife against English or Scots kings included Threave, Hermitage, and Douglas Castles (Douglas), Craignethan (Hamilton), and Caerlaverock (Maxwell).

240   *invy, nor nygh*. CM: *in vy nor ny^t*. A interprets, "nobody might view them with envy," meaning desire was pointless because of their impregnability. I take *note* in the common sense of "make or get use of" (OED, *note*, v.1).

241   *lufsum*. CM: *luffum*.

242   *feir*. CM: *seir*; M reads *schir*. I emend for sense.

255   *ever couth*. CM: *ener couch*.

261   *Schir Spynagrose*. In the *Roman de Perceval*, Arthur is accompanied in the main episode by Bran de Lis, the Brandles of *Jeaste*; in *Gologras* he is replaced by Spynagros. Madden connects the latter (p. 341) with Malory's Sir Epynogrys, but this poet seems rather to have formed his name to echo that of the poem's second hero, Gologras. The character's name (like Gologras) is spelled var-

iously: *Spynagrose* here and at line 812, *Spynagrus* (line 535), *Spinagrus* (line 506), *Spynok* (line 1263), and *Spynagros* (lines 341, 779, and 795). These patterns may reflect no more than a compositor's whim in setting type, but I have chosen the last as the representative spelling.

262   *lord.* CM: *lordis.*

263   *everlesting.* CM: *ener lesting.*

266   *ever.* CM: *ener.*

267   *never.* CM: *nener.*

273   *I mak myne avow.* Arthur's impulsive, public oath takes the form of the speech act that defines chivalric identity within an honor/shame culture. Such public vows constitute the central plot of *Avowyng*; see the introduction to that poem, and lines 127 ff., 313 ff., 425 ff. and notes, and below, lines 292 ff. and note.

274   *more.* Here, and at line 276, *schore*, the rhyme is defective. As A suggests, the difficulty in line 274 might be remedied by reversing the last two words — *more speir* — but the second faulty rhyme word points to some larger problem.

276   *be strenyeit.* CM: *bestren yeit.*

278   *Goddis.* CM: *Cristis*; A emends to *Goddis*, which I follow.

    succeudry. In *Sir Gawain and the Green Knight*, when the latter character, through his initial challenge of a beheading contest, has reduced the fellowship of the Round Table to silence, he asks, "Where is now your sourquydrye and your conquestes?" (line 311). At the conclusion of the romance, the Green Knight explains that the motive of his mission to Arthur's court was "For to assay the surquidré, yif hit soth were" (line 2457: for to test the pride [of the Round Table] and see if it were true). In both cases, *surquidré* suggests a false pride or arrogance linked to chivalry, which the Green Knight works to deflate. In the *Alliterative Morte Arthure*, after Arthur has his dream of the Nine Worthy (see below, lines 1220 ff., especially 1233 ff., and notes), his philosopher explains to him that "thy fortune es passede," for "Thow has schedde myche blode, and schalkes distroyede, / Sakeles, in cirquytrie, in sere kynges landis" (lines 3394, 3398–99: your good fortune is over; you have shed much blood and destroyed people, without cause, in your pride, in many kings' lands). This passage, and the entire denouement of the *Alliterative Morte Arthure*, link chivalric pride with imperialistic, territorial ambitions and with the fall of the Round Table. Though some readers have taken *Sir Gawain and the Green Knight* and the *Alliterative Morte Arthure* as outright condemnations of knighthood or knightly behavior in the late Middle Ages, they seem perhaps to offer — like *Gologras* — a delicate probe of the interdependence of honor, violence, pride, and courtesy, of the political constraints of kingship, state-making and national identity, and of the relation of a chivalric ethos to the values and experience of other estates, classes, and groups in an increasingly heterogeneous society.

279   *knicht . . . with.* CM: *knich . . . wy^t.*

281   *the best . . . brevit.* CM: *thee best . . . beevit.*

282   *The myghty king of Massidone.* Alexander of Macedon, one of the Nine Worthy (see below, lines 1233 ff. and note) was the hero of more medieval narratives than any other figure; throughout Europe and in the Middle East as well, it has been said that Alexander stories were exceeded in popularity only by the Bible. At least ten different works in Middle English and Middle Scots survive.

289   *be licht.* CM: *he licht*; A emends to *be*, which I follow.

290   The demanding rhyme scheme makes clear that this stanza lacks a line following line 290, and that lines are missing as well following lines 331 and 550. Missing lines have not been numbered in the present edition.

292   *trou.* CM: *throu.*

292 ff. Arthur reaffirms here the vow he had made at line 273 (see note), and does so in terms that resemble celebrated oaths made by knights, actual and fictional. In particular, his vow that his body will never "be laid unlaissit to sleip" (line 294) recalls the oath made by Prince Edward (the future Edward II) in 1306, that he would not sleep two nights in the same place until he had made a campaign to the Holy Land. For the traditions associated with such public vows, see *Avowyng*, line 127 and note, and the material cited there, especially Orgelfinger, p. 614.

297 ff.   Arthur's open acceptance of the harm his warfare may cause non-combatants echoes the formulas that describe the effects of his campaigns in the *Alliterative Morte Arthure*:

> Towrres he turnes, and turmentez the pople,
> Wroghte wedewes fulle wlonke wrotherayle synge[n],
> Ofte wery and wepe, and wryngene theire handes

(lines 3153–55: Towers he throws down, and torments the people, made widows most proud to sing of their misery, to curse often and to weep, and to wring their hands). Having Arthur explicitly own responsibility for such consequences highlights the brutality associated with medieval warfare and with chivalric activity in general. Whether the mention of such suffering constitutes a direct critique of knighthood (as Matthews and others have argued) seems less than certain; literary works, vernacular writers, and Latin chroniclers seem often to regard violence as an inevitable condition or by-product of a chivalrous society, so that (as in Froissart) an author can simultaneously exalt knightly exploits and regard its victims as martyrs.

300   *Quhan . . . mude.* CM: *Quhy . . . mynde*; I follow A's emendation for the sake of rhyme.

305   *spurris.* CM: *speirris.*

306   *blonkis.* CM: *bloukis.*

Thai brochit blonkis to thair sidis brist of rede blude. The distinctive alliterative formulas of these two half-lines are repeated at line 754; they occur elsewhere only in *Awntyrs* line 499, and provide evidence for direct connection between the two poems.

308   *Ithandly.* CM: *I thaudly.*

309   *gay.* CM: *pay.* See line 233 and note.

310   *Rone.* CM: *Rome.* Arthur's pilgrimage *ovr the sey* (line 3), *to the cieté of Criste, ovr the salt flude* (line 302) seems certainly to have Jerusalem as its goal, despite the emphasis on passing through Italy (see line 2, note). *Rone* here then would seem to indicate not the city of St. Peter, but the Rhone valley. Further

evidence for this identification occurs at line 1345: *On the riche river of Rone ryot thai maid.* The main episode of *Gologras* is therefore set in southeastern France, after Arthur has made his return from the Holy Land through Tuscany in northwestern Italy.

321   *knichtis.* CM: *kinchtis.*

330   *burgh.* CM: *bnrgh.*

331   *Ressave.* CM: *Ressane.*

The rhyme scheme indicates another omitted line following this (see lines 290 and 550 and notes).

338   *Shir Lancelot de Lake.* Though Malory exalts Lancelot as the preeminent champion of the Round Table, at least among secular knights, he does not appear often in the Gawain romances. The exceptions are the *Stanzaic Morte Arthur* and the Scots romance, *Lancelot of the Laik*; for the latter, see the edition by Alan Lupack, TEAMS Middle English Texts series (Kalamazoo: Medieval Institute Publications, 1994).

339   *Schir Ewin.* Ywain is a central figure in Arthurian romance from Chrétien de Troyes' twelfth-century *Yvain* through the fourteenth-century *Ywain and Gawain*; *Carlisle* mentions him in passing (see line 40, note).

340   *the schore chiftane.* A, following M, suggests "high, noble" for this adjective. I take it as an adjective cognate with *to schore* (line 276), and with the noun of the same spelling, meaning "menace" (see OED, *schore* sb.2, and v.2).

344   *leving.* CM: *leuiug.* A gives *leuing* in his corrigenda.

345   *And.* CM: *Aud.*

356   *yon trew.* CM: *you trew.*

360   *Ane.* CM: *Has*; I follow A's emendation.

368   *Thre knichtis.* CM: *Thre thre kinchtis.*

370   *freschly.* CM: *fresthly.*

374   *knichtis.* CM: *kinchtis.*

380   *swiftly.* CM: *swistly.*

395   *Schir Golagrus.* Though Spynagros has described this knight at some length, this is the first mention of his name. (For spelling, see note on title above). M tentatively connects the name with Malory's Galagars (see *Works*, p. 131); it also distantly resembles the name of a fiendish giant — Golapas — whom Arthur dispatches in the *Alliterative Morte Arthure* (line 2124). It seems to me more likely, however, that the poem uses the associations of the Chateau Orgueilleux (see note at line 2) to name a hero who embodied chivalric honor and pride.

400   *mediatour.* CM: *mediatonr.*

402   *He is.* CM: *He his.*

405   *doughty . . . induring.* CM: *donghty . . . indurnig.*

406   *mony big bike.* A, following earlier editors, in his glossary suggests "*probably* a thickly populated place," taking it as a metaphoric usage of the word derived from OE *biowic*, nest of wild bees. MED provides no help, but OED (*bike*, sb.4) gives a series of citations, almost all Scots, where the word means "swarm of people."

409   *saw.* CM: *faw.*

411   *crownit.* CM: *crovint.*

416   *doughtynes.* CM: *donghtynes.*

419   *quhare wourscip walkis.* This alliterative formula specifies the heavy dependence of a shame culture like chivalry upon the circulation of honor through word of mouth; compare *Sir Gawain and the Green Knight*, "your worchip walkez ayquere" (line 1521).

421   *fangit.* CM: *sangit.*

424   *riches to rigne.* An obscure alliterative formula (compare line 495). A takes *rigne* to mean "to reign" (which fits well enough with the latter line). I take the phrase to mean something like "with power to dispense," suggesting here that in seeking the friendship and homage of Gologras Arthur will stop short of nothing within his power — offering both an open promise and a covert threat.

429   *gracious.* CM: *gracions.*

429 ff.   Gologras' assertion here of hereditary autonomy within his own domain parallels claims made by many individual lords in resisting preemptive appropriations by kings and emperors during the later Middle Ages. When Edward I challenged the lordship of the Earl of Gloucester in Glamorganshire — one of the Celtic territories (in southern Wales) that typically provided new lands through conquest — the Earl countered "that he holds these lands and liberties by his and his ancestors' conquests." Similarly, when Edward claimed lordship over the lands of the Earl of Warenne, the latter asserted, "My ancestors came with William the Bastard and conquered their lands with the sword. The king did not conquer and subject the land by himself, but our forebears were sharers and partners with him." Robert Bartlett discusses the conflicts surrounding lordship through conquest in *The Making of Europe: Conquest, Colonization and Cultural Change: 950–1350* (Princeton: Princeton University Press, 1993), pp. 90 ff.; I have taken the above quotations from his citations. Arthurian romances often built their fictional worlds on these sites of real contest and conquest; in *Awntyrs* Arthur bestows upon Gawain, in compensation for previously appropriated territory that he has now restored to Sir Galeron, "Al the Glamergan londe with greves so grene" (line 665), that is, the very territory whose lordship the Earl of Gloucester had disputed with his king (himself a sponsor of Arthurian recreations).

430   *ever.* CM: *neuer.* I follow A's emendation.

434   *hail.* In its root meaning (whole, sound), *hail* implies not simply "hale" and "hearty," but also uncompromised in autonomy of lordship, entirely possessed of their own estates and not in service to some higher feudal lord.

441   *subjectioun.* CM: *subiectioun*; A reads *subiection.*

448   *na for na distance.* In ME, *distance* usually means "strife" or "discord," and the phrase *withoutin distance* (line 1362, significantly the last line of *Gologras*)

means "indisputably," "forthwith." Yet in both instances in *Gologras* the word has connotations of deference connected to the formal gap or remoteness between lord and subject.

449   *noght*. CM: *nogth*.

456   *unsaught*. CM: *vnsanght*.

459 ff.   The details mentioned here concerning supplies and fortifications constitute the starting point for a realistic description of a drawn-out and destructive besieging of Gologras' castle, which Arthur seems about to initiate (see lines 297 ff., 499 ff. and note). The poem quickly leaves such hints behind, however, turning its back on the grinding if dull conduct of warfare most typical of the late Middle Ages. In its place *Gologras* offers an idealized portrayal of chivalry, a series of duels and jousts that culminates in the battle of the two champions.

461   *alkin wappyns, I wys, that wes for were wroght*. The inventory mentioned here includes artillery — *Pellokis* and *Gapand gunnys of brase* — suggesting the ways in which technology changed the nature of man-to-man combat in the late Middle Ages, and the ways in which chivalry accommodated these new technologies to its style of warfare. Such heavy armaments were deployed (by both defenders and attackers) in the siege warfare that typified many late medieval campaigns. Gunpowder, by increasing the chances of dying by an unknown hand, diminished the potential for honor through violence. Though it mentions these up-to-date contrivances, *Gologras* clearly presents war as a series of individual encounters that are opportunities to earn honor, in the ultimate case by dying at the hands of a renowned, worshipful opponent; see, for example, lines 635 ff., 713 ff. and notes. On the effects of artillery upon knightly combat and the chivalric ethos, see Keen, *Chivalry*, pp. 241–42 and the bibliography cited there.

462   *bowis of bras*. This seems to refer to a cross-bow or perhaps an arbalest, a weapon with a special mechanism (a windlass or craquelin) for drawing and slipping the string. Late medieval cross-bows were made with metal bows, which substantially increased the power with which they might hurl arrows, bolts (perhaps the *ganyeis* of line 465), or stones. Such armaments were typically used in siege warfare, for they were too large and difficult to manage in open-field combat, let alone in individual encounters. Commonly the bow was made of steel. Other metals, like bronze or *bras* (as here) lacked sufficient tensile

strength, and are not mentioned so far as I know in medieval sources; perhaps *bras* here describes the drawing mechanism.

465 *Grundin.* CM: *Grundiu.*

470 *hurdys.* These are apparently scaffolds that the wrights construct in the woods; after transport to the walls of Gologras' castle, they will be used in the siege.

471–72 A points out that defective rhymes demonstrate that lines 471–72 are out of place in CM; I have therefore reversed them in the present edition.

479 *schaw.* CM: *schair*; I follow A's emendation for the sake of rhyme.

485 *lans.* CM: *laus.*

488 *cunysance.* See line 159 and note. The honor of each knight depends upon the recognition by others of his distinctive arms, and then of his deed. The writing of knights' names — a kind of captioned identity for a literate spectatorship — seems out of keeping with the highly visual character of heraldic sign systems.

489 *names writtin.* CM: *mames wrictin.*

494 *wist.* CM, A: *vist.*

499 ff. Arthur vows here to destroy the countryside *with routis*, a kind of pillaging and scorched earth policy typical of English military tactics in France during the Hundred Years War and after; the object of such warfare was to destroy the *rentis* or income a lord might derive from his lands, and thereby to force his submission even when he was not personally vulnerable to attack. This devastation affected most directly the people who lived and worked on the lands; Arthur's second promise — to find alternate livelihood for his victims during a long campaign — is both a generous and uncharacteristic gesture for a medieval king. Such tactics continued as a practice in the border wars between Scotland and England throughout the late Middle Ages. On the *chevauchee*, see *Greene Knight*, line 246 and note, and on border raids see the Introduction, pp. 28–33. I take *notis* here in its primary ME sense of work, occupation.

501 *nine.* CM: *ix.*

504   *force.* CM: *forte* (as in line 536); I follow A's emendation in both cases, who follows M and Trautman.

507   *you.* CM: *yuo.*

508   *saill.* CM: *faill.* I follow A's emendation, which he makes without note.

        wil set upone sevin. Here, and at line 668 — *thai set upone sevin* — this proverbial phrase means to put everything at risk. It refers to the game of hazard (similar to craps), in which a player might stake his entire wager on one throw of the dice. At line 1045 the similar phrase *settis all on sevin* has almost the opposite meaning. See B. J. and H. W. Whiting, *Proverbs, Sentences, and Proverbial Phrases* (Cambridge, Massachusetts, 1968), S359.

514   *myght.* CM: *mygth.*

516   *sicker.* CM: *silker.* I follow A's silent emendation.

519   *upone raw.* A, with his usual directness, comments that this "seems a useless tag . . . [whose] meaning is of the vaguest." But this formulaic phrase is both a descriptive and constitutive feature of alliterative poetry's oral component and of the chivalric honor culture that it exalts. The phrase *upone raw* describes the rhythmic, symmetrical, artificed style of this poetry, with its rhymes, repetitions, echoes, and patterned stanzas, but it names as well the mnemonic principle on which such poetry is composed and performed. When Gawain delivers his message to Gologras *on raw* — poised amidst the splendor and order of his own court, as Arthur, *richest on raw*, is later — he praises Arthur as the greatest lord *to ryme or rekin on raw* (lines 396, 403, 1277). Style, power, meaningful and memorable speech itself, all are dependent upon this articulated order (and upon others seeing, hearing, and confirming such sights and sounds). In the present scene, speaking and understanding are themselves matters of *reknand upone raw*, of remembering, refashioning, revoicing the scattered but already spoken fragments of shared wisdom. By reiterating formulas like *on raw*, the patterned, orderly verses of *Gologras* make clear the equivalence of language and action, of style and substance; moreover, this equivalence marks the exchanges within its narrative descriptions — Gawain before Gologras, Spynagros with Arthur — and its performative demands on its audience, whether in a reading or listening event.

524   *seymly.* CM: *seynily.*

525   *A gome . . . glisnand.* CM: *Agane . . . glifnaud.* A reads *glifnand* in his corrigenda.

535   *suth.* CM: *such.* I follow A's emendation.

536   *force.* CM: *forte* (see note on line 504 above).

540   Spynagros tells Arthur, "Choose a champion" (*makis furth ane man*) to match the knight who has presented himself on the tower.

545   *Gaudifeir. Carlisle* mentions *Syr Gaytefer* (line 43 and note), but he does not otherwise appear as a knight of the Round Table. A points out that his exploits are associated with the cycles of ancient romance (Alexander and Caesar), which are retold in several Scots narratives, and in the French prose romance of *Perceforest.*

550   *gif he nane had.* Precisely what this phrase means is unclear, since as a nobleman of great ancestry (see lines 545–46) Gaudifeir would surely possess all the accoutrements of a knight. Perhaps he acts *as if* starting from scratch, emphasizing the completeness of the arming ritual. The rhyme scheme indicates a line is missing after the present line; see lines 290, 331 and notes.

557   *Galiot. Lancelot of the Laik* (line 302) mentions a Galiot who seems to be the same knight as Malory's Galehaut; the latter's central role within the Arthurian fellowship makes it impossible to consider him the same knight named here as a vassal of Gologras. The alliterating names of Gologras' champions here and in the following scenes (lines 585, 653 ff.) seem to have been invented for this romance.

564   *steil.* A reads *steill.*

572   *ane myle way and maire.* The ME phrase *myle way* (also at line 1119) indicates a measure of time, namely the interval it takes to walk a mile, or about twenty minutes. The poet here specifies that the two knights fought for a slightly longer period.

573   These formulas for the berserker character of chivalric violence are repeated at line 1014, and the b-verse occurs again at line 972.

577   *yhude.* CM: *yhnde.*

578   *mightis.* CM: *nughtis.*

580   *craft.* CM: *crast.*

585   *Schir Rigal of Rone.* A knight apparently otherwise unknown in Arthurian romance. The localization of his lordship — *of Rone* — provides further evidence that the fictional setting for this episode, and for Gologras' castle, is the Rhone valley, in southeastern France. See lines 310 and 597 and notes.

586   *in quert.* A takes *quert* as the fairly common ME word meaning "peace, rest," in which case the line would mean, "until this matter is requited, I will not be at ease." If *quert* means "court," Gologras is making a stronger statement: "until it is requited, I will not be properly lord in my own court." Compare *Awntyrs*, line 257, where the ghost has Guenevere swear to act "Als thou art Quene in thi quert."

590   *never.* CM: *nener.*

591   *graithit.* CM: *graith it.*

597   *Raunald.* A emends to *Rannald* to preserve consistency with subsequent spellings. The *Alliterative Morte Arthure* lists "Sir Raynalde" as one of the knights who accompanies the Roman prisoners to Paris (line 1607); he fights also at the siege in Saxony where one of his companions is "The riche duke of Rowne" (line 1995–96), recalling the title of Rannald's opponent, *Schir Rigal of Rone.*

599   *schroud.* CM: *schrond.*

600   *him.* CM: *hun.*

603   *With.* CM: *Wich.*

611   *knight.* CM: *kinght.*

613   *right.* CM: *rihht.*

614   *Lightly . . . loft.* CM: *Lighly . . . lost.*

624 *in.* CM: *iu.*

635 *faucht.* CM: *fautht.*

635 ff. The death of even a minor character is a rare occurrence in a chivalric romance. Though "chronicle" narratives like the stanzaic and alliterative poems on the death of Arthur, and Malory's *Morte Darthur*, record the deaths of central characters — including Gawain and of course Arthur himself — they do so as part of the narrative underpinning that announces their status as epic or tragedy. These deaths function as moral signals, either of nostalgic loss in the passing of the heroes of chivalry's golden age, or of chastening deficiency in the spectacle of an honorable society's downfall. Occasionally romances seriously contemplate the death of a notable character, as in the life-threatening circumstances that produce the "tappe" that "severed the hyde" in *Sir Gawain and the Green Knight* (lines 2309 ff.), or in the near battle to the death of Sir Galeron and Gawain in *Awntyrs*. *Gologras*, however, quite remarkably presents death as grim and grievous, and yet as the predictable, even inevitable, outcome of chivalric violence; though Arthur and Gologras feel fierce distress at the deaths of Sir Rigal and Sir Rannald (and later at the death of Sir Edmond, lines 726 ff.), there is never any question about the rightness of chivalric combat and killing. Both men die "with mekil honour," are simultaneously buried with fit ceremony, and — most important of all — have achieved a lasting fame in the memory of a worshipful community: "Yet has men thame in mynd for thair manhede" (lines 648 ff.). The narrative in this way simultaneously impresses upon its audience the high cost and the ultimate worth of the honor and violence sponsored by knighthood. See lines 713 ff. and note, Gawain's and Gologras' acceptances of their own deaths (lines 808 and 1035 ff.), and Gologras' long speech that pinpoints the paradoxes of honor entailed in freely giving up a life that one has created through the most strenuous exertions (lines 1201 ff. and notes).

639 *scheild.* CM: *scheid.*

640 *and fel.* CM: *ane fel.*

652 *glisnand.* CM: *glifnand.*

653   *Schir Louys*. The *Alliterative Morte Arthure* mentions *Lowes* (line 4266), who is slain in the final battle with Mordred, though the composer of *Gologras* seems to have invented *Louys* afresh as a retainer of Gologras.

654   *Edmond*. This knight is otherwise unknown, and seems to have been created simply as Ywain's victim; he is apparently not the same champion as *Ewmond* (line 739).

655   *Schir Bantellas*. Again, this otherwise unknown knight, who subdues Arthur's familiar champion Bedwar, suggests by his name the exotic character of Gologras' retinue.

657   *Schir Sanguel*. This champion of Gologras is otherwise unknown.

661   *Schir Lyonel*. As son of Bors of Gaul, and brother to Lancelot's constant companion Bors de Ganys, Lyonel plays a large role in many romances, including Malory's *Morte Darthur*.

662   *athir*. CM: *a thir*.

663   *Schir Bedwar*. Bedevere is brother of Lucan the Butler, and one of Arthur's chief companions; in the *Stanzaic Morte Arthur* and Malory, he survives the final battle with Mordred, attends Arthur at his death, and disposes of Excalibur, Arthur's sword.

664   *nemmyt*. CM: *nenmyt*. In his glossary, A gives the meaning "taken, chosen" (from OE *niman*); but (as the OED citation confirms) this seems to be the past participle of *nemn*, "to be called," in this case, "to be called upon or summoned."

665   *Gyromalance*. In romances associated with Merlin, Gyromalance is the retainer of Amant, who refuses submission to Arthur. There is perhaps pointed irony in his role in *Gologras*, which makes him the vassal of Arthur who subdues Sangwel, the retainer of another lord who refuses homage to Arthur.

668   *scheildis*. CM: *scheidis*.

669   *knightis*. CM: *kinghtis*.

       maid. Broken type in CM makes this a conjectural reading.

674–75   The idiomatic character of these lines makes them difficult to construe. A paraphrases, "Then their horses receive such hurts in their houghs ["hocks," the lower joint of the leg], are so sorely strained, as they stand quaking, checked in their unrest — i.e., pulled up, reined in, though eager to rush on." To me, the lines seem to emphasize not the horses' eagerness, but their frenzy: they suffered such shocks that they stand quaking like horses under great stress who cannot bolt because of their harness.

677   The formulas of these two half-lines, describing the ritualized havoc of battle, repeat with slight variation in lines 755, 847, and 874.

686   *bauldly.* CM: *banldly.*

687   *brymly.* CM: *bryimly,* which A prints. I emend to the usual form of *brym.*

        bent. CM: *beut.*

689   *Throu . . . schuldiris.* CM: *thron . . . schuldis;* I follow A in expanding a mark above *d* in *schuldis* as an abbreviation for *ir.*

692   *grams.* A emends to *granis,* i.e. "groan." Though the form is somewhat odd (*gramys* would be a more likely spelling), *grams* fits the context.

693   *reuth . . . rent.* CM: *renth . . . reut.*

694   *cair . . . knightis.* CM: *thair . . . kinghtis.* A gives *kingthis* in his corrigenda.

696 ff.   The statement that only God knows, and determines, the outcome of the combat reflects assumptions fundamental to a shame/honor culture like that of chivalry. Because violence constitutes the final proof of honor, the combatants must trust not simply that the best man will win, but that the winner will have proved the justice of his cause with God, the ultimate guarantor of such public rituals. Gaudifeir succeeds in rising from the ground and winning his duel with Galiot only "throu Goddis grete mightis" (line 578, above); Gawain's assertion in *Awntyrs,* concerning his combat with Galeron, that "God stond with the right," offers a striking articulation of this conviction; see *Awntyrs* line 471 and note.

698   *govern.* CM: *gonern.*

703   *here.* A argues this is a form of "hire," and takes the line to mean, "they receive great harms and reward or glory." Almost certainly, however, *here* is related to the common ME word *herien*, to ravage or pilage; in earlier ME, *here* in fact means "devastation by war" (see citations in MED).

704   *All toturvit.* CM, M, A: *toturnit.* Skeat (*The Academy*, 6 January 1894, p. 13; cited by A) argues for this emendation on the basis that no such word as *toturnit* exists in English.

706   *swerdis.* CM: *snerdis.*

        The formulas in this line are repeated at line 1106.

710   *Stalwart.* CM: *Scalvart.*

713 ff. Though the syntax is ambiguous, the account makes clear that Gologras' champion *Lowes* captures *Lyonell* (see lines 722 ff.). Here as earlier, *Gologras* takes care to emphasize the parity, even the symmetry, of the combat between the forces of Arthur and of Gologras: two of Arthur's knights are taken captive, while one of Gologras' knights is captured and one is killed. In giving the Arthurian side only a slight advantage, the narration makes Gologras a more formidable, and intriguing, opponent, and leaves questions of "rightness" within the poem and of audience sympathy more difficult to settle. The effect is also to increase the sense of the costliness and genuine loss consequent upon knightly violence, though without openly condemning such combat. See lines 635 ff. and note, and Gologras' speeches at lines 1035 ff. and lines 1201 ff. and notes.

714   *Giromalans.* CM: *Giromalaus.*

720   *Unmanglit.* CM: *Wnmaglit.*

721   The meaning of this line, clearly parallel to line 719, is hard to disentangle. A suggests, "none was so proud of his part that he could boast of it when he left the field, because they had all suffered so severely." I take it to mean almost the opposite: "not one of the knights so proud of his part in the battle did *not* win honor, even when captured" (though to obtain this meaning one has to assume a suppressed second negative).

739   *Schir Agalus.* Malory mentions Sir Agloval, the brother of Perceval, some ten times, but it seems doubtful that Cador's prisoner here is identical to this Arthurian knight.

        Schir Ewmond. This knight of Gologras', whose name recalls that of *Edmond* (line 654, slain by Ywain at line 726), is, except for the present exploit of defeating Owales, unknown.

740   *Schir Mychin, Schir Meligor.* These retainers of Gologras are otherwise unknown in romance.

742   *Schir Hew.* This knight of Gologras' retinue, otherwise unknown, resembles in name Arthur's knight Schir Hewis (line 1246).

745   *fenyeing.* CM: *fenyenig.*

746   *lufsum.* CM: *luffum.*

747   *Cornwel.* CM: *Coruwel.*

        Schir Cador of Cornwel. In the *Alliterative Morte Arthure,* Cador of Cornwall is nephew to Arthur, who brings news of Mordred's treason to the king in Italy; he is father of Constantine, Arthur's successor (see *Carlisle,* line 44 and note). Cador and Constantine are both accused by Guenevere of lack of courtesy in *Awntyrs* (line 96).

748   *Schir Owales.* Since *Owales* (*Owiles,* line 765) is otherwise unknown as an Arthurian knight, his defeat at the hands of Ewmond gives Gologras' side a victory without diminishing the glory of the Round Table.

        Schir Iwell. This Arthurian knight is otherwise unknown.

749   *Schir Myreot.* This seems to be another Arthurian knight invented by the composer of *Gologras.*

        emell. A is inclined to capitalize *Emell* as a proper name, making the fifth champion of the Round Table, matching the five knights named by Gologras. But he is not named again, and line 750 specifies *four* knights.

764   *laught*. CM: *lāght*. The usual expansion would be *langht*, which makes no sense in this context, where *laught* fits appropriately. See note at line 922.

770   *as*. CM: *ad*.

775   *smal*. CM: *swal*, not noted by A.

776   *Arthur*. CM: *Arthnr*.

778   *yone*. CM: *youe*.

779   *sens peir*. CM: *sen speir* (followed by A), which is clearly a faulty word break.

782   *his aune self shall do for his dail*. Spynagros' account pinpoints the tension between Arthur and Gologras, namely the latter's autonomy as a lord holding allegiance to no overlord, and therefore offering implicit challenge to Arthur's kingship.

783   *in this*. CM: *is this*. I follow A's emendation.

798   *to countir*. This seems to be a quasi-technical term of chivalric combat, encompassing a knight's formal engagement with an opponent (compare the action of line 845).

807   *mobil on the mold*. This distinctive alliterative formula occurs only here and in *Awntyrs* line 199 (see note).

809   *he war*. CM: *the war*. I follow A's emendation.

816   *do it*. CM: *doit*.

823   *nevin*. CM: *uevin*.

827   *And*. CM: *Ayd*.

836 ff.   The assignment to Sir Kay of a small but successful part in the ongoing chivalric combat is a feature that distinguishes *Gologras* from all the other verse romances. Here he encounters and defeats, though just barely (see lines 869 ff.), an unknown champion of Gologras. Though this is clearly the preliminary

bout to the central encounter of the poem, it is presented in complete seriousness, enabling Kay to earn an unwonted bit of honor.

857   *flaw*. CM: *fllaw*, with initial two letters printed as a digraph.

872   *harm*. CM: *harim*.

873   *Kynge*. CM: *kynde*. I follow A's obvious emendation.

875 ff.   Arthur's reassuring reception of the unnamed knight, and the immediate attempt to comfort him and staunch his wounds (lines 882 ff.), reinforce the sense that chivalric values like courtesy and graciousness transcend any individual hostility. Though misfortune may overtake an honorable knight (see lines 864 ff.), he retains his worship and status within the chivalric community.

878 ff.   *romanis*. CM: *romams*. See note on line 778 above. The King's citation, within an Arthurian romance, of *romanis [that] I reid* as a source of authority creates a degree of ironic circularity, in which a fictional character cites fiction as a guide to behavior. There is, however, a large body of evidence documenting the broad interdependence of art and life concerning chivalric practices and ideals in the late Middle Ages. Moreover, the King's remark, in idealizing the audience for chivalric romance (suggesting that even monarchs consult them), explicitly points towards difficult questions surrounding their sponsorship and consumption (see General Introduction, pp. 10–23). The King's phrasing in this line, while a common oral formula, confirms the impression that line 879 is a proverb, though it is not recorded by Whiting, *Proverbs*. It would seem to mean something like, "Even well started plans sometimes fail."

880   *pailyeoun*. An odd spelling compounded by a stroke over the final "n"; A reads *pailyeoune*.

884   *fresch*. CM: *fresth*.

889   *silk*. CM: *filk*.

895   *blonk*. CM: *bonlk*.

896   *gold and*. CM: *goldfand*.

909   *thame.* CM: *tha̅m.*

922   *laught.* CM: *langht.*

928   *ma.* CM: *may.* I follow A's emendation.

937   *And claif throw the cantell of the clene schelde.* In the *Alliterative Morte Arthure*, just before receiving his fatal wound from Mordred, Arthur strikes his nephew/son so fiercely that "The cantelle of the clere schelde he kerfes in sondyre" (line 4231). *Awntyrs* adapts this line as well in the description of the combat between Gawain and Galeron: "And clef his shelde shene . . . He clef thorgh the cantell" (lines 520–21).

961   *as lyoune.* The particular comparisons of Gologras — here to a lion, and at line 945, *Alse ferse as the fyre* — extend back (though not in a direct line) to the elaborated epic similes Homer used to characterize fighters like Sarpedon, Hector, and Achilles.

1002   *wondir.* CM: *wndir.*

1012 ff. The abridged, staccato syntax of this crucial stanza, which ends the combat between the main characters, reproduces the dense, chancy, abrupt character of the action. It begins with both champions frenzied from the battle (*witlese and wod*). Gawain makes the first move, striking at Gologras and destroying his shield (just as Gologras had carved Gawain's *In twenty pecis and ma*, line 970). The blow is by no means lethal; however, as Gologras makes a return stroke (line 1020) he loses his footing on what seems an uneven battlefield (lines 1021–22). Fatigue, loss of blood, and the weight of his armor bring him crashing to the ground, and Gawain (in the following stanza) takes the opportunity to demand his surrender. The narrative takes care in this way to suggest that Gologras' defeat does not occur solely because of Gawain's superiority, but is an outcome presided over by circumstances, Fortune, and, ultimately, by God (see lines 508, 578, 635 ff., 696 ff., 1220, 1333 ff., and notes); chivalric renown therefore depends not upon victory, but upon honorable conduct.

1025   *ever.* CM: *ener.*

1031   *life.* CM: *lise.*

1034   *answerit.* CM: *ausnerit*; A incorrectly prints *ansnerit* in his corrigenda.

1039   *ever.* CM: *ener.*

1043   *levin.* CM: *leme.* M emends for rhyme, though A defends the sense of the original reading as "nor look on my (dishonoured) body in the broad light of day."

1045   *God, that settis all on sevin.* This proverbial phrase alludes to the order imposed by the Creator during the seven days of creation. In the *Alliterative Morte Arthure*, Arthur leads his forces against the giants who accompany the Romans: "Thus he settez on sevene with his sekyre knyghttez" (line 2131), restoring order to his army and putting the giants in their place. A cites many additional instances. Compare the similar sounding phrase at lines 508 and 668 (with note at line 508).

1050   *Doutles.* CM: *Dontles.*

1053   *swownit.* CM: *swowint.*

1064   *loft.* CM: *lost.*

1071   *eneuch.* CM: *eneuth.*

1080   *lurk for ane luke.* A paraphrases, "shall make me hide from people's eyes." I take *lurk* to mean not "hide" but "hesitate," with the phrase emphasizing the public, spectacular nature of chivalric honor, which a knight earns *for ane luke*, before the gaze of onlookers.

1095   *yow.* A prints *thow* here and at line 1099, but the first letter is clearly *y*, not thorn.

1105   *souer.* CM: *soner*; I emend for sense.

        gentrice. CM: *gentrite.*

1114   *sic.* CM: *sit.*

1118   *scheith.* CM: *schetlh.*

1119   *way.* CM: *wan.*

        myle way and mare. See note at line 572.

1135   *knighthede.* CM: *kinghthede.*

1138   *presoune.* CM: *presonne.*

1144   *garisoune.* A paraphrases, "Knights made sport and glee of that prize." Citations from MED indicate that *garisoune* may mean "treasure," but usually with reference to material wealth or a particular object (compare *Sir Gawain and the Green Knight*, lines 1255, 1807, 1837); here it seems to refer directly to Gologras' *castel of stane* (line 1125).

1148   *Al thus with murnyng and myrth thai maid melle.* The alliterative phrasing of this line recalls the end of *St. Erkenwald*, where the decomposition of the pagan saint's body causes the assembled throng to feel a mixture of emotions: "Meche mournyng and myrthe was mellyd togeder" (line 350, ed. Ruth Morse [Cambridge: D. S. Brewer, 1975]).

1154   *that.* A expands the abbreviation to *the.*

1165   *quhilk.* A prints *quilk.*

1167   *thai.* CM: *thair.*

1169   *governyng.* CM: *goduernyng.*

1180   *concele.* CM: *coucele.*

1186   *undir.* A prints *under.*

1220   *Sen Fortoune cachis the cours.* Gologras' explanation of his motives for saving his life on the battlefield are less psychological than philosophical. Fortune and her ever-moving wheel, which arbitrarily brings prosperity and ruin, is a common figure in medieval literature and visual art from the time of Boethius (sixth century). The iconography of her wheel often represents four kings (at top, bottom, and sides) marked by verbs that describe shifting phases of rule: "I reign," "I was reigning," "I have reigned," "I will reign." King Arthur has a vivid, prophetic dream of Fortune in the *Alliterative Morte Arthure*, though here her wheel is not populated by anonymous emblematic kings, but by the Nine Worthy (see lines 1233 ff. and note). Gologras' reflections set up an opposition between Fortune's tricky regime, and the orderly providence of Christ (line 1223). But where the traditional Boethian hierarchies firmly establish the superiority of internal to external, of innocence/guilt to honor/shame, Gologras in this instance uses the traditional opposition to define two kinds of externally conferred shame/honor: false knighthood where one acts self-servingly to keep one's life or possessions, and true knighthood which pursues honor while completely disregarding immediate costs or possible gains. The connection between the inscrutable, inevitable chanciness of martial chivalry and the achievement of knightly honor is vividly pictured in one of the elaborate illustrations to Honoré Bonet's *Tree of Battles*: atop a tree filled with armored knights in combat stands Fortune, blind-folded and turning her wheel. At the bottom, slain knights, fallen from the tree, have their souls rescued by angels or are dragged into the mouth of hell. The iconography of the four kings does not appear; their absence makes the image *not* simply a *memento mori*, but an injunction — like Gologras' here — that every true knight should greet his fate — whether life or death, triumph or defeat — with an unflinching equanimity. For a reproduction of this illustration, see Andrea Hopkins, *Knights* (1990; reprint London: Grange, 1993), p. 135.

1231   *And muse in his myrrour.* In *Awntyrs*, the ghost of Guenevere's mother chastizes her daughter in her speech of greeting:

> "Thus am I lyke to Lucefere: takis witnes by mee!
> For al thi fressh foroure
> *Muse on my mirrour*;
> For, king and emperour,
> Thus dight shul ye be"
> (lines 165–69, italics added; see note)

The recurring presentation in chivalric romances of death — especially the deaths of the rich and famous — as a shocking and thereby memorable mirror of life underscores that gaining worship by arms can take place only in the shadow of death. The poems themselves function as mirrors to the aristocratic ideals of chivalry they describe, but they operate through an aesthetic not of mimesis (art imitating life), but of the spectacular (*speculum* is the Latin word for *mirrour*). The brilliant surface, especially of the alliterative poems — their

305

decorated, lapidary descriptive style — mirrors the centrality of public gaze and display within the romances, conveyed, for example, through lavish dress, the jewelled, embroidered accessories of ladies and warriors, and the exhibitionist quality of warfare.

1233 ff. Gologras here allusively invokes the Nine Worthy, a group presented in medieval literature and art as the greatest exemplars of chivalric achievement in history. They included three heathen, three Jews, and three Christians: Hector of Troy, Alexander of Macedon, and Julius Caesar; Joshua, King David, and Judas Maccabeus; Arthur, Charlemagne, and Godfrey of Bouillon. In *The Parlement of the Thre Ages*, Elde, discoursing on the vanity of the world, devotes almost three hundred lines (nearly half the poem) to the Nine Worthy (lines 297–583); see the edition by M. Y. Offord, EETS 246 (Oxford, 1959). Elde's conclusion is "Bot doghetynes when dede comes ne dare noghte habyde" (line 583: when death comes, valor dare not stay), a moral quite opposite to Gologras' assertion that "Ilkane be werk and be will / Is worth his rewarde" (lines 1244–45). The turning point of the *Alliterative Morte Arthure* occurs in Arthur's nightmarish but prophetic vision of the Nine Worthy on Fortune's wheel (lines 3218–3455); in effect the vision telescopes his own rise and fall, making Arthur ironically a moral emblem for the fleeting, precarious character of his own experience. *Gologras*, in omitting the three Christian Worthy, avoids anachronism (since Arthur is, in the course of the present narrative, only achieving his status, and Charlemagne and Godfrey are yet to come) and forgoes prophecy and explicit moralization; instead, the poem substitutes two heroes from the Hebrew Bible, and then compares all these to the modern instances — those heroes who have suffered in the present glorious combat. In drawing on the tradition of the Nine Worthy, *Gologras* accentuates the tension within chivalry between splendor and mortality; in Gologras' interpretation, the mortal limit that these heroes come up against ("merk," line 1237) becomes not a cause for rejection of the world, but a spur to the individual knight to grasp honor in the world without thought for consequences. This emphasis, though unusual within the moral tradition that surrounds the Nine Worthy, entirely typifies the chivalric ethos celebrated in *Gologras*, where knights paradoxically attain lasting worship through deadly violence. Certainly one of the most magnificent representations of the theme of the Nine Worthy must have been the set of tapestries woven in Paris around 1400; the much-reproduced portrait of Arthur shows this worthy crowned and enthroned, with crowns on his robes and on the banner he holds, at once sovereign and set for a fall. It is now in the Cloisters Museum (New York); see frontispiece to *Arthurian Litera-ture in the Middle Ages*, ed. R. S. Loomis (1959; corrected ed., Oxford, 1967).

1246   *Schir Hallolkis*. A speculates that this name might be a corruption of *Schir Owales* (lines 748, 765), and not the introduction of yet another otherwise unknown champion.

        Schir Hewis. This Arthurian knight does not appear elsewhere, though his name is suspiciously similar to that of Gologras' knight, *Schir Hew* (line 742).

1258   *In ony*. CM: *I nony*.

1271   *Lufsum*. CM: *Luffum*.

1272   *rout*. CM: *rent*. I follow A in emending for the sake of rhyme.

1295   *resoune*. CM: *resonne*.

1298   *Conquerour*. CM: *Conquer*.

1300   *wonnyn*. CM: *wounyn*.

1301   *fortoune*. CM: *fortonne*.

1306   *prejudice*. CM: *preuidice*.

1308   *thi*. CM: *the* (abbreviated); I emend for sense.

1312   *than*. CM: *thau*.

1313   *Ronsiwall*. OF Rencesvals, modern Roncevaux or Roncesvalles (in Spain), ME Rouncyvale, the mountain pass in the Pyrenees where Charlemagne's rear guard, led by his nephew Roland and the Emperor's twelve peers (compare line 1334, *douchspere*), was annihilated by the Saracens (Spanish Muslims). The event is celebrated as a glorious chivalric exploit in the *Chanson de Roland*, in ME Charlemagne romances, and in many other retellings.

1318   *ever*. CM: *ener*.

1322   *I*. The pronoun is lacking in CM; I follow A in supplying this.

1324   *fenyeing.* CM: *senyenig.*

1326   *bidding.* CM: *bibding.*

1331   *syll.* CM: *saill.* I follow A in emending for rhyme.

1334   *douchspere.* The word is a variant of *douzeperes*, i.e., "twelve peers," and refers in its origin to the twelve companion knights or paladins who accompanied Charlemagne in the battle recounted in the *Chanson de Roland* (early twelfth century). Since the sixteenth century the word has been used to identify any collection of great knightly champions. See note on line 1313; and see *Awntyrs* line 4 and note.

1355   *thir.* CM: *their.*

1356   *tuiching.* CM: *tiuching.*

       temporalité. This term, which usually refers to estates and possessions of the clergy, or more generally to the domain of secular (versus ecclesiastical) lordship, here seems to be used to clarify the autonomy of Gologras' rule, as a lord who owes allegiance to no superior. This emphasis on separate rule, outside the authority of the monarch, establishes for Gologras a unique position among rivals and opponents in the Gawain romances. In the *Alliterative Morte Arthure* Arthur bestows on an anonymous knight lordship of the region surrounding Toulouse,

> "The tolle and the tachementez, tavernez and other,
> The towne and the tenementez with towrez so hye,
> That towchez to the temporaltee, whiles my tyme lastez"
>   (lines 1568–70).

See the more traditional use in *Turke*, line 161.

1358   *thin.* CM: *ym.*

1362   On the leaf following the end of *Gologras* occurs a "Balade" that runs for two and one half pages. It is a version of a poem, entitled "Rhyme without Accord," attributed to John Lydgate, a fifteenth-century monk and follower of Chaucer. The colophon of *Gologras*, given here immediately after the text, follows the "Balade."

The Greene Knight

Introduction

Sir Gawain and the Green Knight is by acclamation the most subtle, learned, and enjoyable of poems about this chivalric hero, as well as one of the great narrative achievements in the English language. Yet there exists little evidence of its being read from the time of its composition in the later fourteenth century until the edition produced by Madden in 1839. Even if it did find readers, however, this profoundly literate text exercised little influence over the popular Gawain narratives represented in this volume. The kernel story, of a monstrous Green Knight who visits Arthur's court and tests Sir Gawain as the pearl of chivalry, seems to have been popular before its absorption into *Sir Gawain and the Green Knight*, and there is every reason to think it would have continued as a great favorite in the fifteenth and sixteenth centuries. Certainly some of the central motifs of *Sir Gawain and the Green Knight*, like the beheading game in *Turke*, distantly reflect its plot, and there are echoes of its language and phrasing in other poems, like *Awntyrs*.

The best proof for the lasting popularity of this story is by far the present poem, called *The Greene Knight* in order both to connect it and distinguish it from its illustrious predecessor. Scholars have often assumed that *The Greene Knight* represents a quirky retelling of an exceptional narrative, but such a view neglects important evidence. An inventory of Sir John Paston's books from the late 1470s mentions among his titles several of Chaucer's poems, "The Dethe off Arthur," a series of chivalric romances (Arthurian and otherwise), together with "The Greene Knyght" and "my boke off knyghthod . . . [and] makyng off knyghtys, off justys, off torn[aments and] fyghtyng in lystys" (see General Introduction, p. 12). This remarkable library ranges from popular and oral stories to the most literate and learned texts (Paston also owned a copy of Cicero and a number of religious writings); the strong emphasis on chivalry and Arthur is particularly striking in a collection that dates from within ten years of the publication of Malory's *Morte Darthur* in 1485. But Paston likely owned a more literary, and literate, version of *The Greene Knight* than our poem. The surviving text might well be a written record of the sort of recital mentioned by Robert Laneham in a letter describing festivities put on for Queen Elizabeth at Kenilworth in 1575. Laneham offers an account of Captain Cox, a performance artist "hardy as Gawin," who acts, sings, recites, and professes "philosophy both morall and naturall." Cox possesses "at his fingers ends" — that is, within his memory and ready for recital on demand — a vast repertoire of stories, including ballads, songs, perhaps plays, and romances; he knows "king Arthurs book," a huge mix of other chivalric narratives, and "Syr Gawyn." Just which Gawain romance this was is not specified; that it was the story of the Green Knight is entirely plausible, for the Percy Folio Manuscript (where *The Greene Knight* occurs) makes clear that such popular performances provided the precise milieu where the surviving poem was produced.

Although the differences between the two poems leave open the possibility of one or more intermediate versions, the details of *The Greene Knight*'s plot draw directly upon *Sir Gawain and the Green Knight*. In many ways, in fact, *The Greene Knight*, as the later poem, seems almost a summary or guide in its determined spelling out of motives and events, its domestication of the challenging and mysterious, and its explanation of marvels and ambiguities. Yet, just because the surface narrative gives a reader less pause, the poem moves more quickly and gives a more immediate pleasure.

As its opening suggests, *The Greene Knight* was intended for popular recitation. In this, it resembles the other poems in the present collection, as well as other pieces in the Percy Folio Manuscript, where it occurs. The Percy Folio scribe clearly wished to preserve a large group of what were by the mid-seventeenth century ancient romances and entertainments, many of which must have been transmitted orally. The Percy Folio texts are in general more "popular" — marked for oral performance and mixed audiences — than surviving Middle English versions of the same stories. The manuscript contains *Turke, Marriage, Carle,* and *Cornwall* (all included in the present volume), several other stories involving Gawain (including a version of *Libeaus Desconus,* the "Fair Unknown," a romance about Gawain's son Gyngolyn), together with tales of Robin Hood and other heroes. The language of *The Greene Knight* suggests that it was originally composed about 1500 in the South Midlands. It is marked for two fitts (perhaps indicating performance sessions), and falls into eighty-six tail-rhyme stanzas, running *aabccb*.

As in many of the other Gawain romances, the king's nephew stands out as the court's representative in dealing with the mysterious or unknown — in this case, a shape-shifting Green Knight. Given the lack of stir caused by this figure in *The Greene Knight* — he seems more a "jolly sight to seene" (line 79) and a "venterous knight" (line 94) than an ogre or moral inquisitor — it is worth noting that simple reference to a Green Knight might not seem so extraordinary to a medieval audience accustomed to hearing knights identified by their colors or liveries. Green knights turn up in a number of chivalric romances (see note to line 109), including *Carlisle* and Malory; it is only the extraordinary description in *Sir Gawain and the Green Knight*, combining natural, supernatural, and courtly details, that has made the figure of a Green Knight on a green horse seem so completely without precedent. Like Dame Ragnelle and Sir Gromer in *Turke*, Sir Bredbeddle (who appears also in *Cornwall*, where he is called "the Greene Knight," lines 214, 222, 233, and elsewhere) in his transformed state poses a challenge to Arthurian chivalric values, but the easy resolution of this challenge only reinforces the glamour of the Round Table's fellowship.

Yet the strangeness of this outsider in *The Greene Knight* is much modified from *Sir Gawain and the Green Knight*, first of all by the insertion of conventional episodes like the exchange with the porter and the irritable response of Sir Kay to the initial dare. In addition, the multiple temptations, hunts, exchanges, and blows that organize *Sir Gawain and the Green Knight* are here all reduced to single events, and the relations between them, so richly unspecifiable in the earlier poem, are here made unmistakably plain for the audience. All of this makes the poem coalesce and speed toward its conclusion, and this sense of things coming together finds support in motifs of convergence and communion: the Green Knight actually sits down and shares a meal with the Round Table after making his challenge, Sir Bredbeddle is ultimately brought back to Arthur's court and joins its fellowship, and the poem ends with a celebration of the chivalric order of the Knights of the Bath. This perhaps reflects or even imitates the allusion to the Order of the Garter which follows the conclusion of *Sir Gawain and the Green Knight*, though it is striking that Sir John Paston's "boke off knyghthod" contained a detailed account of "Hou Knyghtis of the Bath shulde be made" (see note at line 502). Gawain's knightly role is to encounter the marvelous and bring it within the realm of the familiar; in *The Greene Knight* he succeeds in taming the mystery of Sir Bredbeddle, the dangerous love of his wife, and the magic of her mother.

Text

The Greene Knight survives in a famous post-medieval manuscript, the Percy Folio, now in the British Library (see Bibliography). The Folio volume, about fifteen inches long and five and a half wide, and about two inches thick, was compiled about 1650 in a single hand. This collection, an unparalleled treasury of late medieval and early Renaissance popular compositions, was acquired by the antiquarian Bishop Thomas Percy of Dromore in Ireland (1729–1811). He reported finding the "scrubby, shabby, paper" book "lying dirty on the floor under a Bureau in the Parlour" of his friend Humphrey Pitt of Shiffnal in Shropshire, "being used by the maids to light the fire" (ed. Hales and Furnivall, p. xii). The text of the present edition is based on the

The Greene Knight

Folio, though it makes use of Madden's and Furnivall's prints (see Bibliography). The scribe wrote in a cramped and relatively rapid cursive, and the misadventures of the manuscript have not rendered it any more easily legible. The scribe frequently uses shortened notations for common words (i.e., *k* for *king*). In transcribing texts from the Percy Folio, orthography (including thorns) has been regularized, so that *u/v* and *i/j* appear according to modern usage; abbreviations have been expanded, numerals spelled out, and modern punctuation added.

Select Bibliography

Manuscript

British Library Additional MS 27879 (The Percy Folio). Pp. 203–10.

Editions (arranged chronologically)

Madden, Frederic. 1839. See Bibliography of Editions and Works Cited.

Hales, John W., and Frederick J. Furnivall. 1868. See Bibliography of Editions and Works Cited.

Criticism

Hulbert, J. R. "Syr Gawayn and the Grene Knyght," *Modern Philology* 13 (1915–16), 433–62; 689–730.

Kittredge, George L. *A Study of Gawain and the Green Knight*. Cambridge, 1916.

Day, Mabel. "Introduction." *Sir Gawain and the Green Knight*. Ed. Israel Gollancz. EETS o.s. 210. London: Oxford University Press, 1940. Pp. xxxviii–xxxix. [Discusses parallels and differences between *Sir Gawain and the Green Knight* and *The Greene Knight*.]

The Greene Knight

First Part

	List! wen Arthur he was King,	*Listen! when*
	He had all att his leadinge	*command*
	The broad Ile of Brittaine.	*Island*
	England and Scottland one was,	*united*
5	And Wales stood in the same case,	
	The truth itt is not to layne.	*to conceal*
	He drive allyance out of this Ile.	*drove aliens*
	Soe Arthur lived in peace a while,	
	As men of mickle maine,	*While; great might*
10	Knights strove of their degree,	*disputed about their rank*
	Which of them hyest shold bee;	*highest*
	Therof Arthur was not faine.	*About that; glad*
	Hee made the Round Table for their behove,	*on their behalf*
	That none of them shold sitt above,	
15	But all shold sitt as one,	
	The King himselfe in state royall,	
	Dame Guenever our Queene withall,	
	Seemlye of body and bone.	*Handsome*
	Itt fell againe the Christmase	*happened upon*
20	Many came to that Lords place,	*[That]*
	To that worthye one,	
	With helme on head and brand bright,	*helmet; sword*
	All that tooke order of knight;	*belonged to the knightly class*
	None wold linger att home.	
25	There was noe castle nor manour free	
	That might harbour that companye,	*lodge*
	Their puissance was soe great.	*entourage*

313

Their tents up they pight   *pitched*
For to lodge there all that night;
30   Therto were sett to meate.   *In the same spot were they; feast*

Messengers there came and went
With much victualls verament,   *food truly*
     Both by way and streete.
Wine and wild fowle thither was brought —
35   Within they spared nought   *In all*
     For gold, and they might itt gett.   *if they could get it*

Now of King Arthur noe more I mell,   *speak*
But of a venterous knight I will you tell   *daring*
     That dwelled in the west countrye.
40   Sir Bredbeddle, for sooth he hett: *was called*
He was a man of mickele might   *great strength*
     And Lord of great bewtye.   *beauty*

He had a Lady to his wiffe:
He loved her deerlye as his liffe —   *dearly*
45   Shee was both blyth and blee.   *cheerful; fair of complexion*
Because Sir Gawaine was stiffe in stowre,   *powerful; battle*
Shee loved him privilye paramour,   *secretly and passionately*
     And shee never him see.   *Even though she never had seen him*

Itt was Agostes that was her mother:
50   Itt was witchcraft and noe other
     That shee dealt with all.
Shee cold transpose knights and swaine   *could; servants*
Like as in battaile they were slaine,   *To appear as if*
     Wounded in lim and lightt.   *arm and leg*

55   Shee taught her sonne the knight alsoe   *son-in-law*
In transposed likenesse he shold goe
     Both by fell and frythe.   *moor; woods*
Shee said, "Thou shalt to Arthurs hall,
For there great adventures shall befall
60   That ever saw king or knight."   *As*

The Greene Knight

All was for her daughters sake,
That which she soe sadlye spake   *earnestly*
  To her sonne-in-law the knight:
Because Sir Gawaine was bold and hardye,
65   And therto full of curtesye,   *in addition*
  To bring him into her sight.   *[She wished] to*

The knight said, "Soe mote I thee,   *On my life*
To Arthurs court will I mee hye   *myself hasten*
  For to praise thee right,   *give you your due*
70   And to prove Gawaines points three —   *test*
And that be true that men tell me,   *Whether*
  By Mary most of might."

Earlye, soone as itt was day,
The Knight dressed him full gay,   *got ready with all speed*
75   Umstrode a full good steede;   *Bestrode*
Helme and hawberke both he hent,   *Helmet; armor; took*
A long fauchion verament   *broadsword truly*
  To fend them in his neede.   *wield*

That was a jolly sight to seene,
80   When horsse and armour was all greene,
  And weapon that hee bare.
When that burne was harnisht still,   *knight; completely armed*
His countenance he became right well,   *He was equal to his appearance*
  I dare itt safelye sweare.

85   That time att Carleile lay our King;
Att a Castle of Flatting was his dwelling,
  In the Forrest of Delamore.
For sooth he rode, the sooth to say;   *[i.e., the Green Knight]*
To Carleile he came on Christmas day,
90   Into that fayre countrye.

When he into that place came,
The porter thought him a marvelous groome.   *man*
  He saith, "Sir, wither wold yee?"   *what is your destination*
Hee said, "I am a venterous knight,   *adventure-seeking*

95	And of your King wold have sight,	
	And other lords that heere bee."	
	Noe word to him the porter spake,	
	But left him standing att the gate,	
	And went forth, as I weene,	*suppose*
100	And kneeled downe before the King,	
	Saith, "In lifes dayes old or younge,	
	Such a sight I have not seene!	
	"For yonder att your gates right,"	*just at*
	He saith, "Heer is a venterous knight.	*Here*
105	All his vesture is greene!"	*trappings*
	Then spake the King, proudest in all,	*foremost of*
	Saith, "Bring him into the hall.	
	Let us see what hee doth meane."	*intend*
	When the Greene Knight came before the King,	
110	He stood in his stirrops strechinge,	*raising himself*
	And spoke with voice cleere,	
	And saith, "King Arthur, God save thee	
	As thou sittest in thy prosperitye,	
	And maintaine thine honor!	
115	"Why thou wold me nothing but right,	*Because; do by me*
	I am come hither a venterous knight,	
	And kayred thorrow countrye farr,	*have travelled through*
	To prove poynts in thy pallace	*test*
	That longeth to manhood in everye case	*That are appropriate*
120	Among thy lords deere."	
	The King, he sayd full still	*remained quiet*
	Till he had said all his will.	*he [the Green Knight]*
	Certein thus can he say:	*Firmly; did [Arthur]*
	"As I am true knight and King,	
125	Thou shalt have thy askinge!	*request*
	I will not say thy nay,	*deny thee*

316

"Whether thou wilt on foote fighting, *desire*
Or on steed backe justing, *horseback jousting*
  For love of ladyes gay.
130 If and thine armor be not fine, *And if*
I will give thee part of mine."
  "God amercy, Lord!" can he say: *did*

"Here I make a challenging,
Among the lords both old and younge
135   That worthy beene in weede — *dress*
Which of them will take in hand, *[To see]; respond*
Hee that is both stiffe and stronge *powerful*
  And full good att need.

"I shall lay my head downe —
140 Strike itt of if he can *off*
  With a stroke to garr itt bleed, *make*
For this day twelf monthe another at his. [1]
Let me see who will answer this —
  A knight that is doughtye of deed. *worthy*

145 "For this day twelf month, the sooth to say, *And then on*
Let him come to me and seieth his praye, *make his request*
  Rudlye, or ever hee blin. *Readily or forever be silent*
Whither to come, I shall him tell — *Where*
The readie way to the Greene Chappell:
150   That place I will be in."

The King att ease sate full still,
And all his lords said but litle
  Till he had said all his will.
Upp stood Sir Kay, that crabbed knight,
155 Spake mightye words that were of height, *exaggerated*
  That were both loud and shrill:

---

[1] *In return for a similar stroke at his neck twelve months from this day*

	"I shall strike his necke in tooe,	*two*
	The head away the body froe!"	*from*
	They bade him all be still,	
160	Saith, "Kay, of thy dints make no rouse!	*[They] said; blows; boast*
	Thou wottest full litle what thou does —	*know*
	Noe good, but mickle ill."	*much*
	Eche man wold this deed have done.	*desired to have the quest*
	Up start Sir Gawaine soone,	*immediately*
165	Upon his knees can kneele,	*did*
	He said, "That were great villanye	*It would be great shame*
	Without you put this deede to me,	*Unless; assign*
	My Leege, as I have sayd.	*Sovereign*
	"Remember, I am your sisters sonne."	
170	The King said, "I grant thy boone.	*request*
	But mirth is best att meele:	
	Cheere thy guest, and give him wine,	*Entertain*
	And after dinner, to itt fine,	*bring it [the challenge] to conclusion*
	And sett the buffett well!"	*deliver the blow*
175	Now the Greene Knight is set att meate,	*dinner*
	Seemlye served in his seate,	*Properly*
	Beside the Round Table.	
	To talke of his welfare, nothing he needs:	*With respect to his satisfaction*
	Like a knight himselfe he feeds,	*With knightly manners*
180	With long time reasnable.	*leisurely*
	When the dinner it was done,	
	The King said to Sir Gawaine soone,	*immediately*
	Withouten any fable,	*idle talk*
	He said, "On you will doe this deede,	*And if*
185	I pray Jesus be youre speede!	*aid*
	This knight is nothing unstable."	*weak*
	The Greene Knight his head downe layd;	
	Sir Gawaine, to the axe he braid	*lept*
	To strike with eger will;	*eager determination*
190	He stroke the necke bone in twaine,	

318

The blood burst out in everye vaine,	*vein*
The head from the body fell.	
The Greene Knight his head up hent;	*seized*
Into his saddle wightilye he sprent,	*vigorously; sprang*
195 Spake words both lowd and shrill,	
Saith: "Gawaine! Thinke on thy covenant!	*bargain*
This day twelf monthes see thou ne want	*don't fail*
To come to the Greene Chappell!"	
All had great marvell, that they see	*when*
200 That he spake so merrilye	
And bare his head in his hand.	*carried*
Forth att the hall dore he rode right,	
And that saw both King and knight	
And lords that were in land.	
205 Without the hall dore, the sooth to saine,	*Outside; tell*
Hee set his head upon againe,	
Saies, "Arthur, have heere my hand!	*pledge*
Whensoever the knight cometh to mee,	
A better buffett sickerlye	*certainly*
210 I dare him well warrand."	*guarantee*
The Greene Knight away went.	
All this was done by enchantment	
That the old witch had wrought.	
Sore sicke fell Arthur the King,	
215 And for him made great mourning	*him [Gawain]*
That into such bale was brought.	*trouble*
The Queen, shee weeped for his sake;	
Sorry was Sir Lancelott du Lake,	
And other were dreery in thought	
220 Because he was brought into great perill.	
His mightye manhood will not availe,	
That before hath freshlye fought.	

Sir Gawaine comfort King and Queen
And all the doughtye there bedeene.   *worthy folk gathered together*
225   He bade they shold be still,   *requested; quiet*
Said, "Of my deede I was never feard,   *death; afraid*
Nor yett I am nothing adread,
    I swere by Saint Michaell!

"For when draweth toward my day,
230   I will dresse me in mine array
    My promise to fulfill.
Sir," he saith, "as I have blis,   *as I hope for heaven*
I wott not where the Greene Chappell is: *know*
    Therfore, seeke itt I will!"

235   The royal courtt verament   *truly*
All rought Sir Gawaines intent;   *understood*
    They thought itt was the best.
They went forth into the feild,
Knights that ware both speare and sheeld   *wore*
240   They priced forth full prest.   *pricked (galloped); swiftly*

Some chuse them to justinge,   *chose (decided upon)*
Some to dance, revell, and sing;   *revelry and song*
    Of mirth they wold not rest.
All they swore together in fere,   *as a group*
245   That and Sir Gawaine overcome were,   *if; were killed*
    They wold bren all the west.   *burn all the west country*

Now leave wee the King in his pallace.
The Greene Knight come home is
    To his owne castle.
250   This folke frend when he came home   *These people asked*
What doughtye deeds he had done.   *brave*
    Nothing he wold them tell.

Full well he wist in certaine   *knew*
That his wiffe loved Sir Gawaine,
255   That comelye was under kell.   *caul (cap)*
Listen, lords! And yee will sitt,   *If you'll sit still*

The Greene Knight

And ye shall heere the second Fitt,
What adventures Sir Gawaine befell.

Second Parte

  The day is come that Gawaine must gone.   *be gone*
260 Knights and ladyes waxed wann   *grew pale*
   That were without in that place.   *stood outside*
  The King himselfe siked ill,   *sighed grievously*
  Ther Queen a swounding almost fell,   *Their; into a faint*
   To that jorney when he shold passe.   *journey*

265 When he was in armour bright,
  He was one of the goodlyest knights
   That ever in Brittaine was borne.
  They brought Sir Gawaine a steed,
  Was dapple gray and good att need,
270 I tell withouten scorne.   *in all seriousness*

  His bridle was with stones sett,
  With gold and pearle overfrett,   *overlaid*
   And stones of great vertue.
  He was of a furley kind.   *[The horse]; marvelous*
275 His stirropps were of silke of Ynd;   *India*
   I tell you this tale for true.

  When he rode over the mold,   *[Gawain]; earth*
  His geere glistered as gold.
   By the way as he rode
280 Many furleys he there did see.   *marvels*
  Fowles by the water did flee,   *Birds*
   By brimes and bankes soe broad.   *waters; shores*

  Many furleys there saw hee,   *marvels*
  Of wolves and wild beasts sikerlye;
285 On hunting hee tooke most heede.   *caution*
  Forth he rode, the sooth to tell,
  For to seeke the Greene Chappell;
   He wist not where indeed.   *knew*

The Greene Knight

	As he rode in an evening late,	
290	Riding downe a greene gate,	*pathway*
	A faire castell saw hee,	
	That seemed a place of mickle pride.	
	Thitherward Sir Gawaine can ryde,	*did*
	To gett some harborrowe.	*lodging*
295	Thither he came in the twylight.	
	He was ware of a gentle knight,	*became aware*
	The lord of the place was hee.	
	Meekly to him Sir Gawaine can speake	*did*
	And asked him, "For King Arthurs sake,	
300	Of harborrowe I pray thee!	
	"I am a far labordd knight —	*an utterly exhausted*
	I pray you, lodge me all this night."	
	He sayd him not nay;	*did not say no*
	He tooke him by the arme and led him to the hall.	
305	A poore child can he call,	*did*
	Saith, "Dight well this palfrey."	*Take good care of*
	Into a chamber they went a full great speed.	
	There they found all things readye att need,	
	I dare safelye swere:	
310	Fier in chambers burning bright,	*Fire*
	Candles in chandlers burning light.	*candlesticks*
	To supper they went full yare.	*readily*
	He sent after his Ladye bright	
	To come to supp with that gentle knight,	
315	And shee came blythe withall.	*gladly*
	Forth shee came then anon,	
	Her maids following her eche one	*one by one*
	In robes of rich pall.	*fine purple*
	As shee sate att her supper,	
320	Evermore the Ladye clere	

Sir Gawaine shee looked upon.
When the supper it was done,
   Shee tooke her maids, and to her chamber gone.   *went*

He cheered the knight and gave him wine,
325 And said, "Welcome, by St. Martine!
   I pray you, take itt for none ill!   *to your health*
One thing, Sir, I wold you pray;
What you make soe farr this way?   *brings you to these remote parts*
   The truth you wold me tell.

330 "I am a knight, and soe are yee:
Your concell, an you will tell mee,   *confidence if*
   Forsooth keepe itt I will.
For if itt be poynt of any dread,   *anything worrisome*
Perchance I may helpe att need,
335   Either lowd or still."   *publicly; privately*

For his words that were soe smooth,   *In reply to; polished*
Had Sir Gawaine wist the soothe,   *known the truth*
   All he wold not have told:
For that was the Greene Knight
340 That hee was lodged with that night,
   And harbarrowes in his hold.   *resides; keep*

He saith, "As to the Greene Chappell,   *[Sir Bredbeddle]*
Thitherward I can you tell,
   Itt is but furlongs thre.   *three*
345 The master of it is a venterous knight,   *daring*
And workes by witchcraft day and night,
   With many a great furley.   *wonder*

"If he worke with never soe much frauce,   *Even if he acts; clamor*
He is curteous as he sees cause.   *when he sees fit*
350   I tell you sikerlye,   *surely*
You shall abyde, and take your rest,   *stay in bed late*
And I will into yonder Forrest
   Under the greenwood tree."

	They plight their truthes to beleeve,	*pledged their troth in agreement*
355	Either with other for to deale,	*exchange*
	Whether it were silver or gold.	
	He said, "We two both sworn wil be	*[The Green Knight]*
	Whatsoever God sends you and mee,	
	To be parted on the mold."	*divided evenly on earth*

360	The Greene Knight went on hunting;	
	Sir Gawaine, in the castle beinge,	*remaining*
	Lay sleeping in his bed.	
	Up rose the old witche with hast throwe,	*with all haste*
	And to her dauhter can shee goe,	*daughter did she*
365	And said, "Be not adread!"	*Don't be frightened*

	To her daughter can shee say,	*did*
	"The man that thou hast wisht many a day,	*desired*
	Of him thou maist be sped,	*succeed*
	For Sir Gawaine, that curteous knight,	
370	Is lodged in this hall all night."	
	Shee brought her to his bedd.	

	Shee saith, "Gentle knight, awake!	*[The mother]*
	And for this faire ladies sake,	
	That hath loved thee soe deere,	
375	Take her boldly in thine armes.	
	There is noe man shall doe thee harme."	
	Now beene they both heere.	*Finally; together*

	The Ladye kissed him times thre,	
	Saith, "Without I have the love of thee,	*Unless*
380	My life standeth in dere."	*ruin*
	Sir Gawaine blushed on the Lady bright,	*glanced at*
	Saith, "Your husband is a gentle knight,	*noble*
	By Him that bought mee deare!	*redeemed*

	"To me itt were a great shame	
385	If I shold doe him any grame,	*harm*
	That hath beene kind to mee.	
	For I have such a deede to doe,	

324

That I can neyther rest nor roe,   *relax*
   Att an end till itt bee."   *Until it be finished*

390   Then spake that Ladye gay,
    Saith, "Tell me some of your journey;   *something; mission*
       Your succour I may bee.
    If itt be poynt of any warr,   *matter of warfare*
    There shall noe man doe you noe darr   *injury*
395   And yee wil be governed by mee.   *If; guided*

    "For heere I have a lace of silke: *silken braid*
    It is as white as any milke,
       And of a great value."
    Shee saith, "I dare safelye sweare
400   There shall noe man doe you deere   *harm*
       When you have it upon you."

    Sir Gawaine spake mildlye in the place: *courteously*
    He thanked the Lady and tooke the lace,
       And promised her to come againe.
405   The knight in the Forrest slew many a hind; *doe*
    Other venison he cold none find,   *game he could*
       But wild bores on the plaine,   *Except; flatland*

    Plentye of does and wild swine,
    Foxes and other ravine,   *predators*
410   As I hard true men tell.   *heard*
    Sir Gawaine swore sickerlye,
    "Home to your owne, welcome you bee,
       By Him that harrowes hell!"   *liberates*

    The Greene Knight his venison downe layd;   *kill*
415   Then to Sir Gawaine thus hee said,
       "Tell me anon in heght,   *aloud*
    What noveltyes that you have won,   *new things*
    For heer is plenty of venison."   *meat*
      Sir Gawaine said full right:

420   Sir Gawaine sware, "By St. Leonard!
       Such as God sends, you shall have part!"
          In his armes he hent the Knight,   *grasped*
       And there he kissed him times thre,
       Saith, "Heere is such as God sends mee,
425   By Mary most of might."

       Ever privilye he held the lace: *secretly*
       That was all the villanye that ever was
          Prooved by Sir Gawaine the gay.   *upon*
       Then to bed soone they went,
430   And sleeped there verament   *truly*
          Till morrow itt was day.

       Then Sir Gawaine soe curteous and free,
       His leave soone taketh hee
          Att the Lady soe gaye.
435   Hee thanked her, and tooke the lace,   *kept*
       And rode towards the Chappell apace;
          He knew noe whitt the way.   *not a bit*

       Ever more in his thought he had
       Whether he shold worke as the Ladye bade,   *act*
440   That was soe curteous and sheene.   *radiant*
       The Greene Knight rode another way;
       He transposed him in another array,   *himself in different trappings*
          Before as it was greene.   *green as before*

       As Sir Gawaine rode over the plaine,
445   He hard one high upon a mountaine   *resoundingly (aloud)*
          A horne blowne full lowde.
       He looked after the Greene Chappell: *around for*
       He saw itt stand under a hill
          Covered with evyes about.   *ivies*

450   He looked after the Greene Knight:
       He hard him wehett a fauchion bright,   *sharpen; broad sword*
          That the hills rang about.   *So that*
       The knight spake with strong cheere,   *a stern countenance*

326

Said, "Yee be welcome, Sir Gawaine, heere;   *becomes you; bow*
455 It behooveth thee to lowte."

He stroke, and litle perced the skin,   *pierced a little*
Unneth the flesh within.   *But scarcely [hurt]*
  Then Sir Gawaine had noe doubt.   *no (more) worry*
He saith, "Thou shontest! Why dost thou soe?"   *[The Green Knight]; flinched*
460 Then Sir Gawaine in hart waxed throe: *heart; ferocious*
  Up on his feete can stand,   *did*

And soone he drew out his sword,   *immediately*
And saith, "Traitor! if thou speake a word,
  Thy liffe is in my hand.
465 I had but one stroke att thee,
And thou has had another att mee:
  Noe falshood in me thou found!"

The Knight said withouten laine,   *concealing anything*
"I wend I had Sir Gawaine slaine,   *I do believe I might have*
470 The gentlest knight in this land.
Men told me of great renowne;
Of curtesie thou might have woon the crowne,   *won*
  Above both free and bound,   *unfree*

"And alsoe of great gentrye.   *high nobility*
475 And now thre points be put fro thee: *points of virtue; removed from*
  It is the moe pittye,   *more*
Sir Gawaine, thou was not leele   *loyal (honest)*
When thou didst the lace conceale
  That my wiffe gave to thee.

480 For wee were both, thou wist full well,   *both [bound by the agreement]; knew*
For thou hadst the halfe dale   *portion*
  Of my venerye.   *hunting*
If the lace had never been wrought, [1]
To have slaine thee was never my thought,
485 I swere by God verelye!   *verily*

---

[1] *If (the concealment of) the lace had not happened*

"I wist it well my wiffe loved thee;   *knew*
Thou wold doe me no villanye,
    But nicked her with nay.   *squelched her with "no"*
But wilt thou doe as I bidd thee —
490 Take me to Arthurs court with thee —
    Then were all to my pay."   *satisfaction*

Now are the knights accorded thore.   *there*
To the Castle of Hutton can they fare,
    To lodge there all that night.
495 Earlye on the other day   *next*
To Arthurs court they tooke the way
    With harts blyth and light.   *hearts happy*

All the court was full faine,   *deeply pleased*
Alive when they saw Sir Gawaine;
500   They thanked God abone.   *above*
That is the matter and the case   *reason*
Why Knights of the Bathe weare the lace
    Untill they have wonen their shoen —   *spurs (shoes)*

Or else a ladye of hye estate   *Unless; high*
505 From about his necke shall it take,
    For the doughtye deeds that hee hath done.
It was confirmed by Arthur the King.
Thorrow Sir Gawaines desiringe   *wish*
    The King granted him his boone.   *[the Green Knight] his request*

510 Thus endeth the tale of the Greene Knight.
God, that is soe full of might,
    To heaven their soules bring
That have hard this litle storye   *heard*
That fell some times in the west countrye   *occurred once upon a time*
515   In Arthurs days our King!

Finis.   *The end*

Notes

Abbreviations: P = Percy Folio; BP= Bishop Percy's marginal notes in the MS; M = Madden's edition; F = Furnivall's edition. See Select Bibliography for these editions.

    First Part. The first fitt or section of the poem is not marked by a rubric in the manuscript; I have added a rubric here to correspond with the one the scribe adds after line 258.

2   *all att*. M prints *att all*; though a blot in the MS makes the reading indistinct, it appears that *att* follows *all*.

    leadinge. M disregards the final stoke and prints *leading*.

10   *strove of*. I follow BP; F reads *strong of*, then inserts *strove* as initial word of line 11.

12   Arthur's founding of a *round* table in order to prevent squabbling among his knights about rank, about who "bygan the highe dese" (*Ragnelle*, line 601), is mentioned first in Geoffrey of Monmouth. *Cornwall* begins with Guenevere's demurral concerning Arthur's statement to Gawain that his is "one of the fairest Round Tables / That ever you see with your eye" (lines 3–4).

22   *on head*. P: *& head*; I emend for sense, following F.

27   *puissance*. Through Shakespeare's time, this word is used to designate a crowd or force of people.

28   *they*. P: *the*; F: *thé*. I emend to *they* here and in lines 159, 199, 225, 240, 243, 246, 307, 308, 312, 430, 494, and 497.

31   *came and went*. P: *came went*; I follow F's emendation.

39   *in the west countrye.* The poem sets its action in the northwest midlands, near the Welsh border, with localized references to Hatton and Delamere Forest (see lines 87 and 493 and notes). Arthur's court nonetheless remains at Carlisle (line 85); despite the impression of proximity offered in the poem, this would have been a long northern journey for Sir Bredbeddle.

41   *mickele.* M: *mickel.*

43   *his wiffe.* P: *wis wiffe*; I follow F's emendation.

49   *Agostes.* So far as I know, this name does not occur elsewhere in Arthurian literature, though the connection between her supernatural powers of witch-craft and the consonance of *Agostes* with 'ghostly' is striking. Agostes' counter-part in *Sir Gawain and the Green Knight*, Morgan le Fay, is called 'Argante' in Layamon's *Brut* (see note at line 169).

54   *lightt.* The manuscript is indistinct; M prints *light*, reading only a single "t" in the tangle of strokes. The tail rhyme is clearly defective in the stanza, and *lightt* may have crept in through analogy with rhymes in lines 60, 63, 66, 69, and 72. BP suggested a variation on "lythe," a word for trunk or body which would rhyme with *frythe* (line 57); *licham* (spelled "lygham" in *Alliterative Morte Arthure*, lines 3281, 3286), also meaning body, would fit still better, making the phrase an alliterative tag. The scribe or a later reader seems to have overwritten the "g," but no amount of straining produces a certain or convincing reading.

62   *That which she.* P: *that theye which*; M: *Y^t the witch* (emending the MS, which he reads as *they w^{ch}*); I follow F's emendation.

70   *Gawaines points three.* Gawain's three points are his boldness, his courtesy, and his hardiness.

79   *a jolly sight.* Though Bredbeddle's "horsse and armour was all greene" (line 80), the magic by which Agostes "transpose[s]" his "likenesse" does not seem to transform his person (lines 53, 56); the porter notes that "his vesture is greene" (line 105), and when he meets Gawain for the return blow, Bredbeddle has "transposed him in another array, / Before as it was greene" (lines 442–43). This distinguishes him from the marvelous intruder of *Sir Gawain and the Green Knight*, who (although he bears no arms or armor) is not simply dressed in green, but is "overal enkergrene" (line 150; everywhere bright green) right

330

down to his hair and skin; the uncanny, and potentially mythic or supernatural, character of that Green Knight separates him from Bredbeddle, and helps mark the radical difference in atmosphere and effect between the two poems. See also line 109 and note, below.

87   *the Forrest of Delamore.* Unlike other Gawain romances, which set their adventures in Inglewood Forest near Carlisle, *Greene Knight* specifies places that are in "the west countrye," in particular, in Cheshire. The reference here is to Delamere Forest, east and slightly north of Chester, in which local Cheshire families maintained interests; see B. M. C. Hussain, "Delamere Forest in Later Medieval Times," *Transactions of the Historic Society of Lancashire and Cheshire* 107 (1955), 23–59, and the more general discussion of the region and its cultural life in M. J. Bennett, *Community, Class and Careerism: Cheshire and Lancashire Society in the Age of "Sir Gawain and the Green Knight"* (Cambridge: Cambridge University Press, 1983). In giving Sir Bredbeddle a seemingly brief journey to Arthur's court, the poem presents his manor as bordering upon the Wirral (the peninsula that extends northwest from Chester, between the Rivers Dee and Mersey), the wilds through which Sir Gawain travels to meet the Green Knight in *Sir Gawain and the Green Knight* (line 701). As the further reference to Hutton (line 493 and note) suggests, the locale has only an imaginary connection to Carlisle, despite the assertion of lines 85 and 89. The Castle of Flatting (line 86) remains unidentified.

90   *fayre countrye.* BP emends to *countrye faire,* to improve the rhyme (but not by much).

104   *Heer.* P: *hee*; BP: *there is*; I emend for sense.

109   *the Greene Knight*: As the introduction points out, *Cornwall* expressly refers to Sir Bredbeddle as "the Greene Knight" (lines 214, 222, 233, 267 and 285). Chivalric champions presenting themselves under the name of "Green Knight" occur in several other romances as well: in *Carlisle*, the son of Sir Ironside is apparently referred to as "The Knyght of Armus Grene" (line 45 and 68), and in the same poem Gawain's own livery seems green, for he throws his "manttell of grene" over the small horse of the Carl (line 353). In Malory, Gawain's brother Sir Gareth (fighting as Sir Bewmaynes) has a long encounter with the Grene Knyght (also called Sir Pertholepe; *Works*, pp. 305–10; 314). It is possible that within popular tradition Sir Gawain and his kin had some long-standing association with Green Knights; see note to line 64 of *Carlisle*.

116   *a venterous*. BP adds *knight*, and F so emends, echoing, e.g., line 104.

119   *everye*. M: *eu ye*, though it seems that M's usual abbreviation mark — an ' for *er* — has been omitted (see p. lxix in his edition); this appears to be a typographical error since there is space within the word as printed for the mark to have been added.

169   *your sisters sonne*. Gawain's mother is Arthur's half-sister and the wife of King Lot of Lothian and Orkney, variously called Morgause (in Malory) or Anna. She is mother also of Mordred (by Arthur), and sister to Morgan le Fay, who in *Sir Gawain and the Green Knight* sponsors the transformation of the Green Knight. Morgan is therefore the counterpart of the witch Agostes (line 49), who in the present poem is also the Green Knight's mother-in-law.

181   *it*. M: *itt*.

220   *perill*. M: *pil*, with a stroke through the descender of the *p* as an abbreviation mark for *er* (see his edition, p. lxix).

235   *courtt*. P: *covett*; I follow BP's suggested emendation here. F reads *Couett*, and speculates that this may be *covey* from French *couvée*, i.e., "gathering."

242   *revell*. M prints *karoll*, emending the MS, which he reads as *keuell*.

246   *They wold bren all the west*. The off-hand character of this threat perhaps reflects its anachronistic status. Though *chevauchée* — the systematic devastation of resources and countryside through pillaging and burning — was a feature of chivalric warfare throughout the Middle Ages, such raids would not have been usual in the conduct of royal justice or even private war after the thirteenth century, at least in "the west." On the northern borders, including Carlisle, such destructive raids continued beyond the end of the Middle Ages.

259   The scribe brackets the stanza beginning with this line, and the accompanying rubric reads, *Second parte*.

280   *furleys*. P: *furlegs*; I follow F's emendation.

289   *evening*. P: *eveing*; I follow F's emendation.

304   *Hee*. F: *He*.

323   This stanza lacks its sixth line. Madden supplies a possible filler of his own devising: "Shee tooke her maids [every one,] / And to her chamber [will] gone."

325   *St. Martine.* St. Martin of Tours was one of the most popular saints of the Middle Ages. His best known act, dividing his cape in two to share with a beggar, made him a patron of the poor and an exemplar of charity and hospitality. Perhaps his invocation here, as a welcoming gesture, reflects the nature of his cult; compare line 420 and note.

327   F labels this as line 328, and his numeration is consequently off by a single line from here to the poem's end. Subsequent citations will refer to actual line numbers (as in the present edition) rather than to F's numbers.

348   *frauce.* This word is apparently not recorded in the OED or MED. The meaning, "uproar, noise," seems clear, though the origin is not. MED lists the apparently onomatopoeic verb *fracchen* or *frashen*, "to make a harsh or strident noise," but gives no cognate noun. F connects it to French *frais*, "noise," but it seems more likely connected to French *fracas*, as in modern English "fracas," i.e., "uproar, row."

396   *a lace of silke.* This phrase vividly recalls the third encounter between Gawain and Lady Bertilak in *Sir Gawain and the Green Knight*, where she offers him her "girdel," "a lace" adorned with "grene sylke" (lines 1829 ff.). This *lace* is not a garment, but an elaborately worked, ornamental braid used as a cincture or belt, or perhaps as a fastener (as in "shoelace"). *Lace* meaning cloth worked in delicate patterns seems not to occur in medieval English, and (like "girdle" before twentieth-century American usage) it has no association with intimate apparel; a *luflace* (as in *Sir Gawain and the Green Knight*, lines 1874, 2438) is simply an accessory of dress, though perhaps especially appropriate as a love token because of its woven, interlaced character. In Middle English, *lace* seems to have had as a primary meaning "net" or "snare." Both here and in *Sir Gawain and the Green Knight*, therefore, the repetition of the word may entail a suggestive pun; see R. A. Shoaf, *The Poem as Green Girdle: "Commercium" in "Sir Gawain and the Green Knight"* (Gainesville: University Presses of Florida, 1984).

400   *noe.* F: *no.*

401   *upon.* I follow F, based upon his glimpsing of a stroke in the manuscript that BP did not see.

418   *heer.* P: *heers*; I emend for sense and meter.

420   *St. Leonard.* St. Leonard of Noblac (near Limoges) was widely celebrated as the patron of captives, peasants, pregnant women, and the sick. In *Sir Gawain and the Green Knight*, the invocation of particular saints seems at times coordinated to specific moments in the narrative, though the linking of St. Leonard to the exchange here is not clear. See line 325 above and note.

434   *Att.* M: *At*; the MS is no longer clearly legible, though the spacing seems to support *Att*.

449   *evyes.* P: *euyes*. According to BP, probably "ivies," but conceivably "yews."

459   *shontest.* The interchangability of letter forms makes it possible to read this as "shoutest" (as does Madden). It is a further recollection of *Sir Gawain and the Green Knight* where, when Gawain "schranke a lytel" from the Green Knight's stroke, the latter held back with "wyth a schunt" (line 2268). In reply to the Green Knight's taunt, "Thou art not Gawayn . . . that is so goud halden" [so highly esteemed], Gawain replies, "I schunt onez, / And so wyl I no more" (lines 2270 ff.).

461   *feete.* P: *ffeete*; I emend to single initial *f* rather than capitalize as in lines 352 and 405.

488   *nicked her with nay.* This vivid alliterative formula occurs frequently in late medieval poetry; see *Sir Gawain and the Green Knight*, lines 706 and 2471, and *Gawain and Gologras*, line 115 and note.

493   *the Castle of Hutton.* Hutton (and Hatton) are relatively common place and family names. F suggests this is Hutton manorhouse, in Somerset. Given the other localizing details of *Greene Knight* (see lines 39, 85 ff. and notes, above), it seems more likely that the reference here is to Hatton in Cheshire, some seven miles north of the Delamere Forest. It is perhaps worth noting that there is a Hutton in Inglewood Forest, Cumberland; it is the neighboring village to Hesket, the parish that contains the Tarn Wathelene. Madden considers this the locale intended, and says the "whole of the territory hereabout was romance-ground" (p. 354).

502   *Knights of the Bathe.* This allusion parallels the insertion of the motto of the Order of the Garter at the conclusion of *Sir Gawain and the Green Knight*, which was written only a generation after the Order was founded in the 1340's. Unlike the Garter, which was a formal Order with statutes and distinctive garb, the category "Knights of the Bath" seems to have been used simply to designate knights of special eminence; often this high rank may have been based upon receiving knighthood from the sovereign's hand after an elaborate, ritualized ceremony (including bathing). Froissart makes this connection explicit in his account of the coronation of Henry IV (1399); on that occasion, with full ceremony, the king created forty-six Knights of the Bath. Particular customs — for example, the removal of a white silken shoulder lace or insignia — became associated with the Knights of the Bath. Nonetheless, the formal Order of the Bath was founded only in 1725 by King George I. John Anstis, who wrote a *Historical Essay Upon the Knighthood of the Bath* (London, 1725) and produced the statutes of the Order, made much use of these historical traditions that preceded the actual founding, though he seems not to have known about the allusion in *Greene Knight*. As noted in the Introduction to this poem, Sir John Paston owned a copy of a poem entitled "the Greene Knyght"; in addition, in a separate volume (his "boke off knyghthod"), he owned a description of "Hou Knyghtis of the Bath shulde be made," a detailed formulary specifying just what "our soveraigne lord" the king must do to create knights of this rank. A scribe or reader, finding these volumes side by side in Sir John's library, might well have been struck by similarities between the actual ceremonies of fifteenth-century knighthood and the fictional portrayal in *Greene Knight*, and may have decided to add this "historical" allusion. For a full discussion of this ceremonial, see G. A. Lester, *Sir John Paston's "Grete Boke"* (Cambridge: D. S. Brewer, 1984), pp. 80–83; Lester's account of this "boke off knyghthod" sheds much light on the links between chivalric romance, the ideals and rituals of chivalric behavior, and the role of courtesy, violence, and political manoeuvering in the lives of a late medieval knight and his associates. James C. Risk, in *The History of the Order of the Bath and Its Insignia* (London, 1972), provides a full account of the Order's origins. The use of an Arthurian poem to lend authority to such "Ancient Ceremonials" makes clear how this chivalric material is rewritten for the interests of each generation and audience.

weare. F prints *wear.*

Finis. F: *ffins.*

The Turke and Sir Gawain

Introduction

The Turke and Sir Gawain occurs in the Percy Folio Manuscript, a collection of popular tales including some of the other Gawain romances printed in this volume. Though the surviving copy of the poem dates from around 1650, the language and spellings of the text indicate it was composed around 1500 in the North or North Midlands. The pages of the Percy Folio on which this poem occurs have been mutilated, so that about half of each page, and therefore about half of the poem, is missing. In the text that follows I have offered prose summaries, inevitably somewhat speculative, of the sections that are lost. The features of the story and the details of its telling mark it for oral recitation; the remaining sections of *Turke* fall into tail-rhyme stanzas linked by *aabccb* rhyme scheme, though there are a number of defective stanzas and rhymes. It is a remarkable tribute to the poem's narrative energy, and to its saturation in traditional plots and motifs, that despite its serious losses it remains not simply intelligible, but boisterously engaging.

Like many another romance, *The Turke and Sir Gawain* begins with an intrusive challenge to the tranquility, or perhaps complacency, of the Arthurian court: the "Turk" — an alien figure who is impressively strong but not knightly, and apparently not Christian — demands an exchange of blows. Sir Kay's violent reaction threatens to undo the court's obligations to courtesy, but Gawain's intervention restores the proper chivalric balance of force and graciousness. This combination of raw power yoked to an elaborate code of honor becomes a central theme of the poem, as in *Carlisle* and *Gologras*, although the relation between these chivalric values is not particularly subtle in *Turke*. On the one hand, the "Turk" makes extraordinary demands on Gawain's courtesy and endurance, dragging him through a series of preternatural encounters; on the other, as Gawain's "boy," he performs deeds of exceptional ferociousness in destroying the enemies he finds for his knightly companion. The latter's courtesy and prowess, his self-imposed deference to one who seems strange and therefore inferior, remain intact, even through the final episode of the "Turk's" beheading. This event clearly constitutes a kind of death and rebirth, by means of which the "Turk" undergoes a conversion, becoming in the process a Christian knight. Throughout the romance, the categorical term "Turk" operates as an indeterminate Orientalist stereotype of difference and exoticism; like "Saracen," "Turk" defines otherness through geography, politics, religion and class (see note at line 10 below). Such interchangable usage is common to the late Middle Ages, as, for example, Caxton's translation of *The Foure Sonnes of Aymon* makes clear in refering to "Goddys enmyes, as ben Turques and Sarrasins" (EETS e.s. 45; London, 1884, 1885, p. 348).

Turke ends on a note common to the popular chivalric romances, and to romance in general. The "Turk," restored to his proper knightly identity as Sir Gromer (a figure who turns up in *Ragnelle* and in Malory), is brought into the fold of Arthurian chivalry and Arthurian political fealty. Sir Gromer's installation as the new and proper King of the Isle of Man not only converts the alien figure — the "Turk" — to familiar Christian knighthood, but presumably it demystifies the Isle of Man, changing it from a magic kingdom into a recognizable and accessible feature of the Arthurian (and contemporary) landscape. Gawain's courteous behavior at the end of the poem also helps make clear why he is such a crucial hero for the Arthurian court. When Sir Gromer and King Arthur attempt to make him "King of Man" (line 322 — certainly a resonant title), he rejects the offer, protesting, "I never purposed to be noe King" (line 326). His suitability for adventure depends upon his being closely connected to the king, as his nephew and champion, but also on his being free of the constraints of leadership; Gawain must continually refuse rule in order to be open to reckless daring and marvelous adventure. Since he is not at the center of the court, he can journey to the most remote and fabulous places without threatening social integrity by his absence; since he is not a ruler, he needn't concern himself with the dull virtues of prudence, justice, and peacemaking. As a free agent with the widest possible scope for his dealings, Gawain typifies popular notions of chivalric virtues, but he is able to test these, to show their nature and durability, in repeated encounters with marvelous opponents and exotic locales.

Text

The Turke and Sir Gawain occurs in the Percy Folio Manuscript, pp. 38–46 (described in the introductory material to *The Greene Knight*). The text of the present edition reflects the dilapidated state of the MS; half of each page on which *The Greene Knight* was written was ripped out of the volume to start fires, and the ill treatment it received before Bishop Percy rescued it has left pages blotted and stained from damp. All of this has made the forms of the cramped scribal hand at points ambiguous or illegible. The writing seems also to have deteriorated since Madden and Furnivall examined the Percy Folio for their nineteenth-century editions; I have sometimes followed their readings for letters or entire words that now appear indistinct or indecipherable. Orthography has been regularized, so that "u"/ "v" and "i"/"j" appear according to modern usage; abbreviations have been expanded, numerals spelled out, and modern punctuation and capitalization added.

Select Bibliography

Manuscript

British Library Additional MS 27879 (The Percy Folio). Pp. 38–46.

Editions (arranged chronologically)

Madden, Frederic. 1839. See Bibliography of Editions and Works Cited.

Hales, John W., and Frederick J. Furnivall. 1868. See Bibliography of Editions and Works Cited.

Williams, Jeanne Myrle Wilson. "A Critical Edition of 'The Turke & Gowin.'" Ph.D. Diss. University of Southern Mississippi, 1988. (*Dissertation Abstracts International* 49 (1988) 815A.) [I have not seen a copy of this edition.]

Criticism

Jost, Jean E. "The Role of Violence in *Aventure*: 'The Ballad of King Arthur and the King of Cornwall' and 'The Turke and Gowin.'" *Arthurian Interpretations* 2.2 (1988), 47–57.

Lyle, E. B. "*The Turk and Gawain* as Source of Thomas of Ercledoune." *Forum for Modern Language Studies* 6 (1970), 98–102.

The Turke and Sir Gawain

Listen, lords, great and small,
What adventures did befall
   In England, where hath beene   *there were (once)*
Of knights that held the Round Table   *[Some] knights*
5 Which were doughty and profittable,   *stalwart and worthy*
   Of kempys cruell and keene.   *warriors fierce and courageous*

All England, both East and West,   *[Throughout]*
Lords and ladyes of the best,
   They busked and made them bowne.   *came and went*
10 And when the King sate in seate —   *sat*
Lords served him att his meate —
   Into the hall a burne there came.   *warrior*

He was not hye, but he was broad,   *tall*
And like a Turke he was made   *(i.e., a pagan)*
15   Both legg and thye;   *thigh*
And said, "Is there any will, as a brother,   *who wishes through mutual consent*
To give a buffett and take another?   *blow*
   And iff any soe hardy bee?"   *Might there be*

Then spake Sir Kay, that crabbed knight,   *sulky*
20 And said "Man, thou seemest not soe wight,   *powerful*
   If thou be not adread.   *Given that*
For there beene knights within this hall
With a buffett will garr thee fall,   *make*
   And grope thee to the ground.   *drop*

25 "Give thou be never soe stalworth of hand   *If; ever so stalwart*
I shall bring thee to the ground,   *overcome you*
   That dare I safely sweare."
Then spake Sir Gawaine, that worthy knight,
Saith, "Cozen Kay, thou speakest not right —   *Cousin*
30   Lewd is thy answere!   *Uncouth*

The Turke and Sir Gawain

"What and that man want of his witt?	*What if; be deficient in*
Then litle worshipp were to thee pitt	*honor; allotted*
If thou shold him forefore."	*destroy*
Then spake the Turke with words thraw,	*angry*
35 Saith, "Come the better of your tow,	*two*
Though ye be breme as bore . . .	*fierce as a wild boar*

[At this point about half a page of the story is missing; Gawain enters into a sworn agreement to trade blows (apparently without weapons) with the Turk. He strikes his blow, but the return blow by the Turk is postponed.]

"This buffett thou hast . . .	
Well quitt that it shall be.	*repaid*
And yett I shall make thee thrise as feard	*three times as afraid*
40 As ever was man on middlearth,	
This Court againe ere thou see."	*before*
Then said Gawaine, "My truth I plight,	*troth I pledge*
I dare goe with thee full right,	*[That]; resolutely*
And never from thee flye;	*flee*
45 I will never flee from noe adventure,	
Justing, nor noe other turnament,	*Jousts*
Whilest I may live on lee."	*unharmed*
The Turke tooke leave of King with crowne;	
Sir Gawaine made him ready bowne,	*himself ready for travel*
50 His armor and his steed.	
They rode northwards two dayes and more.	
By then Sir Gawaine hungred sore;	*sorely*
Of meate and drinke he had great need.	
The Turke wist Gawaine had need of meate,	*understood*
55 And spake to him with words great,	
Hawtinge uppon hee;	*Raising himself on high*
Says "Gawaine, where is all thy plenty?	*riches*
Yesterday thou wast served with dainty,	*were; delicacies*
And noe part thou wold give me,	

341

60	"But with buffett thou did me sore;	*made*
	Therefore thou shalt have mickle care,	*great*
	And adventures shalt thou see.	
	I wold I had King Arthur heere,	
	And many of thy fellowes in fere	*together*
65	That behaves to try mastery."[1]	

	He led Sir Gawaine to a hill soe plaine.	*in the open*
	The earth opened and closed againe —	
	Then Gawaine was adread.	
	The merke was comen, and the light is gone:	*darkness*
70	Thundering, lightning, snow, and raine,	
	Therof enough they had.	*Of those*

	Then spake Sir Gawaine and sighed sore:	
	"Such wether saw I never afore	
	In noe stead there I have beene stood."	*place where*

[Again at this point a half page is missing. The storms seem a preliminary test. Gawain endures them, and accepts instruction from the Turk, and is then allowed to proceed to the mysterious castle.]

75	". . . made them noe answere	
	But only unto mee."	

	To the Castle they then yode.	*went*
	Sir Gawaine light beside his steed,	*dismounted*
	For horsse the Turke had none.	
80	There they found chamber, bower, and hall,	
	Richly rayled about with pale,	*arrayed with elegant cloths*
	Seemly to look uppon.	*handsome*

	A bord was spred within that place:	*table*
	All manner of meates and drinkes there was	
85	For groomes that might it againe.	*men; gain*
	Sir Gawaine wold have fallen to that fare,	*taken up that food*

---

[1] *Who deserve to have their prowess tested*

342

The Turke and Sir Gawain

The Turke bad him leave for care;   *[But]; refrain because of harm*
   Then waxt he unfaine.   *became [Gawain] unhappy*

Gawaine said, "Man, I marvell have   *am astonished*
90   That thou may none of these vittells spare,   *foods dispense*
     And here is soe great plentye.
   Yett have I more mervaile, by my fay,   *faith*
   That I see neither man nor maid,
     Woman nor child soe free.

95   "I had lever now att mine owne will   *rather*
   Of this fayre meate to eate my fill
     Then all the gold in Christenty."   *[have]; Christendom*
   The Turke went forth, and tarryed nought;
   Meate and drinke he forth brought,
100   Was seemly for to see.

He said, "Eate, Gawaine, and make thee yare.   *ready*
   In faith, or thou gett victalls more   *before; food*
     Thou shalt both swinke and sweate.   *toil*
   Eate, Gawaine, and spare thee nought!"
105   Sir Gawaine eate as him good thought,
     And well he liked his meate.

He dranke ale, and after wine.
   He saith, "I will be att thy bidding baine   *ready*
     Without bost or threat.   *Without (need for)*
110   But one thing I wold thee pray:
   Give me my buffett and let me goe my way.
     I wold not longer be hereatt.

[Another half page is missing at this point. The Turk refuses to allow Gawain to conclude the bargain by receiving his return blow. Instead he asks that Gawain accompany him to the Isle of Man.]

Ther stood a bote and . . .   *boat*
   Sir Gawaine left behind his steed,
115   He might noe other doe.

The Turke and Sir Gawain

The Turke said to Sir Gawaine,
"He shal be here when thou comes againe —
   I plight my troth to thee —
Within an hower, as men tell me."   *hour*
120   They were sailed over the sea:
   The Turke said, "Gawaine, hee!   *hasten*

"Heere are we withouten scath.   *harm*
But now beginneth the great othe,   *the fulfillment of our compact*
   When we shall adventures see."
125   He lett him see a castle faire;
   Such a one he never saw yare,   *before*
    Noewher in noe country.

The Turke said to Sir Gawaine
"Yonder dwells the King of Man,
130   A heathen soldan is hee.   *sultan*

"With him he hath a hideous rout   *throng*
Of giants strong and stout
   And uglie to looke uppon.
Whosoever had sought farr and neere
135   As wide as the world were,
   Such a companye he cold find none.

"Many aventures thou shalt see there,
Such as thou never saw yare   *before*
   In all the world about.
140   Thou shalt see a tenisse ball   *tennis ball [so large]*
That never knight in Arthurs hall
   Is able to give it a lout.   *blow*

"And other adventures there are moe.   *more*
Wee shall be assayled ere we goe,   *absolved (of sin) before*
145   Therof have thou noe doute.

"But and yee will take to me good heed,   *if*
I shall helpe you in time of need.
   For ought I can see   *anything*

There shall be none soe strong in stower   *battle*
150   But I shall bring thee againe to hi . . .

[Another half page is missing here. After these reassurances, Gawain accompanies the Turk into the Castle of the King of Man where he is met with verbal assaults.]

. . . "Sir Gawaine stiffe and stowre,   *fierce*
How fareth thy unckle King Arthur,
    And all his company?
And that Bishopp Sir Bodwine   *Baldwin*
155   That will not let my goods alone,
    But spiteth them every day?   *spoils*

"He preached much of a Crowne of Thorne;
He shall ban the time that he was borne   *curse*
    And ever I catch him may.   *If*
160   I anger more att the spiritually   *clergy*
In England, not att the temporaltie,   *lords*
    They goe soe in theire array.   *lavish clothes*

"And I purpose in full great ire   *intend; wrath*
To brenn their clergy in a fire   *burn*
165   And punish them to my pay.   *satisfaction*
Sitt downe, Sir Gawaine, at the bord."   *table*
Sir Gawaine answered at that word,
    Saith, "Nay, that may not be,

"I trow not a venturous knight shall   *do not think a daring*
170   Sitt downe in a kings hall
    Adventures or you see."   *before*
The King said, "Gawaine, faire mot thee fall!   *may good things befall you*
Goe feitch me forth my tennisse ball,
    For play will I and see."   *see what happens*

175   They brought it out without doubt.
With it came a hideous rout   *huge throng*
    Of gyants great and plenty;
All the giants were there then
Heire by the halfe then Sir Gawaine,   *Higher; than*
180   I tell you withouten nay.   *without doubt*

The Turke and Sir Gawain

There were seventeen giants bold of blood,
And all thought Gawaine but litle good.
   When they thought with him to play.
All the giants thoughten then
185   To have strucke out Sir Gawaines braine.
   Help him God that best may!

The ball of brasse was made for the giants hand;
There was noe man in all England
   Were able to carry it . . .

[In a missing section, Gawain defeats the giants at tennis with the help of the Turk, who ends by pummeling one of the giants.]

190   . . . and sticked a giant in the hall   *stabbed*
   That grysly can hee grone.   *gruesomely did*
The King sayd, "Bray away this axeltree,   *Take; staff*
For such a boy I never see.   *[i.e., the Turk]*
   Yett he shal be assayed better ere he goe —

195   "I told you, soe mote I the —   *may I prosper*
With the three adventure, and then no more
   Befor me at this tide."   *time*

Then there stood amongst them all
A chimney in the Kings hall   *free-standing fireplace*
200   With barres mickle of pride.   *iron bars great in strength*
There was laid on in that stond   *stand*
Coales and wood that cost a pound,   *in large quantity*
   That upon it did abide.   *lie*

A giant bad Gawaine assay,   *give it a try*
205   And said, "Gawaine, begin the play —
   Thou knowest best how it shold be!
And afterwards when thou hast done,
I trow you shal be answered soone   *matched*
   Either with boy or me.   *[i.e., the Turk]*

210 "A great giant, I understand,
Lift up the chimney with his hand   *[Should be able to]*
    And sett it downe againe fairly."   *easily*

Sir Gawaine was never soe adread
Sith he was man on midle earth,   *since*
215   And cryd on God in his thought.
Gawaine unto his boy can say   *did*
"Lift this chimney — if you may —
    That is soe worthily wrought."   *massively*

Gawaines boy to it did leape,
220   And gatt itt by the bowles great,   *charcoal holders*
And about his head he it flang.   *flung*
Thris about his head he it swang   *Thrice*
    That the coals and the red brands . . .

[In a missing half page the Turk completes his victory in the second contest,
twirling the hot fireplace above his head. He then clothes himself in a garment
of invisibility to accompany Gawain as the King of Man leads him to the final
challenge. Here, a giant threatens Gawain.]

". . . saw of mickle might   *great*
225   And strong were in battell.

"I have slaine them thorrow my mastery,   *(i.e., other knights)*
And now, Gawaine, I will slay thee,
    And then I have slaine all the flower.   *elite (of chivalry)*
There went never none againe no tale to tell,   *none ever returned*
230 Nor more shalt thou, thoe thou be fell,   *Any more than; though; fierce*
    Nor none that longeth to King Arthur."   *belong*

The Turke was clad invissible gay: *clothed with wonderful invisibility*
No man cold see him withouten nay,   *without doubt*
He was cladd in such a weede.   *garment*
235 He heard their talking lesse and more: *altogether*
And yet he thought they shold find him there   *feel his presence*
When they shold do that deed.

347

Then he led him into steddie   *(i.e., the King led Gawain); a spot*
Werhas was a boyling leade,   *Where; [cauldron of] molten lead*
240   And welling uppon hie: *seething*
And before it a giant did stand
With an iron forke in his hand,
   That hideous was to see.

The giant that looked soe keene   *fierce*
245   That before Sir Gawaine had never seene   *[one so fierce]*
   Noe where in noe country.
The King saide to the giant thoe,   *then*
"Here is none but wee tow;   *two*
   Let see how best may bee."   *do your best*

250 When the giant saw Gawaines boy there was,
He leapt and threw, and cryed "Alas,   *writhed*
   That he came in that stead!"   *this place*
Sir Gawaines boy to him lept,
And with strenght up him gett,   *took*
255   And cast him in the lead.

With an iron forke made of steele
He held him downe wondorous weele,   *well*
   Till he was scalded to the dead.   *death*
Then Sir Gawaine unto the King can say,   *did*
260 "Without thou wilt agree unto our law,   *Unless*
   Eatein is all thy bread."   *(i.e., your time is up)*

The King spitt on Gawaine the knight.
With that the Turke hent him upright   *seized him as he stood*
   And into the fyer him flang,   *fire*
265 And saide to Sir Gawaine at the last,
"Noe force, Master, all the perill is past!   *No worry*
   Thinke not we tarrie too longe . . .

[In a missing half page, Gawain and the Turk apparently move quickly to another part of the Castle, where captives have been magically imprisoned. The Turk then, instead of taking the return blow at Gawain to which he is entitled, requests that Gawain deliver a sword stroke that would behead him.]

The Turke and Sir Gawain

	He tooke forth a bason of gold	*basin*
	As an Emperour washe shold,	*Such as*
270	As fell for his degree.	*it suited his rank*
	He tooke a sword of mettle free,	*metal noble*
	Saies "If ever I did any thing for thee,	*[And] says*
	Doe for me in this stead:	*Help me; case*
	Take here this sword of steele	
275	That in battell will bite weele,	
	Therwith strike of my head."	*[And] with it; off*
	"That I forefend!" said Sir Gawaine,	*forbid*
	"For I wold not have thee slaine	
	For all the gold soe red."	
280	"Have done, Sir Gawaine! I have no dread.	*Enough*
	But in this bason let me bleed,	
	That standeth here in this steed,	*place*
	"And thou shalt see a new play,	*turn of events*
	With helpe of Mary that mild mayd	
285	That saved us from all dread."	
	He drew forth the brand of steele	
	That in battell bite wold weele,	
	And there stroke of his head.	*off*
	And when the blood in the bason light,	*fell*
290	He stood up a stalwortht Knight	
	That day, I undertake,	*dare say*
	And song "'Te Deum Laudamus' —	*sang*
	Worshipp be to our Lord Jesus	
	That saved us from all wracke!	*ruin*
295	"A! Sir Gawaine! Blessed thou be!	
	For all the service I have don thee,	
	Thou hast well quitt it me."	*repaid*
	Then he tooke him by the hand,	
	And many a worthy man they fand	*encountered*
300	That before they never see.	*had seen*

	He said, "Sir Gawaine, withouten threat	*with all courtesy*
	Sitt downe boldly at thy meate,	
	And I will eate with thee.	
	Ladyes all, be of good cheere:	
305	Eche ane shall wend to his owne deer	*one; go; dear*
	In all hast that may be.	*haste*

"First we will to King Arthurs hall,
And soone after your husbands send we shall
   In country where they beene;   *have lived*
310 There they wold . . . abide.

[In another missing section, the process of liberating the chivalric captives continues with the return to Arthur's court.]

"Thus we have brought seventeen ladys cleere   *handsome*
That there were left in great danger,
   And we have brought them out."

Then sent they for theire husbands swithe,   *quickly*
315 And every one tooke his oune wife,   *own*
   And lowlye can they lowte,   *humbly did they bow*
And thanked the two knights and the King,
And said they wold be at theire bidding
   In all England about.

320 Sir Gromer kneeld upon his knee,
Saith "Sir King, and your wil be,   *if it be your will*
   Crowne Gawaine King of Man."   *[of the Isle] of Man*
Sir Gawaine kneeld downe by,   *next to Sir Gromer*
And said "Lord, nay, not I;
325   Give it him, for he it wan.

"For I never purposed to be noe King,
Never in all my livinge,
   Whilest I am a living man."
He said, "Sir Gromer, take it thee,   *(i.e., Arthur); for yourself*
330 For Gawaine will never King bee
   For no craft that I can."   *argument I may make*

Thus endeth the tale that I of meane,   *had in mind*
Of Arthur and his knightes keene
   That hardy were and free.
335   God give them good life far and neere   *to them (i.e., the audience)*
That such talking loves to heere!
   Amen for Charity!

Fins.   *The end*

Notes

Abbreviations: P = Percy Folio; BP= Bishop Percy's marginal notes in the MS; M = Madden's edition; F = Furnivall's edition. See Select Bibliography for these editions.

10 ff.   The appearance of a strange, potentially threatening figure as preliminary to a great feast occurs frequently in Arthurian romance. See note at line 169 below. The "Turk" as emblem of festive exoticism occurs also in civic pageants at Gloucester; in 1595 the chamberlains paid ten shillings to cover expenses "for a wagon in the pageant and for the turke," the latter clearly a figure whose lavish dress conveyed his exotic, and entirely conventionalized, strangeness (*Cumberland, Westmorland, Gloucestershire: Records of the Early English Drama*, eds. Audrey W. Douglas and Peter Greenfield [Toronto: University of Toronto Press, 1986], p. 313). The "Turk" also appears as a character in many of the folk plays that originated in the Middle Ages. Surviving versions of Sword Dances, St. George Plays, and other mummings include "The Turk," "The Turkish Knight," "The Turkish Champion," "Turkey Snipe," and so on, a boisterous figure who stands as the enemy of the plays' comically chivalric Christian heroes (see Alex Helm, *The English Mummers' Play* [Woodbridge, UK: D. S. Brewer, 1981], pp. 34, 76, 80, with other examples as well).

12   *came.* The word has been written over, perhaps by BP. P may originally have read *taite*, which M gives. F reads the corrected form as *cane* (which he notes means *came*).

18   *iff.* I follow M's reading; F reads *Gift*, taking the ampersand for "g".

25   *Give . . . hand.* M: *Gine . . . hands.*

35   *your.* P: *yo*ᵘ; F reads the abbreviation as *your*, which I follow.

39   *thrise.* P: *ʒise.*

40   *on middlearth.* M: *in middlearth.*

Notes

51   *northwards*. M: *northward*.

56   *Hawtinge*. M: *Lawtinge*, and adds *Lawghinge?* in his note.

59   *part*. M: *that* (the letter "thorn" with superscript "t"), though F's *part* seems accurate.

62   *shalt*. M: *shall*.

74   *beene stood*. M's reading of the line ends with *beene*, though additional (undecipherable) letters appear at the end of the line; here and at later breaks, F seems to have been able to make out more of the text, and I follow his reconstructions.

75   *made them noe answere*. M's line begins *noe answere*.

77   The mysterious adventures within this depopulated Castle, which is inside a hill and surrounded by *merke* (line 69), parallel events in other romances, especially (in the motifs of dangerous feasts) those associated with the Holy Grail. The entrance to the other world through an earthly, seemingly natural portal — "a hill," "The earth opened and closed again" (lines 66–67) — occurs in a wide variety of narratives beginning with Homer and Virgil, but is especially common in stories with Celtic connections. In the Breton *lai*, *Sir Orfeo*, the hero rides "In at a roche [cliff]" to enter fairyland (ed. A. J. Bliss, 2nd ed. [Oxford: Clarendon, 1966]; see Bliss's comment, pages xxxviii ff.).

79   *horsse*. M: *horse*.

    Whether the Turk lacked a horse during the entire journey (see line 51) or has lost his horse only at this point seems uncertain, but what is clear is the contrast between Sir Gawain as knight — mounted warrior — and the Turk as powerful, and even magical, but not chivalric. In line 114, the romance significantly notes that Gawain must abandon his horse. *Jeaste* makes a point of noting the discomfiture that follows upon each combat when a knight (including Gawain, in the last encounter) loses his horse.

82   *look*. M: *looke*.

113   *Ther stood a bote and*. M's line ends with *stood a*.

121   *hee*. M: *hoe*, in the sense of "stop" ("whoa").

124   *we*. P: *he*; I emend for sense.

        see. P: *doe*; I emend for rhyme.

128   Here, and at lines 143, 195, and 210 occur defective three-line stanzas, all linked by tail-rhyme to the previous or succeeding stanza (making four potential nine-line stanzas). Other defective stanzas (e.g., at lines 37 and 74) are clearly the result of losses in the MS. See also line 219 and note.

129   *the King of Man*. Despite the characterization of the King as a *heathen soldan* (line 130), the reference seems clearly to locate this enemy on the Isle of Man in the Solway Firth; this is (as line 51 suggests) off the northwest coast of England, near Scotland. The Isle of Man is opposite Cumberland, the county which contains Carlisle, Inglewood Forest, the Tarn Wathelene, and other locations repeatedly associated with Arthurian legend in the popular Gawain romances. Man was one of the "Southern Islands," in contrast to the northern islands (which included the Orkneys, by tradition one of Sir Gawain's ancestral homes). The Manx people, originally of Celtic descent, intermarried with Scandinavian invaders, and lived under their own king, who did homage to the kings of Norway and Scotland. English control of Man began about 1290, during the reign of Edward I, though it passed back to the Scots several times during the next half century. Several English knights ruled the Manx people (by appointment of the king or purchase of the Manx crown) before 1400; in 1406 Henry IV made Sir John Stanley the hereditary King of Man, and members of this family governed the island through the eighteenth century. The chivalric exploits that led the king to appoint Sir John as ruler of the Manx people parallel those celebrated in romances (see General Introduction, pp. 33–34).

144   *Wee shall be assayled*. Though this form might, in its context, be taken as "assailed" — i.e., "we shall be attacked before we finish" — I have interpreted it as a spelling of "assoil," meaning "absolve." The Turk's concern for Christian absolution suggests the superficiality of his role as exotic stereotype within the narrative. He serves clearly as a "stage Saracen," whose strangeness works to set off the hero and offset some of the plot's predictability. Within the action, though the Turk seems Gawain's adversary, he cooperates in the adventures he orchestrates to advance Christendom: he calls the King of Man a "heathen soldan" (line 130, and note at line 129), destroys the King when he

Christianity (lines 263 ff.), and spontaneously calls upon the Virgin Mary before his transformation. The covert alliance of the Turk with the conventional Christian ethos of the poem is only thinly veiled, therefore, by his exotic appearance.

150 The line breaks off, with fragment of a word beginning *hi* visible.

154 *that Bishopp Sir Bodwine.* This reference to a Baldwin who is by title both a bishop and a knight seems unarguably to assume a single identity for the Bishop Baldwin who accompanies Gawain in *Carlisle*, and the knight who exchanges vows with Arthur, Kay, and Gawain in *Avowyng*. See *Carlisle*, line 28 and note, and *Avowyng*, line 74 and note.

160 ff. This attack on the *spiritually* or clergy in England and *not att the temporaltie* seems, both in its very terms and in its unmotivated appearance at this point in the poem, to be a post-Reformation insertion into the text, and in this resembles the outburst in *Carle*, lines 269 ff.

169 Gawain's refusal to begin the feast until he witnesses an adventure is a commonplace of French and English chivalric romance. It occurs notably at the outset of *Sir Gawain and the Green Knight* and in Malory's tale of Sir Gareth (*Works*, p. 293); the beginning of the present poem more distantly echoes the convention. See note at line 10.

172 *thee.* P: *then*; I emend to restore the common idiom.

181 *seventeen.* M: *ix.*

192 *axeltree.* The word refers literally to an axle for wheels; here it seems to be an instrument — a huge staff perhaps — used by the Turk in the tennis game and in combat against the giant.

194 *assayed.* M: *aflayed.*

194 ff. The three lines that follow, and constitute a separate short stanza, continue the sentence begun in line 194. The sense is, "He shall be more fully put to the test before he leaves — as I've said, so help me — with the three adventures, and no more, with me as witness, right now."

195   *soe mote I the.* M and F read *tho*, which almost rhymes with *more* (line 196). The letter form is sufficiently ambiguous to allow reading *the*; though not at all a rhyme, grammatically and idiomatically this is precisely the form the context demands.

199   *the.* F reads *they*, which seems possible, though there is a blot on the line.

220   *bowles.* M: *bowler.* The last line of this stanza is lost because of a missing half-page, but the rhyme scheme of the surviving five lines is defective.

222   *Thris.* P: 3^{is}.

226   *them.* M: *then.*

232   *gay.* M suggests *gray.*

250   The Turk seems to rematerialize at this point, as the giant's dismay suggests.

257   *wondorous.* M: *wonderous.*

261   *Eatein.* M: *eaten.*

262   The King's pointed rejection of Christianity, symbolized by his spitting on Gawain, casts him in the role of *heathen soldan* (line 130), as adapted from popular verse romances associated with Charlemagne and the conquest of the Saracens (to whom the Turk would be equivalent). In *The Sowdone of Babylon*, when Laban, the chief enemy of the Christian West, is offered baptism, he spits into the font, and is promptly beheaded. See line 3167 of Alan Lupack's edition of *The Sultan of Babylon*, in *Three Middle English Charlemagne Romances* (Kalamazoo: Medieval Institute Publications, 1990), p. 92.

269   *washe.* M: *was he.*

271   The act of disenchantment, where by delivering a return blow Sir Gawain changes the Turk back into Sir Gromer, is a version of the folk motif called the Beheading Game. It vividly recalls the beheading scenes in *Sir Gawain and the Green Knight* and *Carle*, and calls attention to the missing scene in *Carlisle*. Moreover, the metamorphosis to a true self as the climax of the romance resonates as well with the endings of *Ragnelle*, *Marriage*, and *The Greene Knight*.

292   *Te Deum Laudamus.* This is a Latin hymn of praise to the Father and Son, often (though falsely) attributed to St. Ambrose and associated with the baptism of St. Augustine. It dates probably from the fifth century, and was widely familiar from its use in the daily offices and in the liturgies for various feasts and ceremonies. It was also frequently used to conclude popular festivities and plays, where its singing emphasized the solidarity of the Christian community. The transformed Sir Gromer's spontaneous performance of the hymn here signals his restoration to Christian knighthood.

299   *many a worthy man.* Apparently the defeat of the King of Man, with his preternatural powers, together with the transformation of the Turk, liberates those other knights and ladies whom the King had defeated, captured, and enchanted; see above, lines 226 ff. The actual restoration of these knights and ladies to their proper identities parallels the scene in *Carlisle* (lines 517 ff.), and its counterpart in *Carle* (lines 409 ff.), where the Carle shows Gawain the liveries and bones of the knights he has slain. Unlike the beheading of the Turk, the disenchantment of the Carle, who also had been "transformed soe" (*Carle*, line 410), does not result in the liberation of a tyrant's victims, only in prayers for their souls. The freeing of the captive ladies (to which Sir Gromer refers in lines 304 ff.) resembles the episode at Le Chastel de Pesme Avanture in Chrétien de Troyes' *Yvain* (lines 51 ff.), which is reproduced in the English *Ywain and Gawain.* In the English version, Ywain arrives at the Castel of the Hevy Sorow (line 2933), confronts a porter, defeats two "fowl felouns," and releases the women of "Maydenland" (line 3010): " 'Maidens,' he said, 'God mot yow se, / And bring yow wele whare ye wald be' " (lines 3355–56). This episode in *Turke* also recalls Lancelot's release of Gawain's brother Gaherys and sixty-four other knights of the Round Table from captivity within Sir Terquyne's castle, and his freeing of "three score ladyes and damesels" by the defeat of "two grete gyauntis" (Malory, *Works*, pp. 265–72).

301 ff.   The willingness of the transformed Sir Gromer to share a meal with Gawain contrasts with the Turk's interruption of the court's feast (lines 10 ff.) which he is not asked to join, and with the apparent refusal of the Turk to partake in the meal he serves Gawain at the depopulated castle (lines 83 ff.). The shared meal signifies the restoration of Gromer's proper individual identity, and the confirmation of the generalized cultural identity he and Gawain take part in as Christian knights.

310   *There they wold . . . abide.* This line is not now at all legible. I follow the text as given by F. M provides no text for this line.

318   *they.* P: *the.*

320   *Sir Gromer.* This knight of the Round Table is apparently identical with Sir Gromer Somer Joure of *Ragnelle* (see line 62 and note) and Malory's Sir Gromore Somyr Ioure (*Works* p. 1164), an ally of Galeron of Galloway (see *Awntyrs*, line 417 and note).

The Marriage of Sir Gawain

Introduction

Marriage follows *Cornwall* and *Turke* in the Percy Folio manuscript. It has suffered the same fate as those two poems: half of each page of the text had been torn out for use in starting fires sometime before Bishop Percy acquired the volume. In plot, *Marriage* closely resembles *Ragnelle* and the versions of the same story told in Gower's *Confessio Amantis* and Chaucer's *Wife of Bath's Tale*, so that despite the losses the main points of the narrative remain clear. In fact, *Marriage* presents a retelling bolder and balder than any of the others. The characters play exaggerated parts: Arthur's antagonist is not knightly, but a threatening thug "With a great club upon his backe"; the lady "in red scarlett" is simply monstrous; Kay at first is totally disgusted, and at the end filled with brotherly congratulation; Gawain is impeccably courteous. In the same way, motives and reactions are unhesitatingly named by the narrative: Arthur says he was afraid to fight, he offers Gawain in marriage before the lady even expresses an interest, and the crux of the story — what women most desire — turns out to be a tautology, for "a woman will have her will": she wants what she wants.

As a proper ballad, *Marriage* maintains the fundamental simplicity of the plot. There are none of the literary touches that Gower adds, or the learned allusions to Ovid, Dante, and Boethius of Chaucer's version. Likewise, *Marriage* forgoes the narrative replications and the thematic and verbal repetitions that mark *Ragnelle* as a popular romance and complicate its possible meanings. The interlocking sets of masculine social relations held in place through *Ragnelle*'s plot do not surface in *Marriage*; indeed, the nameless antagonist calls his nameless sister "a misshappen hore" and promises to burn her "in a fyer" if he catches her. The lady's plight, whereby like a witch she "looked soe foule and . . . was wont / On the wild more to goe" (lines 184–85), comes about through a bad marriage: her father, an "old knight . . . marryed a younge lady" who in fairy-tale fashion proceeded to turn her competition (or her children's competition for inheritance) into a creature "most like a feend of hell" (line 182). The wicked stepmother appears also in *Ragnelle* and in Gower's version.

The Marriage of Sir Gawain

Like the majority of Gawain romances, *Marriage* places Arthur's court at Carlisle (line 1), and sets its action in Inglewood Forest, and specifically at the Tarn Wathelene (lines 32, 51). Arthur is presumably hunting when he encounters the "bold barron," as are the main characters in *Ragnelle, Carlisle, Awntyrs*, and several others in this group of romances. These linkages of plot and detail do not, however, demonstrate that *Marriage* is a popular refashioning of an earlier written or literary narrative. The Percy Folio poem may well be the record of one more retelling of a story that had been popular at least from the time of King Edward I, and that, in addition to giving rise to a group of literary renditions, must have circulated widely in oral performances throughout the Middle Ages and the Renaissance. As such, it bears witness to Gawain's huge celebrity with an astonishing variety of audiences, and across centuries of enormous cultural change. The social milieu and the precise nature of the performance represented by *Marriage* are vividly defined in the fictional portrayal that Howard Pyle inserts into his *Merry Adventures of Robin Hood* (1883); in this children's narrative, Robin's first adventure is a meeting in a tavern with a Tinker-minstrel, who sings "an ancient ballad of the time of good King Arthur, called the Marriage of Sir Gawaine, which you may some time read, yourself, in stout English of early times" (New York: Dover, 1968, p. 19). Pyle's portrayal of this impromptu performance before a tavern audience at the edge of Sherwood Forest likely corresponds to the sort of setting in which the compiler of the Percy Folio Manuscript heard the version of *Marriage* that he wrote down.

Like *Cornwall, Marriage* is composed in ballad meter, namely four-line stanzas rhyming *xaxa*. The lines tend not to fall into regular metrical feet; instead they alternate, with four-stress unrhymed lines followed by three-stress lines containing the rhyming final word. As the oral sources of the meter would suggest, the poetry is most effective when read aloud; lines that "sound" clumsy when not vocalized take on life in spoken form.

Text

The Marriage of Sir Gawain survives, though mutilated, in the Percy Folio Manuscript, pp. 46–52 (described in the introductory material to *The Greene Knight*). In transcribing the cramped and fading hand, I have been aided by the editions of Madden, Furnivall and Hales, and Child, and I have sometimes followed their readings and reconstructions for letters and words that now appear indistinct or indecipherable. I have regularized orthography, so that *u/v* and *i/j* appear according to modern usage; abbreviations have been silently expanded, numerals spelled out, and modern punctuation and capitalization added.

Introduction

Select Bibliography

Manuscript

British Library Additional MS 27879 (The Percy Folio). Pp. 46–52.

Editions (arranged chronologically)

Hales, John W., and Frederick J. Furnivall. 1868. See Bibliography of Editions and Works Cited.

Child, Francis James. 1884. See Bibliography of Editions and Works Cited.

Lupack, Alan. "The Marriage of Sir Gawaine." In *Modern Arthurian Literature: An Anthology of English and American Arthuriana from the Renaissance to the Present*, ed. Alan Lupack. New York and London: Garland, 1992, pp. 108–18. [A reprint of the reconstructed version by Bishop Percy (first published in his *Reliques*, 1765), in which Percy supplied from his own invention the missing portions of the surviving fragment in the Percy Folio Manuscript.]

Shepherd, Stephen H. A., ed. *Middle English Romances*. New York: Norton, 1995. Pp. 380–87. [I have not been able to examine a copy of this edition.]

Criticism

Coomaraswamy, Amanda K. "On the Loathly Bride." *Speculum* 20 (1945), 391–404.

Garbáty, Thomas J. "Rhyme, Romance, Ballad, Burlesque, and the Confluence of Form." *Fifteenth-Century Studies: Recent Essays*, ed. Robert F. Yeager. Hamden, Connecticut: Archon Books, 1984. Pp. 283–301. [A discussion of the generic relation between ballad and romance in *Wedding* and *Marriage*.]

The Marriage of Sir Gawain

Kinge Arthur lives in merry Carleile,   *Carlisle*
   And seemely is to see,
And there he hath with him Queene Genever,
   That bride soe bright of blee.   *woman; countenance*

5   And there he hath with Queene Genever,   *has been*
   That bride soe bright in bower,   *chamber*
And all his barons about him stoode
   That were both stiffe and stowre.   *brave*

The King kept a royall Christmasse
10   Of mirth and great honor,
And when . . .

[In a missing half page, Arthur arranges a hunt; he is accosted by a Baron — an armed warrior — who demands the King fulfill a quest.]

"And bring me word what thing it is
   That a woman most desire.
This shal be thy ransome, Arthur," he sayes,
15   "For Ile have noe other hier."   *I will; recompense*

King Arthur then held up his hand   *gave his hand (in agreement)*
   According thene as was the law;   *custom*
He tooke his leave of the Baron there,
   And homward can he draw.   *did*

20   And when he came to merry Carlile,
   To his chamber he is gone;
And ther came to him his cozen Sir Gawaine   *kinsman*
   As he did make his mone.   *lament*

And there came to him his cozen Sir Gawaine,
25 That was a curteous knight: *Who*
"Why sigh you soe sore, uncle Arthur," he said,
"Or who hath done thee unright?"   *wrong*

"O peace, O peace, thou gentle Gawaine,
That faire may thee beffall,
30 For if thou knew my sighing soe deepe,   *knew [the cause of]*
Thou wold not mervaile att all.

"For when I came to Tearne Wadling,   *Tarn Wathelene*
A bold Barron there I fand   *encountered*
With a great club upon his backe,
35 Standing stiffe and strong.

"And he asked me wether I wold fight,
Or from him I shold begone —
Or else I must him a ransome pay   *(In which case)*
And soe depart him from.

40 "To fight with him I saw noe cause,
Methought it was not meet,   *suitable*
For he was stiffe and strong withall,   *indeed*
His strokes were nothing sweete.

"Therefor this is my ransome, Gawaine,
45 I ought to him to pay: *owe*
I must come againe, as I am sworne,
Upon the New Yeers Day.

"And I must bring him word what thing it is . . .

[Here a half page is missing. Arthur and Gawain spend their time searching for an answer to the Baron's question, and collect a sheaf of answers, none satisfactory. Finally, Arthur sets out for his New Year's meeting.]

Then King Arthur drest him for to ryde   *prepared himself*
50 In one soe rich array
Toward the foresaid Tearne Wadling,
That he might keepe his day.

363

And as he rode over a more,   *moor*
    Hee see a lady where shee sate   *sat*
55 Betwixt an oke and a greene hollen: *holly*
    She was cladd in red scarlett.

Then there as shold have stood her mouth,   *where*
    Then there was sett her eye;
The other was in her forhead fast,
60   The way that she might see.

Her nose was crooked and turnd outward,
    Her mouth stood foule awry;
A worse formed lady than shee was,
    Never man saw with his eye.

65 To halch upon him, King Arthur,   *greet him*
    This lady was full faine,   *eager*
But King Arthur had forgott his lesson,   *was at a loss for words*
    What he shold say againe.   *again (i.e., in reply)*

"What knight art thou," the lady sayd,
70   "That will not speak to me?
Of me be thou nothing dismayd
    Tho I be ugly to see.

"For I have halched you curteouslye,   *greeted*
    And you will not me againe;   *not [greet] me in turn*
75 Yett I may happen, Sir Knight," shee said,   *turn out*
    "To ease thee of thy paine."

"Give thou ease me, lady," he said,   *If*
    Or helpe me any thing,   *in any way*
Thou shalt have gentle Gawaine, my cozen,
80   And marry him with a ring."

"Why, if I help thee not, thou noble King Arthur,
    Of thy owne hearts desiringe,
Of gentle Gawaine . . .

The Marriage of Sir Gawain

[The lady agrees to the marriage bargain, and tells Arthur what women most desire. The King proceeds to his appointed meeting.]

And when he came to the Tearne Wadling
85   The Baron there cold he finde,   *could*
With a great weapon on his backe,
    Standing stiffe and stronge.

And then he tooke King Arthurs letters in his hands   *written answers*
    And away he cold them fling,   *did*
90   And then he puld out a good browne sword,   *bright*
    And cryd himselfe a king.   *declared*

And he sayd, "I have thee and thy land, Arthur,
    To doe as it pleaseth me,
For this is not thy ransome sure: *recompense*
95   Therfore yeeld thee to me."

And then bespoke him noble Arthur,
    And bad him hold his hand,   *bade*
"And give me leave to speake my mind
    In defence of all my land."

100   He said, "As I came over a more,
    I see a lady where shee sate
Betweene an oke and a green hollen;
    Shee was clad in red scarlett.

"And she says, 'A woman will have her will,
105   And this is all her cheef desire.'
Doe me right, as thou art a baron of sckill: *by me; proper*
    This is thy ransome and all thy hyer."

He sayes, "An early vengeance light on her!   *(The Baron)*
    She walkes on yonder more —
110   It was my sister that told thee this,
    And she is a misshappen hore!   *whore*

365

"But heer Ile make mine avow to God   *here I will; oath*
    To doe her an evill turne,
For an ever I may thate fowle theefe gett,   *if*
115   In a fyer I will her burne."   *fire*

[Having satisfactorily answered the Baron's question, Arthur returns to court. He gathers his knights and returns to the lady in the forest, though he appears to have informed Gawain alone of his marriage pact.]

The Second Part

Sir Lancelott and Sir Steven bold
    They rode with them that day,
And the formost of the company   *[among]*
    There rode the steward Kay.

120   Soe did Sir Banier and Sir Bore,
    Sir Garrett with them soe gay,
Soe did Sir Tristeram that gentle knight,
    To the forrest fresh and gay.

And when he came to the greene forrest,
125   Underneath a greene holly tree
Their sate that lady in red scarlet
    That unseemly was to see.

Sir Kay beheld this ladys face,
    And looked uppon her swire: *neck*
130   "Whosoever kisses this lady," he says,
    "Of his kisse he stands in feare."   *kiss's outcome*

Sir Kay beheld the lady againe,
    And looked upon her snout:
"Whosoever kisses this lady," he saies,
135   "Of his kisse he stands in doubt."   *fear*

"Peace cozen Kay," then said Sir Gawaine,
    "Amend thee of thy life.

The Marriage of Sir Gawain

For there is a knight amongst us all
    That must marry her to his wife."

140   "What! Wedd her to wiffe!" then said Sir Kay.
    "In the divells name anon,
    Gett me a wiffe where ere I may,   *wherever*
    For I had rather be slaine!"   *destroyed*

Then some tooke up their hawkes in hast,
145   And some tooke up their hounds,
    And some sware they wold not marry her   *swore*
    For citty nor for towne.

And then bespake him noble King Arthur,   *spoke out*
    And sware there by this day:
150   "For a litle foule sight and misliking . . .

[After Arthur's speech, Gawain announces his intention to marry the lady. All return to the court, the marriage is celebrated, and the lady and Gawain retire to their marriage bed. Faced with Gawain's sexual reticence, the lady metamorphoses into a beautiful young woman, and then offers Gawain a choice.]

Then she said, "Choose thee, gentle Gawaine,
    Truth as I doe say,
    Wether thou wilt have me in this liknesse   *appearance*
    In the night or else in the day."

155   And then bespake him gentle Gawaine,
    With one soe mild of moode,   *With a demeanor ever so*
    Sayes, "Well I know what I wold say —
    God grant it may be good!

"To have thee fowle in the night   *[I choose]*
160   When I with thee shold play;   *make love*
    Yet I had rather, if I might,
    Have thee fowle in the day."

"What! When lords goe with ther feires," shee said,   *companions*
    "Both to the ale and wine?

The Marriage of Sir Gawain

165   Alas! Then I must hyde my selfe,
       I must not goe withinne."   *into the hall (public space)*

    And then bespake him gentle Gawaine,   *spoke out*
       Said, "Lady, thats but a skill: *trick (i.e., trial response)*
    And because thou art my owne lady,
170   Thou shalt have all thy will."

    Then she said, "Blesed be thou gentle Gawain,
       This day that I thee see,
    For as thou see me att this time,
       From hencforth I wil be.   *remain*

175   "My father was an old knight.
       And yett it chanced soe
    That he marryed a younge lady
       That brought me to this woe.

    "Shee witched me, being a faire young lady,   *bewitched*
180   To the greene forrest to dwell,
    And there I must walke in womans liknesse,
       Most like a feeind of hell.   *like a monstrous woman*

    "She witched my brother to a carlish B. . . .   *churlish B[aron?]*

[The lady continues her explanation, and then she and Gawain consummate the marriage. In the morning Kay comes to check on Gawain's welfare, and Gawain explains his wife's history.]

    "That looked soe foule, and that was wont   *accustomed*
185   On the wild more to goe.   *moor*

    "Come kisse her, brother Kay," then said Sir Gawaine,
       "And amend thé of thy liffe: *thee*
    I sweare this is the same lady
       That I marryed to my wiffe."

190   Sir Kay kissed that lady bright,
       Standing upon his feete;

He swore, as he was trew knight,
   The spice was never soe sweete.

"Well, cozen Gawaine," sayes Sir Kay,
195   "Thy chance is fallen arright,   *luck*
For thou hast gotten one of the fairest maids
   I ever saw with my sight."

"It is my fortune," said Sir Gawaine.
   "For my uncle Arthurs sake,
200   I am glad as grasse wold be of raine,
   Great joy that I may take."

Sir Gawaine tooke the lady by the one arme,
   Sir Kay tooke her by the tother;   *the other*
They led her straight to King Arthur
205   As they were brother and brother.

King Arthur welcomed them there all,
   And soe did Lady Genever his Queene,
With all the knights of the Round Table
   Most seemly to be seene.

210   King Arthur beheld that lady faire
   That was soe faire and bright.
He thanked Christ in Trinity
   For Sir Gawaine that gentle knight.

Soe did the knights, both more and lesse,
215   Rejoyced all that day,
For the good chance that hapened was
   To Sir Gawaine and his lady gay.   *handsome*

Fins.   *The End*

Notes

Abbreviations: P = Percy Folio Manuscript; M = Madden's edition; FH = Furnivall's and Hales' edition; C = Child's edition. See Select Bibliography for these editions.

29   *beffall.* M: *befall*; the stroke for the second *f* appears blurred.

32   *Tearne Wadling.* The Tarn Wathelene (a tarn is a small lake) is mentioned in *Avowyng* (lines 131, 338) and *Awntyrs* (line 2), and again in lines 51 and 84 of the present romance. Though Inglewood Forest, where this lake is located, is the setting of *Ragnelle*, the Tarn itself is not mentioned in that romance.

87   *stronge.* Though elsewhere rhymes are strained, this stanza seems clearly deficient.

116   *Sir Steven.* This is a knight otherwise unknown in Arthurian romance.

120   *Sir Banier and Sir Bore.* Madden suggests the first name is a misnomer for Beduer or Bedyvere (Bedevere), brother of Lucan the Butler and Arthur's constable, but perhaps this is Sir Ban (or Bayan), the father of Lancelot. The second is Bors de Gaynes, Lancelot's loyal companion.

121   *Sir Garrett.* This is Gareth, Gawain's brother and loyal supporter of Lancelot, by whom he is inadvertently killed in the rescue of Guenevere.

122   *Sir Tristeram.* A celebrated hero in many Arthurian tales, Sir Tristan is the son of Melyodas and nephew of King Mark of Cornwall.

143   *slaine.* FH: *shaine*, with the suggestion that the word may be a variant of *shent*, *slaine*, or *shamed*.

163   *feires.* The scribal forms are unclear; M, C read *seires*, and emend to *feires*, which I follow. FH give *squires*.

174 *hencforth.* M: *henceforth.*

175 ff. The plot of *Marriage* more closely resembles a traditional fairy tale in making the source of evil simply a wicked stepmother rather than the entanglements of an Arthurian court intrigue.

182 *feeind.* M reads the apparent extra minum as *i*, which seems right; FH, C: *feend.*

192 *swore.* M: *sayes*, without explanation, though *swore* seems clear in P.

The Carle of Carlisle

Introduction

Like *The Marriage of Sir Gawain*, *The Carle of Carlisle* is a post-medieval version of a surviving tail-rhyme romance. Besides giving witness to the continuing appeal of chivalric plots among popular audiences, *Carle* is especially valuable for including a crucial episode that the extant version of *Sir Gawain and the Carle of Carlisle* omits. This is the beheading scene (lines 379 ff.), which resembles similar motifs in *Turke*, *Greene Knight*, and *Sir Gawain and the Green Knight*. In *Carle*, Gawain's obliging beheading of his host is the act of courtesy that breaks the spell, restoring the erstwhile good warrior to his proper identity. The transformation also strongly resembles the climactic events in *Ragnelle* and *Marriage*, whereby a beautiful and noble maiden is likewise saved from "nigromancy." In a popular story like *Carle*, the beheading episode precipitates a Frog Prince metamorphosis; the tale presents this less as a rudimentary psychology — a change of heart — than as a complete change of character, or rather a return from the monstrous to a true identity. The surviving text of *Carlisle*, however, omits this consequential scene, which the *Carle* convincingly shows was a feature of the established plot. In *Carlisle*, the Carle must simply vow to reform himself, which makes for a much less vivid and memorable turnabout.

Carlisle and *Carle* are not directly related to one another as source or derivative, and so give evidence for still another medieval version of the story in some lost common ancestor. *Carle* recalls *Avowyng* (and *Carlisle*) in bringing Sir Gawain together with Kay and Baldwin, and, in common with many of the other popular Gawain romances, it makes the area surrounding Carlisle in Cumberland, near the Scottish border, the setting for Arthurian adventure. As *Carle* makes clear, the point of the story is to prove Gawain's worthiness as a knight, to show that his courtesy indeed justifies his reputation and the chivalry of the Round Table. Both the courtesy and the hardiness of Arthur's knights are put to the test by the seeming bluffness of the Carle; his "lodlye" appearance and behavior (line 182) make him, like Ragnelle, not only monstrous but uncouth and uncourtly. In the end, however, the poem presents the Carle's challenges not as conflicts of values between knights and churls, but as the result of magical plotting; its undoing of the spell simply confirms the superiority of chivalry. Not only does the chivalric code absorb the Carle's rude

373

buffets and demands, it actually transforms him to a properly compassionate and honorable knight. Gawain's courteous submission — his deliberate control of his personal strength and his political and social superiority — demonstrates not simply that every Carle's home is his castle, but that true knighthood cuts across and consolidates class distinctions. By the conclusion, the audience sees the Carle not as an enemy of knighthood, but as another of the knights of the Round Table. The other motifs of reconciliation in the poem — Gawain's marriage to the Carle's daughter, and the Carle's feasting of Arthurian knighthood — are then simply themes within the larger movement of the romance plot towards reunion and restored identity. These normative motifs also help clarify the meaning of the central episode, for though the Carle's apparently eccentric hospitality seems to violate or distend ordinary expectations, its effect is to allow the standards of chivalric conduct to prevail.

Text

The Carle of Carlisle appears in the Percy Folio Manuscript, dating from the middle of the seventeenth century (see introduction to *The Greene Knight*). The poem is not preserved in formal ballad stanzas, but simply in rhyming couplets. See Bibliography for other editions.

Select Bibliography

Manuscript

British Library Additional MS 27879 (The Percy Folio). Pp. 448–55.

Editions (arranged chronologically)

Madden, Frederic. 1839. See Bibliography of Editions and Works Cited.

Hales, John W., and Frederick J. Furnivall. 1868. See Bibliography of Editions and Works Cited.

The Carle of Carlisle

	Listen to me a litle stond —	*while*
	Yee shall heare of one that was sober and sound.	*trustworthy and brave*
	Hee was meeke as maid in bower,	*maiden in a chamber*
	Stiffe and strong in every stoure.	*battle*
5	Certes, withouten fable,	*Surely*
	He was one of the Round Table.	
	The knights name was Sir Gawaine,	
	That much worshipp wan in Brittaine.	*won*
	The Ile of Brittaine called is	
10	Both England and Scottland iwis.	*indeed*
	Wales is an angle to that ile,	*corner*
	Where King Arthur sojorned a while,	*stayed*
	With him twenty-four knights told	*[And]; all told (in number)*
	Besids barrons and dukes bold.	
15	The King to his bishopp gan say,	*did*
	"Wee will have a Masse today —	
	Bishopp Bodwim shall itt done.	*perform*
	After to the forrest wee will gone,	
	For now itts grass-time of the yeere:	*it's time when the deer are fattened*
20	Barrons bold shall breake the deere."	*dress*
	Faine theroff was Sir Marrocke,	*Glad*
	Soe was Sir Kay, the knight stout.	
	Faine was Sir Lancelott Du Lake;	
	Soe was Sir Percivall, I undertake.	*dare say*
25	Faine was Sir Ewaine	
	And Sir Lott of Lothaine;	
	Soe was the Knight of Armes Greene	
	And alsoe Sir Gawaine the sheene.	*brilliant one*
	Sir Gawaine was Steward in Arthurs hall:	
30	Hee was the curteous knight amongst them all.	*most courteous*
	King Arthur and his cozen Mordred,	*kinsman; [were there]*
	And other knights withouten lett.	*without end*

The Carle of Carlisle

	Sir Lybius Disconyus was there	*The Fair Unknown*
	With proud archers lesse and more.	
35	Blanch Faire and Sir Ironside,	
	And many knights that day can ryde.	*did*
	And Ironside, as I weene,	
	Gate the Knight of Armour Greene,	*Begot*
	Certes, as I understand,	
40	Of a faire lady of Blaunch Land.	
	Hee cold more of honor in warr	*knew*
	Then all the knights that with Arthur weare.	*were*
	Burning dragons he slew in land	*on land*
	And wilde beasts, as I understand.	
45	Wilde beares he slew that stond:	*time*
	A hardyer knight was never found.	
	He was called in his dayes	
	One of King Arthurs fellowes.	
	Why was hee called Ironsyde?	
50	For ever armed wold he ryde;	
	Hee wold allwais armes beare,	
	For gyants and hee were ever att warr.	
	Dapple-coulour was his steede,	*Spotted*
	His armour, and his other weede.	*attire*
55	Azure of gold he bare	
	With a griffon lesse or more,	
	And a difference of a molatt	
	He bare in his crest allgate. [1]	
	Wheresoever he went, east nor west,	
60	He never forsooke man nor beast.	
	Beagles keenely away they ran;	*Hunting dogs*
	The King followed affter with many a man.	
	The grayhounds out of the leashe;	*[were released]*
	They drew downe the deere of grasse.	*in meadows*
65	Fine tents in the feild were sett:	
	A merry sort there were mett	*crowd*
	Of comely knights of kind.	*by nature*

---

[1] Lines 55–58: *He bore arms of blue and gold, / [Emblazoned] with several griffins, / And the distinguishing mark of a mullet (i.e., star) / He always bore on his crest* (see note)

	Uppon the bent there can they lend,	*field; linger*
	And by noone of the same day	
70	A hundred harts on the ground lay.	
	Then Sir Gawaine and Sir Kay	
	And Bishopp Bodwin, as I heard say,	
	After a redd deere they rode	
	Into a forrest wyde and brode.	
75	A thicke mist fell them among	
	That caused them all to goe wronge.	
	Great moane made then Sir Kay	
	That they shold loose the hart that day:	
	That red hart wold not dwell.	*stay behind*
80	Hearken what adventures them beffell.	
	Full sore they were adread	
	Ere they any lodginge had.	*Before*
	Then spake Sir Gawaine:	
	"This labour wee have had in vaine.	
85	This red hart is out of sight —	
	Wee meete with him no more this night.	
	I reede wee of our horsses do light,	*from*
	And lodge wee heere all this night.	
	Truly itt is best, as thinketh mee,	
90	To lodge low under this tree."	
	"Nay!" said Kay, "Goe wee hence anon!	*now*
	For I will lodge whersoere I come;	*wherever*
	For there dare no man warne me	*forbid me*
	Of whatt estate soever hee bee."	
95	"Yes," said the Bishopp, "that wott I well.	*know*
	Here dwelleth a carle in a castele.	*Nearby; churl*
	The Carle of Carlile is his name;	
	I know itt well, by St. Jame.	
	Was there never man yett soe bold	
100	That durst lodge within his hold	*castle*
	But and if hee scape with his liffe away	*But if only*
	Hee ruleth him well, I you say."	*does very well*
	Then said Kay, "All in fere	*together*
	To goe thither is my desire.	
105	For and the Carle be never so bolde,	*no matter whether*
	I thinke to lodge within his hold.	

377

	For if he jangle and make itt stout,	*complain and resist*
	I shall beate the Carle all about.	
	And I shall make his bigging bare	*dwelling*
110	And doe to him mickle care.	*cause for him*
	And I shall beate him, as I thinke,	
	Till he both sweate and stinke."	
	Then said the Bishopp, "So mote I fare,	*However I*
	Att his bidding I wil be yare."	*[Kay's]; ready*
115	Gawaine said, "Lett be thy bostlye fare,	*noisy claims*
	For thou dost ever waken care.	*stir up*
	If thou scape with thy liffe away	
	Thou rules thee well, I dare say."	
	Then said Kay, "That pleaseth mee;	*That's fine with me*
120	Thither let us ryde all three.	
	Such as hee bakes, such shall hee brew;	
	Such as hee shapes, such shall hee sew;	*intends*
	Such as he breweth, such shall he drinke."	
	"That is contrary," said Gawaine, "as I thinke.	*perverse*
125	But if any faire speeche will he gaine,	*respond to*
	Wee shall make him lord within his owne.	*own [castle]*
	If noe faire speech will avayle,	*profit [us]*
	Then to karp on Kay wee will not faile."	*complain*
	Then said the Bishopp, "That senteth mee.	*I assent*
130	Thither lett us ryde all three."	
	When they came to the Carles gate,	
	A hammer they found hanging theratt.	
	Gawaine hent the hammer in his hand	*took*
	And curteouslye on the gates dange.	*knocked*
135	Forth came the porter with still fare	*quietly*
	Saying, "Who is soe bold to knocke there?"	
	Gawaine answered him curteouslye:	
	"Man," hee said, "that is I.	
	Wee be two knights of Arthurs inn	*household*
140	And a bishopp, no moe to min.	*mention*
	Wee have rydden all day in the forrest still	*desolate*
	Till horsse and man beene like to spill.	*perish*
	For Arthurs sake, that is our Kinge,	
	Wee desire my Lord of a nights lodginge	
145	And harbarrow till the day att morne	*hospitality*

That wee may scape away without scorne."   *harm*
Then spake the crabbed knight Sir Kay: *prickly*
"Porter, our errand I reede the say,   *advise you to convey our mission*
Or else the castle gate wee shall breake
150 And the keyes thereof to Arthur take."
The porter sayd with words throe,   *angry*
"Theres no man alive that dares doe soe.
If a hundred such as thou his death had sworne,
Yett he wold ryde on hunting tomorne."   *tomorrow*
155 Then answered Gawain, that was curteous aye,
"Porter, our errand I pray thee say."
"Yes," said the porter, "withouten fayle,
I shall say your errand full well."
As soone as the porter the Carle see   *saw the Carl*
160 Hee kneeled downe upon his knee.
"Yonder beene two knights of Arthurs in   *household*
And a bishopp, no more to myn.
They have roden all day in the forrest still
That horsse and man is like to spill.   *perish*
165 They desire you for Arthurs sake, their King,
To grant them one nights lodginge
And herberrow till the day att morne,
That they may scape away without scorne."
"Noething greeves me," sayd the Carle, "without doubt,
170 But that the knights stand soe long without."   *outside*
With that the porter opened the gates wyde,
And the knights rode in that tyde.   *time*
Their steeds into the stable are tane;   *taken*
The knights into the hall are gone.
175 Heere the Carle sate in his chaire on hye
With his legg cast over the other knee.
His mouth was wyde and his beard was gray;
His lockes on his shoulders lay.
Betweene his browes, certaine,
180 Itt was large there a spann.   *as broad there as*
With two great eyen brening as fyer,
Lord, hee was a lodlye syer.   *loathly sire (lord)*
Over his sholders he bare a bread   *Across; breadth*
Three taylors yards, as clarkes doe reede.   *reckon*

185	His fingars were like to teddar-stakes,	*thick pegs*
	And his hands like breads that wives may bake.	
	Fifty cubitts he was in height.	
	Lord, he was a lothesome wight!	*creature*
	When Sir Gawaine that Carle see	
190	He halched him full curteouslye	*greeted*
	And saith, "Carle of Carlile, God save thee	
	As thou sittes in thy prosperitye."	
	The Carle said, "As Christ me save,	
	Yee shall be welcome for Arthurs sake.	
195	Yet is itt not my part to doe soe,	
	For Arthur hath beene ever my foe.	
	He hath beaten my knights and done them bale	*hurt*
	And send them wounded to my owne hall.	*sent*
	Yett the truth to tell I will not leane,	*lie*
200	I have quitt him the same againe."	*requited (given him back)*
	"That is a kind of knave," said Kay, "without leasing,	*churl's nature; lying*
	Soe to revile a noble king."	*reproach*
	Gawaine heard and made answere,	
	"Kay, thou sayest more then meete weere."	*right*
205	With that they went further into the hall,	
	Where bords were spredd and covered with pall.	*tables; rich cloth*
	And four welpes of great ire	
	They found lying by the fire.	
	There was a beare that did rome,	*wander unleashed*
210	And a bore that did whett his tushes fome;	*boar; foamy tusks*
	Alsoe a bull that did rore,	
	And a lyon that did both gape and rore —	
	The lyon did both gape and gren.	*glare and snarl*
	"O peace, whelpes," said the Carle then.	
215	For that word that the Carle did speake	
	The four whelpes under the bord did creepe.	*table*
	Downe came a lady faire and free	
	And sett her on the Carles knee.	
	One whiles shee harped, another whiles song	*For a time*
220	Both of paramours and lovinge amonge.	*among other subjects*
	"Well were that man," said Gawaine, "that ere were borne	*ever*
	That might lye with that lady till day att morne."	
	"That were great shame," said the Carle free,	

      "That thou sholdest doe me such villanye."

225   "Sir," said Gawaine, "I sayd nought."

      "No, man!" said the Carle; "More thou thought."[1]

      Then start Kay to the flore   *got up*

      And said hee wold see how his palfrey fore.   *fared*

      Both corne and hay he found lyand,   *spread about*

230   And the Carles palfrey by his steed did stand.

      Kay tooke the Carles palfrey by the necke,

      And soone hee thrust him out att the hecke.   *stall door*

      Thus Kay put the Carles fole out,

      And on his backe he sett a clout.   *struck a blow*

235   Then the Carle himselfe hee stood thereby

      And sayd, "This buffett, man, thou shalt abuy."   *pay for*

      The Carle raught Kay such a rapp   *delivered*

      That backward he fell flatt.

      Had itt not beene for a feald of straw,

240   Kayes backe had gone in two.

      Then said Kay, "And thow were without thy hold, *If; own castle*

      Man, this buffett shold be deere sold."   *dearly paid for*

      "What," sayd the Carle, "dost thou menace me?   *threaten*

      I swere by all the soules sicerlye,   *surely*

245   Man, I swere further thore: *then*

      If I heere any malice more

      For this one word that thou hast spoken,   *Beyond*

      Itt is but ernest thou hast gotten."   *a token*

      Then went Kay into the hall,

250   And the Bishopp to him can call,   *did*

      Saith, "Brother Kay, where you have beene?"

      "To looke my palfrey, as I weene."

      Then said the Bishopp, "Itt falleth me   *It happens*

      That my palfrey I must see."

255   Both corne and hay he found lyand

      And the Carles palffrey, as I understand.

      The Bishopp tooke the Carles horsse by the necke,

      And soone hee thrust him out att the hecke.   *stall door*

      Thus he turned the Carles fole out   *warhorse*

---

[1] *"You imagined more (than you said)"*

381

260	And on his backe he sett a clout,	
	Sais, "Wend forth, fole, in the devills way.	
	Who made thee soe bold with my palfrey?"	
	The Carle himselfe he stood thereby:	
	"Man, this buffett thou shalt abuy."	*[And said]*
265	He hitt the Bishopp upon the crowne	*head*
	That his miter and he fell downe.	
	"Mercy," said the Bishopp, "I am a clarke!	*ordained priest*
	Somewhatt I can of Christs werke."	*I have some power through*
	He saith, "By the clergye I sett nothing,	*(The Carle) says*
270	Nor yett by thy miter nor by thy ringe.	
	It fitteth a clarke to be curteous and free	*befits*
	By the conning of his clergy."	*knowledge*
	With that the Bishopp went into the hall,	
	And Sir Gawaine to him can call,	*did*
275	Saith, "Brother Bishopp, where have you beene?"	
	"To looke my palfrey, as I weene."	*look after; guess*
	Then sayd Sir Gawaine, "Itt falleth mee	
	That my palfreye I must needs see."	
	Corne and hay he found enoughe lyand,	
280	And the Carles fole by his did stand.	
	The Carles fole had beene forth in the raine;	
	Therof Sir Gawaine was not faine.	*glad*
	Hee tooke his mantle that was of greene	
	And covered the fole, as I weene;	
285	Sayth, "Stand up, fole, and eate thy meate.	*[He] says; food*
	Thy master payeth for all that wee heere gett."	
	The Carle himselfe stood thereby	
	And thanked him of his curtesye.	
	The Carle tooke Gawaine by the hand,	
290	And both together in the hall they wend.	*made their way*
	The Carle called for a bowle of wine,	
	And soone they settled them to dine.	
	Seventy bowles in that bowle were —	*might be put*
	He was not weake that did itt beare.	*lift*
295	Then the Carle sett itt to his chin	
	And said, "To you I will begin."	*For*
	Fifteen gallons he dranke that tyde	*time*
	And raught to his men on every side.	*And passed it*

Then the Carle said to them anon,

300 "Sirrs, to supper gett you gone."

Gawaine answered the Carle then,

"Sir, att your bidding wee will be ben."   *happy*

"If you be bayne att my bidding   *happy*

You honor me without leasinge."   *lie*

305 They washed all and went to meate

And dranke the wine that was soe sweete.

The Carle said to Gawaine anon,

"A long speare see thou take in thy hand:

Att the buttrye dore take thou thy race,   *pantry door prepare your attack*

310 And marke me well in middest the face."   *aim at*

"A," thought Sir Kay, "that that were I,   *if only*

Then his buffett he shold deere abuy!"

"Well," quoth the Carle, "when thou wilt thou may, *whenever you're ready*

When thou wilt thy strenght assay."   *make trial*

315 "Well, Sir," said Kay, "I said nought."

"Noe," said the Carle, "but more thou thought."

Then Gawaine was full glad of that,

And a long spere in his hand he gatt.

Att the buttery dore he tooke his race   *prepared his attack*

320 And marked the Carle in the middst the face.

The Carle saw Sir Gawaine come in ire   *with violence*

And cast his head under his speare.   *ducked*

Gawaine raught the wall such a rapp   *made against*

The fyer flew out and the speare brake;   *sparks*

325 He stroke a foote into the wall of stone.

A bolder barron was there never none.

"Saft," said the Carle, "thow was to radd."   *Soft; quick*

"I did but, Sir, as you me bade."   *only*

"If thou had hitt me as thou had ment,   *aimed to*

330 Thou had raught me a fell dint."   *given*

The Carle tooke Gawaine by the hand,

And both into a chamber they wend.

A full faire bed there was spred:

The Carles wiffe therin was laid.

335 The Carle said, "Gawaine, of curtesye

Gett into this bedd with this faire ladye.

Kisse thou her thrice before mine eye:

Looke thou doe no other villanye."
The Carle opened the sheetes wyde.
340   Gawaine gott in by the ladyes syde;
Gawaine over her put his arme —
With that his flesh began to warme.
Gawaine had thought to have made infare.   *intercourse*
"Hold!" quoth the Carle, "Man, stopp thee!
345   Itt were great shame," quoth the Carle, "for me
That thou sholdest doe me such villanye.
But arise up, Gawaine, and goe with me;
I shall bring thee to a fairer lady then ever was shee."
The Carle tooke Gawaine by the hand;
350   Both into another chamber they wend.
A faire bedd there found they spred,
And the Carles daughter therin laid.
Saith, "Gawaine, now for thy curtesye
Gett thee to bedd to this faire lady."
355   The Carle opened the sheetes wyde;
Sir Gawaine gott in by the ladyes side.
Gawaine put his arme over that sweet thing.
"Sleepe, daughter," sais the Carle, "on my blessing."   *says; with*
The Carle turned his backe and went his way
360   And lockt the dore with a silver kaye.
On the other morning when the Carle rose   *next*
Unto his daughters chamber he goes.
"Rise up, Sir Gawaine, and goe with mee,
A marvelous sight I shall lett thee see."
365   The Carle tooke him by the hand,
And both into another chamber they wend.
And there they found many a bloody serke   *battle shirt*
Which were wrought with curyous werke.   *designs*
Fifteen hundred dead mens bones
370   They found upon a rooke att once.   *rock*
"Alacke!" quoth Sir Gawaine; "What have beene here?"   *has happened*
Saith, "I and my welpes have slaine all there."   *[The Carl] says; these*
Then Sir Gawaine, curteous and kind,
He tooke his leave away to wend
375   And thanked the Carle and the ladyes there
Right as they worthy were.   *Accordingly*

"Nay," said the Carle, "wee will first dine,
And then thou shalt goe with blessing mine." *depart*
After dinner, the sooth to say,
380   The Carle tooke Gawaine to a chamber gay
Where were hanginge swords towe. *two*
The Carle soone tooke one of tho
And sayd to the knight then,
"Gawaine, as thou art a man,
385   Take this sword and stryke of my head." *off*
"Nay," said Gawaine, "I had rather be dead.
For I had rather suffer pine and woe *pain*
Or ever I wold that deede doe."
The Carle sayd to Sir Gawaine,
390   "Looke thou doe as I thee saine,
And therof be not adread.
But shortly smite of my head: *in short order; off*
For if thou wilt not doe itt tyte *quickly*
For ssooth thy head I will ofsmyte." *strike off*
395   To the Carle said Sir Gawaine,
"Sir, your bidding shall be done."
He stroke the head the body froe: *from*
And he stood up a man thoe *then*
Of the height of Sir Gawaine —
400   The certaine soothe, withouten laine. *lie*
The Carle sayd, "Gawaine, God blese thee!
For thou hast delivered mee
From all false witchcrafft —
I am delivred att the last.
405   By nigromancé thus was I shapen *magic (necromancy); transformed*
Till a knight of the Round Table
Had with a sword smitten of my head,
If he had grace to doe that deede. *my permission*
Itt is forty winters agoe *years*
410   Since I was transformed soe.
Since then none lodged within this woonn *dwelling*
But I and my whelpes driven them downe. *Except that; destroyed*
And but if hee did my bidding soone *unless*
I killed him and drew him downe,
415   Every one but only thee.

	Christ grant thee of his mercye:	*[some] of*
	He that the world made reward thee this,	*[for] this*
	For all my bale thou hast turned to blisse.	*sorrow*
	Now will I leave that lawe;	*custom*
420	There shall no man for me be slawe.	*through; slain*
	And I purpose for their sake	
	A chantrey in this place to make,	
	And five preists to sing for aye	
	Untill itt be doomesday.	
425	And Gawaine, for the love of thee	
	Every one shall bee welcome to me."	*traveler*
	Sir Gawaine and the young lady clere,	
	The Bishopp weded them in fere.	*together*
	The Carle gave him for his wedding	*for celebration of the*
430	A staffe, a miter, and a ringe.	
	He gave Sir Kay, that angry knight,	
	A blood-red steede and a wight.	*powerful (one)*
	He gave his daughter, the sooth to say,	
	An ambling white palfrey:	
435	The fairest hee was on the mold;	
	Her palfrey was charged with gold.	*laden*
	Shee was soe gorgeous and soe gay	*handsome*
	No man cold tell her array.	*could justly describe*
	The Carle commanded Sir Gawaine to wend	
440	And say unto Arthur our King	
	And pray him that hee wold,	
	For His love that Judas sold	*[i.e., Jesus]*
	And for His sake that in Bethelem was borne,	
	That hee wold dine with him tomorne.	*[Arthur with the Carl]*
445	Sir Gawaine sayd the Carle unto,	
	"For ssooth, I shall your message doe."	*perform*
	Then they rode singing by the way	
	With the ladye that was gay.	*handsome*
	They were as glad of that lady bright	
450	As ever was fowle of the daylyght.	
	They told King Arthur where they had beene,	
	And what adventures they had seene.	
	"I thanke God," sayd the King, "cozen Kay,	
	That thou didst on live part away."	*get out alive*

455	"Marry," sayd Sir Kay againe,	*Indeed*
	"Of my liffe I may be faine.	*glad*
	For His love that was in Bethlem borne	
	You must dine with the Carle tomorne."	
	In the dawning of the day they rode:	
460	A merryer meeting was never made.	
	When they together were mett,	
	Itt was a good thing, I you hett.	*promise*
	The trumpetts plaid att the gate,	
	With trumpetts of silver theratt.	*right there*
465	There was all manner of minstrelsye —	
	Harpe, gyttorne, and sowtrye.	*(stringed instruments)*
	Into the hall the King was fett	*escorted*
	And royallye in seat was sett.	
	By then the dinner was readye dight;	*prepared*
470	Tables were covered all on height.	*Tables on trestles were all set*
	Then to wash they wold not blinn,	*hold off*
	And the feast they can beginn.	*did*
	There they were mached arright,	*paired*
	Every lady against a knight,	
475	And minstrells sate in windowes faire	*at window seats*
	And playd on their instruments cleere.	
	Minstrells for worshipp att every messe	*banquet*
	Full lowd they cry, "Largnesse!"	*Largess (give generously)*
	The Carle bade the King, "Doe gladlye,	*Enjoy*
480	For heere yee gett great curtesye."	
	The King said, "By Seint Michaell,	
	This dinner liketh me full well."	*pleases*
	He dubd the Carle a knight anon.	*made*
	He gave him the country of Carlile soone,	*immediately*
485	And made him Erle of all that land,	
	And after knight of the Table Round.	
	The King said, "Knight, I tell thee	
	Carlile shall thy name bee."	
	When the dinner was all done,	
490	Every knight tooke his leave soone	
	To wend forward soberlye	
	Home into their owne countrye.	
	He that made us all with His hand,	

Both the sea and the land,
495 Grant us all for His sake
This false world to forsake —
And out of this world when wee shall wend
To heavens blisse our soules bringe.
God grant us grace itt may soe bee.
500 Amen, say all, for charitye.

FINIS. *The End*

Notes

Abbreviations: P = Percy Folio; M = Madden's edition; HF = Hales' and Furnivall's edition; K = Kurvinen's edition. See Select Bibliography for these editions.

19 *grass-time*. The term refers to the "grease" time, when herds have fattened; see explanation of this idiom, and of the assay or "breaking" of the deer in *Ragnelle*, line 46 note.

20 *breake the deere*. This term is frequently used for the prescribed, almost ritualized, dressing of the dead animal. *Sir Gawain and the Green Knight* (lines 1325 ff.) offers a striking and detailed account, in which *brek* occurs at line 1333; briefer descriptions of the hunt appear in *Ragnelle* (lines 46 ff.), *Carlisle* (lines 29 ff., 85–87, 103 ff.), *Avowyng* (lines 25 ff.), and *Awntyrs* (lines 5 ff.).

21 ff. On the catalogue of knights, see notes on the corresponding passage in *Carlisle*, lines 34 ff.

31 *cozen Mordred*. In *Cornwall*, line 1, Arthur calls Gawain "cuzen" or kinsman; see note on *Carlisle*, line 49, which refers to "The Kyngus uncull, Syr Mordrete."

55 ff. Sir Ironside's coat of arms consists of a field of blue, emblazoned in gold with *a griffon lesse or more*. The phrase *lesse or more*, which may have been composed for metrical rather than descriptive purposes, seems to suggest arms decorated with more than one griffin, though how the animals are arranged is unclear. *Lesse or more* may indicate the presence of an inescutcheon, i.e. one smaller coat of arms set within a larger to signify a family connection, or, geratting, where the family symbol or totem is repeated across the field of the coat. The griffin, a mythical beast, may symbolize the traits of the bearer, as is suggested in John Trevor's fifteenth-century Welsh *Llyfr Arfau* [*Book of Arms*]: "A griffon borne in arms signifies that the first to bear it was a strong, pugnacious man in whom were found two distinct natures and qualities: for the griffon is a bird in its head and talons and resembles an eagle, and its hind part

389

is like that of a lion" (in Evan John Jones' *Medieval Heraldry: Some Fourteenth-Century Heraldic Works* [Cardiff, Wales: William Lewis, 1903], p. 45). Also, Lycurgus, the King of Thrace in Chaucer's Knight's Tale, is intimidatingly described as glaring around "lik a grifphon" (line 2133). Ironside's coat of arms contains a *difference*, or cadence mark designed to distinguish it from that of his father or other senior kinsman. In this case it is a mullet, a figure resembling a five-pointed star (cp. with Gawain's pentangle [line 664] in *Sir Gawain and the Green Knight*), which became the particular mark of the third son of a family: "originally the mullet was a spur rowel, from the French word *molette*, but it now has a stereotyped form and more often symbolizes a star" (J. P. Brooke-Little, *An Heraldic Alphabet*, rev. ed., [London: Robson Books, 1985], p. 145). Griffins, either as crests or ornamentation, appear elsewhere in Arthurian poems in association with Gawain. In *Awntyrs*, this hero bears arms engraved with *griffons of golde* (line 509). In *Libeaus Desconus*, Arthur gives Gawain's son (i.e., The Fair Unknown) "a rich sheeld all over gilte / with a griffon soe gay" (lines 92–93 in Hales' and Furnivall's edition of the Percy Folio [see Bibliography of Editions and Works Cited], vol. 2, p. 419); in the Cotton version of this romance (edited by Mills [see Bibliography of Editions and Works Cited]) "Lybeau Desconus" receives a golden shield with a griffin (lines 78–81). Interestingly, there also exists a fifteenth-century depiction of a coat of arms composed of a green field emblazoned with three gold griffins registered to "SIR GAWAYNE *the good knyght*" (Harleian MS 2169; this is reproduced in *The Ancestor: A Quarterly Review of County and Family History, Heraldry and Antiquities* 3 [1902], p. 192; see also General Introduction, note 21). The description of Ironside's arms in both *Carlisle* and *Carle* suggests by its placement some confusion with the distinct armorial bearings associated with Gawain and his kin. See *Awntyrs*, line 509 and note, and *Carlisle*, lines 82 ff. and note. Baron Simon de Montagu (d. 1317) bore arms resembling those of Sir Ironside, composed of blue and gold, with, depending on the particular campaign, either one or two griffins — the animal assumed to be the symbol of his house, which died out in 1428.

61 *they*. P: *the*; HF prints *thé* in instances where the scribal spelling *the* represents "they." I emend to *they* here and at lines 73, 81, 82, and 459. Elsewhere the scribe uses *they* as the form of the demonstrative adjective or the definite article. I have emended this spelling to *the* at lines 63, 170, 171, 215, 216, 287, 289, 290, 295, 299, 331, 345, 349, 359, 365, and 375.

121 ff. All these remarks are proverbial; see *Carlisle* line 160 and note.

125   *gaine*. This is a broken rhyme, whose meaning is unclear. M in a note suggests the emendation *him* for *he*, which would give, "win him [the Carl] over." *gaine* may be the adverbial form (meaning "back," "in return") used as a verb, giving "reply to," "respond to"; or it may be the noun *gein*, "reward," "profit" (whose northern form, *gawin*, would suit the rhyme) used as a verb, giving "reward," "respond favorably to."

152   *Theres*. K: *There's*, with no indication of punctuation in P.

179 ff.   Given the obviously fantastic dimensions of the Carle, who is clearly a fairy-tale giant, it may seem pointless to note that his size here far exceeds that in *Carlisle*: here his shoulders are nine feet broad (rather than six), and he is seventy-five feet tall (as opposed to twenty-seven in *Carlisle*; see lines 256 ff.).

269   This overt anti-clerical (or, more precisely, anti-episcopal in its focus on *miter* and *ringe*) outburst seems to reflect a post-Reformation rather than a medieval attitude. In *Carlisle*, when Baldwin claims a similar benefit of clergy, the Carle simply attacks his want of courtesy. *Turke*, lines 154 ff., contains a similar intrusive anti-clericalism.

309   *race*. In *Carlisle*, the Carl asks Gawain to "take thy passe," to take his position at the door.

367   *bloody serke*. This is a traditional phrase; see note at line 535 of *Carlisle*.

379 ff.   The beheading scene, by which the Carle is "delivered . . . From all false witch-crafft" (lines 402–03) is inexplicably missing from *Carlisle*. The manner of disenchantment resembles the similar episode in *Turke* (see lines 271 ff. and note). The Carle's revelation that he had been "by nigromancé . . . shapen" (line 405) echoes Ragnelle's use of the same term; see *Ragnelle*, line 691 and note.

The Jeaste of Sir Gawain

Introduction

The *Jeaste of Sir Gawain* combines two widely separated but interwoven episodes from a twelfth-century French poetic romance, the anonymous continuation of Chrétien de Troyes' *Perceval*. In this poem, Gawain's union with an unknown woman leads many years later to combat with her brother, Bran de Lys (Brandles in *Jeaste*); this encounter ends, however, when the sister of Bran de Lis intervenes, presenting to her lover and her brother the son she has borne to Gawain, Ginglain (called elsewhere Le Bel Inconnu, or, as in *Carlisle*, Libeaus Desconus, The Fair Unknown). In the end, Arthur inducts Bran de Lys into the fellowship of the Round Table. The Middle English *Jeaste* stitches together these relatively minor components of Gawain's part in the much larger story of the Grail, and, by omitting the reconciliation that ends the episodes in the French romance, turns them into a stark series of trials of Gawain's martial prowess. Gawain's role in the *Jeaste* therefore differs somewhat from his character as the knight of *troth* in other Middle English romances; here he more closely resembles the French Gauvain, whose exploits often involve, or even start with, love affairs. The surviving transcription of the poem lacks the opening episode. In the original French, this was a *chanson d'aventure*, a chance meeting while wandering in the woods; in the *Jeaste*, Gawain may have been part of an Arthurian hunt ("chase," line 2), as in *Ragnelle*, *Carlisle*, *Awntyrs*, *Avowyng*, and other romances. Gawain's venture into the woods (not localized here as Inglewood Forest, or connected to Carlisle) transmutes from the pursuit of wild creatures to the stalking of a strange lady in a pavilion. In his study of the narrative core of *Ragnelle* and other loathly lady stories, Eisner suggests that the quest to discover what women most desire traditionally began with a seduction or a rape, as Chaucer's *Wife of Bath's Tale* in fact does. On this argument, an episode like the one that opens the *Jeaste* would have been an integral part of *Ragnelle*; the union of a strange woman with Gawain or another hero would thus have formed the kernel story that initiates the action in a widely known Arthurian romance. (All but Gower's version of the story explicitly connect the tale to the Round Table.)

Despite its amorous beginnings, however, the *Jeaste* is not at all about romantic love. The succession of combats that make up the plot of the *Jeaste* spell out the nature of honor among men. Yet the least active figure — the nameless sister/ daughter/lover — turns out to be the pivotal character, through whom male relations of power and honor receive definition. Retaining the love (and the body) of the woman constitutes Gawain's best proof of manhood, for it brings Sir Gylbert to confess, "Therfore I dare well saye he ys a manne" (line 315). The fundamental cause that sets the anonymous lady's male relations against Gawain is that he has improperly taken from them her "love" — that is, her sexual person, in which they have proprietary rights. The father claims that in possessing the daughter without permission, Gawain has "done *me* great vyllanye" and "done *me* muche dyshonoure" (lines 18, 26; my italics), and that her "loss," physical and symbolic, harms him more than the loss of his own blood (line 102). Through proper conduct — by testing each other out according to the rules of chivalric combat, "all gentlenes to fullfyll" (line 427) — Gawain, Gylbert, Gyamoure, Terrye, and Brandles establish their proper identities, their names as worshipful knights. Like *Ragnelle*, the *Jeaste* dramatizes the signal function of Woman as the medium by which men establish relations among themselves: in the French poem the woman eventually returns, bearing a son, and so consolidates the bond between Gauvin and Bran de Lys, whereas here, after being beaten "bothe backe and syde" (line 509), the lady vanishes, without name or trace:

> Than the lady gate her awaye —
> They sawe her never after that daye;
> She went wandrynge to and fro.
> (lines 524–26)

Sir Gylbert and his sons are left to lick their wounds, and Gawain returns "home" to the court (line 529) to share his adventures with his uncle, King Arthur.

In its attention to individual combat and martial prowess as the staple of the plot, the *Jeaste* resembles *Gologras*. But here each of the four fights is compressed into a formulaic exchange of blows, so that *Jeaste* lacks the spectacular and lavish details that themselves constitute chivalric encounter in the Scots poem. A chivalric residue is apparent in the repeated focus upon the knights' discomfort and disgrace in their unhorsing, and the accompanying emphasis upon the identity of these fighters as mounted warriors. But the *Jeaste* indicates its popular status by its very title: "jeaste" (more often spelled "geste," from Latin *gesta*, "things done," memorable or heroic deeds) is a generic title for a romance of derring-do. By the end of the Middle Ages it had, at least among literary writers, come to mean a popular or degraded form of chivalric romance, and was well on its way to attaining its modern meaning of "jest," a frivolous or laughable story.

Introduction

The Jeaste of Syr Gawayne comes down to us in a copy written out by an Arthurian enthusiast of the Elizabethan age; this copy was itself based upon an earlier sixteenth-century print of the poem, perhaps that entered in the Stationers' Register (1557 or 1558), licensing John Kynge to print a book of this title. Still another copy was printed by Thomas Petyt (date unknown); of this, one leaf survives, corresponding to the last fifty-three lines of the surviving transcript. The *Jeaste*'s language indicates it was composed in the second half of the fifteenth century in the South Midlands. It is composed in remarkably regular six-line tail-rhyme stanzas, running *aabccb*. The *Jeaste*'s survival in multiple copies — hand-written and printed, medieval (at least in origin) and Renaissance — bears further witness to Gawain's enduring popularity as a hero. As a thoroughly popular production, the *Jeaste* takes its place in the company of other post-medieval versions of chivalric romances, like those of the Percy Folio Manuscript. One can easily imagine it entertaining the same audiences who enjoyed the performances of Captain Cox in the 1570s (see General Introduction); indeed, the Captain was just the sort of reader and performer who might have carried such a story in his collection "bound with a whipcord," ready for recitation.

Text

The *Jeaste* survives in an incomplete, hand-written version (dated 1564), probably made from a now lost print issued by John Kynge in 1557 or 1558 (Oxford, Bodley MS 21835, formerly Douce 261). The final leaf of a second print, issued by Thomas Petyt, has also survived (London, British Library MS Harley 5927 Arts 32). The manuscript transcription is signed E.B., and contains some drawings as well as several other romances (*Isumbras*, *Degaré*, and *Eglamoure*), all apparently also copied from early prints. The hand is clear, formal, italic script, with few abbreviations. The *Jeaste* has been printed previously only once, in Madden's edition. I note differences between the manuscript and the print in the notes.

Select Bibliography

Manuscripts

Oxford, Bodley MS 21835 (formerly Douce 261).

London, British Library MS Harley 5927 Arts 32.

The Jeaste of Sir Gawain

Editions (arranged chronologically)

Madden, Frederic. 1839. See Bibliography of Editions and Works Cited.

Child, Francis James. 1884. See Bibliography of Editions and Works Cited.

Criticism

Bennett, R. E. "Sources of *The Jeaste of Syr Gawayne*." *Journal of English and Germanic Philology* 33 (1934), 57–63.

The Jeaste of Sir Gawain

	And sayde, "I dreede no threte;	*fear*
	I have founde youe here in my chase."	*hunt*
	And in hys armes he gan her brace,	*embrace*
	With kyssynge of mowthes sweete.	
5	There Syr Gawayne made suche chere,	*was so good mannered*
	That greate frendeshyp he founde there,	*affection*
	With that fayre lady so gaye;	*gracious*
	Suche chere he made, and suche semblaunce	*proper conduct*
	That longed to love, he had her countenaunce	*was appropriate to; favor*
10	Withoute any more delaye.	
	He had not taryed with her longe,	
	But there came a knyght tall and stronge;	
	Unto the pavylion he wente.	
	He founde Syr Gawayne with that lady fayre:	
15	"Syr knyght, thow makest an evyll repayre	*visit*
	That wyll make the shente.	*leave you ruined*
	Yt ys my doughter that thow lyest by.	
	Thowe hast done me great vyllanye —	
	Amende yt mayst thou nought.	
20	Thou haste greate fortune with that dame:	*success*
	Tyll nowe never man coulde for shame.[1]	
	I see, Syr knyght, that thou hast wrought,	*what; done*
	Wherefore I see fortune ys thy frynde.	*friend*
	But hastely unto harnes nowe thou wynde."	*armor; go*
25	Than sayed that bolde knyght:	*(i.e., the father)*

---

[1] *Until now no man has been able (to have sexual relations with her) because of her modesty*

397

"Thou hast done me muche dyshonoure,
And may not amende yt, by Mary floure!   *flower [of women]*
Therefore hastelye the dyght."   *prepare yourself*

Than bespake Syr Gawayne, and thus he sayde:
30 "I suppose I have the love of the mayde,   *agree that*
Suche grace on her have I founde.   *with her*
But and youe be her father deere,   *if*
Syr, amendes nowe wyll I make here,
As I am to knyghthode bounde.

35 Nowe all forewardes I wyll fullfyll,   *obligations*
And make amendes youe untyll,   *to you*
And lette me passe quyte."   *If you allow me to leave free and clear*
"Naye," sayed the olde knyght than.   *then*
"Fyrst wyll we assaye oure myghtes as we can,   *prowess*
40 Or else yt were a dyspyte."   *an outrage*

Nowe sayde Gawayne, "I graunte yt the,
Sythe yt none otherwise wyll be:
Nedes must that nedes shall."   *What will be must be*
He toke hys stronge horse by the brydle,
45 And lyghtly lepte into the saddle,
As a knyght good and royall.

He toke a spere that was greate and stronge,
And forthe he wente, a large furlonge,
And turned hys horse with mayne.   *strength*
50 They feutred theyr speares, these knyghtes good,   *braced their spears for combat*
And russhed together with eger moode,   *fierce resolve*
Above on the mountayne.

Gawayne smotte thys knyght so soore,   *struck; harshly*
That hys horse with strenght he overthrewe thore,   *there*
55 And on the grounde he laye upright.   *stretched out*
Syr Gawayne turned hys horse agayne
And sayde, "Syr knyght, wyll ye any more fayne?"   *do you desire any more*
"Naye," he sayed, for he ne myght.

"I yelde me, Syr knyght, into thy hande,
60 For thou arte to styffe for me to stande.   *too powerful; withstand*
My lyfe thou graunte me."   *please grant*
"On thys covenaunte," Syr Gawayne sayde: *agreement*
"That ye do no harme unto the mayde,
I am agreed that yt so be.

65 "Also ye shall swere on my swerde here,
That none armes agaynst me ye shall beare,
Neyther todaye nor tonyght.
And then take your horse, and wende your waye,
And I shall do the best that I maye,
70 As I am a trewe knyght."

There thys knyght sware, and dyd passe;   *went off*
Syr Gylbert called he was,
A ryche earle, styffe and stoure.   *strong*
He sayde, "Syr kngyht, take good kepe,   *stay on guard*
75 For better shalt thou be assayled or thou slepe,   *before*
With many a sharpe shoure."   *attack*

Than sayd Gawayne, "I beleve right well.
Whan they come, youe shall here tell   *take account*
Howe the game shall goo.   *sword play*
80 I am nowe here in my playnge —   *ready for contest*
I wyll not go awaye for no threatynge,
Or that I will feele more woo." [1]

Than Syr Gylberte wente hys waye.
Hys horse was gone downe the valaye,
85 On foote he must hym abyde;   *remain*
He yode downe, without wordes more.   *went*
The strokes greaved hym full soore;
That bated muche hys pryde.   *abated*

---

[1] *Before (or until) I suffer painful defeat*

Syr Gawayne had smytten hym in the sholderblade;
90   After hys walkynge the blode out shade.   *Because of; flowed*
He rested hym under a tree.
He had not rested hym but a lyttell space,
But one of hys sonnes came to that place —
Syr Gyamoure called was he.

95   "Father," he sayde "what ayleth youe nowe?
Hathe any man in thys forrest hurte youe?
Me thynke full faste ye blede!"
"Yea, sonne," he sayde, "by Goddes grame!   *wrath*
A knyght hath done me spyte and shame,   *dishonor*
100   And lost I have my stede.   *steed*

"Also he hath layne by thy syster, by the Rode!   *Cross*
That greveth me more than shedynge of my blode,
And the dyspyte was well more: *outrage was still greater*
And he hath made me to sweare
105   That todaye none armes shall I beare,
Agaynst hym, by Goddes ore!"   *mercy*

"Father, nowe be of good chere,
And I shall rewarde hym, as ye shall here,   *requite*
As I am a trewe knyght!
110   He shall beate me, or I shall beate hym.
I shall hym beate be he never so grymme,   *fierce*
And hys death todyght."   *bring about*

"Lett be, sonne Gyamoure, nowe I the praye!   *Stop; you*
Thou speakest more than thou maye: *should*
115   That shalt thoue feele soone.   *you*
There shalt thoue mete with a knyght stronge
That wyll paye hys lyveray large and longe,   *make good on his reputation*
Or thy journey be all done."   *Before your encounter*

"Nowe farewell, father," Gyamoure sayde.
120   He toke the waye to hys syster the mayde
As fast as he myght on the gate;   *path*
Unto the pavylion he toke the waye,

The Jeaste of Sir Gawain

There as Syr Gawayne and hys syster laye,　　　　　　　　*Who; strife*
That thought on no debate.

125　"Aryse," he sayed, "thou knyght stronge of hande,
And geve me battaylle on thys lande.
Hye the fast anone right!　　　　　　　　*Hasten; immediately*
Thou hast hurte my father todaye,
And layne by my syster, that fayre may:　　　　　　　　*maiden*
130　Therfore thy deathe ys dyght."　　　　　　　　*ordained*

Than sayde Gawayne, "Though yt be so,
Amendes I wyll make or that I goo,　　　　　　　　*before I go further*
Yf that I have mysdone.
Better yt ys nowe to accorde right,　　　　　　　　*agree in justice*
135　Than we two nowe in battayll shulde fyght.
Therfore go from me soone."　　　　　　　　*right away*

"Nay," sayed Gyamoure, "that shall not bee.
That daye, knyght, shalt thow never see,
For to suffer suche a skorne.　　　　　　　　*[That I should] suffer such dishonor*
140　Aryse in haste, and that anone,
For with the wyll I fyght alone,
As God lett me be borne!"　　　　　　　　*God made me*

Gawayne sawe no better bote,　　　　　　　　*solution then*
And wyghtelye he lepte on foote.　　　　　　　　*nimbly*
145　Hys horse was fast hym bye;
Into the saddle wightelye he sprente,　　　　　　　　*sprang*
And in hys hande hys speare he hentte,　　　　　　　　*seized*
And loked full egerlye.　　　　　　　　*fiercely*

Eyther turned hys horse than awaye　　　　　　　　*Each one*
150　A furlonges lenght, I dare well saye,
Above on the mountayne.
They ranne together, those knightes good,
That theyr horses sydes ranne on bloode,
Eyther to other, certayne.　　　　　　　　*Each against*

155　What nedeth nowe more tale to tell?
　　　Gawayne smotte hym with hys speare so well,
　　　That he fell flatte to the grounde;
　　　Hys horse was fyers, and went hys waye, *vigorous*
　　　And hurte was the knyght ther as he laye.
160　Syr Gawayne asked hym in that stounde: *at that point*

　　　"Syr knight wyll ye any more?"
　　　"Naye," he sayde, "I am hurte so sore
　　　I maye not my selfe welde. *get full control of myself*
　　　I yelde me, syr knyght, and save my lyfe,
165　For with the I wyll no more stryffe, *wish*
　　　For thowe hast wonne the felde."

　　　"Syr, on thys covenaunte I the graunte,
　　　So ye wyll make me faythe and warraunte, *give me good faith; guarantee*
　　　Todaye agaynst me no armes to beare:
170　Sweare thys othe on my swearde bright." *sword*
　　　"Yes," he sayde, "I wyll, as I am trewe knight,
　　　That thys daye I wyll not youe deare. *hurt*

　　　"Nowe fare well, knyght, so God me amende!
　　　For I see fortune ys thy great frende —
175　That sheowith in the todaye; *is obvious through your actions*
　　　There ys no bote to stryve agayne, *fight again*
　　　For thou arte a knyght full stronge of mayne. *might*
　　　Fare well, and have good daye."

　　　Thus Gyamoure wente downe the mountayne hye.
180　On foote he wente full werelye; *wearily*
　　　Hys father soone hym spyed.
　　　"A! wellcome," he sayed, "my sonne Gyamoure.
　　　Me thynke thou hast not spede well thys stoure; *fared; in this battle*
　　　That full well I see thys tyde. *at this time*

185　"Thou went on horsebacke, lyke a good knyght,
　　　And nowe I see thou arte dolefully dyght; *sorrowfully served*
　　　That maketh all my care."
　　　"Father," he sayde, "yt wyll none otherwise be.

| | Yonder knyght hath wonne me in warre so fre, | *defeated; honorable combat* |
| 190 | And hathe wounded me full sore. | |

	"Forsothe," sayde Gyamoure, "I wyll not lye,	
	He ys a stronge knyght, bolde and hardye.	
	Of Arthures courte I trowe he ys;	*guess*
	I suppose on of the Rounde Table,	*[he is] one*
195	For at nede he ys both stronge and hable.	*in a pinch; able*
	So have I founde hym, withouten mysse."	*make no mistake*

	Right so as they spake the one to the other,	
	There came to them the seconde brother,	
	Syr Tyrry was hys name;	
200	He came rydynge on a jolye coursyer,	*warhorse*
	Dryvinge by leapes, as the wylde fyer.	*Galloping*
	The knyght was of good fame.	*renowned*

	He was not ware of hys father deare,	
	But hys brother called hym neare,	
205	And sayde, "Syr, nowe abyde!"	
	He than turned hys horse, that knyght so gaye,	
	By leapes out of straye;	*aside*
	Hys hearte was full of pryde.	

	Than founde he hys father all blodye,	
210	And hys brother was wounded syckerlye.	*indeed*
	In hys hearte he began to be syke:	*sick*
	"A! Syr, who hath wounded youe?" quod he;	
	"Avenged on hym nowe wyll I be,	
	That shall hym myslyke."	*So that it shall hurt him*

215	"Iwys, sonne, yt ys a knyght stronge	
	That hath done us thys wronge,	
	Above on the mountayne.	
	He hath me wounded passynge soore,	*with extreme pain*
	And I trowe thy brother he hathe well more,	*even more*
220	And by thy syster he hathe layne.	

Therfore go nowe, as a knyght good,
And avenge the shedynge of thy fathers blood,
As faste as ever thou maye.
Loke that thou fayle not for no cowardyse,
225 But mete hym in the myghtyest wyse,   *take him on; way*
For he ys good at asaye."   *in combat*

"I see well, father, he ys a knyght stronge.
But he hathe done youe greate wronge   *If he had not done*
Yt wolde be harde hym to wynne;   *defeat*
230 But never the later I shall do my myght.   *nonetheless; utmost*
Hys strenght assaye nowe I shall in fyght,   *test*
Yf he were of the devyls kynne."   *Even if; kin*

Thys knyght Syr Terry turned hys horse,
And up the mountayne he rode with force,
235 As fast as he myght dryve.
He came to the pavylion, with greate pryde:
"Have done, syr knyght! Thy horse bestryde,
For with the I am at stryve."   *at enmity*

Syr Gawayne loked out at the pavylyon doore,
240 And sawe thys knyght armed hym before;
To hym he sayed verelye: *truly*
"Syr, yf I have ought to youe offended,
I am ready to make yt to be amended,
By mylde mother Marye!"

245 "Naye, syr knyght, yt maye not so be.
Therfore make the ready faste to me,
In all the haste that thou maye;   *you may*
For be God that me dere bought,   *by God who saved me*
Make amendes mayest thou nought.
250 Therfore nowe lett us playe."   *join in battle*

Gawayne sawe none other bote than;   *solution*
Hys horse he toke as a worthye man,
And into the saddle he sprente;
He toke hys horse with a greate randone, —   *mounted; rush*

255	"Nowe, Syr knyght, lette me have done,	*make proof*
	What in youre hearte ys mente."	

"Lo! Here I am," sayde Syr Terrye,
"For to the I have greate envye."   *anger*
And together gan they dasshe —
260 They russhed together with suche debate   *such a clash*
That marveyll yt was howe that they sate,   *stayed mounted*
They gave suche a crasshe!

Syr Terrye spake in that place,   *groaned*
And Gawayne fought faste in that race,   *charge*
265 And throughe the sholder hym pyght;   *pierced*
And caste hym over the horse backe,
That in the earth hys helme stacke,   *stuck*
That nyghe hys death he was dyght.   *near; left*

Syr Gawayne than sayed on hyght: *aloud*
270 "Syr knyght, wyll ye any more fyght?"
He aunswered hym, "Naye!
I am so soore hurte I may no more stande.
Therfore I yelde me into thy hande;
Of mercye I the praye."

275 "What," sayde Gawayne, "ys that youre boast greate?   *that [the outcome of]*
I wende youe woulde have foughten tyll ye had sweate!   *[worked up a] sweat*
Ys youre strenght all done?"
"Yea, syr, in fayth, so God me nowe save!
Of me thou mayste no more crave,   *demand*
280 For all my myght ys gone.

"Thou haste today wonne thre knyghtes,   *defeated*
The father, and two sonnes, that well fyghtes,
Worshypfullye under thy shyelde.   *In honorable chivalric combat*
And yf thou maye wynne oure eldest brother,
285 I call thee the best knyght, and none other,
That ever fought in fyelde.   *on the field*

"For he ys full wyght, I warne youe welle: *powerful, I advise you*
He endureth better than doth the steele,

405

    And that shalte thou soone see.

290   But he be thy matche, I can not knowe,

    Of knyghthode thoue haste no felowe, [1]

    On my fayth I ensure thee."

    "Nowe," quod Gawayne, "lette hym be.   *leave him aside*

    And, Syr knyght, make an othe to me,

295   That this daye thou do me no greve;   *harm*

    And thou shalt passe fro me all quyte,   *free*

    Where as ys nowe thy moste delyght,   *Which is; greatest desire*

    Withoute any moore repreve."   *rebuke*

    Syr Terrye sayde, "Therto I graunte.

300   Farewell nowe! God be thy warrante."   *safekeeping*

    Full weykelye he wente on foote;   *feebly*

    He lefte never tyll he came there,   *stopped*

    Where as hys father and Gyamoure were,

    That carefull heartes had, God wote.   *sorrowful; knows*

305   Than bespake Gyamoure, hys yongest brother:

    "Syr, thou hast gotten as we have, and non other;   *received*

    That knewe I well yt shoulde so be."

    "By God!" sayd Syr Terrye, "so nowe yt ys.

    He ys a devyll, forsothe ywys,   *for absolute certainty*

310   And that ys proved on me."

    "Yea," quod Syr Gylbart, that Earle so olde;

    "He ys a knyght bothe stronge and bolde,

    And fortune ys hys frende;

    My doughters love he hath clene wanne.   *completely*

315   Therfore I dare well saye he ys a manne,

    Whereever that he wende."   *may go*

    As they thre stode thus talkynge,

    They hearde a manne full loude synge,

    That all the woode ronge: *rung*

---

[1] Lines 290–91: *If he is not a match for you, I cannot think / That you have an equal in knighthood*

320 "That ys my sonne Brandles so gaye;   *[Gylbert says:]*
      Whan he seeth us in suche araye,
      He wyll leave hys songe."

      By than they sawe the knight comynge;
      A grene boughe in hys hande he dyd brynge,
325 Syttynge on a joylye coursyere.   *warhorse*
      Hys horse was trapped in redde velvett;   *decked out*
      Many ouches of golde theron was sette.   *ornaments*
      Of knyghthode he had no peere.

      Allso hys horse was armed before —   *in front*
330 The headde and the brest, and no more,
      And that in fyne steele.
      Hymselfe was armed passynge sure,   *most stoutly*
      In harneys that woulde strokes endure,   *armor*
      That had bene proved right wele.

335 Thys knyght bare on hys hedde a pomell gaye.   *an ornamental boss*
      Syttynge on hys horse, stertynge oute of the waye, *changing his course*
      By leapes he came aboute.   *turned around*
      A shyelde he had, that was of renowne: *remarkable*
      He bare theryn a blacke fawcowne;   *falcon*
340 The shyelde was of sylver withoute.   *on the outside*

      Also in hys hande a spere he bare,
      Bothe stronge and longe, I make youe ware,   *tell you*
      And of a trustye tree;   *reliable wood*
      There was an headde theron of steele wrought,
345 The best that myght be made or bought,
      And well assayed had be.   *tried out; been*

      Theron of pleasaunce a kercheyf dyd honge; *handsomely a pennon did hang*
      I wote yt was more than thre elles longe,   *about twelve feet*
      Enbrodered all withe golde.
350 He was a knyght of large and lenght,   *big and tall*
      And proved well of muche strenght,
      Assaye hym whoso woulde.   *Test*

Spurres of golde also he had on,
And a good swerde, that wolde byte abone.   *above [all others]*
355 Thus came he dryvynge,   *in a rush*
Tyll he came there as hys father was;
Whan he all sawe, he sayde, "Alas!
Thys ys an evyll tydynge."   *piece of news*

Whan he sawe hys father all blodye,
360 And hys two brethern hurte full syckerlye,
"Alas!" sayde Brandles than,
"Who hath done youe suche a dyspite?   *dishonor*
Tell me in haste, that I maye yt quyte,   *repay*
For my hearte ys wo begone."

365 Than saide the father, "Sonne, I shall the tell:
All thys hathe done a knyght full fell,   *dangerous*
And layne by thy syster also.
He beete me fyrst, and them all,
And made us swere that we ne shall
370 Thys daye do hym no wo."

Nowe saide Brandles, "Thys ys yll come!   *bad luck*
I ensure youe by my holydome,   *spiritual welfare*
I shall prove hys myght;   *test out*
Were he as stronge as Sampson was,
375 In fayth shall I never from hym pas,   *turn away*
Tyll the one of us to death be dyght."   *marked for death*

"Yea, sonne Brandles, thou shalt not soo.
Thoughe he have done wronge, lett hym goo.
The knyght ys passynge sure;   *stalwart without measure*
380 I wyll not for more than I wyll sayne   *than I can say*
See the, Syr Brandels, there slayne,
For I warraunte the he wyll endure.   *assure you; prevail*

"The knyght ys stronge, and well fight can,
And when he hathe at hande a man,   *at advantage*
385   He wyll do hym none yll.
But gentle wordes speake agayne,   *in return*
And do hym no harme ne mayne,   *violence*
Thus gentyll he ys in skyll."   *So noble; in knightly behavior*

"Nowe lette hym be," sayde Brandles than;   *(i.e., whatever he is)*
390   "Sone shall we see yf he be a manne,"
And sayed "Have good daye."
Streyght to the pavylyon he rode;
That sawe the mayden as she stode,
That yt was her brother gaye.

395   "Syr knyght," she sayde, "here cometh one,
Yt wyl be harde hym to overgone —   *overcome*
Beholde nowe and see:
Yonder cometh one wyll dure in fyght;   *endure*
I warraunte ye sawe never a better knight
400   Than ye shall fynde hym, syckerlye.   *surely*

"Beholde nowe my brother, Syr Brandles.
He ys in warre full slye, ywys,   *skillful*
And that thowe shalt fynde;
Me thynke hym passynge lyke a knyght.
405   Have no drede ye shall fynde hym wight,   *doubt; powerful*
Nowe under thys lynde."   *linden tree*

"By God!" sayde Gawayne, "he ys full lyke   *just the sort*
To abyde a buffette and to stryke,   *withstand*
And of hys handes a man.   *in his strength a warrior*
410   I sawe not or nowe thys yeares thre,   *before*
A man more lyke a man to be,
By God and by Saynt Johan!"

Right so Syr Brandles, the knyght gaye,   *gracious*
Spake on hyghe, and thus gan saye: *aloud*
415   "Where arte thou, good Squyer?
Come forthe in haste," he sayde on hyght,

"For with the will I fyght.   *you*
A newe game thoue shalt leere.   *learn*

"Thou haste done me dysworship greate,   *dishonor*
420   And mayst not nowe amendement gette;
Yt ys no tyme of peace to speake."
Syr Gawayne saide, "Syr, I the praye,
Let me make amendes, and youe maye,   *if you please*
Or thou begynne thys wreke.   *vengeance*

425   "Syr, and I have ought mysdone,   *if*
Tell me, and it shal be amended soone,
All gentlenes to fullfyll.   *noble obligation*
I have bene bestad todaye full soore;   *sorely beset*
Shame yt were to prove me any moore.   *test*
430   But here I am at youre wyll."

"Ywys," quod Brandles, "that ys sothe.   *Indeed*
But I must nedes holde myne othe,   *oath*
Thou haste done so yll —
My father and my brethren thou hast beaten bothe.
435   To accorde with the I were therof lothe,
My worshippe to fullfyll."   *[If I wish] to maintain my honor*

Nowe sayed Gawayne, "Sythe yt ys so,
I muste nedes me dryve ther to.   *enter into combat*
Thys daye God lende me grace,
440   For my worde shall do none advauntage: *negotiation will gain*
Let us see howe well we can outrage,   *fight furiously*
Yf I maye dare ought in thys trace."   *course*

"Gramarcy," sayde Brandles, "in good faye,   *Great thanks; faith*
Nowe shall youe see me make good playe.
445   Of knighthode thou hast no peere;   *equal*
I am right gladde thou hast myght,
But sorye I am we lacke the dayelyght.   *sorry*
But amended ys my cheere."   *Nonetheless; mood*

They fought together, those knightes good;
450   Throughe theyr haburgeons ran out the redde blode,   *coats of mail*

That pytté yt was to see;
They fought together with suche yre,   *fury*
That after flamed out the fyre.   *sparks*
They spake of no mercye.

455   Thus full longe than gan they fyght,
Tyll at the laste they wanted lyght;   *lacked daylight*
They wyste not what to done.   *knew*
Than sayde Syr Brandles, that knyght so gaye:
"Syr knyght, we wante lyght of the daye;
460   Therfore I make my mone.   *protest*

"Yf we fyght thus in the darke together
Throughe myshappe the one myght sle the other;   *bad luck; slay*
And therefore by myne assent,
Lett us sweare on oure sweardes bothe,   *swords*
465   Where that we mete for leyfe or lothe,   *Wherever; love or hate*
Yf that we mete in present,   *soon*

"Never to leave the battayll tyll the one be slayne." *one of us*
"I assent me therunto," than sayde Gawayne,
"And ye wyll that yt so be."   *If; wish*
470   Than sayde Syr Brandles, "I may none other do,
For suche promesse I made my father unto;
Therefore thys othe make we.

"I wotte there ys no stroke that thou gavest me,   *know*
But I shall quyte yt full syckerlye —   *repay; surely*
475   And thou arte not in my debte.
Full large of lyveray thou arte, syr knyght —   *powerful in combat*
Never none that proved so well my myght;   *No other ever tested*
We bene even as we mette.   *as equal as when*

"Lett us make an othe on our swerdes here,
480   In that place we mete, farre or nere,
Even there as ether other may fynde,   *either*
Even so we shall do the battayle utterlye."   *to the death*
"I holde," sayde Gawayne, "by mylde Marye!   *promise*
And thus we make an ende."

411

485   Syr Gawayne put up hys swerde than:
       "Syr knight, be frende to that gentle woman,
       As ye be gentle knyght."
       "As for that," sayde Brandles than,
       "She hathe caused today, pardye, much shame.   *by God*
490   Yt ys pyttye she hathe her syght."   *she is yet alive*

       "Syr knyght," sayde Gawayne, "have good daye,
       For on foote I have a longe waye,
       And horse were wonders deare;   *badly wounded*
       Some tyme good horses I have good wone,   *captured*
495   And nowe on foote I muste nedes gone.
       God in haste amende my chere!"   *situation*

       Syr Gawayne was armed passynge heavy;
       On fote myght he not endure, trewely.
       Hys knyfe he toke in hande;
500   Hys armure good he cutte hym fro,
       Els on foote myght he not goo.
       Thus with care was he bande.   *beset (bound)*

       Leave we nowe of Syr Gawayne in wo,
       And speake we more of Syr Brandles tho.   *then*
505   When he with hys syster mette
       He sayed, "Fye on the, harlot stronge!
       Yt ys pyttie thou lyvest so longe.
       Strypes harde I wyll the sette."   *A lashing; give*

       He bete her bothe backe and syde.   *beat*
510   And than woulde he not abyde,   *stay longer*
       But to hys father streight he wentte,
       And he asked hym how he fared.
       He sayde, "Sonne, for the have I cared;   *you; worried*
       I wende thou haddest be shente."   *thought; perished*

515   Brandles sayde, "I have beate my syster,
       And the knyght, I made hym sweare
       Than whan we mete agayne,
       He and I wyll together fyght

| | Tyll that we have spended our myght, | *exhausted* |
| 520 | And that one of us be slayne." | |

So home they went all foure together,
And eche of them helped other,
As well as they myght go.
Than the lady gate her awaye —   *went off by herself*
525 They sawe her never after that daye;
She went wandrynge to and fro.

Also Syr Gawayne on hys partye,   *for his part*
On foote he went full werylye,   *wearily*
Tyll he to the courte came home.
530 All hys adventures he shewed the Kinge,   *disclosed*
That with those foure knyghtes he had fyghtynge,
And eche after other alone.   *in single combat*

And after that tyme they never mette more;   *encountered again*
Full gladde were those knightes therfore.
535 So there was made the ende.

I praye God geve us good reste,
And those that have harde thys lyttel Jeste,
And in hye heaven to be dwellynge; [1]
And that we all maye, upon domesdaye,
540 Come to the blysse that lasteth aye,
Where we maye here thy Aungels synge.

AMEN.

Here endeth the Jeaste of Syr Gawayne.

---

[1] Lines 536–38: *I pray that God give good rest to us / And to all who have heard this little Jeaste, / And (that all) may come to dwell in high heaven*

Notes

Abbreviations: B = Bodley MS; H = surviving leaf of printed edition in the Harley Collection, British Library; M = Madden's edition. See Select Bibliography for these editions.

1   *And sayde. Jeaste* clearly begins in the midst of a conversation between the nameless lady and Gawain, indicating the loss of the opening episode. The context clearly indicates that Gawain has come upon the lady in her forest pavilion while hunting, and has made amorous overtures. She warns him of possible reprisals by her father and brothers, but Gawain dismisses these threats in the opening lines of the surviving text.

5   *suche.* M: *such.*

42   Following this line, the remainder of this page is taken up with a drawing showing two mounted knights, in armor with lances; one (obviously Gawain) unhorses the other. The drawings (see lines 147, 274, 357, 452, and 503 and notes) were executed by a talented amateur with archaic realism, in a pseudo-medieval style, and illustrate the enthusiastic response chivalric romance might elicit in the sixteenth century.

50   *feutred.* B: *fentred*; M emends without comment.

57   *fayne.* B: *sayne*; I emend for sense.

73   *and stoure.* M suggests reading *in stoure.*

74 ff. Gylbert here gives Gawain warning that he will soon have to fight the three sons.

103   *dyspyte.* M: *despyte.*

109   *a trewe knyght.* M: *trewe knyght.*

414

147   Another picture takes up the remainder of the page, showing a mounted knight with lance and a second knight — clearly Gyamoure at this point in the narrative — unhorsed and seated on the ground, but still holding his lance.

176   *stryve*. B: *stryde*; I follow the suggested emendation from M's notes.

207   *out of straye*. Tyrry turns his horse "astray," abruptly aside from the path on which he had been riding. For the use of this phrase, see *Gologras* line 19 and note.

233   *Thys*. This line begins with an enlarged capital *T* against a shaded background, four lines of text in size.

275   The entire page above this line is taken up with a drawing that closely resembles that on folio 17b; in it a mounted knight holds his lance against a knight seated on the ground (in this case, Terrye), while the latter knight's horse looks on.

284   *oure*. M: *our*.

288   *than*. B: *that*; I follow M's emendation.

295   Under line 293 a rule is drawn across the page, and line 295 is inserted to the right of line 294, remedying what is clearly a skip by the copyist.

320   *Brandles*. In the continuation to Chrétien's *Perceval*, Gawain fights and then reconciles with a knight named Bran de Lys; this same knight accompanies Arthur in the episode that forms the source of the first part of *Gologras* (though in the Scots poem Arthur's companion is named Spynagros). *Carlisle* names *Syr Brancheles* (line 64) among the roster of knights associated with Arthur. In Malory, Lancelot rescues a knight of this name (*Braundeles*) from Tarquyn (*Works*, pp. 268, 344 ff.). In addition, Malory declares that two of Gawain's three sons — Sir Florence and Sir Lovell — "were begotyn uppon sir Braundeles syster " (*Works*, p. 1147), reflecting a narrative tradition that prolongs the relationship between Gawain and this woman long beyond the brief encounter of *Jeaste*. In *Ragnelle*, the third son listed by Malory — Sir Gyngalyn — is born of the union between that heroine and Gawain; see *Ragnelle*, line 799 ff. and note.

324   When the Green Knight appears before Arthur's court in *Sir Gawain and the Green Knight*, "in his on honde he hade a holyn bobbe, / That is grattest in grene when grevez ar bare / And an ax in his other" (lines 206–8: in his one hand he had a sprig of holly, which is greenest when the trees are bare, and an ax in the other). Carrying a bough signals peaceful intentions, though Brandles also holds a spear (line 341).

329   *Allso*. M: *Also*.

350   *of large*. The phrase means "of (considerable) size"; compare *Gologras* line 241, "The land wes likand in large."

357   The remainder of the page following this line is taken up by a drawing, showing three armored knights on foot, with a fourth mounted holding a spear with pennon attached. Their raised visors make their faces visible, and one, no doubt Gylbert, is bearded.

383 ff.   Sir Gylbert seems to say that Gawain defeats and treats honorably all those that approach him violently; but if one speaks courteously to him from the outset, Gawain shows nothing but courtesy.

389   Another enlarged capital against a shaded background, this one six lines in size, begins this line.

451   *yt*. B: *ys*; I follow M's emendation.

453   The entire page above this line contains a drawing of two armored knights (Gawain and Brandles) on foot, fighting each other with swords drawn and visors up.

489   *pardye much shame*. H: *moch shame parde*.

491   *sayde Gawayne*. H: *syr Gawayne*.

491 ff.   Having fought to a draw with Brandles, and lost his horse in the duel (as he does in *Awntyrs*; see lines 540 ff.), Gawain seems to feel he can no longer remain in the pavilion with the lady. He therefore departs on foot, after cutting away the heavy armor a mounted knight would wear for combat.

493   *And horse were wonders.* H: *an horse were me wonder.*

495   *And.* H: *But.*

         I muste nedes. H: *nedes must I.*

499   *hande.* H: *hende.*

502   *bande.* H: *bonde.* Following this line, the rest of the page is occupied by a drawing of a knight in armor, holding a staff with one hand and grasping the arm of a woman (clothed in distinctively Elizabethan dress) with the other. These must be Brandles and the nameless sister.

503   *nowe of Syr.* H: *now syr.* This line begins with an enlaged capital *L* against a shaded background, three lines long.

507   *pyttie thou.* H: *pyttie that thou.*

508   *wyll the sette.* H: *wyll sette.*

509   *He bete her.* H: *And bete the.*

512   *And he asked.* H: *Then he axed.*

514   *wende thou haddest be.* H: *wende that thou haddest ben.*

517   *Than whan.* H: *That whan.*

519   *Tyll that we.* H: *Tyll we.*

         our. H: *eche our.*

521   *all foure together.* H: *all together.*

527   *on.* H: *in.*

530   *hys adventures.* H: *this adventure.*

533   *And after.* H: *After.*

534   *those knightes.* H: *these partyes*; M: *knyghtes.*

535   *there was.* H: *was there.*

536   *us.* H: *us al.*

538   *to.* H: *for to.*

539   *all maye, upon.* H: *all upon.*

541   *thy.* H: *the.* Following *AMEN* there is another drawing by the same hand, show-
       ing marvelous creatures holding a shield with three fleurs-de-lis. A rectangle at
       the center surrounds the explicit, above which are the initials *E B*, perhaps
       those of the copyist and illustrator. The other romances in the manuscript —
       Isumbras, *Degaré*, and *Eglamour* — are written in the same distinctive hand,
       with drawings of the same sort, though none of the other romances contains a
       signature or initials. The date 1564 appears at the conclusion of *Eglamour*.

King Arthur and King Cornwall

Introduction

As a story of fantastic knightly adventure, *King Arthur and King Cornwall* resembles Chaucer's Squire's Tale and other popular romances like *Sir Launfal*. The Arthurian knights gain victory by getting control of a magical horse, sword, and horn; to come by these, they must first gain mastery (through a kind of religious ritual or white magic) over a seven-headed sprite who serves King Cornwall, improbably named Burlow Beanie. To seal their victory, Sir Gawain vows to carry Cornwall's daughter back with them to Little Britain. The magical elements are embedded within an overt contest of honor and prowess between the knights of the Round Table and Cornwall's court; a series of ritualized public boasts, serving both as speeches and as acts that define heroic behavior, initiate this contest. The plot begins when Guenevere challenges Arthur's boast to Gawain that his Round Table excels all others. The King (here ruler of Little Britain, or Brittany, rather than England) and his entourage travel in disguise through "many a strange country" (line 33) until they reach the palace of King Cornwall; once again, Arthur's rival in an English narrative is the lord of a marginal, Celtic territory in Britain. Cornwall's boasts — of the daughter he fathered on Guenevere, his magical possessions, and his general superiority to Arthur — openly offend the chivalric honor of the Round Table, and demand reprisal. This redress occurs first in the form of counterboasts, in which the Arthurian knights stake their reputation on living up to their bold words. Afterwards, Sir Bredbeddle nearly suffers defeat in combat with the monster, but then snatches victory through an exorcism of sorts. *Cornwall* ends with each of the knights achieving his vow, through the assistance of the monster.

In making boasts or vows the essence of chivalric honor, *Cornwall* resembles *Avowyng* (and to some extent *Ragnelle*, *Gologras*, *Sir Gawain and the Green Knight*, *Jeaste*, and other poems where fulfilling one's spoken word controls the story). In upholding the excellence of Arthurian chivalry, however, the fragmentary *Cornwall* contains no twists, suspense, or reconciliations. King Cornwall is a false braggart, and the knights of the Round Table easily accomplish their vows and dispatch him. (In Arthurian tradition, the King of Cornwall is Mark, uncle — mother's brother — of Sir Tristan, who is the King's rival for the love of Isolde of Ireland.) But neither

419

King Arthur and King Cornwall

King Arthur nor Sir Gawain is the hero of this poem, though in the first lines Arthur refers to their typifying heroic relationship of mother's brother-sister's son. Instead, the central figure is Sir Bredbeddle, the former antagonist of Sir Gawain in *The Greene Knight*, now a full companion of the Round Table. As the Green Knight, Bredbeddle is Arthur's great champion, and he dominates the action in the second half of the poem — much of which consists of uproarious knock-about between the Green Knight and the demonic Burlow Beanie. Sir Gawain plays a relatively small role in *Cornwall*; his vow, unfulfilled in the surviving text, to "worke my will" (line 155) with Cornwall's daughter, recalls his rakish character in the later French romances, or in *Jeaste*. Nevertheless, the very naming of Bredbeddle as the Green Knight makes clear that the composer assumed the audience's familiarity with the romances of Sir Gawain.

King Arthur and King Cornwall survives in the Percy Folio Manuscript. Like *Turke*, it occurs in that section of the volume where about half of each page had been ripped out to start fires, and so lacks about half its content; as a result, a story that was already more attentive to large motifs and bold turns of plot than to subtle details has lost a number of crucial events. *Cornwall* redeploys an array of traditional features of romance story. In particular, the pilgrimage, the boasts (or "gabs"), and the encounter with a magically powerful opponent resemble medieval anecdotes told about Charlemagne, though similar episodes also occur in Arthurian narratives like *Gologras* and *Turke*. Yet *Cornwall* may not have come by these elements through specific literary sources. Instead, its plot may reflect motifs connected to Arthurian legend from its origins, or, perhaps most likely of all, it may simply represent a reworking of elements popularly associated with the knights of the Round Table in the late Middle Ages. Whether the seventeenth-century ballad retells a medieval romance of Gawain and Arthur, or improvises its own image of medieval chivalry on the basis of notions that earlier Arthurian romances had put in circulation, *Cornwall* strongly conveys the enduring glamour of the Round Table's might and magic. It also reiterates a basic romance paradigm, by which the king and his chief knights journey to a strange, outlying territory, defeat the monstrous forces they encounter, and bring that formerly mysterious place into the governance of the monarch. This process of appropriation or domestication finds its ultimate symbol in Gawain's possessing Cornwall's daughter; forced marriage becomes the means of bringing this wayward creature back under the control of her legitimate (if not biological) father, and of joining the recalcitrant fringe to the center.

Cornwall preserves a rough version of ballad meter. It falls mainly into quatrains rhyming *xaxa*, though the a-rhyme sometimes continues into an additional couplet, producing some six-line stanzas. The metrical feet and the number of stresses in each line are irregular, though much of the verse falls into the ballad formula of a four-stress line followed by a three-stress line.

Text

King Arthur and King Cornwall survives (with the losses mentioned above) in the Percy Folio Manuscript, pp. 24–31 (described in the introductory material to *The Greene Knight*). The cramped hand and blotted lines have become more difficult to read over time; in transcribing the text, I have made full use of the nineteenth-century editions of Madden, Furnivall and Hales, and Child, sometimes following their readings where the script now seems indistinct or indecipherable. I have regularized orthography so that *u/v* and *i/j* appear according to modern usage; abbreviations have been expanded, numerals spelled out, and modern punctuation and capitalization added.

Select Bibliography

Manuscript

British Library Additional MS 27879 (The Percy Folio). Pp. 24–33.

Editions (arranged chronologically)

Madden, Frederic. 1839. See Bibliography of Editions and Works Cited.

Hales, John W., and Frederick J. Furnivall. 1868. See Bibliography of Editions and Works Cited.

Child, Francis James. 1884. See Bibliography of Editions and Works Cited.

Criticism

Jost, Jean E. "The Role of Violence in *Aventure*: 'The Ballad of King Arthur and the King of Cornwall' and 'The Turke and Gowin.'" *Arthurian Interpretations* 2.2 (1988), 47–57.

Krappe, Alexander Haggerty. "Mediaeval Literature and the Comparative Method." *Speculum* 10 (1935), 270–76.

King Arthur and King Cornwall

. . . .

Saies, "Come here cuzen Gawaine so gay;   *Says; handsome*
   My sisters sonne be yee;
For you shall see one of the fairest Round Tables
   That ever you see with your eye."

5   Then bespake Lady Queen Guenever,   *spoke out*
   And these were the words said shee:
"I know where a Round Table is, thou noble King,
   Is worth thy Round Table and other such three.

"The trestle that stands under this Round Table," she said,
10   "Lowe downe to the mould,   *near the earth*
It is worth thy Round Table, thou worthy King,
   Thy halls, and all thy gold.

"The place where this Round Table stands in,
   It is worth thy castle, thy gold, thy fee;   *estate*
15   And all good Litle Britaine."   *Brittany*

"Where may that Table be, Lady?" quoth hee,
   "Or where may all that goodly building be?"
"You shall it seeke," shee sayd, "till you it find,
   For you shall never gett more of me."

20   Then bespake him noble King Arthur,
   These were the words said hee:
"Ile make mine avow to God,   *I will*
   And alsoe to the Trinity,

"Ile never sleepe one night, there as I doe another,   *I will; two consecutive nights*
25   Till that Round Table I see!
Sir Marramiles and Sir Tristeram,
   Fellowes that ye shall bee;

"Weele be clad in palmers weede,   *We will; pilgrims' dress*
   Five palmers we will bee;
30 There is noe outlandish man will us abide,   *stay among us*
   Nor will us come nye."

Then they rived east and they rived west,   *traveled*
   In many a strange country;

Then they tranckled a litle further,   *wandered*
35   They saw a battle new sett;   *just arranged*
   "Now, by my faith," saies noble King Arthur,
   . . . well mett

[Half a page is missing. After martial adventures and further travel, Arthur and his pilgrim-knights come to the castle of King Cornwall]

But when he cam to this . . . C . . ,
   And to the palace gate,
40 Soe ready was ther a proud porter,
   And met him soone therat.

Shooes of gold the porter had on,
   And all his other rayment was unto the same.   *of the same material*
"Now, by my faith," saies noble King Arthur,
45   "Yonder is a minion swaine."   *dainty boy*

Then bespake noble King Arthur,
   These were the words says hee:
"Come hither, thou proud porter,
   I pray thee come hither to me.

50 "I have two poore rings of my finger,
   The better of them Ile give to thee: *I will*
Tell who may be Lord of this castle," he sayes,
   "Or who is Lord in this cuntry?"

"Cornewall King," the porter sayes;
55   "There is none soe rich as hee;
Neither in Christendome, nor yet in heathennest,   *among pagans*
   None hath soe much gold as he."

And then bespake him noble King Arthur,
    These were the words sayes hee:

60   "I have two poore rings of my finger,
    The better of them Ile give thee,
If thou wilt greete him well, Cornewall King,
    And greete him well from me.

"Pray him for one nights lodging, and two meales meate,   *food*
65   For His love that dyed uppon a tree;   *(i.e., Jesus)*
A une ghesting, and two meales meate,   *single [night's] hospitality*
    For His love that dyed uppon a tree,

"A une ghesting of two meales meate,
    For His love that was of Virgin borne,
70   And in the morning that we may scape away,   *depart*
    Either without scath or scorne."   *harm or disgrace*

Then forth has gone this proud porter,
    As fast as he cold hye;   *hasten*
And when he came befor Cornewall King,
75   He kneeled downe on his knee.

Sayes, "I have beene porterman at thy gate   *[He]*
    This thirty winter and three . . .

[Half a page is missing. The disguised Arthur and his knights are brought into King Cornwall's presence and a series of probing verbal exchanges takes place.]

    . . . our Lady was borne.
Then thought Cornewall King,
80   These palmers had beene in Brittaine.

Then bespake him Cornwall King,
    These were the words he said there:
"Did you ever know a comely King,
    His name was King Arthur?"

85   And then bespake him noble King Arthur,

These were the words said hee:
"I doe not know that comly King,
But once my selfe I did him see."
Then bespake Cornwall King againe;
90   These were the words said he:

Sayes, "Seven yeere I was clad and fed,
In Litle Brittaine, in a bower.   *room*
I had a daughter by King Arthurs wife,
That now is called my flower.
95   For King Arthur, that kindly cockward,   *cuckold*
Hath none such in his bower.

"For I durst sweare, and save my othe,   *keep my oath*
That same lady soe bright,   *[is] so splendid*
That a man that were laid on his death bed
100   Wold open his eyes on her to have sight."[1]
"Now, by my faith," sayes noble King Arthur,
"And thats a full faire wight!"   *she is; being*

And then bespake Cornewall againe,
And these were the words he said:
105   "Come hither, five or three of my knights,
And feitch me downe my steed;
King Arthur, that foule cockeward,   *cuckold*
Hath none such, if he had need.

"For I can ryde him as far on a day,
110   As King Arthur can doe any of his on three.
And is it not a pleasure for a King
When he shall ryde forth on his journey?

"For the eyes that beene in his head,
They glister as doth the gleed."   *burning ember*

---

[1] *Would come back from the dead just to lay eyes on her*

115   "Now, by my faith," says noble King Arthur,
        That is a well faire steed."

[Half a page is missing. King Cornwall continues with his insulting proofs of his superiority to Arthur, and then all agree to retire to bed.]

        "Nobody say . . .
        But one thats learned to speake."   *(i.e., courteous)*

        Then King Arthur to his bed was brought,
120   A greeived man was hee,   *grieved*
        And soe were all his fellowes with him.
        From him they thought never to flee.

        Then take they did that lodly boome,   *(i.e., Cornwall's household); monstrous sprite*
        And under thrub chadler closed was hee.   *within a chest on which was a candle*
125   And he was set by King Arthurs bedside,
        To heere theire talke and theire cumunye,   *hear; conversation*

        That he might come forth, and make proclamation,
        Long before it was day.
        It was more for King Cornwalls pleasure,
130   Then it was for King Arthurs pay.   *benefit*

        And when King Arthur in his bed was laid,
        These were the words said hee:
        "Ile make mine avow to God,   *I will*
        And alsoe to the Trinity,
135   That Ile be the bane of Cornwall Kinge,   *sworn enemy (killer)*
        Litle Brittaine or ever I see!"   *before I see again*

        "It is an unadvised vow," saies Gawaine the gay,   *rash*
        "As ever King hard make I: *heard*
        But wee that beene five Christian men,   *We are only*
140   Of the Christen faith are wee —
        And we shall fight against anoynted king
        And all his armorie."   *army*

And then bespake him noble Arthur,
    And these were the words said he:
145   "Why, if thou be afraid, Sir Gawaine the gay,
    Goe home, and drinke wine in thine owne country."

The Third Part

And then bespake Sir Gawaine the gay,
    And these were the words said hee:
"Nay, seeing you have made such a hearty vow,
150   Heere another vow make will I.

"Ile make mine avow to God,
    And alsoe to the Trinity,
That I will have yonder faire lady
    To Litle Brittaine with mee.

155   "Ile hose her homly to my hurt,   *clasp her close to my heart*
    And with her Ile worke my will."

[Half a page is missing. Arthur and his companions discover the sprite hidden in their chamber, and prepare to try to subdue it.]

These were the words sayd he:
    "Befor I wold wrestle with yonder feend,   *would; fiend*
It is better be drowned in the sea."

160   And then bespake Sir Bredbeddle,
    And these were the words said he:
"Why, I will wrestle with yon lodly feend!   *loathsome*
    God, my governor thou wilt bee."   *guide*

Then bespake him noble Arthur,
165   And these were the words said he:
"What weapons wilt thou have, thou gentle knight?
    I pray thee tell to me."

He sayes, "Collen brand Ile have in my hand, *A sword from Cologne*
 And a Millaine knife fast by me knee;   *Milanese*
170 And a Danish axe fast in my hands —
 That a sure weapon I thinke wil be."

Then with his Collen brand that he had in his hand
 The bunge of the trubchandler he burst in three; *opening of the candle tub*
With that start out a lodly feend,   *leaped*
175 With seven heads, and one body.

The fyer towards the element flew   *heavens*
 Out of his mouth, where was great plentie.
The knight stoode in the middle, and fought, *midst*
 That it was great joy to see,

180 Till his Collaine brand brake in his hand,
 And his Millaine knife burst on his knee;
And then the Danish axe burst in his hand first,
 That a sur weapon he thought shold be.   *trusty*

But now is the knight left without any weapons.
185 And alacke! it was the more pitty.
But a surer weapon then had he one,
 Had never lord in Christentye:
And all was but one litle booke —   *(i.e., the Bible)*
 He found it by the side of the sea.

190 He found it at the seaside,
 Wrucked upp in a floode;   *Left; tide*
Our Lord had written it with His hands,
 And sealed it with His bloode.

[In a missing section of a half page, Bredbeddle exorcises the sprite through the power of the sacred page. After requiring him to appear in a less frightening aspect, he prepares to make the sprite work for Arthur's benefit.]

"That thou doe not s . . .
195 But ly still in that wall of stone   *lie*

Till I have beene with noble King Arthur,
    And told him what I have done."

And when he came to the Kings chamber,
    He cold of his curtesie;   *was mindful of*
200   Says, "Sleepe you? Wake you, noble King Arthur?
    And ever Jesus waken yee!"

"Nay, I am not sleeping, I am waking" —
    These were the words said hee:
"For thee I have card. How hast thou fared?   *cared (been concerned)*
205   O gentle knight, let me see."

The knight wrought the King his booke,   *produced for*
    Bad him behold, reede, and see;   *bade*
And ever he found it on the backside of the leafe,   *surely*
    As noble Arthur wold wish it to be.

210   And then bespake him King Arthur:
    "Alas, thow gentle knight, how may this be —
That I might see him in the same licknesse   *likeness (appearance)*
    That he stood unto thee?"

And then bespake him the Greene Knight,
215   These were the words said hee:
"If youle stand stifly in the battell stronge,   *you will*
    For I have won all the victory."

Then bespake him the King againe,
    And these were the words said hee:
220   "If wee stand not stifly in this battell strong,
    Wee are worthy to be hanged all on a tree."

Then bespake him the Greene Knight,
    These were the words said he:
Saies, "I doe conjure thee, thou fowle feend,
225   In the same licknesse thou stood unto me."   *[To appear again]*

With that start out a lodly feend,
 With seven heads, and one body;
The fier towards the element flaugh   *flew*
 Out of his mouth, where was great plenty.

230 The knight stood in the middle p . . .

[Half a page is missing, in which Bredbeddle and the sprite go several more
rounds, with the knight finally gaining complete mastery.]

  . . . they stood the space of an houre,
   I know not what they did.

  And then bespake him the Greene Knight,
   And these were the words said he:
235 Saith, "I conjure thee, thou fowle feend,
   That thou feitch downe the steed that we see."   *fetch; saw*

  And then forth is gone Burlow Beanie,   *(the monster's name)*
   As fast as he cold hie;   *hasten*
  And feitch he did that faire steed,
240   And came againe by and by.

  Then bespake him Sir Marramiles,
   And these were the words said hee:
  "Riding of this steed, brother Bredbeddle,
   The mastery belongs to me."

245 Marramiles tooke the steed to his hand,
   To ryd him he was full bold;   *ride*
  He cold noe more make him goe   *could*
   Then a child of three yeere old.

  He laid uppon him with heele and hand,
250   With yard that was soe fell;   *riding crop; violent*
  "Helpe! Brother Bredbeddle!" says Marramile,
   "For I thinke he be the devill of hell.

"Helpe! Brother Bredbeddle!" says Marramile,
   "Helpe! for Christs pittye!
255 For without thy help, brother Bredbeddle,
   He will never be rydden thorrow me."   *by*

Then bespake him Sir Bredbeddle,
   These were the words said he:
"I conjure thee, thou Burlow Beane,
260   Thou tell me how this steed was riddin in his country."
He saith, "There is a gold wand
   Stands in King Cornwalls study windowe.

"Let him take that wand in that window,
   And strike three strokes on that steed;
265 And then he will spring forth of his hand
   As sparke doth out of gleede."   *burning ember*

And then bespake him the Greene Knight . . .

[Half a page is missing. With the help of the sprite, Bredbeddle and his companions take possession of the horse and Cornwall's other magical objects, and learn the mysteries that enable their use.]

A lowd blast he may blow then.

And then bespake Sir Bredebeddle,
270   To the feend these words said hee:
Says, "I conjure thee, thou Burlow Beanie,
   The powder box thou feitch me."

Then forth is gone Burlow Beanie
   As fast as he cold hie;
275 And feich he did the powder box,
   And came againe by and by.

Then Sir Tristeram tooke powder forth of that box,
   And blent it with warme sweet milke;   *mixed*
And there put it unto that horne,
280   And swilled it about in that ilke.   *swished; same [horn]*

Then he tooke the horne in his hand,
    And a lowd blast he blew.
He rent the horne up to the midst —   *split*
    All his fellowes this they knew.

285   Then bespake him the Greene Knight,
    These were the words said he:
Saies, "I conjure thee, thou Burlow Beanie,
    That thou feitch me the sword that I see."

Then forth is gone Burlow Beanie,
290   As fast as he cold hie,
And feitch he did that faire sword,
    And came againe by and by.

Then bespake him Sir Bredbeddle,
    To the King these words said he:
295   "Take this sword in thy hand, thou noble King Arthur!
    For the vowes sake that thou made Ile give it thee.

"And goe strike off King Cornewalls head,
    In bed were he doth lye."
Then forth is gone noble King Arthur,
300   As fast as he cold hye;
And strucken he hath off King Cornwalls head,
    And came againe by and by.

He put the head upon a swords point . . .

[Another half page is missing. Having slain Cornwall, the knights seize his possessions. Sir Gawain takes Cornwall's daughter, and the companions return to Arthur's court in Little Britain.]

Notes

Abbreviations: P = Percy Folio MS; BP = Bishop Percy's marginal glosses in the MS; C = Child's edition; M = Madden's edition; HF = Hales' and Furnivall's edition. See Select Bibliography for these editions.

1   *Saies.* The first line of the surviving copy was cut off when Percy sent the manuscript to the binder; Percy restored this line to the text from memory. The opening section of the poem has been lost through the mutilation of the Percy Folio.

3   *one of the fairest Round Tables.* Arthur's founding of a *round* table in order to prevent squabbling among his knights about rank, about who "bygan the highe dese" (*Ragnelle,* line 601), is mentioned first in Geoffrey of Monmouth's *History.* Guenevere's demur from Arthur's claim to Gawain here is peculiarly ironic, since it initiates the plot of *Cornwall* by starting a squabble over the ranking of round tables themselves.

18   *sayd.* HF, C: *says.* The scribal form is unclear; I agree with M in reading it as an oddly formed *d.*

26   *Sir Marramiles.* A knight apparently otherwise unknown in Arthurian legend. Sir Tristan, one of the most prominent of Arthurian knights, is the nephew of Mark, King of Cornwall.

29   *Five palmers.* Gawain and Bredbeddle make up the full complement of five knights.

32   *they rived.* P: *thé.* I emend this scribal spelling of *they* here and at lines 114, 122, and 284.

34   *tranckled.* BP: *travelled* with an asterisk in the margin.

51   *The.* P: *they;* I follow M's emendation.

433

66   *A une ghesting of.* M: *A bue ghesting.*

68   *A une ghesting of.* M reads as in line 66, emending *of* to *and*; C remarks "the first two words are hard to make out," and reads them as *A une*, but emends to modernized *Of one*. I leave the MS reading, since its meaning appears sufficiently plain.

69   *borne.* HF: *boirne.*

72   *has.* P: *his*; M, C emend to *is*; I follow the reading of HF.

79–80   I have made two lines of what is written as a single long line in P.

81   *Cornwall.* So C, HF; M reads *Cornewall*, but the MS is too faint to confirm this spelling.

92   *Litle Brittaine.* This is the usual English designation for Brittany (French *Bretagne*, the Roman territory of Armorica), across the English Channel from Cornwall. The Bretons preserved many Celtic traditions associated with Arthur; an English prose romance, *Arthur of Little Britain* (translated in the early sixteenth century from a fourteenth-century French source by John Bourchier, Lord Berners), sets Arthur's adventures in Brittany.

95   *cockward.* One of the problems that haunts Arthur's reign in romance and chronicle is that he produces no legitimate heir; the question of succession to the throne therefore produces open strife, usually involving Mordred, Arthur's son by his sister. In his novel *The Lyre of Orpheus* (New York: Viking, 1988), Robertson Davies describes the production of an opera, *Arthur the Cuckold*, whose Arthurian themes of sexual anxiety and rivalry are reproduced in the novel's central plot.

124   *thrub chadler.* P's reading here has become faint; though the spelling at line 173 — *trubchandler* — is more distinct, the meaning of this word is not at all clear in either case. M reads as a single word, and emends to *thrubchandler*, without comment; HF conjecture, "a kind of tub?" C emends to *rub-chadler*, commenting that he is "unable to make anything of *thrub, thub*"; he goes on to give elaborate philological arguments for the meaning "rubbish barrel" (p. 279). *bunge* (line 173) confirms that this is some sort of stoppered container; I assume from the context of the poem that this is used as a stand next to

Arthur's bed, on which a candle is placed. Burlow Beanie has been enclosed within by Cornwall's men (lines 123 ff.) in order to spy upon Arthur's company.

147 ff.   *The Third Part.* The division is noted in the left margin, apparently by the scribe rather than BP. Whatever other rubrics there may have been have been lost in the torn-out pages.

155   *homly.* M: *hourly*; C adopts this apparent misreading by M as an emendation.

165   *the.* P: *they.*

201   *waken.* M: *watch* (apparently misled by the descender from the line above that touches *n*).

206 ff.   It is not clear whether Bredbeddle conveys to Arthur words of magical power (perhaps even the sprite's name), or, as seems more likely, somehow shows him an image of what the sprite looked like before its metamorphosis. In the lines that follow, Burlow Beanie upon request transforms back into its monstrous form, only to be domesticated for a final time by Bredbeddle.

214   *the Greene Knight.* The reference to Sir Bredbeddle by this title suggests that the composer and his audience were familiar with *The Greene Knight*, which makes Bredbeddle its hero.

228   *towards.* M: *towarde.*

236   *Burlow Beanie*: This alliterative title apparently names a combination monster-genie who serves Cornwall. The source and meaning of the name are obscure. It recalls formulaic phrases like "burlokest blonke" (applied to Gawain's horse, Grissell, in *Awntyrs*, line 548), "borelych bole" (*Sir Gawain and the Green Knight*, line 766), or especially "borly berne" (stout, burly warrior), which occurs in several alliterative poems. Child connects Burlow Beanie to the Billie Blin, a household demon who appears in several surviving ballads (see p. 279, and discussion at p. 67). As a figure of the comic grotesque, Burlow Beanie might be compared to a character in the repertoire of Victorian street players, "Billy Barlow"; Henry Mayhew records the carnivalesque dress and the semi-improvisatory performance of this figure in his lengthy conversation with a Billy Barlow impersonator from the "street business" (*London Labour and the London Poor* [1861; rpt. New York: Dover, 1968], vol. 3, pp. 138–39). The

pageants, narratives, and performances Mayhew records in this section would seem to be the direct descendants of the popular recitations offered by Captain Cox and his troupe at Kenilworth (see General Introduction).

256   *thorrow me.* The scribe has abbreviated the form before *me* as a *p* with a stroke over it, usually indicating Latin *pro* ("for") or *per* ("through"). M expands to *for*; HF give *pro me*; C expands to *for*, following M. "Through" seems the most appropriate expansion, and I have followed scribal spelling from elsewhere in P.

295   *King Arthur.* As usual, *King* is abbreviated as *K* in P; in this case, *Arthur* is also abbreviated as *a* (standing apart from the end of the line). M omits *Arthur*.

302   The motif of impaling an opponent's head on a spear or sword occurs in Chrétien de Troyes' *Erec*, *Le Bel Inconnu*, and elsewhere; see Loomis' *Arthurian Literature*, p. 358.

Glossary

air *before, earlier, ever*
and *if*
-and *-ing* (present participle ending)
aryghte *correctly*
a(i)ther *either*
aune *own*
aw *to owe, deserve*

baith *both*
bairn *man, warrior, knight*
bauld *bold, courageous*
be *by*
be chesun of *for the sake of*
bedene *together*
beild *protection*
beli(e)fe *quickly*
berne, beirne *man, warrior, knight*
bird(e), byrd *woman, lady*
birny *chain mail*
boure *private chamber, bedroom*
braid *to draw, pull out*
brym *fierce*
bugell *bugle*
burne *knight, man*
busken *to set out, go, hasten, prepare,
fit out, dress, dispatch*

cair *care, sorrow*
can, con *did* (past auxiliary), *did order,
did bring to pass*
cary, caryis, caryit *to move off, go*
cleir *clear, open, beautiful*

dalis *dales, valleys*
daw *day*
de *to die*
deir *dear*
dellis *dells, wooded valleys*
dere *costly*
dight *prepared, ordained, decked out*
dighten *to prepare, make ready, arrange,
set, dress, outfit*
doughty *strong, stalwart*
dounis *downs, rolling country*
dred, dreid *fear, doubt*
dredless *certainly, without question*

fayr(e), feir, feyr *fair, beautiful*
fele *many*
fell *skin, complexion, visage, look*
fer *far*
fere, feir *fellow;* **in fere, in feir**
together
fir *far*
firth *woods, forest*
fold *earth, creation*
force *strength*
forthi *therefore, and so*
freik, freke *man, warrior, knight*

gais *goes*
gart *did, caused to happen*
gate *path, way*
gay *gracious, lively, handsome, generous*
geir *armor, weapons, gear*

437

Glossary

glemand *shining, gleaming*

gome, gomes, gomys *man (men), warrior(s), knight(s)*

graith(en) *to prepare, make ready, go, take oneself*

graithly *immediately*

grund *ground, foundation*

hart *heart*

hathil *man, warrior, nobleman*

hee *high;* **on hee** *aloud*

heynd *noble, courteous, handsome; (n.) noble warrior, knight*

helm(e) *helmet*

hertly *fervently*

hewit *hacked, slashed, hewed, struck*

hie, hee *to hasten*

hie, hy *high, lofty*

holtes *woods*

ich *each, every*

ilk *each; the same*

iwis, ywis *certainly, indeed*

kene *eager, vigorous, bold*

kith *kinspeople, loyal supporters*

layne *to conceal;* **not to layne** *to tell the truth, indeed*

ledis *people, loyal supporters, vassals*

leid *lord*

leid *to lead*

lesing, leasing *lie, falsehood;* **without lesing** *no lie, assuredly*

light *dismount, alight, set on, attack*

lykand *pleasing, handsome*

loft *high;* **on loft** *aloud, loudly, above*

lodely *loathsome, frightful*

lowd *loud, loudly*

mayn(e) *strength*

mair *more*

matens *morning prayers, liturgical services*

meik *meek, submissive, courteous*

melen *to speak, talk, converse*

melle *struggle, combat, melee*

mellen *to mix, struggle, fight*

mete *food, meal*

myld *courteous; (n.) a courteous person*

mold *earth;* **on mold** *on earth, in the world, anywhere*

mony *many, many a*

namyt *named, called, reputed*

of *off*

off *of*

ovr, our *over*

or *before, ere*

peir *peer, equal*

quha *who*

quhare *where*

quhen *when*

quethin *whether*

quhilk *which, which one, this, this one*

quhill *while, until*

rad *quickly, impetuously*

raw *row, order;* **on raw** *in order, in an orderly manner*

raid *rode*

rathe *quickly*

raughte *reached, provided*

438

Glossary

renke *warrior, knight*

rial(e) *royal, kingly;* the rial(e) *the king*

rich *powerful;* (n.) *a powerful person, a knight*

rought *made, prepared, reached*

roy *king*

sa *so*

sail(l) *hall, lord's chamber*

sale *hall, lord's chamber*

sall *shall*

sare *grievously*

schaft *spear, lance, shaft*

schalk *warrior, knight*

s(c)hene *shining, handsome, brilliant;* (n.) *a noble person, a knight*

s(c)here *bright*

schir *sir*

schire *bright*

sege *man, warrior, knight*

sen *since, because*

sertainly *certainly, absolutely*

sethen *afterwards, since*

sey *sea, water*

seymly *becoming, handsome, seemly*

sengeoury *lordship*

sicht *sight, spectacle*

sikerly *surely, truly*

soth(e) *true*

steil *steel, armor, chain mail*

stern *bold, terrible;* (n.) *a bold warrior*

strife *strong, powerful;* (n.) *a fierce warrior*

stint(e) *stop*

stode *stood, stood still*

stound *interval, time*

stour *fierce, angry;* (n.) *battle, combat*

streme *water, ocean, stream*

tene *hurtful, greivious, noisome*

thai, thay *those*

the *you, thee*

thee *to thrive, prosper;* so mote I thee *as I prosper, on my life*

thir *these*

thretty *thirty*

thrid *third*

tong(e) *tongue*

toure *tower*

traist *trusty, faithful, worthy;* (n.) *trust*

wedis *clothes, dress, armor*

weir *doubt;* but weir *without doubt, to be sure, you may be certain*

weir *were (past tense of "to be")*

weynt *went*

wend *go, take one's way,*

wene *know, understand, think*

wer(re) *war battle, combat*

wy *person, warrior*

wyghte *strong, able, vigorous*

wyg(g)hte *person, being*

wy(is) *warrior(s)*

wite *know*

wytt *with*

wod(e) *mad, angry, violent*

wraithly *angrily, fiercely*

wroht *angry*

wroght *caused, made, wrought*

wundir *fantastically, extremely, unusually*

yaul *yowl, scream*

yhere *year*

ywis *truly, indeed*

Volumes in the Middle English Texts Series

The Floure and the Leafe, The Assembly of Ladies, The Isle of Ladies, ed. Derek Pearsall (1990)

Three Middle English Charlemagne Romances, ed. Alan Lupack (1990)

Six Ecclesiastical Satires, ed. James M. Dean (1991)

Heroic Women from the Old Testament in Middle English Verse, ed. Russell A. Peck (1991)

The Canterbury Tales: Fifteenth-Century Continuations and Additions, ed. John M. Bowers (1992)

Gavin Douglas, *The Palis of Honoure*, ed. David Parkinson (1992)

Wynnere and Wastoure and The Parlement of the Thre Ages, ed. Warren Ginsberg (1992)

The Shewings of Julian of Norwich, ed. Georgia Ronan Crampton (1994)

King Arthur's Death: The Middle English Stanzaic Morte Arthur and *Alliterative Morte Arthure*, ed. Larry D. Benson and Edward E. Foster (1994)

Lancelot of the Laik and Sir Tristrem, ed. Alan Lupack (1994)

Sir Gawain: Eleven Romances and Tales, ed. Thomas Hahn (1995)

The Middle English Breton Lays, ed. Anne Laskaya and Eve Salisbury (1995)

Sir Perceval of Galles and Ywain and Gawain, ed. Mary Flowers Braswell (1995)

Four Middle English Romances: Sir Isumbras, Octavian, Sir Eglamour of Artois, Sir Tryamour, ed. Harriet Hudson (1996)

The Poems of Laurence Minot (1333–1352), ed. Richard H. Osberg (1996)

Medieval English Political Writings, ed. James M. Dean (1996)

The Book of Margery Kempe, ed. Lynn Staley (1996)

Amis and Amiloun, Robert of Cisyle, and Sir Amadace, ed. Edward E. Foster (1997)

The Cloud of Unknowing, ed. Patrick J. Gallacher (1997)

Robin Hood and Other Outlaw Tales, ed. Stephen Knight and Thomas Ohlgren (1997)

The Poems of Robert Henryson, ed. Robert L. Kindrick (1997)

Moral Love Songs and Laments, ed. Susanna Greer Fein (1998)

John Lydgate, *Troy Book: Selections*, ed. Robert R. Edwards (1998)

Thomas Usk, *The Testament of Love*, ed. R. Allen Shoaf (1998)

Prose Merlin, ed. John Conlee (1998)

Middle English Marian Lyrics, ed. Karen Saupe (1998)

Four Romances of England: King Horn, Havelok the Dane, Bevis of Hampton, Athelston, ed. Ronald B. Herzman, Graham Drake, and Eve Salisbury (1999)

John Metham, *Amoryus and Cleopes*, ed. Stephen F. Page (1999)

The Assembly of Gods: Le Assemble de Dyeus, or Banquet of Gods and Goddesses, with the Discourse of Reason and Sensuality, ed. Jane Chance (1999)

Thomas Hoccleve, *The Regiment of Princes*, ed. Charles R. Blyth (1999)

John Capgrave, *The Life of St. Katherine*, ed. Karen A. Winstead (1999)

John Gower, *Confessio Amantis, Volume 1*, ed. Russell A. Peck (2000)

Other TEAMS Publications

Documents of Practice Series:

Love and Marriage in Late Medieval London, by Shannon McSheffrey (1995)

A Slice of Life: Selected Documents of Medieval English Peasant Experience, edited, translated, and with an introduction by Edwin Brezette DeWindt (1996)

Sources for the History of Medicine in Late Medieval London, by Carole Rawcliffe (1996)

Regular Life: Monastic, Canonical, and Mendicant Rules, selected with an introduction by Douglas J. McMillan and Kathryn Smith Fladenmuller (1997)

Commentary Series:

Commentary on the Book of Jonah, by Haimo of Auxerre, translated with an introduction by Deborah Everhart (1993)

Medieval Exegesis in Translation: Commentaries on the Book of Ruth, translated with an introduction by Lesley Smith (1996)

Nicholas of Lyra's Apocalypse Commentary, translated with an introduction and notes by Philip D. W. Krey (1997)

Rabbi Ezra Ben Solomon of Gerona: Commentary on the Song of Songs and Other Kabbalistic Commentaries, selected, translated, and annotated by Seth Brody (1998)

To order please contact:

MEDIEVAL INSTITUTE PUBLICATIONS
Western Michigan University
Kalamazoo, MI 49008–3801
Phone (616) 387–8755
FAX (616) 387–8750

http://www.wmich.edu/medieval/mip/mipubshome/html